Readings in Ecology and Feminist Theology

Readings in Ecology and Feminist Theology

*Mary Heather MacKinnon
and Moni McIntyre, Editors*

Sheed & Ward
Kansas City

Sheed & Ward™ is a service of The National Catholic Reporter Publishing Company.

———————————◆———————————

Library of Congress Cataloguing-in-Publication Data

Readings in ecology and feminist theology / Mary Heather MacKinnon,
　　Moni McIntyre, editors.
　　　　p. cm.
　　　ISBN: 1-55612-762-6 (pbk. : alk. paper)
　　　1. Ecofeminism. 2. Ecofeminism—Religious aspects—Christianity.
　　3. Feminist theology. I. MacKinnon, Mary Heather, 1945-　.
　　II. McIntyre, Moni, 1948-　.
　　HQ1233.R43 1995
　　261.8'362'082—dc20　　　　　　　　　　　　　　　　　95-14283
　　　　　　　　　　　　　　　　　　　　　　　　　　　　　　　CIP

———————————◆———————————

Published by:　Sheed & Ward
　　　　　　　115 E. Armour Blvd.
　　　　　　　P.O. Box 419492
　　　　　　　Kansas City, MO 64141-6492

To order, call: (800) 333-7373

Cover design by Emil Antonucci.

Contents

Acknowledgements v

Introduction ix

Part I
Early Voices

1. *Valerie Saiving* – The Human Situation: A Feminine View . . 3

2. *Rachel Carson* – The Obligation to Endure 19

3. *Lynn White, Jr.* – The Historical Roots of Our Ecologic Crisis . 25

4. *Sherry B. Ortner* – Is Female to Male as Nature Is to Culture? . 36

5. *H. Paul Santmire* – Ecology, Justice, and Theology 56

6. *Thomas Berry* – The Dynamics of the Future: Reflections on the Earth Process 63

7. *Rosemary Radford Ruether* – The Biblical Vision of the Ecological Crisis 75

8. *Carolyn Merchant* – Epilogue 82

Part II
Further Conversation

9. *Rosemary Radford Ruether* – Toward an Ecological-Feminist Theology of Nature 89

10. *Susan Griffin* – Split Culture 94

11. *Karen J. Warren* – Feminism and Ecology: Making Connections 105

12. *Michael E. Zimmerman* – Feminism, Deep Ecology and Environmental Ethics 124

13. *Ynestra King* – The Ecology of Feminism and the Feminism of Ecology 150

14. *Vandana Shiva* – Development, Ecology, and Women 161

15. *Karen J. Warren* – The Power and the Promise of Ecological Feminism 172

16. *Mary Anne Hinsdale* – Ecology, Feminism, and Theology . . . 196

17. *Ivone Gebara* – Cosmic Theology: Ecofeminism and Panentheism 208

18. *Shamara Shantu Riley* – Ecology Is a Sistah's Issue Too: The Politics of Emergent Afrocentric Ecowomanism 214

Part III
Postmodern Horizons

19. *John B. Cobb, Jr.* – Ecology, Science, and Religion: Toward a
    Postmodern Worldview 233
20. *Brian Swimme* – The Cosmic Creation Story 249
21. *Joanna Macy* – The Ecological Self: Postmodern Ground for
    Right Action 259
22. *Michael J. Himes and Kenneth R. Himes* – The Sacrament of
    Creation: Toward an Environmental Theology 270
23. *Grace M. Jantzen* – Healing Our Brokenness: The Spirit and
    Creation 284
24. *Jay B. McDaniel* – Six Characteristics of a Postpatriarchal
    Christianity 299
25. *Sallie McFague* – An Earthly Theological Agenda 327
26. *Anne M. Clifford* – Feminist Perspectives on Science: Implications
    for an Ecological Theology of Creation 334
27. *Mary Heather MacKinnon* – Experience and God 361
28. *Moni McIntyre* – Toward a Theological Perspective on the
    Implicate Order of David Bohm 376

Acknowledgements

Grateful acknowledgement is given for copyright reprint permissions as follows:

"The Human Situation: A Feminine View," by Valerie Saiving, reprinted from *The Journal of Religion* 40 (April, 1960):100-112. Reprinted by permission of The University of Chicago Press.

"The Obligation to Endure," from *Silent Spring*, by Rachel Carson. Copyright© 1962 by Rachel L. Carson, renewed 1990 by Roger Christie. Reprinted by permission of Houghton Mifflin Co. All rights reserved.

"The Historical Roots of Our Ecological Crisis," by Lynn White, Jr., from *Science*, 1 Report, Vol. 155, 1967, pp. 1203-07. Copyright 1967 by AAAS. Reprinted by permission.

"Is Female to Male as Nature Is to Culture?" by Sherry B. Ortner, reprinted from *Woman, Culture, and Society*, edited by Michelle Zimbalist Rosaldo and Louise Lamphere. Copyright© 1974 by the Board of Trustees of the Leland Stanford Junior University. Reprinted by permission of the publishers, Stanford University Press.

"Ecology, Justice and Theology," by H. Paul Santmire. Copyright© 1976 by Christian Century Foundation. Reprinted by permission from the may 12, 1976 issue of *The Christian Century*.

"The Dynamics of the Future: Reflections on the Earth Process," by Thomas Berry. Reprinted by permission from the Volume 12: Michaelmas 1976 issue of *Monastic Studies*.

"The Biblical Vision of the Ecological Crisis," by Rosemary Radford Ruether. Copyright© 1978 by Christian Century Foundation. Reprinted by permission from the November 22, 1978 issue of *The Christian Century*.

"Epilogue," by Carolyn Merchant, appeared originally in *The Death of Nature: Women, Ecology, and the Scientific Revolution*, by Carolyn Merchant. Copyright© 1980 by Carolyn Merchant. Reprinted by permission of HarperCollins Publishers, Inc.

"Toward an Ecological Feminist Theology of Nature," is reprinted from *Sexism and God-Talk: Toward a Feminist Theology*. Copyright© 1983 by Rosemary Radford Ruether. Reprinted by permission of Beacon Press.

"Split Culture," by Susan Griffin; "The Ecology of Feminism and the Feminism of Ecology," by Ynestra King; and "Development, Ecology, and Women," by Vandana Shiva, are reprinted from *Healing the Wounds: The Promise of Ecofeminism*, ed. by Judith Plant (Toronto: Between the Lines, 1989). Reprinted by permission of New Society Publishers.

Dedicated to
Evelyn Collins
Reference Librarian
University of St. Michael's College
Toronto, Ontario
and all gracious persons who make research possible

Introduction

ALTHOUGH IT WOULD BE DIFFICULT TO TRACE THE VERY BEGINNING of human exploitation of the planet, it is somewhat less difficult to trace the beginning of serious reflection in North America on the human penchant for destruction of the earth. Such analysis has spawned a movement of sizable interdisciplinary proportions.

One of the areas most profoundly touched by study of the ecological crisis is theology. Members of the Judeo-Christian tradition in particular have been blamed for a good deal of the present ecological crisis. This blame has been placed on these believers primarily because of their scriptural claims as well as their subsequent actions and traditions. Conversations both implicating and absolving biblical traditions have expanded considerably during the past several decades.

The result has been not only extraordinary gains in scientific and religious insights, but also a shift in the way theology is perceived by several of its adherents and opponents. Prior to the frequency of North American voices in the 1960s, there was very little obvious concern for the woes of the earth from an ecological standpoint. Sermons were seldom if ever preached on the theological merits of conserving the goods of the earth. Theologians did not rise to prominence because of their attention to earthly concerns. Christian theology books emphasized heaven as the destiny of human beings, and people were exhorted to keep separate the realms of matter and spirit.

Things have changed somewhat, however. With the publication of several key books and articles, attitudes have begun to change. Both ecology and liberation theologies have focused our attention on things of this earth. God is perceived as one vitally concerned with the affairs of human beings. Creation is heralded as God's gift to us, one we may not absently or consciously abuse. While heaven has not been displaced entirely, it has at least shared the spotlight with things of this earth. This approach to reality has added a new dimension to theology if indeed it has not entirely replaced some of its traditional assumptions.

As Christian educators, we have felt the need for an anthology that could be used at the advanced undergraduate and graduate levels that introduces students to some of the contemporary issues and voices in ecology and those in theology that relate especially to ecology. Consequently, the authors selected for this volume have spoken within the past 35 years. Our omission of other scholars is not intended in any way to posit a claim that only contemporary voices have spoken to the foundational issues raised in our time. While it is true that many voices have spoken

ix

throughout human history to alert the human community to the consequences of its destructive ways and to the faulty philosophical foundations for its plunder, we have included critical works by only a limited number of those important voices.

This anthology chronicles historical developments in this century of our current realization of the integral relationship of ecology to theology. The readings are divided into three sections and are arranged chronologically within each section.

The first section contains works by some of the most often cited authors who link the future of our planet to our perceptions of the human, the earth, and the divine. The articles were selected with their enduring value in mind.

Essays in the second section feature authors who make further connections among feminism, ecology, and the sacred. Their multifaceted commitment to ecofeminism reflects an awareness of its global implications.

The third section shows the growing influence of postmodern consciousness on the conversations within the fields of ecology, science, and theology. Like those in the previous sections, these authors bring new insights and challenges to traditional theological categories.

We wish to let these writers speak on their own without our interpretation of them or making connections between the essays. They represent a wide but not exhaustive variety of contributors to the field of ecology and theology. They are some of the ones we have found most helpful in our teaching and learning. Practical and technical considerations have rendered it impossible to include all the essays that we would have liked.

As white North American academics, our selection of articles reflects many of those authors and issues which we have deemed important to further the discussion among those who care for God and creation. We are professed Roman Catholic women religious, and we teach in our birth countries, although we were educated in both countries.

Mary Heather MacKinnon, SSND
Halton Roman Catholic Separate
School Board
Burlington, Ontario

Moni McIntyre, IHM
Duquesne University
Pittsburgh, Pennsylvania

Part I

Early Voices

1

The Human Situation:
A Feminine View

Valerie Saiving Goldstein

I AM A STUDENT OF THEOLOGY; I AM ALSO A WOMAN. PERHAPS IT STRIKES you as curious that I put these two assertions beside each other, as if to imply that one's sexual identity has some bearing on his theological views. I myself would have rejected such an idea when I first began my theological studies. But now, thirteen years later, I am no longer as certain as I once was that, when theologians speak of "man," they are using the word in its generic sense. It is, after all, a well-known fact that theology has been written almost exclusively by men. This alone should put us on guard, especially since contemporary theologians constantly remind us that one of man's strongest temptations is to identify his own limited perspective with universal truth.

I purpose to criticize, from the viewpoint of feminine experience, the estimate of the human situation made by certain contemporary theologians. Although the views I shall outline receive their most uncompromising expression in the writings of Anders Nygren and Reinhold Niebuhr, I believe that they represent a widespread tendency in contemporary theology to describe man's predicament as rising from his separateness and the anxiety occasioned by it and to identify sin with self-assertion and love with selflessness.

The human condition, according to many contemporary theologians, is universally characterized by anxiety, for, while man is a creature, subject to the limitations of all finite existence, he is different from other creatures because he is free. Although his freedom is qualified by his participation in the natural order, he is not simply bound by inherited instinct to a repetitious living – out of the life – pattern common to all members of the species. Instead, he can stand apart from the world and survey it, envision multiple possibilities and make choices, elaborate his own private ends and imagine larger harmonies, destroy given natural structures and create new ones in their place. This freedom of man, which is the source of his historical and cultural creativity, is also the source of

3

his temptation to sin. For man's freedom, which from another point of view can be called his individuality and his essential loneliness, brings with it a pervasive fear for the survival of the self and its values. Sin is the self's attempt to overcome that anxiety by magnifying its own power, righteousness, or knowledge. Man knows that he is merely a part of the whole, but he tries to convince himself and others that he is the whole. He tries, in fact, to become the whole. Sin is the unjustified concern of the self for its own power and prestige; it is the imperialistic drive to close the gap between the individual, separate self and others by reducing those others to the status of mere objects which can then be treated as appendages of the self and manipulated accordingly. Sin is not an occasional, isolated act but pervades everything man does, even those acts which he performs for the most pure and "unselfish" motives. For the human creature has a marvelous capacity for blinding himself to the fact that, no matter how altruistic his goals may be, he always inserts his own limited individual goals into his attempts to achieve them.

Love is the precise opposite of sin. It is the true norm of human existence and the one real solution to the fundamental predicament in which man stands. Love, according to these theologians, is completely self-giving, taking no thought for its own interests but seeking only the good of the other. Love makes no value judgments concerning the other's worth; it demands neither merit in the other nor recompense for itself but gives itself freely, fully, and without calculation. Love is unconditional forgiveness; concerning the one to whom it is given, it beareth all things, believeth all things, hopeth all things, endureth all things. Love is personal; it is the concrete relatedness of an I to a *Thou,* in which the I casts aside all its particularities, all its self-affirmations, everything which separates it from the *Thou,* and becomes wholly receptive to the other.

It is important, I think, to emphasize that the foregoing analysis of the human situation and the definitions of love and sin which accompany it are mutually dependent concepts. The kind of love described is normative and redemptive precisely insofar as it answers to man's deepest need. If human nature and the human situation are not as described by the theologians in question, then the assertion that self-giving love is the law of man's being is irrelevant and may even be untrue. To the extent that contemporary theology has, in whole or in part, described the human condition inaccurately, to that same extent is its doctrine of love in question.

It is my contention that there are significant differences between masculine and feminine experience and that feminine experience reveals in a more emphatic fashion certain aspects of the human situation which are present but less obvious in the experience of men. Contemporary theological doctrines of love have, I believe, been constructed primarily upon the basis of masculine experience and thus view the human condition from the male standpoint. Consequently, these doctrines do not provide an adequate interpretation of the situation of women – nor, for that matter, of men, especially in view of certain fundamental changes now taking place in our own society.

But can we speak meaningfully about feminine experience as something fundamentally different from masculine experience? Is there such a thing as an underlying feminine character structure which always and everywhere differs from the basic character structure of the male? Are not all distinctions between the sexes, except the purely biological ones, relative to a given culture? Are we not all, men and women alike, members of a single species?

Of course it would be ridiculous to deny that there is a structure of experience common to both men and women, so that we may legitimately speak of the "human situation" without reference to sexual identity. The only question is whether we have described the human situation correctly by taking account of the experiences of both sexes. We know, too, that we can no longer make any hard-and-fast distinctions between the *potentialities* of men and women as such. The twentieth century has witnessed the shattering of too many of our traditional conceptions of sexual differences for us any longer to ignore the tremendous plasticity of human nature. But perhaps the most telling evidence of all that every distinction between the sexes above the physiological level is purely arbitrary comes from the descriptions given by cultural anthropologists of many primitive societies whose ideas about the behavior appropriate to each sex are widely different from, and in many instances contradictory to, those held in our own tradition.

And yet, curiously enough, it is the anthropologists themselves who have begun in recent years to question the assumption that the characters of men and women are essentially alike in all respects. It is even more startling to note that among them are two women of unquestioned professional competence.

It was Ruth Benedict – who in *Patterns of Culture* stressed the relativity of the character ideals held by various societies and the inability of science to account for their diversity on a biological basis – who also wrote these words: "To me it seems a very terrible thing to be a woman." And again: "Nature lays a compelling and very distressing hand upon woman, and she struggles in vain who tries to deny it or escape it – life loves the little irony of proving it upon the very woman who has denied it; she can only hope for success by working according to Nature's conception of her make-up – not against them."[1]

Margaret Mead's concern with the problem of sex differentiation has been expressed in much of her research and writing. In 1935 she published *Sex and Temperament in Three Primitive Societies,*[2] in which she came to the conclusion that there are no natural – that is to say, innate – differences between the character traits of men and women. Rather, the way any particular society defines masculinity and femininity is by a purely arbitrary assignment to one or the other sex of qualities to which members of either sex could be trained with equal ease.

Fourteen years later Margaret Mead published *Male and Female,* in which she returned to the problem, but this time from a slightly different perspective:

> In every known society, mankind has elaborated the biological division of labour into forms often very remotely related to the original biological differences that provided the original clues. . . . Sometimes one quality has been assigned to one sex, sometimes to the other. . . . Whether we deal with small matters or with large, with the frivolities of ornament and cosmetics or the sanctities of man's place in the universe, we find this great variety of ways often flatly contradictory one to the other, in which the roles of the two sexes have been patterned.

> But we always find the patterning. We know of no culture that has said, articulately, that there is no difference between men and women except in the way they contribute to the creation of the next generation; that otherwise in all respects they are simply human beings with varying gifts, no one of which can be exclusively assigned to either sex. . . .

> So . . . we are faced with a most bewildering and confusing array of apparently contradictory evidence about sex differences. We may well ask: Are they important? Do real differences exist, in addition to the obvious anatomical and physical ones – but just as biologically based – that may be masked by the learnings appropriate to any given society, but which will nevertheless be there? Will such differences run through all of men's and all of women's behaviour?[3]

Miss Mead answers this question in the affirmative, not because she has found new evidence which contradicts the evidence presented in her earlier book, but because she has put the question in a different way. Instead of asking the question most of us ask: "Are character differences between the sexes the result of heredity or environment, of biology or culture?" she asks, rather, whether there may not be certain basic similarities in the ways in which men and women in every culture have experienced what it means to be a man or to be a woman. Cultures may and do superimpose upon the fundamental meanings of sex membership other ideas which are irrelevant or contradictory to the basic structure of sexuality. Nevertheless, if such regularities do exist, then we may find that, underneath the specific additions which each culture has imposed, there remains a substratum or core of masculine and feminine orientations which, if too drastically contradicted by the superstructure, may threaten the very existence of the society and its members.

In my description of a few of these biocultural differences between masculine and feminine experience, I shall draw heavily upon Margaret Mead's analysis because I personally find it most illuminating. Nevertheless, I wish to make it clear that I am not attempting to summarize her thought, which is far too complex to present fully here, nor (since even anthropologists are not in agreement in these matters) do I present her as an authority. Primarily, what I shall say is based upon my own experience and observation as it has been clarified and substantiated by Miss Mead and by a number of other writers, including Helene Deutsch,[4] Erich Fromm,[5] and Theodor Reik[6] (Psychoanalysts), Talcott Parsons[7] (sociologist), and Ashley Montagu[8] (anthropologist).

What, then, are the distinctions between the experiences of men and the experiences of women as they occur in any human society, and in what way do these contribute to the formation of differences between the masculine and the feminine character and orientation?

We must begin with the central fact about sexual differences: that in every society it is women – and only women – who bear children. Further, in every society the person closest to the infant and young child is a woman. This fact, based on the physiology of lactation, remains true even in our own culture, in which the formula has so largely replaced the mother's breast.

The close relationship between mother and infant plays the first and perhaps the most important role in the formation of masculine and feminine character, for it means that the person with whom the child originally identifies himself is a woman. Both male and female children must learn to overcome this initial identification by differentiating themselves from the mother. But the kind and degree of differentiation required of the boy are strikingly different from what is required of the girl. The little girl learns that, although she must grow up (become a separate person), she will grow up to be a woman, like her mother, and have babies of her own; she will, in a broad sense, merely take her mother's place. She learns, too, that she will attain womanhood quite naturally – merely by the maturation of her body. In fact, she already is a woman, if in miniature, and must therefore be protected against the premature exploitation of her femininity. And so the emphasis for the girl is upon the fact that she *is* a female and that all she needs to do to realize her full femininity is to wait.

The boy's process of differentiation from his mother is much more complex and difficult. He learns not only that he must grow up but that he must grow up to be a man; that men are different from women, since they do not have babies; and that he must therefore become quite a different sort of creature from his mother. Instead of imitating her, he must relinquish completely his original identification with her. He also finds that, while he is not and never will be a woman, neither is he yet a man. It will be many years before he can perform sexually as a man, and therefore he does not need to be guarded, like his sister, against sexual activity before he is ready for it. He is thus permitted far greater freedom than the girl. But this freedom has its drawbacks for him, since along with it goes a certain set of standards which he must meet before he will be judged to have achieved manhood. He must learn this or that skill, acquire this or that trait or ability, and pass this or that test of endurance, courage, strength, or accomplishment. He must *prove* himself to be a man. True, he has certain advantages over the girl, particularly in the fact that he has visible organs which demonstrate his sex. But, on the whole, the process of self-differentiation plays a stronger and more anxiety-provoking role in the boy's maturation than is normally the case for the girl. Growing up is not merely a natural process of bodily maturation; it is, instead, a challenge which he must meet, a proof he must furnish by means of performance, achievement, and activity directed toward the external world. And even so his reward for achieving manhood is not easily grasped in imagination. It is quite obvious to a child what motherhood is; it is not nearly so obvious what it means to be a father.

This early divergence between masculine and feminine sexual development is repeated, reinforced, and elaborated in later stages of the individual's life. For instance, the girl's history as a female is punctuated and authenticated by a series of definite, natural, and irreversible bodily occurrences: first menstruation, defloration, childbirth, menopause. Each of these events, to be sure, occasions anxiety for the girl and thus might seem to be the female equivalent of the constant anxiety regarding his maleness which besets the boy. Yet these physiological events which mark the woman's life have a reassuring aspect, too, for each of them is concrete, unmistakable proof of her femaleness. The boy's history will provide no such dramatic, once-for-all physical signals of his masculinity.

Even more significant are the differences between male and female roles in the various aspects of adult sexuality. The processes of impregnation, pregnancy, childbirth, and lactation have a certain passivity about them; they are things which *happen* to a woman more than things that she *does*. The sexual act itself, for example, has for her this basically passive quality. The woman, of course, *may* take an active role, but it is not necessary for her to do so, either to satisfy the man or to fulfill her reproductive function. In fact, she may be quite without desire or may even have strong feelings of revulsion, and yet she may, for any number of reasons, submit to the man – sometimes with sufficient grace so that he is completely unaware of her feelings. In the extreme case – rape – the passive structure of female sexuality unquestionably appears. The case is quite otherwise for the male, whose *active* desire and *active* performance in the sexual act is absolutely required for its completion. And here again the demand for performance is coupled with an inevitable anxiety; in order to prove his maleness, he *must* succeed in what he has undertaken – and it is possible for him to fail.

Considered in terms of its reproductive consequences, the sexual act has greatly different meanings for men and women. The male's part in the creation of a child seems indirect and is completed very quickly, while a woman's participation is direct, immediate, and prolonged. It is true that we now know as scientific fact what some primitive peoples have only suspected and others denied: that the man's role in reproduction is essential and that his genetic contribution is equal to the woman's. Yet the birth of a child is never an absolute guaranty to a man of his maleness, as it is to a woman of her femaleness. For, while there can be no doubt as to who is the mother of the child, "paternity remains, with all our modern biological knowledge, as inferential as it ever was, and considerably less ascertainable than it has seemed to be in some periods of history."[9] There is a sense, too, in which woman's biological creativity appears to present a challenge to a man; he perhaps feels his inability to bear children as a deficiency for which he must compensate by other kinds of creativity.

The man's sense of his own masculinity, then, is throughout characterized by uncertainty, challenge, and the feeling that he must again and again prove himself a man. It also calls for a kind of objective achievement and a greater degree of self-differentiation and self-development than are required of the woman *as* woman. In a sense, masculinity is an endless process of *becoming,* while in femininity the emphasis is on *being.* Another way of putting the distinction is that woman is more closely bound to nature than is man. This has advantages and disadvantages for her as a human being. The advantages lie in her greater degree of natural security and the lesser degree of anxiety to which she is subject, both of which make it easier, all other things being equal, for her to enter into loving relationships in which self-concern is at a minimum. Yet if it is true, as Niebuhr says, that man stands at the juncture of nature and spirit, then woman's closeness to nature is a measure of the distance she must travel to reach spirit. That she, too, is a free human being is proved by the fact that she can reject the feminine role; but, having chosen it, she has chosen a kind of bondage which is not involved in a man's acceptance of his sexual identity.

For masculinity can with good reason be defined as the distance between spirit and nature. Because of his less direct and immediate role in the reproductive process, including nurture during the long period of human infancy, man is, in his greater freedom, necessarily subject to a kind of anxiety – and, consequently, to a kind of creative drive – which is experienced more rarely and less intensely by most women.

I have drawn the distinctions between masculine and feminine experience in the sharpest possible terms in order to clarify the divergence between them. But it is important to remind ourselves of the countless changes which have been rung on these basic themes in human societies.

Every culture, we have said, superimposes upon the necessities of sexual roles a whole structure of masculine and feminine character traits. Many of these addenda are only tenuously related to the foundation on which they rest, and they may even be completely contradictory to that foundation. When this phenomenon is carried to its extreme, so that women, for example, are educated by their society to despise the functions of child-bearing and nurture, then the society is in grave danger of bringing about its own destruction. Similarly, where procreation is valued so highly that men attempt to participate directly in the processes of pregnancy, birth, and the rearing of children to the exclusion of other kinds of creative activity, the social fabric again becomes dangerously weak. Both types of society have been discovered among preliterate peoples,[10] and, as we shall see, our own society has not escaped the tendency to overvalue the traits characteristic to one or the other sex.

The truth is, of course, that there is no impassable gulf between the ways in which men and women may look at themselves and at their world. Just as sexuality is not the whole of human existence, so the individual's sense of his own identity is not derived solely from his sexual role. Human beings of both sexes have certain basic experiences in common from earliest infancy – hunger and satiety, constriction and freedom, defenselessness and power, resentment and love. Men and women can and do learn from each other, too; women can be aggressive and ambitious, and men can be fatherly. Neither sex is exempt from anxiety, and both experience the temptations of passivity. Yet the individual's sense of being male or female, which plays such an important part in the young child's struggle for self-definition, can never be finally separated from his total orientation to life; in those cases – which are the majority – in which adult men and women accept and are able to actualize their respective sexual roles, the characterological tendencies based on sex membership are reinforced and strengthened. This is surely the reason why, although there have been women philosophers, musicians, and murderers, there have been no female Platos, Bachs, or Hitlers. It is also the reason why even those men who enjoy being fathers most fully can scarcely be imagined as finding complete self-fulfillment in fatherhood. "A woman, as Madame de Staël remarked, either has children or writes books."[11] As for men, Margaret Mead has observed:

> In every known human society the male's need for achievement can be recognized. Men may cook, or weave or dress dolls or hunt humming-birds, but if such activities are appropriate occupations of men, then the whole society, men and women alike, votes them as important. When the same occupations are performed by women, they are regarded as less important. In a great number of human societies men's sureness of their sex role is tied up with their right, or ability, to practice some activity that women are not allowed to practice. Their male-

ness, in fact, has to be underwritten by preventing women from entering some field or performing some feat. Here may be found the relationship between maleness and pride; that is, a need for prestige that will outstrip the prestige which is accorded to any woman. There seems no evidence that it is necessary for men to surpass women in any specific way, but rather that men do need to find reassurance in achievement, and because of this connection, cultures frequently phrase achievement as something that women do not or cannot do, rather than directly as something which men do well.

The recurrent problem of civilization is to define the male role satisfactorily enough – whether it be to build gardens or raise cattle, kill game or kill enemies, build bridges or handle bank-shares – so that the male may in the course of his life reach a solid sense of irreversible achievement, of which his childhood knowledge of the satisfactions of childbearing have given him a glimpse. In the case of women, it is only necessary that they be permitted by the given social arrangements to fulfill their biological role, to attain this sense of irreversible achievement. If women are to be restless and questing, even in the face of childbearing, they must be made so through education. If men are ever to be at peace, ever certain that their lives have been lived as they were meant to be, they must have, in addition to paternity, culturally elaborated forms of expression that are lasting and sure. Each culture – in its own way – has developed forms that will make men satisfied in their constructive activities without distorting their sure sense of their masculinity. Fewer cultures have yet found ways in which to give women a divine discontent that will demand other satisfactions than those of childbearing.[12]

It seems to me that a more realistic appraisal of contemporary theological doctrines of sin and love is possible against this general background, for the prevalent theologies today were created by men who lived amid the tensions of a hypermasculine culture. What is usually called the "modern era" in Western civilization, stretching roughly from the Renaissance and Reformation up to very recent times and reaching the peak of its expression in the rise of capitalism, the industrial revolution, imperialism, the triumphs of science and technology, and other well-known phenomena of the eighteenth, nineteenth, and twentieth centuries – this modern era can be called the "masculine age par excellence," in the sense that it emphasized, encouraged, and set free precisely those aspects of human nature which are peculiarly significant to men. It placed the highest value on external achievement, on the creation of structures of matter and meaning, on self-differentiation and the separation of man from nature. By its emphasis on laissez faire competition and economic uncertainty, on scientific and geographic explorations, on the widening of the gulf between family relationships, on the one hand, and the public life of business and politics, on the other – by these and many more innovations, the modern era presented a heightened challenge to men; and, by the same token, it increased their natural sense of insecurity and anxiety. It was a masculine era, too, in the degree to which it devalued the functions of women and children and the whole reproductive process. It thereby provoked a new restlessness in women, too.[13]

It is clear that many of the characteristic emphases of contemporary theology – its definition of the human situation in terms of anxiety, estrangement, and the conflict between necessity and freedom; its identification of sin with pride, will-to-power, exploitation, self-assertiveness, and the treatment of others as objects rather than persons; its conception of redemption as restoring to man what he fundamentally lacks (namely, sacrificial love, the I-Thou relationship, the primacy of the personal, and, ultimately, peace) – it is clear that such an analysis of man's dilemma was profoundly responsive and relevant to the concrete facts of modern man's existence. Insofar as modern woman, too, increasingly accepted the prevailing values of the age and took on the challenges and opportunities, risks and insecurities of participation in the masculine world, this theology spoke directly to her condition also. And, since the most striking features of modern culture were but heightened expressions of one aspect of the universal human situation, the adequacy of this theology as a description of man's fundamental predicament seemed assured.

As a matter of fact, however, this theology is not adequate to the universal human situation; its inadequacy is clearer to no one than to certain contemporary women. These women have been enabled, through personal experience and education, to transcend the boundaries of a purely feminine identity. They now stand closer to the juncture of nature and spirit than was possible for most women in the past. They believe in the values of self-differentiation, challenge, and adventure and are not strangers to that "divine discontent" which has always driven men. Yet these same women value their femininity also; they do not wish to discard their sexual identity but rather to gather it up into a higher unity. They want, in other words, to be both women *and* full human beings.

Many of these women, who were brought up to believe in the fundamental equality of the sexes and who were given the same kind of education and the same encouragement to self-realization as their male contemporaries, do not really discover until they marry and bear children – or, perhaps, have been forced to admit to themselves that they never will marry – that there are real differences between the masculine and feminine situations which cannot be blamed upon a cultural lag in the definitions of femininity or upon the "selfishness" and "stupidity" of men. It is only at this point, when the ultimate actualization of their specific sexuality must be either accepted or given up for good, that they become aware of the deep need of almost every woman, regardless of her personal history and achievements or her belief in her own individual value, to surrender her self-identity and be included in another's "power of being." And, if she is fortunate enough to bear a child, she very soon discovers that the one essential, indispensable relationship of a mother to her child is the I-Thou relationship. In infancy the very existence of the child depends upon the mother's ability to transcend her own patterns of thought, feeling, and physical need. As Margaret Mead puts it, "The mother who must learn that the infant who was but an hour ago a part of her own body is now a different individual, with its own hungers and its own needs, and that if she listens to her own body to interpret the child, the child will die, is schooled in an irreplaceable school."[14] At a later stage in the child's life, too, the essential relationship continues to be one of love. To take just one example – the least sentimental one, perhaps – the child, when he has learned to talk, is almost constantly absorbed in trying to understand the world around him. It is so full of strange and wonderful and lovely and terrifying things. He is full of questions, and upon his learning the true and adequate answers to them depends the whole process of acculturation upon which the uniqueness of human societies rests. But, in order to answer a child's eager questions, the mother must be able to transcend her own habitual patterns of thought; she must meet the child where *he* is at that moment. It is absolutely impossible to communicate with a young child without in some way abandoning one's own perspective and looking at the world through *his* eyes.

A mother who rejoices in her maternal role – and most mothers do most of the time – knows the profound experience of self-transcending love. But she knows, too, that it is not the whole meaning of life. For she learns not only that it is impossible to sustain a perpetual I-Thou relationship but that the attempt to do so can be deadly. The moments, hours, and days of self-giving must be balanced by moments, hours, and days of withdrawal into, and enrichment of, her individual selfhood if she is to remain a whole person. She learns, too, that a woman can give too much of herself, so that nothing remains of her own uniqueness; she can become merely an emptiness, almost a zero, without value to herself, to her fellow men, or, perhaps, even to God.

For the temptations of woman *as woman* are not the same as the temptations of man *as man,* and the specifically feminine forms of sin – "feminine" not because they are confined to women or because women are incapable of sinning in other ways but because they are outgrowths of the basic feminine character structure – have a quality which can never be encompassed by such terms as "pride" and "will-to-power." They are better suggested by such items as triviality, distractibility, and diffuseness; lack of an organizing center or focus; dependence on others for one's own self-definition; tolerance at the expense of standards of excellence; inability to respect the boundaries of privacy; sentimentality, gossipy sociability, and mistrust of reason – in short, underdevelopment or negation of the self.

This list of specifically feminine sins could be extended. All of them, however, are to be understood as merely one side of the feminine coin. For just as man's distance from nature is the precondition of his creativity, on the one hand, and his self-concern, on the other, so does woman's closeness to nature have dipolar potentialities. Her sureness of her own femininity and thus of her secure place in the scheme of things may, if she accepts the feminine role with joy, enable her to be a source of strength and refreshment to her husband, her children, and the wider community. If she has been brought up to devalue her femininity, on the other hand, this same sense that for her "anatomy is destiny" may create an attitude of stolid and sterile resignation, a feeling that there is no use in trying. Again, the fact that her whole growth toward womanhood has the character of an inevitable process of bodily maturation rather than that of a challenge and a task may lead her to dissipate herself in activities which are merely trivial. Yet it is the same lack of creative drive which may make it possible for her to perform cheerfully the thousand-and-one routine tasks – the woman's work which is never done – which someone must do if life is to go on. Her capacity for surrendering her individual concerns in order to serve the immediate needs of others – a quality which is so essential to the maternal role – can, on the other hand, induce a kind of diffuseness of purpose, a tendency toward being easily distracted, a failure to discriminate between the more and the less important, and an inability to focus in a sustained manner on the pursuit of any single goal.[15] Her receptivity to the moods and feelings of others and her tendency to merge her selfhood in the joys, sorrows, hopes, and problems of those around her are the positive expressions of an aspect of the feminine character which may also take the negative forms of gossipy sociability, dependence on others (such as husband or children) for the definition of her values, or a refusal to respect another's right to privacy. And her capacity for forgiving love, for cherishing all her children equally without regard to beauty, merit, or intelligence, can also express itself in a kind of indiscriminate tolerance which suspects or rejects all objective criteria of excellence.

All this is not meant to constitute an indictment of the feminine character as such. I have no wish, certainly, to add to the burden of guilt which has been heaped upon women – by themselves as well as by men – for centuries. My purpose, indeed, as far as it concerns women in particular, is quite the opposite. It is to awaken theologians to the fact that the situation of woman, however similar it may appear on the surface of our contemporary world to the situation of man and however much it may be echoed in the life of individual men, is, at bottom, quite different – that the specifically feminine dilemma is, in fact, precisely the opposite

of the masculine. Today, when for the first time in human history it really
seems possible that those endless housewifely tasks – which, along with
the bearing and rearing of children, have always been enough to fill the
whole of each day for the average woman – may virtually be eliminated;
today, when at last women might seem to be in a position to begin to be
both feminine and fully developed, creative human beings; today, these
same women are being subjected to pressures from many sides to return
to the traditional feminine niche and to devote themselves wholly to the
tasks of nurture, support, and service of their families. One might expect
of theologians that they at least not add to these pressures. One might
even expect them to support and encourage the woman who desires to be
both a woman and an individual in her own right, a separate person some
part of whose mind and feelings are inviolable, some part of whose time
belongs strictly to herself, in whose house there is, to use Virginia
Woolf's marvelous image, "a room of one's own." Yet theology, to the
extent that it has defined the human condition on the basis of masculine
experience, continues to speak of such desires as sin or temptation to sin.
If such a woman believes the theologians, she will try to strangle those
impulses in herself. She will believe that, having chosen marriage and
children and thus being face to face with the needs of her family for
love, refreshment, and forgiveness, she has no right to ask anything for
herself but must submit without qualification to the strictly feminine role.

Perhaps, after all, the contemporary woman who wants to participate
in the creative tasks of the world outside her home – those tasks upon
which mankind has built all that is distinctively human, that is, history
and culture – and yet remain a woman is attempting an impossible task.
Perhaps the goal we should set ourselves is to rear our daughters in the
older way, without too much formal education and without encouraging
them to be independent, differentiated, free human beings of whom some
contribution is expected other than the production of the next generation.
If we could do this, our daughters might be able to find secure fulfillment in a simple femininity. After all, the division of labor between the
sexes worked fairly well for thousands of years, and we may be only asking for trouble by trying to modify that structure.

And yet I do not think we can turn back this particular clock. Nor
do I think that the feminine dilemma is of concern only to women. To
understand it is important for men, too, not only because it is a loss to
every man when a woman fails to realize her full self-identity, but because there is, it seems to me, a growing trend in contemporary life toward the feminizing of society itself, including men as well as women.

To document and explore this trend would require a lengthy exposition beyond the scope of the present paper. I can only refer here briefly
to two recent analyses of contemporary Western culture which have impressed me greatly in this connection. Neither of these books – David

Riesman's *The Lonely Crowd*[16] and Hannah Arendt's *The Human Condition*[17] – deals with the masculine-feminine theme as such, yet both of them see a quite recent shift in the fundamental orientation of our present society, one which presages an era as different from what we call the "modern age" as the modern age differs from the medieval. And the analysis of each presents, in its own way, the picture of a society in which the character traits inherent in femininity are being increasingly emphasized, encouraged, and absolutized, just as the modern era raised the essentially masculine character traits to their highest possible power. Lionel Trilling has noted the same trend in our contemporary life and has characterized both its virtues and its dangers with great clarity:

> Our culture is in process of revision, and of revision in a very good and right direction, in the direction of greater openness, greater socialization, greater cooperativeness, greater reasonableness. There are, to be sure, tendencies to be observed which go counter to this one, but they are not, I believe, so momentous as the development of the tendency toward social peace. It must always seem ill-natured to raise any question at all about this tendency. It goes against the grain to do so. . . . The American educated middle class is firm in its admiration of non-conformity and dissent. The right to be nonconformist, the right to dissent, is part of our conception of community. Everybody says so: in the weekly, monthly, quarterly magazines and in *The New York Times,* at the cocktail party, at the conference of psychiatrists, at the conference of teachers. How good this is, and how right! And yet, when we examine the content of our idea of non-conformity, we must be dismayed at the smallness of the concrete actuality this very large idea contains. The rhetoric is as sincere as it is capacious, yet we must sometimes wonder whether what is being praised and defended is anything more than the right to have had some sympathetic connection with Communism ten or twenty years ago. . . . We cannot really imagine non-conformity at all, not in art, not in moral or social theory, certainly not in the personal life – it is probably true that there never was a culture which required so entire an eradication of personal differentiation, so bland a uniformity of manner. Admiring non-conformity and loving community, we have decided that we are all non-conformists together. We assert the right of our egos to court adventure without danger and of our superegos to be conscientious without undue strain.
>
> We make, I think, what is in many ways a very attractive culture, but we really cannot imagine what it means to take an intellectual chance, or to make an intellectual mistake, or to have a real intellectual difference. You have but to read our novels to understand that we have a growing sense of the cooperative virtues and a diminishing sense of the self that cooperates.[18]

It is true that the kind of "selflessness" and "community" described here is hardly what the theologians who identify love with selflessness and community mean when they speak of the redemptive power of love. yet there is no mistaking the fact that there is a strong similarity between theology's view that salvation lies in selfless love and contemporary man's growing tendency to avoid any strong assertion of the self as over against others and to merge his individual identity in the identities of others. In truth, the only element that is lacking in the latter picture is the theological presupposition of man's inherent sinfulness, the stubborn refusal of the individual human being to give up his individuality and separateness and to unite in harmonious love. But, if this refusal to become selfless is wholly sinful, then it would seem that we are obliged to try to overcome it; and, when it is overcome, to whatever extent this may be possible, we are left with a chameleon-like creature who responds to others but has no personal identity of his own.

If it is true that our society is moving from a masculine to a feminine orientation, then theology ought to reconsider its estimate of the human condition and redefine its categories of sin and redemption. For a feminine society will have its own special potentialities for good and evil, to which a theology based solely on masculine experience may well be irrelevant.

Notes

1. Quoted by Clyde Kluckhohn in a review of Margaret Mead, *An Anthropologist at Work: Writings of Ruth Benedict* (Boston: Houghton Mifflin Co., 1959), *New York Times Book Review,* May 31, 1959.

2. New York: William Morrow & Co., 1935.

3. Margaret Mead, *Male and Female* (New York: New American Library, 1959, by arrangement with William Morrow & Co. [originally published in 1949]), pp. 16-17.

4. Helene Deutsch, *Psychology of Women* (New York: Grune & Stratton, 1944), Vols. I and II.

5. Erich Fromm, "Sex and Character," in Ruth Nanda Anshen (ed.), *The Family: Its Function and Destiny* (New York: Harper & Bros., 1949), chap. xix.

6. Theodor Reik, *Of Love and Lust* (New York: Grove Press, 1957, by arrangement with Farrar, Straus & Cudahy [originally published in 1949]).

7. Talcott Parsons, "The Social Structure of the Family," in Anshen (ed.), *op. cit.,* pp. 186-88.

8. Ashley Montagu, *The Natural Superiority of Women* (New York: Macmillan Co., 1953).

9. Mead, *Male and Female,* p. 125.

10. See, among others, Mead, *ibid., passim.*

11. Robert Briffault, *The Mothers* (New York: Macmillan Co., 1927), II, 443.

12. Mead, *Male and Female,* pp. 125-26.

13. This point is discussed at some length by Ferdinand Lundberg and Marynia F. Farnham, M.D., *Modern Woman, the Lost Sex* (New York: Grosset & Dunlap, 1959, by arrangement with Harper & Bros. [originally published in 1947]).

14. Mead, *Male and Female,* p. 284.

15. "The tendency to identification sometimes assumes very valuable forms. Thus, many women put their qualities, which may be excellent, at the disposal of their object of identification. . . . They prefer to love and enjoy their own qualities in others. . . . There are women endowed with rich natural gifts that cannot, however, develop beyond certain limits. Such women are exposed to outside influences and changing identifications to such an extent that they never succeed in consolidating their achievements. Instead of making a reasonable choice among numerous opportunities at their disposal, they constantly get involved in confusion that exerts a destructive influence on their own lives and the lives of those around them" (Deutsch, *op. cit.,* pp. 132-33).

16. New York: Doubleday & Co., 1950, by arrangement with Yale University Press (originally published in 1950).

17. Chicago: University of Chicago Press, 1958.

18. Lionel Trilling, *Freud and the Crisis of Our Culture* (Boston: Beacon Press, 1955), pp. 50-53.

2

The Obligation to Endure

Rachel Carson

THE HISTORY OF LIFE ON EARTH HAS BEEN A HISTORY OF INTERACTION between living things and their surroundings. To a large extent, the physical form and the habits of the earth's vegetation and its animal life have been molded by the environment. Considering the whole span of earthly time, the opposite effect, in which life actually modifies its surroundings, has been relatively slight. Only within the moment of time represented by the present century has one species – man – acquired significant power to alter the nature of his world.

During the past quarter century this power has not only increased to one of disturbing magnitude but it has changed in character. The most alarming of all man's assaults upon the environment is the contamination of air, earth, rivers, and sea with dangerous and even lethal materials. This pollution is for the most part irrecoverable; the chain of evil it initiates not only in the world that must support life but in living tissues is for the most part irreversible. In this now universal contamination of the environment, chemicals are the sinister and little-recognized partners of radiation in changing the very nature of the world – the very nature of its life. Strontium 90, released through nuclear explosions into the air, comes to earth in rain or drifts down as fallout, lodges in soil, enters into the grass or corn or wheat grown there, and in time takes up its abode in the bones of a human being, there to remain until his death. Similarly, chemicals sprayed on croplands or forests or gardens lie long in soil, entering into living organisms, passing from one to another in a chain of poisoning and death. Or they pass mysteriously by underground streams until they emerge and, through the alchemy of air and sunlight, combine into new forms that kill vegetation, sicken cattle, and work unknown harm on those who drink from once pure wells. As Albert Schweitzer has said, "Man can hardly even recognize the devils of his own creation."

It took hundreds of millions of years to produce the life that now inhabits the earth – eons of time in which that developing and evolving and diversifying life reached a state of adjustment and balance with its surroundings. The environment, rigorously shaping and directing the life it supported, contained elements that were hostile as well as supporting.

Certain rocks gave out dangerous radiation; even within the light of the sun, from which all life draws its energy, there were short-wave radiations with power to injure. Given time – time not in years but in millennia – life adjusts, and a balance has been reached. For time is the essential ingredient; but in the modern world there is no time.

The rapidity of change and the speed with which new situations are created follow the impetuous and heedless pace of man rather than the deliberate pace of nature. Radiation is no longer merely the background radiation of rocks, the bombardment of cosmic rays, the ultraviolet of the sun that have existed before there was any life on earth; radiation is now the unnatural creation of man's tampering with the atom. The chemicals to which life is asked to make its adjustment are no longer merely the calcium and silica and copper and all the rest of the minerals washed out of the rocks and carried in rivers to the sea; they are the synthetic creations of man's inventive mind, brewed in his laboratories, and having no counterparts in nature.

To adjust to these chemicals would require time on the scale that is nature's; it would require not merely the years of a man's life but the life of generations. And even this, were it by some miracle possible, would be futile, for the new chemicals come from our laboratories in an endless stream; almost five hundred annually find their way into actual use in the United States alone. The figure is staggering and its implications are not easily grasped – 500 new chemicals to which the bodies of men and animals are required somehow to adapt each year, chemicals totally outside the limits of biologic experience.

Among them are many that are used in man's war against nature. Since the mid-1940's over 200 basic chemicals have been created for use in killing insects, weeds, rodents, and other organisms described in the modern vernacular as "pests"; and they are sold under several thousand different brand names.

These sprays, dusts, and aerosols are now applied almost universally to farms, gardens, forests, and homes – nonselective chemicals that have the power to kill every insect, the "good" and the "bad," to still the song of birds and the leaping of fish in the streams, to coat the leaves with a deadly film, and to linger on in soil – all this though the intended target may be only a few weeds or insects. Can anyone believe it is possible to lay down such a barrage of poisons on the surface of the earth without making it unfit for all life? They should not be called "insecticides," but "biocides."

The whole process of spraying seems caught up in an endless spiral. Since DDT was released for civilian use, a process of escalation has been going on in which ever more toxic materials must be found. This has happened because insects, in a triumphant vindication of Darwin's principle of the survival of the fittest, have evolved super races immune to the particular insecticide used, hence a deadlier one has always to be developed – and then a deadlier one than that. It has happened also because, for reasons to be described later, destructive insects often undergo a "flareback," or resurgence, after spraying, in numbers greater than before. Thus the chemical war is never won, and all life is caught in its violent crossfire.

Along with the possibility of the extinction of mankind by nuclear war, the central problem of our age has therefore become the contamination of man's total environment with such substances of incredible potential for harm – substances that accumulate in the tissues of plants and animals and even penetrate the germ cells to shatter or alter the very material of heredity upon which the shape of the future depends.

Some would-be architects of our future look toward a time when it will be possible to alter the human germ plasm by design. But we may easily be doing so now by inadvertence, for many chemicals, like radiation, bring about gene mutations. It is ironic to think that man might determine his own future by something so seemingly trivial as the choice of an insect spray.

All this has been risked – for what? Future historians may well be amazed by our distorted sense of proportion. How could intelligent beings seek to control a few unwanted species by a method that contaminated the entire environment and brought the threat of disease and death even to their own kind? Yet this is precisely what we have done. We have done it, moreover, for reasons that collapse the moment we examine them. We are told that the enormous and expanding use of pesticides is necessary to maintain farm production. Yet is our real problem not one of *overproduction?* Our farms, despite measures to remove acreages from production and to pay farmers *not* to produce, have yielded such a staggering excess of crops that the American taxpayer in 1962 is paying out more than one billion dollars a year as the total carrying cost of the surplus-food storage program. And is the situation helped when one branch of the Agriculture Department tries to reduce production while another states, as it did in 1958, "It is believed generally that reduction of crop acreages under provisions of the Soil Bank will stimulate interest in use of chemicals to obtain maximum production on the land retained in crops."

All this is not to say there is no insect problem and no need of control. I am saying, rather, that control must be geared to realities, not to mythical situations, and that the methods employed must be such that they do not destroy us along with the insects.

The problem whose attempted solution has brought such a train of disaster in its wake is an accompaniment of our modern way of life. Long before the age of man, insects inhabited the earth – a group of extraordinarily varied and adaptable beings. Over the course of time since man's advent, a small percentage of the more than half a million species of insects have come into conflict with human welfare in two principal ways: as competitors for the food supply and as carriers of human disease.

Disease-carrying insects become important where human beings are crowded together, especially under conditions where sanitation is poor, as in time of natural disaster or war or in situations of extreme poverty and deprivation. Then control of some sort becomes necessary. It is a sobering fact, however, as we shall presently see, that the method of massive chemical control has had only limited success, and also threatens to worsen the very conditions it is intended to curb.

Under primitive agricultural conditions the farmer had few insect problems. These arose with the intensification of agriculture – the devotion of immense acreages to a single crop. Such a system set the stage for explosive increases in specific insect populations. Single-crop farming does not take advantage of the principles by which nature works; it is agriculture as an engineer might conceive it to be. Nature has introduced great variety into the landscape, but man has displayed a passion for simplifying it. Thus he undoes the built-in checks and balances by which nature holds the species within bounds. One important natural check is a limit on the amount of suitable habitat for each species. Obviously then, an insect that lives on wheat can build up its population to much higher levels on a farm devoted to wheat than on one in which wheat is intermingled with other crops to which the insect is not adapted.

The same thing happens in other situations. A generation or more ago, the towns of large areas of the United States lined their streets with the noble elm tree. Now the beauty they hopefully created is threatened with complete destruction as disease sweeps through the elms, carried by a beetle that would have only limited chance to build up large populations and to spread from tree to tree if the elms were only occasional trees in a richly diversified planting.

Another factor in the modern insect problem is one that must be viewed against a background of geologic and human history: the spreading of thousands of different kinds of organisms from their native homes to invade new territories. This worldwide migration has been studied and graphically described by the British ecologist Charles Elton in his recent book *The Ecology of Invasions*. During the Cretaceous Period, some hundred million years ago, flooding seas cut many land bridges between continents and living things found themselves confined in what Elton calls "colossal separate nature reserves." There, isolated from others of their kind, they developed many new species. When some of the land masses were joined again, about 15 million years ago, these species began to move out into new territories – a movement that is not only still in progress but is now receiving considerable assistance from man.

The importation of plants is the primary agent in the modern spread of species, for animals have almost invariably gone along with the plants, quarantine being a comparatively recent and not completely effective innovation. The United States Office of Plant Introduction alone has introduced almost 200,000 species and varieties of plants from all over the world. Nearly half of the 180 or so major insect enemies of plants in the United States are accidental imports from abroad, and most of them have come as hitchhikers on plants.

In new territory, out of reach of the restraining hand of the natural enemies that kept down its numbers in its native land, an invading plant or animal is able to become enormously abundant. Thus it is no accident that our most troublesome insects are introduced species.

These invasions, both the naturally occurring and those dependent on human assistance, are likely to continue indefinitely. Quarantine and massive chemical campaigns are only extremely expensive ways of buying time. We are faced, according to Dr. Elton, "with a life-and-death need not just to find new technological means of suppressing this plant or that animal"; instead we need the basic knowledge of animal populations and their relations to their surroundings that will "promote an even balance and damp down the explosive power of outbreaks and new invasions."

Much of the necessary knowledge is now available but we do not use it. We train ecologists in our universities and even employ them in our governmental agencies but we seldom take their advice. We allow the chemical death rain to fall as though there were no alternative, whereas in fact there are many, and our ingenuity could soon discover many more if given opportunity.

Have we fallen into a mesmerized state that makes us accept as inevitable that which is inferior or detrimental, as though having lost the will or the vision to demand that which is good? Such thinking, in the words of the ecologist Paul Shepard, "idealizes life with only its head out of water, inches above the limits of toleration of the corruption of its own environment. . . . Why should we tolerate a diet of weak poisons, a home in insipid surroundings, a circle of acquaintances who are not quite our enemies, the noise of motors with just enough relief to prevent insanity? Who would want to live in a world which is just not quite fatal?"

Yet such a world is pressed upon us. The crusade to create a chemically sterile, insect-free world seems to have engendered a fanatic zeal on the part of many specialists and most of the so-called control agencies. On every hand there is evidence that those engaged in spraying operations exercise a ruthless power. "The regulatory entomologists . . . function as prosecutor, judge and jury, tax assessor and collector and sheriff to enforce their own orders," said Connecticut entomologist Neely Turner. The most flagrant abuses go unchecked in both state and federal agencies.

It is not my contention that chemical insecticides must never be used. I do contend that we have put poisonous and biologically potent chemicals indiscriminately into the hands of persons largely or wholly ignorant of their potentials for harm. We have subjected enormous numbers of people to contact with these poisons, without their consent and often without their knowledge. If the Bill of Rights contains no guarantee that a citizen shall be secure against lethal poisons distributed either by private individuals or by public officials, it is surely only because our forefathers, despite their considerable wisdom and foresight, could conceive of no such problem.

I contend, furthermore, that we have allowed these chemicals to be used with little or no advance investigation of their effect on soil, water, wildlife, and man himself. Future generations are unlikely to condone our lack of prudent concern for the integrity of the natural world that supports all life.

There is still very limited awareness of the nature of the threat. This is an era of specialists, each of whom sees his own problem and is unaware of or intolerant of the larger frame into which it fits. It is also an era dominated by industry, in which the right to make a dollar at whatever cost is seldom challenged. When the public protests, confronted with some obvious evidence of damaging results of pesticide applications, it is fed little tranquilizing pills of half truth. We urgently need an end to these false assurances, to the sugar coating of unpalatable facts. It is the public that is being asked to assume the risks that the insect controllers calculate. The public must decide whether it wishes to continue on the present road, and it can do so only when in full possession of the facts. In the words of Jean Rostand, "The obligation to endure gives us the right to know."

3

The Historical Roots
of Our Ecologic Crisis

Lynn White, Jr.

A CONVERSATION WITH ALDOUS HUXLEY NOT INFREQUENTLY PUT ONE AT the receiving end of an unforgettable monologue. About a year before his lamented death he was discoursing on a favorite topic: Man's unnatural treatment of nature and its sad results. To illustrate his point he told how, during the previous summer, he had returned to a little valley in England where he had spent many happy months as a child. Once it had been composed of delightful grassy glades; now it was becoming overgrown with unsightly brush because the rabbits that formerly kept such growth under control had largely succumbed to a disease, myxomatosis, that was deliberately introduced by the local farmers to reduce the rabbits' destruction of crops. Being something of a Philistine, I could be silent no longer, even in the interests of great rhetoric. I interrupted to point out that the rabbit itself had been brought as a domestic animal to England in 1176, presumably to improve the protein diet of the peasantry.

All forms of life modify their contexts. The most spectacular and benign instance is doubtless the coral polyp. By serving its own ends, it has created a vast undersea world favorable to thousands of other kinds of animals and plants. Ever since man became a numerous species he has affected his environment notably. The hypothesis that his fire-drive method of hunting created the world's great grasslands and helped to exterminate the monster mammals of the Pleistocene from much of the globe is plausible, if not proved. For 6 millennia at least, the banks of the lower Nile have been a human artifact rather than the swampy African jungle which nature, apart from man, would have made it. The Aswan Dam, flooding 5000 square miles, is only the latest stage in a long process. In many regions terracing or irrigation, overgrazing, the cutting of forests by Romans to build ships to fight Carthaginians or by Crusaders to solve the logistics problems of their expeditions, have profoundly changed some ecologies. Observation that the French landscape falls into two basic types, the open fields of the north and the *bocage* of the south and west, inspired Marc Bloch to undertake his classic study of medieval agricultural methods. Quite unintentionally, changes in human ways often affect nonhuman nature. It has been noted, for example, that the advent of the automobile eliminated huge flocks of sparrows that once fed on the horse manure littering every street.

The history of ecologic change is still so rudimentary that we know little about what really happened, or what the results were. The extinction of the European aurochs as late as 1627 would seem to have been a simple case of overenthusiastic hunting. On more intricate matters it often is impossible to find solid information. For a thousand years or more the Frisians and Hollanders have been pushing back the North Sea, and the process is culminating in our own time in the reclamation of the Zuider Zee. What, if any, species of animals, birds, fish, shore life, or plants have died out in the process? In their epic combat with Neptune have the Netherlanders overlooked ecological values in such a way that the quality of human life in the Netherlands has suffered? I cannot discover that the questions have ever been asked, much less answered.

People, then, have often been a dynamic element in their own environment, but in the present state of historical scholarship we usually do not know exactly when, where, or with what effects man-induced changes came. As we enter the last third of the 20th century, however, concern for the problem of ecologic backlash is mounting feverishly. Natural science, conceived as the effort to understand the nature of things, had flourished in several eras and among several peoples. Similarly there had been an age-old accumulation of technological skills, sometimes growing rapidly, sometimes slowly. But it was not until about four generations ago that Western Europe and North America arranged a marriage between science and technology, a union of the theoretical and the empirical approaches to our natural environment. The emergence in widespread practice of the Baconian creed that scientific knowledge means technological power over nature can scarcely be dated before about 1850, save in the chemical industries, where it is anticipated in the 18th century. Its acceptance as a normal pattern of action may mark the greatest event in human history since the invention of agriculture, and perhaps in nonhuman terrestrial history as well.

Almost at once the new situation forced the crystallization of the novel concept of ecology; indeed, the word *ecology* first appeared in the English language in 1873. Today, less than a century later, the impact of our race upon the environment has so increased in force that it has changed in essence. When the first cannons were fired, in the early 14th century, they affected ecology by sending workers scrambling to the forests and mountains for more potash, sulfur, iron ore, and charcoal, with some resulting erosion and deforestation. Hydrogen bombs are of a different order: a war fought with them might alter the genetics of all life on this planet. By 1285 London had a smog problem arising from the burning of soft coal, but our present combustion of fossil fuels threatens to change the chemistry of the globe's atmosphere as a whole, with consequences which we are only beginning to guess. With the population explosion, the carcinoma of planless urbanism, the now geological deposits of sewage and garbage, surely no creature other than man has ever managed to foul its nest in such short order.

There are many calls to action, but specific proposals, however worthy as individual items, seem too partial, palliative, negative: ban the bomb, tear down the billboards, give the Hindus contraceptives and tell them to eat their sacred cows. The simplest solution to any suspect change is, of course, to stop it, or, better yet, to revert to a romanticized past: make those ugly gasoline stations look like Anne Hathaway's cottage or (in the Far West) like ghost-town saloons. The "wilderness area" mentality invariably advocates deep-freezing an ecology, whether San Gimignano or the High Sierra, as it was before the first Kleenex was dropped. But neither atavism nor prettification will cope with the ecologic crisis of our time. What shall we do? No one yet knows. Unless we think about fundamentals, our specific measures may produce new backlashes more serious than those they are designed to remedy.

As a beginning we should try to clarify our thinking by looking, in some historical depth, at the presuppositions that underlie modern technology and science. Science was traditionally aristocratic, speculative, intellectual in intent; technology was lower-class, empirical, action-oriented. The quite sudden fusion of these two, towards the middle of the 19th century, is surely related to the slightly prior and contemporary democratic revolutions which, by reducing social barriers, tended to assert a functional unity of brain and hand. Our ecologic crisis is the product of an emerging, entirely novel, democratic culture. The issue is whether a democratized world can survive its own implications. Presumably we cannot unless we rethink

The Western Traditions of Technology and Science

One thing is so certain that it seems stupid to verbalize it: both modern technology and modern science are distinctively *Occidental*. Our technology has absorbed elements from all over the world, notably from China; yet everywhere today, whether in Japan or in Nigeria, successful technology is Western. Our science is the heir to all the sciences of the past, especially perhaps to the work of the great Islamic scientists of the Middle Ages, who so often outdid the ancient Greeks in skill and perspicacity: al-Razi in medicine, for example; or ibn-Haytham in optics; or Omar Khayyám in mathematics. Indeed, not a few works of such geniuses seem to have vanished in the original Arabic and to survive only in medieval Latin translations that helped to lay the foundations for later

Western developments. Today, around the globe, all significant science is
Western in style and method, whatever the pigmentation or language of
the scientists.

A second pair of facts is less well recognized because they result
from quite recent historical scholarship. The leadership of the West, both
in technology and in science, is far older than the so-called Scientific
Revolution of the 17th century or the so-called Industrial Revolution of
the 18th century. These terms are in fact outmoded and obscure the true
nature of what they try to describe – significant stages in two long and
separate developments. By A.D. 1000 at the latest – and perhaps, feebly,
as much as 200 years earlier – the West began to apply water power to
industrial processes other than milling grain. This was followed in the
late 12th century by the harnessing of wind power. From simple beginnings, but with remarkable consistency of style, the West rapidly expanded its skills in the development of power machinery, labor-saving devices, and automation. Those who doubt should contemplate that most
monumental achievement in the history of automation: the weight-driven
mechanical clock, which appeared in two forms in the early 14th century.
Not in craftsmanship but in basic technological capacity, the Latin West
of the later Middle Ages far outstripped its elaborate, sophisticated. and
esthetically magnificent sister cultures, Byzantium and Islam. In 1444 a
great Greek ecclesiastic, Bessarion, who had gone to Italy, wrote a letter
to a prince in Greece. He is amazed by the superiority of Western ships,
arms, textiles, glass. But above all he is astonished by the spectacle of
waterwheels sawing timbers and pumping the bellows of blast furnaces.
Clearly, he had seen nothing of the sort in the Near East.

By the end of the 15th century the technological superiority of
Europe was such that its small, mutually hostile nations could spill out
over all the rest of the world, conquering, looting, and colonizing. The
symbol of this technological superiority is the fact that Portugal, one of
the weakest states of the Occident, was able to become, and to remain for
a century, mistress of the East Indies. And we must remember that the
technology of Vasco da Gama and Albuquerque was built by pure empiricism, drawing remarkably little support or inspiration from science.

In the present-day vernacular understanding, modern science is supposed to have begun in 1543, when both Copernicus and Vesalius published their great works. It is no derogation of their accomplishments,
however, to point out that such structures as the *Fabrica* and the *De revo-
lutionibus* do not appear overnight. The distinctive Western tradition of
science, in fact, began in the late 11th century with a massive movement
of translation of Arabic and Greek scientific works into Latin. A few notable books – Theophrastus, for example – escaped the West's avid new
appetite for science, but within less than 200 years effectively the entire
corpus of Greek and Muslim science was available in Latin, and was be-

ing eagerly read and criticized in the new European universities. Out of criticism arose new observation, speculation, and increasing distrust of ancient authorities. By the late 13th century Europe had seized global scientific leadership from the faltering hands of Islam. It would be as absurd to deny the profound originality of Newton, Galileo, or Copernicus as to deny that of the 14th century scholastic scientists like Buridan or Oresme on whose work they built. Before the 11th century, science scarcely existed in the Latin West, even in Roman times. From the 11th century onward, the scientific sector of Occidental culture has increased in a steady crescendo.

Since both our technological and our scientific movements got their start, acquired their character, and achieved world dominance in the Middle Ages, it would seem that we cannot understand their nature or their present impact upon ecology without examining fundamental medieval assumptions and developments.

Medieval View of Man and Nature

Until recently, agriculture has been the chief occupation even in "advanced" societies; hence, any change in methods of tillage has much importance. Early plows, drawn by two oxen, did not normally turn the sod but merely scratched it. Thus, crossplowing was needed and fields tended to be squarish. In the fairly light soils and semiarid climates of the Near East and Mediterranean, this worked well.

But such a plow was inappropriate to the wet climate and often sticky soils of northern Europe. By the latter part of the 7th century after Christ, however, following obscure beginnings, certain northern peasants were using an entirely new kind of plow, equipped with a vertical knife to cut the line of the furrow, a horizontal share to slice under the sod, and a moldboard to turn it over. The friction of this plow with the soil was so great that it normally required not two but eight oxen. It attacked the land with such violence that cross-plowing was not needed, and fields tended to be shaped in long strips.

In the days of the scratch-plow, fields were distributed generally in units capable of supporting a single family. Subsistence farming was the presupposition. But no peasant owned eight oxen: to use the new and more efficient plow, peasants pooled their oxen to form large plow-teams, originally receiving (it would appear) plowed strips in proportion to their contribution. Thus, distribution of land was based no longer on the needs of a family but, rather, on the capacity of a power machine to till the earth. Man's relation to the soil was profoundly changed. Formerly man had been part of nature; now he was the exploiter of nature. Nowhere else in the world did farmers develop any analogous agricultural implement. Is it coincidence that modern technology, with its ruthlessness toward nature, has so largely been produced by descendants of these peasants of northern Europe?

This same exploitive attitude appears slightly before A.D. 830 in Western illustrated calendars. In older calendars the months were shown as passive personifications. The new Frankish calendars, which set the style for the Middle Ages, are very different: they show men coercing the world around them – plowing, harvesting, chopping trees, butchering pigs. Man and nature are two things, and man is master.

These novelties seem to be in harmony with larger intellectual patterns. What people do about their ecology depends on what they think about themselves in relation to things around them. Human ecology is deeply conditioned by beliefs about our nature and destiny – that is, by religion. To Western eyes this is very evident in, say, India or Ceylon. It is equally true of ourselves and of our medieval ancestors.

The victory of Christianity over paganism was the greatest psychic revolution in the history of our culture. It has become fashionable today to say that, for better or worse, we live in "the post-Christian age." Certainly the forms of our thinking and language have largely ceased to be Christian, but to my eye the substance often remains amazingly akin to that of the past. Our daily habits of action, for example, are dominated by an implicit faith in perpetual progress which was unknown either to Greco-Roman antiquity or to the Orient. It is rooted in, and is indefensible apart from, Judeo-Christian teleology. The fact that Communists share it merely helps to show what can be demonstrated on many other grounds: that Marxism, like Islam, is a Judeo-Christian heresy. We continue today to live, as we have lived for about 1700 years, very largely in a context of Christian axioms.

What did Christianity tell people about their relations with the environment?

While many of the world's mythologies provide stories of creation, Greco-Roman mythology was singularly incoherent in this respect. Like Aristotle, the intellectuals of the ancient West denied that the visible world had had a beginning. Indeed, the idea of a beginning was impossible in the framework of their cyclical notion of time. In sharp contrast, Christianity inherited from Judaism not only a concept of time as non-repetitive and linear but also a striking story of creation. By gradual stages a loving and all-powerful God had created light and darkness, the heavenly bodies, the earth and all its plants, animals, birds, and fishes. Finally, God had created Adam and, as an afterthought, Eve to keep man from being lonely. Man named all the animals, thus establishing his dominance over them. God planned all of this explicitly for man's benefit and rule: no item in the physical creation had any purpose save to serve man's purposes. And, although man's body is made of clay, he is not simply part of nature: he is made in God's image.

Especially in its Western form, Christianity is the most anthropocentric religion the world has seen. As early as the 2nd century both Tertullian and Saint Irenaeus of Lyons were insisting that when God shaped Adam he was foreshadowing the image of the incarnate Christ, the Second Adam. Man shares, in great measure, God's transcendence of nature. Christianity, in absolute contrast to ancient paganism and Asia's religions (except, perhaps, Zoroastrianism), not only established a dualism of man and nature but also insisted that it is God's will that man exploit nature for his proper ends.

At the level of the common people this worked out in an interesting way. In Antiquity every tree, every spring, every stream, every hill had its own *genius loci,* its guardian spirit. These spirits were accessible to men, but were very unlike men; centaurs, fauns, and mermaids show their ambivalence. Before one cut a tree, mined a mountain, or dammed a brook, it was important to placate the spirit in charge of that particular situation, and to keep it placated. By destroying pagan animism, Christianity made it possible to exploit nature in a mood of indifference to the feelings of natural objects.

It is often said that for animism the Church substituted the cult of saints. True; but the cult of saints is functionally quite different from animism. The saint is not *in* natural objects; he may have special shrines, but his citizenship is in heaven. Moreover, a saint is entirely a man; he can be approached in human terms. In addition to saints, Christianity *of* course also had angels and demons inherited from Judaism and perhaps, at one remove, from Zoroastrianism. But these were all as mobile as the saints themselves. The spirits in natural objects, which formerly had protected nature from man, evaporated. Man's effective monopoly on spirit in this world was confirmed, and the old inhibitions to the exploitation of nature crumbled.

When one speaks in such sweeping terms, a note of caution is in order. Christianity is a complex faith, and its consequences differ in differing contexts. What I have said may well apply to the medieval West, where in fact technology made spectacular advances. But the Greek East, a highly civilized realm of equal Christian devotion, seems to have produced no marked technological innovation after the late 7th century, when Greek fire was invented. The key to the contrast may perhaps be found in a difference in the tonality of piety and thought which students of comparative theology find between the Greek and the Latin Churches. The Greeks believed that sin was intellectual blindness, and that salvation was found in illumination, orthodoxy – that is, clear thinking. The Latins, on the other hand, felt that sin was moral evil, and that salvation was to be found in right conduct. Eastern theology has been intellectualist. Western theology has been voluntarist. The Greek saint contemplates; the Western saint acts. The implications of Christianity for the conquest of nature would emerge more easily in the Western atmosphere.

The Christian dogma of creation, which is found in the first clause of all the Creeds, has another meaning for our comprehension of today's ecologic crisis. By revelation, God had given man the Bible, the Book of Scripture. But since God had made nature, nature also must reveal the divine mentality. The religious study of nature for the better understanding of God was known as natural theology. In the early Church, and always in the Greek East, nature was conceived primarily as a symbolic system through which God speaks to men: the ant is a sermon to sluggards; rising flames are the symbol of the soul's aspiration. This view of nature was essentially artistic rather than scientific. While Byzantium preserved and copied great numbers of ancient Greek scientific texts, science as we conceive it could scarcely flourish in such an ambiance.

However, in the Latin West by the early 13th century natural theology was following a very different bent. It was ceasing to be the decoding of the physical symbols of God's communication with man and was becoming the effort to understand God's mind by discovering how his creation operates. The rainbow was no longer simply a symbol of hope first sent to Noah after the Deluge: Robert Grosseteste, Friar Roger Bacon, and Theodoric of Freiberg produced startlingly sophisticated work on the optics of the rainbow, but they did it as a venture in religious understanding. From the 13th century onward, up to and including Leibnitz and Newton, every major scientist, in effect, explained his motivations in religious terms. Indeed, if Galileo had not been so expert an amateur theologian he would have got into far less trouble: the professionals resented his intrusion. And Newton seems to have regarded himself more as a theologian than as a scientist. It was not until the late 18th century that the hypothesis of God became unnecessary to many scientists.

It is often hard for the historian to judge, when men explain why they are doing what they want to do, whether they are offering real reasons or merely culturally acceptable reasons. The consistency with which scientists during the long formative centuries of Western science said that the task and the reward of the scientist was "to think God's thoughts after him" leads one to believe that this was their real motivation. If so, then modern Western science was cast in a matrix of Christian theology. The dynamism of religious devotion, shaped by the Judeo-Christian dogma of creation, gave it impetus.

An Alternative Christian View

We would seem to be headed toward conclusions unpalatable to many Christians. Since both *science* and *technology* are blessed words in our contemporary vocabulary, some may be happy at the notions, first, that, viewed historically, modern science is an extrapolation of natural theology and, second, that modern technology is at least partly to be explained as an Occidental, voluntarist realization of the Christian dogma of man's transcendence of, and rightful mastery over, nature. But, as we now recognize, somewhat over a century ago science and technology – hitherto quite separate activities – joined to give mankind powers which, to judge by many of the ecologic effects, are out of control. If so, Christianity bears a huge burden of guilt.

I personally doubt that disastrous ecologic backlash can be avoided simply by applying to our problems more science and more technology. Our science and technology have grown out of Christian attitudes toward man's relation to nature which are almost universally held not only by Christians and neo-Christians but also by those who fondly regard themselves as post-Christians. Despite Copernicus, all the cosmos rotates around our little globe. Despite Darwin, we are *not,* in our hearts, part of the natural process. We are superior to nature, contemptuous of it, willing to use it for our slightest whim. The newly elected Governor of California, like myself a churchman but less troubled than I, spoke for the Christian tradition when he said (as is alleged), "when you've seen one redwood tree, you've seen them all." To a Christian a tree can be no more than a physical fact. The whole concept of the sacred grove is alien to Christianity and to the ethos of the West. For nearly 2 millennia Christian missionaries have been chopping down sacred groves, which are idolatrous because they assume spirit in nature.

What we do about ecology depends on our ideas of the man-nature relationship. More science and more technology are not going to get us out of the present ecologic crisis until we find a new religion, or rethink our old one. The beatniks, who are the basic revolutionaries of our time, show a sound instinct in their affinity for Zen Buddhism, which conceives of the man-nature relationship as very nearly the mirror image of the Christian view. Zen, however, is as deeply conditioned by Asian history as Christianity is by the experience of the West, and I am dubious of its viability among us.

Possibly we should ponder the greatest radical in Christian history since Christ: Saint Francis of Assisi. The prime miracle of Saint Francis is the fact that he did not end at the stake, as many of his left-wing followers did. He was so clearly heretical that a General of the Franciscan Order, Saint Bonaventura, a great and perceptive Christian, tried to suppress the early accounts of Franciscanism. The key to an understanding of

Francis is his belief in the virtue of humility – not merely for the individual but for man as a species. Francis tried to depose man from his monarchy over creation and set up a democracy of all God's creatures. With him the ant is no longer simply a homily for the lazy, flames a sign of the thrust of the soul toward union with God; now they are Brother Ant and Sister Fire, praising the Creator in their own ways as Brother Man does in his.

Later commentators have said that Francis preached to the birds as a rebuke to men who would not listen. The records do not read so: he urged the little birds to praise God, and in spiritual ecstasy they flapped their wings and chirped rejoicing. Legends of saints, especially the Irish saints, had long told of their dealings with animals but always, I believe, to show their human dominance over creatures. With Francis it is different. The land around Gubbio in the Apennines was being ravaged by a fierce wolf. Saint Francis, says the legend, talked to the wolf and persuaded him of the error of his ways. The wolf repented, died in the odor of sanctity, and was buried in consecrated ground.

What Sir Steven Ruciman calls "the Franciscan doctrine of the animal soul" was quickly stamped out. Quite possibly it was in part inspired, consciously or unconsciously, by the belief in reincarnation held by the Cathar heretics who at that time teemed in Italy and southern France, and who presumably had got it originally from India. It is significant that at just the same moment, about 1200, traces of metempsychosis are found also in western Judaism, in the Provençal *Cabbala*. But Francis held neither to transmigration of souls nor to pantheism. His view of nature and of man rested on a unique sort of pan-psychism of all things animate and inanimate, designed for the glorification of their transcendent Creator, who, in the ultimate gesture of cosmic humility, assumed flesh, lay helpless in a manger, and hung dying on a scaffold.

I am not suggesting that many contemporary Americans who are concerned about our ecologic crisis will be either able or willing to counsel with wolves or exhort birds. However, the present increasing disruption of the global environment is the product of a dynamic technology and science which were originating in the Western medieval world against which Saint Francis was rebelling in so original a way. Their growth cannot be understood historically apart from distinctive attitudes toward nature which are deeply grounded in Christian dogma. The fact that most people do not think of these attitudes as Christian is irrelevant. No new set of basic values has been accepted in our society to displace those of Christianity. Hence we shall continue to have a worsening ecologic crisis until we reject the Christian axiom that nature has no reason for existence save to serve man.

The greatest spiritual revolutionary in Western history, Saint Francis, proposed what he thought was an alternative Christian view of nature and man's relation to it: he tried to substitute the idea of the equality of all creatures, including man, for the idea of man's limitless rule of creation. He failed. Both our present science and our present technology are so tinctured with orthodox Christian arrogance toward nature that no solution for our ecologic crisis can be expected from them alone. Since the roots of our trouble are so largely religious, the remedy must also be essentially religious, whether we call it that or not. We must rethink and refeel our nature and destiny. The profoundly religious, but heretical, sense of the primitive Franciscans for the spiritual autonomy of all parts of nature may point a direction. I propose Francis as a patron saint for ecologists.

4

Is Female to Male
as Nature Is to Culture?*

Sherry B. Ortner

MUCH OF THE CREATIVITY OF ANTHROPOLOGY DERIVES FROM THE TENSION
between two sets of demands: that we explain human universals, and that
we explain cultural particulars. By this canon, woman provides us with
one of the more challenging problems to be dealt with. The secondary
status of woman in society is one of the true universals, a pan-cultural
fact. Yet within that universal fact, the specific cultural conceptions and
symbolizations of woman are extraordinarily diverse and even mutually
contradictory. Further, the actual treatment of women and their relative
power and contribution vary enormously from culture to culture, and over
different periods in the history of particular cultural traditions. Both of
these points – the universal fact and the cultural variation – constitute
problems to be explained.

My interest in the problem is of course more than academic: I wish
to see genuine change come about, the emergence of a social and cultural
order in which as much of the range of human potential is open to
women as is open to men. The universality of female subordination, the
fact that it exists within every type of social and economic arrangement
and in societies of every degree of complexity, indicates to me that we
are up against something very profound, very stubborn, something we
cannot rout out simply by rearranging a few tasks and roles in the social
system, or even by reordering the whole economic structure. In this paper
I try to expose the underlying logic of cultural thinking that assumes the

*   The first version of this paper was presented in October 1972 as a lecture in the course
"Women: Myth and Reality" at Sarah Lawrence College. I received helpful comments from
the students and from my co-teachers in the course: Joan Kelly Gadol, Eva Kollisch, and
Gerda Lerner. A short account was delivered at the American Anthropological Association
meetings in Toronto, November 1972. Meanwhile, I received excellent critical comments from
Karen Blu, Robert Paul, Michelle Rosaldo, David Schneider, and Terence Turner, and the
present version of the paper, in which the thrust of the argument has been rather significantly
changed, was written in response to those comments. I, of course, retain responsibility for its
final form. The paper is dedicated to Simone de Beauvoir, whose book *The Second Sex*
(1953), first published in French in 1949, remains in my opinion the best single
comprehensive understanding of "the woman problem."

inferiority of women; I try to show the highly persuasive nature of the logic, for if it were not so persuasive, people would not keep subscribing to it. But I also try to show the social and cultural sources of that logic, to indicate wherein lies the potential for change.

It is important to sort out the levels of the problem. The confusion can be staggering. For example, depending on which aspect of Chinese culture we look at, we might extrapolate any of several entirely different guesses concerning the status of women in China. In the ideology of Taoism, *yin,* the female principle, and *yang,* the male principle, are given equal weight; "the opposition, alternation, and interaction of these two forces give rise to all phenomena in the universe" (Siu, 1968: 2). Hence we might guess that maleness and femaleness are equally valued in the general ideology of Chinese culture.[1] Looking at the social structure, however, we see the strongly emphasized patrilineal descent principle, the importance of sons, and the absolute authority of the father in the family. Thus we might conclude that China is the archetypal patriarchal society. Next, looking at the actual roles played, power and influence wielded, and material contributions made by women in Chinese society – all of which are, upon observation, quite substantial – we would have to say that women are allotted a great deal of (unspoken) status in the system. Or again, we might focus on the fact that a goddess, Kuan Yin, is the central (most worshipped, most depicted) deity in Chinese Buddhism, and we might be tempted to say, as many have tried to say about goddess-worshipping cultures in prehistoric and early historical societies, that China is actually a sort of matriarchy. In short, we must be absolutely clear about *what* we are trying to explain before explaining it.

We may differentiate three levels of the problem:

1. The universal fact of culturally attributed second-class status of woman in every society. Two questions are important here. First, what do we mean by this; what is our evidence that this is a universal fact? And second, how are we to explain this fact, once having established it?

2. Specific ideologies, symbolizations, and socio-structural arrangements pertaining to women that vary widely from culture to culture. The problem at this level is to account for any particular cultural complex in terms of factors specific to that group – the standard level of anthropological analysis.

3. Observable on-the-ground details of women's activities, contributions, powers, influence, etc., often at variance with cultural ideology (although always constrained within the assumption that women may never be officially preeminent in the total system). This is the level of direct observation, often adopted now by feminist-oriented anthropologists.

This paper is primarily concerned with the first of these levels, the problem of the universal devaluation of women. The analysis thus depends not upon specific cultural data but rather upon an analysis of "culture" taken generically as a special sort of process in the world. A discussion of the second level, the problem of cross-cultural variation in conceptions and relative valuations of women, will entail a great deal of cross-cultural research and must be postponed to another time. As for the third level, it will be obvious from my approach that I would consider it a misguided endeavor to focus only upon women's actual though culturally unrecognized and unvalued powers in any given society, without first understanding the overarching ideology and deeper assumptions of the culture that render such powers trivial.

The Universality of Female Subordination

What do I mean when I say that everywhere, in every known culture, women are considered in some degree inferior to men? First of all, I must stress that I am talking about *cultural* evaluations; I am saying that each culture, in its own way and on its own terms, makes this evaluation. But what would constitute evidence that a particular culture considers women inferior?

Three types of data would suffice: (1) elements of cultural ideology and informants' statements that *explicitly* devalue women, according them, their roles, their tasks, their products, and their social milieu less prestige than are accorded men and the male correlates; (2) symbolic devices, such as the attribution of defilement, which may be interpreted as *implicitly* making a statement of inferior valuation; and (3) social-structural arrangements that exclude women from participation in or contact with some realm in which the highest powers of the society are felt to reside.[2] These three types of data may all of course be interrelated in any particular system, though they need not necessarily be. Further, any one of them will usually be sufficient to make the point of female inferiority in a given culture. Certainly, female exclusion from the most sacred rite or the highest political council is sufficient evidence. Certainly, explicit cultural ideology devaluing women (and their tasks, roles, products, etc.) is sufficient evidence. Symbolic indicators such as defilement are usually sufficient, although in a few cases in which, say, men and women are equally polluting to one another, a further indicator is required – and is, as far as my investigations have ascertained, always available.

On any or all of these counts, then, I would flatly assert that we find women subordinated to men in every known society. The search for a genuinely egalitarian, let alone matriarchal, culture has proved fruitless. An example from one society that has traditionally been on the credit side of this ledger will suffice. Among the matrilineal Crow, as Lowie (1956) points out, "Women . . . had highly honorific offices in the Sun Dance; they could become directors of the Tobacco Ceremony and played, if anything, a more conspicuous part in it than the men; they sometimes played the hostess in the Cooked Meat Festival; they were not debarred from sweating or doctoring or from seeking a vision" (p. 61). Nonetheless, "Women [during menstruation] formerly rode inferior horses and evidently this loomed as a source of contamination, for they were not allowed to approach either a wounded man or men starting on a war party. A taboo still lingers against their coming near sacred objects at these times" (p. 44). Further, just before enumerating women's rights of participation in the various rituals noted above, Lowie mentions one particular Sun Dance Doll bundle that was not supposed to be unwrapped by a woman (p. 60). Pursuing this trail we find: "According to all Lodge Grass informants and most others, the doll owned by Wrinkled-face took precedence not only of other dolls but of all other Crow medicines whatsoever. . . . This particular doll was not supposed to be handled by a woman" (p. 229).[3]

In sum, the Crow are probably a fairly typical case. Yes, women have certain powers and rights, in this case some that place them in fairly high positions. Yet ultimately the line is drawn: menstruation is a threat to warfare, one of the most valued institutions of the tribe, one that is central to their self-definition; and the most sacred object of the tribe is taboo to the direct sight and touch of women.

Similar examples could be multiplied ad infinitum, but I think the onus is no longer upon us to demonstrate that female subordination is a cultural universal; it is up to those who would argue against the point to bring forth counterexamples. I shall take the universal secondary status of women as a given, and proceed from there.

Nature and Culture[4]

How are we to explain the universal devaluation of women? We could of course rest the case on biological determinism. There is something genetically inherent in the male of the species, so the biological determinists would argue, that makes them the naturally dominant sex; that "something" is lacking in females, and as a result women are not only naturally subordinate but in general quite satisfied with their position, since it affords them protection and the opportunity to maximize maternal pleasures, which to them are the most satisfying experiences of life. Without going into a detailed refutation of this position, I think it fair to say that it has failed to be established to the satisfaction of almost anyone in academic anthropology. *This is to say, not that biological facts are ir-*

relevant, or that men and women are not different, but that these facts and differences only take on significance of superior/inferior within the framework of culturally defined value systems.

If we are unwilling to rest the case on genetic determinism, it seems to me that we have only one way to proceed. We must attempt to interpret female subordination in light of other universals, factors built into the structure of the most generalized situation in which all human beings, in whatever culture, find themselves. For example, every human being has a physical body and a sense of nonphysical mind, is part of a society of other individuals and an inheritor of a cultural tradition, and must engage in some relationship, however mediated, with "nature," or the nonhuman realm, in order to survive. Every human being is born (to a mother) and ultimately dies, all are assumed to have an interest in personal survival, and society/culture has its own interest in (or at least momentum toward) continuity and survival, which transcends the lives and deaths of particular individuals. And so forth. It is in the realm of such universals of the human condition that we must seek an explanation for the universal fact of female devaluation.

I translate the problem, in other words, into the following simple question. *What could there be in the generalized structure and conditions of existence, common to every culture, that would lead every culture to place a lower value upon women?* Specifically, my thesis is that woman is being identified with – or, if you will, seems to be a symbol of – something that every culture devalues, something that every culture defines as being of a lower order of existence than itself. Now it seems that there is only one thing that would fit that description, and that is "nature" in the most generalized sense. Every culture, or, generically, "culture," is engaged in the process of generating and sustaining systems of meaningful forms (symbols, artifacts, etc.) by means of which humanity transcends the givens of natural existence, bends them to its purposes, controls them in its interest. We may thus broadly equate culture with the notion of human consciousness, or with the products of human consciousness (i.e., systems of thought and technology), by means of which humanity attempts to assert control over nature.

Now the categories of "nature" and "culture" are of course conceptual categories – one can find no boundary out in the actual world between the two states or realms of being. And there is no question that some cultures articulate a much stronger opposition between the two categories than others – it has even been argued that primitive peoples (some or all) do not see or intuit any distinction between the human cultural state and the state of nature at all. Yet I would maintain that the universality of ritual betokens an assertion in all human cultures of the specifically human ability to act upon and regulate, rather than passively move with and be moved by, the givens of natural existence. In ritual, the purposive manipulation of given forms toward regulating and sustaining order, every culture asserts that proper relations between human existence and natural forces depend upon culture's employing its special powers to regulate the overall processes of the world and life.

One realm of cultural thought in which these points are often articulated is that of concepts of purity and pollution. Virtually every culture has some such beliefs, which seem in large part (though not, of course, entirely) to be concerned with the relationship between culture and nature (see Ortner, 1973, n.d.). A well-known aspect of purity/pollution beliefs cross-culturally is that of the natural "contagion" of pollution; left to its own devices, pollution (for these purposes grossly equated with the unregulated operation of natural energies) spreads and overpowers all that it comes in contact with. Thus a puzzle – if pollution is so strong, how can anything be purified? Why is the purifying agent not itself polluted? The answer, in keeping with the present line of argument, is that purification is effected in a ritual context; purification ritual, as a purposive activity that pits self-conscious (symbolic) action against natural energies, is more powerful than those energies.

In any case, my point is simply that every culture implicitly recognizes and asserts a distinction between the operation of nature and the operation of culture (human consciousness and its products); and further, that the distinctiveness of culture rests precisely on the fact that it can under most circumstances transcend natural conditions and turn them to its purposes. Thus culture (i.e., every culture) at some level of awareness asserts itself to be not only distinct from but superior to nature, and that sense of distinctiveness and superiority rests precisely on the ability to transform – to "socialize" and "culturalize" – nature.

Returning now to the issue of women, their pan-cultural second-class status could be accounted for, quite simply, by postulating that women are being identified or symbolically associated with nature, as opposed to men, who are identified with culture. Since it is always culture's project to subsume and transcend nature, if women were considered part of nature, then culture would find it "natural" to subordinate, not to say oppress, them. Yet although this argument can be shown to have considerable force, it seems to oversimplify the case. The formulation I would like to defend and elaborate on in the following section, then, is that women are seen "merely" as being *closer* to nature than men. That is, culture (still equated relatively unambiguously with men) recognizes that women are active participants in its special processes, but at the same time sees them as being more rooted in, or having more direct affinity with, nature.

The revision may seem minor or even trivial, but I think it is a more accurate rendering of cultural assumptions. Further, the argument cast in these terms has several analytic advantages over the simpler formulation; *I shall discuss these later. It might simply be stressed here that the revised argument would still account for the pan-cultural devaluation of women, for even if women are not equated with nature, they are none-theless seen as representing a lower order of being, as being less tran-scendental of nature than men are. The next task of the paper, then, is to consider why they might be viewed in that way.*

Why Is Woman Seen as Closer to Nature?

It all begins of course with the body and the natural procreative functions specific to women alone. We can sort out for discussion three levels at which this absolute physiological fact has significance: (1) woman's *body and its functions,* more involved more of the time with "species life," seem to place her closer to nature, in contrast to man's physiology, which frees him more completely to take up the projects of culture; (2) woman's body and its functions place her in *social roles* that in turn are considered to be at a lower order of the cultural process than man's; and (3) woman's traditional social roles, imposed because of her body and its functions, in turn give her a different *psychic structure,* which, like her physiological nature and her social roles, is seen as being closer to nature. I shall discuss each of these points in turn, showing first how in each instance certain factors strongly tend to align woman with nature, then indicating other factors that demonstrate her full alignment with culture, the combined factors thus placing her in a problematic inter-mediate position. It will become clear in the course of the discussion why men seem by contrast less intermediate, more purely "cultural" than women. And I reiterate that I am dealing only at the level of cultural and human universals. These arguments are intended to apply to generalized humanity; they grow out of the human condition, as humanity has experi-enced and confronted it up to the present day.

1. Woman's physiology seen as closer to nature. This part of my argument has been anticipated with subtlety, cogency, and a great deal of hard data, by de Beauvoir (1953). De Beauvoir reviews the physiological structure, development, and functions of the human female and concludes that "the female, to a greater extent than the male, is the prey of the species" (p. 60). She points out that many major areas and processes of the woman's body serve no apparent function for the health and stability of the individ-ual; on the contrary, as they perform their specific organic functions, they are often sources of discomfort, pain, and danger. The breasts are irrele-vant to personal health; they may be excised at any time of a woman's life. "Many of the ovarian secretions function for the benefit of the egg, promoting its maturation and adapting the uterus to its requirements; in re-spect to the organism as a whole, they make for disequilibrium rather than for regulation – the woman is adapted to the needs of the egg rather than to her own requirements" (p. 24). Menstruation is often uncomfortable, sometimes painful; it frequently has negative emotional correlates and in any case involves bothersome tasks of cleansing and waste disposal; and – a point that de Beauvoir does not mention – in many cultures it interrupts a woman's routine, putting her in a stigmatized state involving various restrictions on her activities and social contacts. In pregnancy many of the woman's vitamin and mineral resources are channeled into nourishing the fetus, depleting her own strength and energies. And finally, childbirth itself is painful and dangerous (pp. 24-27 *passim*). In sum, de Beauvoir concludes that the female "is more enslaved to the species than the male, her animality is more manifest" (p. 239).

While de Beauvoir's book is ideological, her survey of woman's physiological situation seems fair and accurate. It is simply a fact that proportionately more of woman's body space, for a greater percentage of her lifetime, and at some – sometimes great – cost to her personal health, strength, and general stability, is taken up with the natural processes surrounding the reproduction of the species.

De Beauvoir goes on to discuss the negative implications of woman's "enslavement to the species" in relation to the projects in which humans engage, projects through which culture is generated and defined. She arrives thus at the crux of her argument (pp. 58-59):

> Here we have the key to the whole mystery. On the biological level a species is maintained only by creating itself anew; but this creation results only in repeating the same Life in more individuals. But man assures the repetition of Life while transcending Life through Existence [i.e., goal-oriented, meaningful action]; by this transcendence he creates values that deprive pure repetition of all value. In the animal, the freedom and variety of male activities are vain because no project is involved. Except for his services to the species, what he does *is* immaterial. Whereas in serving the species, the human male also remodels the face of the earth, he creates new instruments, he invents, he shapes the future.

In other words, woman's body seems to doom her to mere reproduction of life; the male, in contrast, lacking natural creative functions, must (or has the opportunity to) assert his creativity externally, "artificially," through the medium of technology and symbols. In so doing, he creates relatively lasting, eternal, transcendent objects, while the woman creates only perishables – human beings.

This formulation opens up a number of important insights. It speaks, for example, to the great puzzle of why male activities involving the destruction of life (hunting and warfare) are often given more prestige than the female's ability to give birth, to create life. Within de Beauvoir's framework, we realize it is not the killing that is the relevant and valued aspect of hunting and warfare; rather, it is the transcendental (social, cultural) nature of these activities, as opposed to the naturalness of the process of birth: "For it is not in giving life but in risking life that man is raised above the animal; that is why superiority has been accorded in humanity not to the sex that brings forth but to that which kills" (*ibid.*).

Thus if male is, as I am suggesting, everywhere (unconsciously) associated with culture and female seems closer to nature, the rationale for these associations is not very difficult to grasp, merely from considering the implications of the physiological contrast between male and female. At the same time, however, woman cannot be consigned fully to the category of nature, for it is perfectly obvious that she is a full-fledged human being endowed with human consciousness just as a man is; she is half of the human race, without whose cooperation the whole enterprise would collapse. She may seem more in the possession of nature than man, but having consciousness, she thinks and speaks; she generates, communicates, and manipulates symbols, categories, and values. She participates in human dialogues not only with other women but also with men. As Lévi-Strauss says, "Woman could never become just a sign and nothing more, since even in a man's world she is still a person, and since insofar as she is defined as a sign she must [still] be recognized as a generator of signs" (1969a: 496).

Indeed, the fact of woman's full human consciousness, her full involvement in and commitment to culture's project of transcendence over nature, may ironically explain another of the great puzzles of "the woman problem" – woman's nearly universal unquestioning acceptance of her own devaluation. For it would seem that, as a conscious human and member of culture, she has followed out the logic of culture's arguments and has reached culture's conclusions along with the men. As de Beauvoir puts it (p. 59):

> For she, too, is an existent, she feels the urge to surpass, and her project is not mere repetition but transcendence towards a different future – in her heart of hearts she finds confirmation of the masculine pretensions. She joins the men in the festivals that celebrate the successes and victories of the males. Her misfortune is to have been biologically destined for the repetition of Life, when even in her own view Life does not carry within itself its reasons for being, reasons that are more important than life itself.

In other words, woman's consciousness – her membership, as it were, in culture – is evidenced in part by the very fact that she accepts her own devaluation and takes culture's point of view.

I have tried here to show one part of the logic of that view, the part that grows directly from the physiological differences between men and women. Because of woman's greater bodily involvement with the natural functions surrounding reproduction, she is seen as more a part of nature than man is. Yet in part because of her consciousness and participation in human social dialogue, she is recognized as a participant in culture. Thus she appears as something intermediate between culture and nature, lower on the scale of transcendence than man.

2. *Woman's social role seen as closer to nature.* Woman's physiological functions, I have just argued, may tend in themselves to motivate[5] a view of woman as closer to nature, a view she herself, as an observer of herself and the world, would tend to agree with. *Woman creates naturally from within her own being, whereas man is free to, or forced to, create artificially, that is, through cultural means, and in such a way as to sustain culture.* In addition, I now wish to show how woman's physiological functions have tended universally to limit her social movement, and to confine her universally to certain social contexts which *in turn* are seen as closer to nature. That is, not only her bodily processes but the social situation in which her bodily processes locate her may carry this significance. And insofar as she is permanently associated (in the eyes of culture) with these social milieux, they add weight (perhaps the decisive part of the burden) to the view of woman as closer to nature. I refer here of course to woman's confinement to the domestic family context, a confinement motivated, no doubt, by her lactation processes.

Woman's body, like that of all female mammals, generates milk during and after pregnancy for the feeding of the newborn baby. The baby cannot survive without breast milk or some similar formula at this stage of life. Since the mother's body goes through its lactation processes in direct relation to a pregnancy with a particular child, the relationship of nursing between mother and child is seen as a natural bond, other feeding arrangements being seen in most cases as unnatural and makeshift. Mothers and their children, according to cultural reasoning, belong together. Further, children beyond infancy are not strong enough to engage in major work, yet are mobile and unruly and not capable of understanding various dangers; they thus require supervision and constant care. Mother is the obvious person for this task, as an extension of her natural nursing bond with the children, or because she has a new infant and is already involved with child-oriented activities. *Her own activities are thus circumscribed by the limitations and low levels of her children's strengths and skills:*[6] she is confined to the domestic family group; "woman's place is in the home."

Woman's association with the domestic circle would contribute to the view of her as closer to nature in several ways. In the first place, the sheer fact of constant association with children plays a role in the issue; one can easily see how infants and children might themselves be considered part of nature. Infants are barely human and utterly unsocialized; like animals they are unable to walk upright, they excrete without control, they do not speak. Even slightly older children are clearly not yet fully under the sway of culture. They do not yet understand social duties, responsibilities, and morals; their vocabulary and their range of learned skills are small. One finds implicit recognition of an association between children and nature in many cultural practices. For example, most cultures have initiation rites for adolescents (primarily for boys; I shall return to this point below), the point of which is to move the child ritually from a less than fully human state into full participation in society and culture; many cultures do not hold funeral rites for children who die at early ages, explicitly because they are not yet fully social beings. Thus children are likely to be categorized with nature, and woman's close association with children may compound her potential for being seen as closer to nature herself. It is ironic that the rationale for boys' initiation rites in many cultures is that the boys must be purged of the defilement accrued from being around mother and other women so much of the time, when in fact much of the woman's defilement may derive from her being around children so much of the time.

The second major problematic implication of women's close association with the domestic context derives from certain structural conflicts between the family and society at large in any social system. The implications of the "domestic/public opposition" in relation to the position of women have been cogently developed by Rosaldo,[7] and I simply wish to show its relevance to the present argument. The notion that the domestic unit – the biological family charged with reproducing and socializing new members of the society – is opposed to the public entity – the superimposed network of alliances and relationships that *is* the society – is also the basis of Lévi-Strauss's argument in the *Elementary Structures of Kinship* (1969a). Lévi-Strauss argues not only that this opposition is present in every social system, but further that it has the significance of the opposition[8] between nature and culture. The universal incest prohibition and its ally, the rule of exogamy (marriage outside the group), ensure that "the risk of seeing a biological family become established as a closed system is definitely eliminated; the biological group can no longer stand apart, and the bond of alliance with another family ensures the dominance of the social over the biological, and of the cultural over the natural" (p. 479). And although not every culture articulates a radical opposition between the domestic and the public as such, it is hardly contestable that the domestic is always subsumed by the public; domestic units are allied with one another through the enactment of rules that are logically at a higher level than the units themselves; this creates an emergent unit – society – that is logically at a higher level than the domestic units of which it is composed.

Now, since women are associated with, and indeed are more or less confined to, the domestic context, they are identified with this lower order of social/cultural organization. What are the implications of this for the way they are viewed? First, if the specifically biological (reproductive) function of the family is stressed, as in Lévi-Strauss's formulation, then the family (and hence woman) is identified with nature pure and simple, as opposed to culture. But this is obviously too simple; the point seems more adequately formulated as follows: the family (and hence woman) represents lower-level, socially fragmenting, particularistic sort of concerns, as opposed to interfamilial relations representing higher-level, integrative, universalistic sorts of concerns. Since men lack a "natural" basis (nursing, generalized to child care) for a familial orientation, their sphere of activity is defined at the level of interfamilial relations. And hence, so the cultural reasoning seems to go, men are the "natural" proprietors of religion, ritual, politics, and other realms of cultural thought and action in which universalistic statements of spiritual and social synthesis are made. Thus men are identified not only with culture, in the sense of all human creativity, as opposed to nature; they are identified in particular with culture in the old fashioned sense of the finer and higher aspects of human thought – art, religion, law, etc.

Here again, the logic of cultural reasoning aligning woman with a lower order of culture than man is clear and, on the surface, quite compelling. At the same time, woman cannot be fully consigned to nature, for there are aspects of her situation, even within the domestic context, that undeniably demonstrate her participation in the cultural process. It goes without saying, of course, that except for nursing newborn infants (and artificial nursing devices can cut even this biological tie), there is no reason why it has to be mother – as opposed to father, or anyone else – who remains identified with child care. But even assuming that other practical and emotional reasons conspire to keep woman in this sphere, it is possible to show that her activities in the domestic context could as logically put her squarely in the category of culture.

In the first place, one must point out that woman not only feeds and cleans up after children in a simple caretaker operation; she in fact is the primary agent of their early socialization. It is she who transforms newborn infants from mere organisms into cultured humans, teaching them manners and the proper ways to behave in order to become full-fledged members of the culture. On the basis of her socializing functions alone, she could not be more a representative of culture. Yet in virtually every society there is a point at which the socialization of boys is transferred to the hands of men. The boys are considered, in one set of terms or another, not yet "really" socialized; their entrée into the realm of fully human (social, cultural) status can be accomplished only by men. We still see this in our own schools, where there is a gradual inversion in the proportion of female to male teachers up through the grades: most kindergarten teachers are female; most university professors are male.[9]

Or again, take cooking. In the overwhelming majority of societies cooking is the woman's work. No doubt this stems from practical considerations – since the woman has to stay home with the baby, it is convenient for her to perform the chores centered in the home. But if it is true, as Lévi-Strauss has argued (1969b), that transforming the raw into the cooked may represent, in many systems of thought, the transition from nature to culture, then here we have woman aligned with this important culturalizing process, which could easily place her in the category of culture, triumphing over nature. Yet it is also interesting to note that when a culture (e.g., France or China) develops a tradition of *haute cuisine* – *"real"* cooking, as opposed to trivial ordinary domestic cooking – the high chefs are almost always men. Thus the pattern replicates that in the area of socialization – women perform lower-level conversions from nature to culture, but when the culture distinguishes a higher level of the same functions, the higher level is restricted to men.

In short, we see once again some sources of woman's appearing more intermediate than man with respect to the nature/culture dichotomy. Her "natural" association with the domestic context (motivated by her natural lactation functions) tends to compound her potential for being viewed as closer to nature, because of the animal-like nature of children, and because of the infrasocial connotation of the domestic group as against the rest of society. Yet at the same time her socializing and cooking functions within the domestic context show her to be a powerful agent of the cultural process, constantly transforming raw natural resources into cultural products. Belonging to culture, yet appearing to have stronger and more direct connections with nature, she is once again seen as situated between the two realms.

3. Woman's psyche seen as closer to nature. The suggestion that woman has not only a different body and a different social locus from man but also a different psychic structure is *most controversial.* I will argue that she probably *does* have a different psychic structure, but I will draw heavily on Chodorow's paper (in Rosaldo and Lamphere, *Woman, Culture, and Society*) to establish first that her psychic structure need not be assumed to be innate; it can be accounted for, as Chodorow convincingly shows, by the facts of the probably universal female socialization experience. Nonetheless, if we grant the empirical near universality of a "feminine psyche" with certain specific characteristics, these characteristics would add weight to the cultural view of woman as closer to nature.

It is important to specify what we see as the dominant and universal aspects of the feminine psyche. If we postulate emotionality or irrationality, we are confronted with those traditions in various parts of the world in which women functionally are, and are seen as, more practical, pragmatic, and this-worldly than men. One relevant dimension that does seem pan-culturally applicable is that of relative concreteness vs. relative abstractness: the feminine personality tends to be involved with concrete feelings, things, and people, rather than with abstract entities; it tends toward personalism and particularism. A second, closely related, dimension seems to be that of relative subjectivity vs. relative objectivity: Chodorow cites Carlson's study (1971), which concludes that "males represent experiences of self, others, space, and time in individualistic, objective, and distant ways, while females represent experiences in relatively interpersonal, subjective, immediate ways" (cf. *op. cit,* Rosaldo and Lamphere, p. 56, quoting Carlson, p. 270). Although this and other studies were done in Western societies, Chodorow sees their findings on the differences between male and female personality – roughly, that men are more objective and inclined to relate in terms of relatively abstract categories, women more subjective and inclined to relate in terms of relatively concrete phenomena – as "general and nearly universal differences" (p. 43).

But the thrust of Chodorow's elegantly argued paper is that these differences are not innate or genetically programmed; they arise from nearly universal features of family structure, namely that "women, universally, are largely responsible for early child care and for (at least) later female socialization" (p. 43) and that "the structural situation of child rearing, reinforced by female and male role training, produces these differences, which are replicated and reproduced in the sexual sociology of adult life" (p. 44). Chodorow argues that, because mother is the early socializer of both boys and girls, both develop "personal identification" with her, i.e., diffuse identification with her general personality, behavior traits, values, and attitudes (p. 51). A son, however, must ultimately shift to a masculine role identity, which involves building an identification with the father. Since father is almost always more remote than mother (he is rarely involved in child care, and perhaps works away from home much of the day), building an identification with father involves a "positional identification," i.e., identification with father's male role as a collection of abstract elements, rather than a personal identification with father as a real individual (p. 49). Further, as the boy enters the larger social world, he finds it in fact organized around more abstract and universalistic criteria (cf. *op. cit,* Rosaldo and Lamphere, pp. 28-29; Chodorow, p. 58), as I have indicated in the previous section; thus his earlier socialization prepares him for, and is reinforced by, the type of adult social experience he will have.

For a young girl, in contrast, the personal identification with mother, which was created in early infancy, can persist into the process of learning female role identity. Because mother is immediate and present when the daughter is learning role identity, learning to be a woman involves the continuity and development of a girl's relationship to her mother, and sustains the identification with her as an individual; it does not involve the learning of externally defined role characteristics (cf. *op. cit,* Rosaldo and Lamphere, Chodorow, p. 51). This pattern prepares the girl for, and is fully reinforced by, her social situation in later life; she will become involved in the world of women, which is characterized by few formal role differences (cf. *op. cit,* Rosaldo and Lamphere, p. 29), and which involves again, in motherhood, "personal identification" with *her* children. And so the cycle begins anew. ·

Chodorow demonstrates to my satisfaction at least that the feminine personality, characterized by personalism and particularism, can be explained as having been generated by social-structural arrangements rather than by innate biological factors. The point need not be belabored further. But insofar as the "feminine personality" has been a nearly universal fact, it can be argued that its characteristics may have contributed further to the view of women as being somehow less cultural than men. That is, women would tend to enter into relationships with the world that culture might see as being more "like nature" – immanent and embedded in things as given – than "like culture" – transcending and transforming things through the superimposition of abstract categories and transpersonal values. Woman's relationships tend to be, like nature, relatively unmediated, more direct, whereas man not only tends to relate in a more mediated way, but in fact ultimately often relates more consistently and strongly to the mediating categories and forms than to the persons or objects themselves.

It is thus not difficult to see how the feminine personality would lend weight to a view of women as being "closer to nature." Yet at the same time, the modes of relating characteristic of women undeniably play a powerful and important role in the cultural process. For just as relatively unmediated relating is in some sense at the lower end of the spectrum of human spiritual functions, embedded and particularizing rather than transcending and synthesizing, yet that mode of relating also stands at the upper end of that spectrum. Consider the mother-child relationship. Mothers tend to be committed to their children as individuals regardless of sex, age, beauty, clan affiliation, or other categories in which the child might participate. Now any relationship with this quality – not just mother and child but any sort of highly personal, relatively unmediated commitment – may be seen as a challenge to culture and society "from below," insofar as it represents the fragmentary potential of individual loyalties vis-à-vis the solidarity of the group. But it may also be seen as embodying the synthesizing agent for culture and society "from above," in that it represents generalized human values above and beyond loyalties to particular social categories. Every society must have social categories that transcend personal loyalties, but every society must also generate a sense of ultimate moral unity for all its members above and beyond those social categories. Thus that psychic mode seemingly typical of women, which tends to disregard categories and to seek "communion" (cf. *op. cit,* Rosaldo and Lamphere, Chodorow, p. 55, following Bakan, 1966) directly and personally with others, although it may appear infracultural from one point of view, is at the same time associated with the highest levels of the cultural process.

The Implications of Intermediacy

My primary purpose in this paper has been to attempt to explain the universal secondary status of women. Intellectually and personally, I felt strongly challenged by this problem; I felt compelled to deal with it before undertaking an analysis of woman's position in any particular society. Local variables of economy, ecology, history, political and social structure, values, and world view – these could explain variations within this universal, but they could not explain the universal itself. And if we were not to accept the ideology of biological determinism, then explanation, it seemed to me, could only proceed by reference to other universals of the human cultural situation. Thus the general outlines of the approach – although not of course the particular solution offered – were determined by the problem itself, and not by any predilection on my part for global abstract structural analysis.

I argued that the universal devaluation of women could be explained by postulating that women are seen as closer to nature than men, men being seen as more unequivocally occupying the high ground of culture. The culture/nature distinction is itself a product of culture, culture being minimally defined as the transcendence, by means of systems of thought and technology, of the natural givens of existence. This of course is an analytic definition, but I argued that at some level every culture incorporates this notion in one form or other, if only through the performance of ritual as an assertion of the human ability to manipulate those givens. In any case, the core of the paper was concerned with showing why women might tend to be assumed, over and over, in the most diverse sorts of world views and in cultures of every degree of complexity, to be closer to nature than men. Woman's physiology, more involved more of the time with "species of life"; woman's association with the structurally subordinate domestic context, charged with the crucial function of transforming animal-like infants into cultured beings; "woman's psyche," appropriately molded to mothering functions by her own socialization and tending toward greater personalism and less mediated modes of relating – all these factors make woman appear to be rooted more directly and deeply in nature. At the same time, however, her "membership" and fully necessary participation in culture are recognized by culture and cannot be denied.

Thus she is seen to occupy an intermediate position between culture and nature.

This intermediacy has several implications for analysis, depending upon how it is interpreted. First, of course, it answers my primary question of why woman is everywhere seen as lower than man, for even if she is not seen as nature pure and simple, she is still seen as achieving less transcendence of nature than man. Here intermediate simply means "middle status" on a hierarchy of being from culture to nature.

Second, intermediate may have the significance of "mediating," i.e., performing some sort of synthesizing or converting function between nature and culture, here seen (by culture) not as two ends of a continuum but as two radically different sorts of processes in the world. The domestic unit – and hence woman, who in virtually every case appears as its primary representative – is one of culture's crucial agencies for the conversion of nature into culture, especially with reference to the socialization of children. Any culture's continued viability depends upon properly socialized individuals who will see the world in that culture's terms and adhere more or less unquestioningly to its moral precepts. The functions of the domestic unit must be closely controlled in order to ensure this outcome; the stability of the domestic unit as an institution must be placed as far as possible beyond question. (We see some aspects of the protection of the integrity and stability of the domestic group in the powerful taboos against incest, matricide, patricide, and fratricide.[10]) Insofar as woman is universally the primary agent of early socialization and is seen as virtually the embodiment of the functions of the domestic group, she will tend to come under the heavier restrictions and circumscriptions surrounding that unit. Her (culturally defined) intermediate position between nature and culture, here having the significance of her *mediation* (i.e., performing conversion functions) between nature and culture, would thus account not only for her lower status but for the greater restrictions placed upon her activities. In virtually every culture her permissible sexual activities are more closely circumscribed than man's, she is offered a much smaller range of role choices, and she is afforded direct access to a far more limited range of its social institutions. Further, she is almost universally socialized to have a narrower and generally more conservative set of attitudes and views than man, and the limited social contexts of her adult life reinforce this situation. This socially engendered conservatism and traditionalism of woman's thinking is another – perhaps the worst, certainly the most insidious – mode of social restriction, and would clearly be related to her traditional function of producing well-socialized members of the group.

Finally, woman's intermediate position may have the implication of greater symbolic ambiguity (cf. *op. cit,* Rosaldo and Lamphere). Shifting our image of the culture/nature relationship once again, we may envision culture in this case as a small clearing within the forest of the larger natural system. From this point of view, that which is intermediate between culture and nature is located on the continuous periphery of culture's clearing; and though it may thus appear to stand both above and below (and beside) culture, it is simply outside and around it. We can begin to understand then how a single system of cultural thought can often assign to woman completely polarized and apparently contradictory meanings, since extremes, as we say, meet. That she often represents both life and death is only the simplest example one could mention.

For another perspective on the same point, it will be recalled that the psychic mode associated with women seems to stand at both the bottom and the top of the scale of human modes of relating. The tendency in that mode is to get involved more directly with people as individuals and not as representatives of one social category or another; this mode can be seen as either "ignoring" (and thus subverting) or "transcending" (and thus achieving a higher synthesis of) those social categories, depending upon the cultural view for any given purpose. Thus we can account easily for both the subversive feminine symbols (witches, evil eye, menstrual pollution, castrating mothers) and the feminine symbols of transcendence (mother goddesses, merciful dispensers of salvation, female symbols of justice, and the strong presence of feminine symbolism in the realms of art, religion, ritual, and law). Feminine symbolism, far more often than masculine symbolism, manifests this propensity toward polarized ambiguity – sometimes utterly exalted, sometimes utterly debased, rarely within the normal range of human possibilities.

If woman's (culturally viewed) intermediacy between culture and nature has this implication of generalized ambiguity of meaning characteristic of marginal phenomena, then we are also in a better position to account for those cultural and historical "inversions" in which women are in some way or other symbolically aligned with culture and men with nature. A number of cases come to mind: the Sirionó of Brazil, among whom, according to Ingham (1971: 1098), "nature, the raw, and maleness" are opposed to "culture, the cooked, and femaleness";[11] Nazi Germany, in which women were said to be the guardians of culture and morals; European courtly love, in which man considered himself the beast and woman the pristine exalted object – a pattern of thinking that persists, for example, among modern Spanish peasants (see Pitt-Rivers, 1961; Rosaldo, cf. *op. cit,* Rosaldo and Lamphere). And there are no doubt other cases of this sort, including some aspects of our own culture's view of women. Each such instance of an alignment of women with culture rather than nature requires detailed analysis of specific historical and ethnographic data. But in indicating how nature in general, and the feminine mode of interpersonal relations in particular, can appear from certain points of view to stand both under and over (but really simply outside of) the sphere of culture's hegemony, we have at least laid the groundwork for such analyses.

In short, the postulate that woman is viewed as closer to nature than man has several implications for further analysis, and can be interpreted in several different ways. If it is viewed simply as a *middle* position on a scale from culture down to nature, then it is still seen as lower than culture and thus accounts for the pan-cultural assumption that woman is lower than man in the order of things. If it is read as a *mediating* element in the culture-nature relationship, then it may account in part for the cultural tendency not merely to devalue woman but to circumscribe and restrict her functions, since culture must maintain control over its (pragmatic and symbolic) mechanisms for the conversion of nature into culture. And if it is read as an *ambiguous* status between culture and nature, it may help account for the fact that, in specific cultural ideologies and symbolizations, woman can occasionally be aligned with culture, and in any event is often assigned polarized and contradictory meanings within a single symbolic system. Middle status, mediating functions, ambiguous meaning – all are different readings, for different contextual purposes, of woman's being seen as intermediate between nature and culture.

Conclusions

Ultimately, it must be stressed again that the whole scheme is a construct of culture rather than a fact of nature. Woman is not "in reality" any closer to (or further from) nature than man – both have consciousness, both are mortal. But there are certainly reasons why she appears that way, which is what I have tried to show in this paper. The result is a (sadly) efficient feedback system: various aspects of woman's situation (physical, social, psychological) contribute to her being seen as closer to nature, while the view of her as closer to nature is in turn embodied in institutional forms that reproduce her situation. The implications for social change are similarly circular: a different cultural view can only grow out of a different social actuality; a different social actuality can only grow out of a different cultural view.

It is clear, then, that the situation must be attacked from both sides. Efforts directed solely at changing the social institutions – through setting quotas on hiring, for example, or through passing equal-pay-for-equal-work laws – cannot have far-reaching effects if cultural language and imagery continue to purvey a relatively devalued view of women. But at the same time efforts directed solely at changing cultural assumptions – through male and female consciousness-raising groups, for example, or through revision of educational materials and mass-media imagery – cannot be successful unless the institutional base of the society is changed to support and reinforce the changed cultural view. Ultimately, both men and women can and must be equally involved in projects of creativity and transcendence. Only then will women be seen as aligned with culture, in culture's ongoing dialectic with nature.

Notes

1. It is true of course that *yin*, the female principle, has a negative valence. Nonetheless, there is an absolute complementarity of *yin* and *yang* in Taoism, a recognition that the world requires the equal operation and interaction of both principles for its survival.

2. Some anthropologists might consider this type of evidence (social-structural arrangements that exclude women, explicitly or de facto, from certain groups, roles, or statuses) to be a subtype of the second type of evidence (symbolic formulations of inferiority). I would not disagree with this view, although most social anthropologists would probably separate the two types.

3. While we are on the subject of injustices of various kinds, we might note that Lowie secretly bought this doll, the most sacred object in the tribal repertoire, from its custodian, the widow of Wrinkled-face. She asked $400 for it, but this price was "far beyond [Lowie's] means," and he finally got it for $80 (p. 300).

4. With all due respect to Lévi-Strauss (1969a,b, and *passim*).

5. Semantic theory uses the concept of motivation of meaning, which encompasses various ways in which a meaning may be assigned to a symbol because of certain objective properties of that symbol, rather than by arbitrary association. In a sense, this entire paper is an inquiry into the motivation of the meaning of woman as a symbol, asking why woman may be unconsciously assigned the significance of being closer to nature. For a concise statement on the various types of motivation of meaning, see Ullman (1963).

6. A situation that often serves to make her more childlike herself.

7. Cf. Michelle Zimbalist Rosaldo and Louise Lamphere, eds., *Woman, Culture, and Society.* Stanford University Press, 1974.

8. David M. Schneider (personal communication) is prepared to argue that the incest taboo is not universal, on the basis of material from Oceania. Let us say at this point, then, that it is virtually universal.

9. I remember having my first male teacher in the fifth grade, and I remember being excited about that – it was somehow more grown-up.

10. Nobody seems to care much about sororicide – a point that ought to be investigated.

11. Ingham's discussion is rather ambiguous itself, since women are also associated with animals: "The contrasts man/animal and man/woman are evidently similar . . . hunting is the means of acquiring women as well as animals" (p. 1095). A careful reading of the data suggests that both women and animals are mediators between nature and culture in this tradition.

5

Ecology, Justice and Theology Beyond the Preliminary Skirmishes

H. Paul Santmire

Out of today's environmental issues a theological dispute has arisen – one that could bode serious ill for the life and mission of the church if it gives rise to polarization.

ONLY IN ITS INFANCY – OR PERHAPS ITS LATENCY PERIOD – THE ECOLOGY movement has come under attack on every side. The Daughters of the American Revolution condemn its "communist tendencies." Utilities and other corporate interests, in a parade of TV advertisements defending atomic power plants and off-shore oil wells, suggest that environmentalists are sincere but misguided "reformers." Workers in such fields as the aerospace industry, championed most vocally by Senator Henry Jackson, are profoundly disturbed by what the senator refers to as "ecological extremists." At the other end of the political spectrum, activists and political organizers charge that the movement is a white middle-class copout. Meanwhile, within the ranks of the ecology movement itself, the fervor that sparked the first Earth Day and the publication of the *Environmental Handbook* in 1970 seems to have died down.

Out of these environmental issues a theological dispute has arisen – one that could bode serious ill for the life and mission of the church if it gives rise to a full-fledged polarization. The debate between those who maintain an interest in "ecological theology" and the more firmly established exponents of "political theology" must be resolved without delay. At a time when spiritual discouragement, pietistic fervor, narcissistic monetary preoccupation, and quietistic political withdrawal are increasingly in evidence within the churches, we can ill afford a frenetic dispute between two theological movements dedicated, overall, to radical re-formation of both church and society.

I

The preliminary questions have focused on the issue of survival versus justice.

56

Ecological theologians have, as a rule, taken seriously the predictions of crisis advanced by responsible scientists. They have also been influenced by the much-contested argument of Lynn White, Jr., and others that the classical Western theological tradition has proved ecologically problematic. Writing with a sense of urgency, they have sought to develop new theological approaches to nature, emphasizing, in varying degrees, the politics of justice.

Political theologians, on the other hand, have tended either to ignore ecological problems altogether or to regard them as expressions of unresolved political or economic problems. They have been suspicious of much of the literature associated with the ecology movement, seeing it as an expression of First World ideology, as yet another way of keeping oppressed peoples in their places. Political theologians have often implied and sometimes directly stated that theologians with ecological interests must be politically naïve or insensitive. Guilt by association has been a frequently invoked form of polemics – and an effective one, since the ecology movement has been a bizarre congeries of political reactionaries, romantic conservationists, political cop-outs, solitary poets, anarchic lifestylers, as well as genuine political radicals, serious-minded reformers, and level-headed natural scientists.

To move the discussion beyond these preliminary skirmishes, let me offer the following basis for a working consensus.

First, it should be acknowledged that there is a strong tendency within the ecology movement to give "survival," understood in conservative, even elitist terms, pre-eminence in our national policies. The increasing popularity of the "lifeboat ethic," championed by Garrett Hardin and others, is only the latest expression of a trend. This tendency must be fought at every turn in the name of social justice. Generally social justice must be given priority over survival in our theological hierarchy of values (here the way of the cross can be paradigmatic). Survival should then come next in importance, since obviously there can be no social justice without survival of the human species.

Second, it should be noted that exponents of ecological theology are not necessarily bound to accept the traditional, conservative, organic, hierarchical model for society. This model has been pointedly identified by Richard Neuhaus:

> Ecology deals not with the interaction of human power, but with man's relation to the nature of which he is a part. It is at heart apolitical, although its concerns may lead to political engagement. The ecological archetype sees man in his unity, forced to solidarity in the face of a common threat. The ecologists call us to the struggle for survival. The revolutionaries scorn survival in the struggle for a new order *[In De-*

fense of People: Ecology and the Seduction of Radicalism (Macmillan. 1971), p. 70].

It is quite possible for an ecological theologian to argue self-consciously on the basis of a political "root metaphor," rather than an organic metaphor. Also, the question must be raised whether all revised uses of the organic model (e.g., by John Cobb or Kenneth Cauthen) are by definition reactionary, or so geared to evolution that they have no room for or interest in revolution. Simply because the organic metaphor has had politically undesirable ramifications in the past should not disqualify it forever as an object for theological reflection and argumentation. Each theology must be judged on its own merits.

Third, in contrast to the hasty judgments about the extent of the ecological crisis expressed by some of the more politically oriented theologians, it must be agreed that there is an environmental crisis of profound dimensions facing the planet today. The life-support system of our species is threatened, and it is the poor who first bear the weight of the crisis (e.g., poisonous air for the slum-dwellers of New York city, famine for the impoverished of Bangladesh). So it is not a question of either ecology or justice, but both/and. The environmental crisis is a hard fact that we all must acknowledge, however disdainful we may be of ecological doom-sayers or countercultural faddists, however politically radical we may consider ourselves.

II

Preliminary debates and misunderstandings aside, then, a number of fundamental theological and ethical issues related to the ecological crisis require sustained critical reflection by both ecological and political theologians.

First is the historical and sociocritical task. It has been widely assumed by those concerned with the ecological crisis that Western theology, except for certain isolated figures like St. Francis, is ecologically bankrupt. Yet there seems to be good evidence (a) that such an assumption is historically inaccurate; that our own Western theological tradition, particularly in its pre-modern expressions, has been replete with rich ecological dimensions, which we ignore to our own impoverishment; (b) that Western theology is only one factor among many that helped to set the stage for the contemporary ecological crisis; and (c) that those who assume that the Western theological tradition is to blame for our present environmental situation are discounting the culpability of the structures of modern scientific-technological industrialism (capitalist or Marxist), and the stake of the affluent classes which benefit most from that system. The importance of research in these areas as a foundation for substantive theological reflection should not be underestimated.

Among the areas of study most urgently requiring attention is biblical theology. Virtually all of the most renowned biblical scholars of our era – the names of G. Ernest Wright and Rudolf Bultmann come to mind – either have not investigated the biblical theology of nature or have "discovered" that the biblical approach to nature is substantially the same as the modern theological approach. Nature, then, has been presented as "the servant of history" or the "stage for history" in much modern writing about biblical theology. But there is evidence – beginning with Genesis 1, where we are told that God looked at the *whole* creation and saw that it was good – that biblical thinking is not nearly so anthropocentric as many interpreters of the Bible have supposed. But if nature is not merely a stage for history, what is it? In what sense does nature have a role in the sweep of God's history with God's creation, as it is depicted in the Bible? The time is overdue for biblical scholars to examine the Old and New Testaments anew, raising ecological as well as political questions.

The *second* and perhaps most fundamental area requiring joint attention by ecological and political theologians is the problem of properly conceptualizing and expressing the relationship between nature and history. The ecological theologian sometimes falls prey to the traditional romantic danger of submerging the distinctively human dimension of the created order in nature, thereby undercutting the biblical norm of social justice. On the other hand, political theologians are sometimes prone to the opposite danger, so historicizing their conceptualization of reality that nature comes to be treated, as it generally was in 19th century continental Protestant thought and on into the 20th century, as a *mere stage* for history. But this kind of theology plays into the hands of the exploiters of the biosphere, especially the dominant classes in the affluent West. In the modern West, the acting on the stage of nature has become so destructive (for the sake of "progress," "a constantly increasing gross national product," "development," "exploitation of new resources") that it threatens to destroy the stage itself. The carrying capacities of our ecological platform are finite. That platform is a delicate living matrix out of which the human species evolved and on which it is still dependent for life. Too much emphasis on history, therefore, pushes us in the direction of ecological collapse. But if theologians are to develop theologies with a tangible and comprehensive ecological dimension, how should they conceptualize and express the realities of nature and history and their interrelationship?

III

Third is the whole problem of finding a fundamental imagery or root-metaphor that can embody both ecological and political concerns. Whitehead once observed that there is a hidden imaginative background behind even the most refined and abstract of philosophical systems. His observation is even more valid for theology, given the theologian's self-conscious use of mythological and narrative materials. What imagery, then, can best do justice to both our ecological and our political interests?

The traditional "City of God" imagery can be politically helpful, but it tends to mold theological thought in an insular-anthropocentric fashion, virtually excluding any meaningful substantive interpretation of nature. The various metaphors from nature, on the other hand – organism, process, body, ground of being – tend to rule out full explication of the historical dimension as it is attested by the biblical writers. Still another alternative, the biblical and classical theological image "the Kingdom of God," seems to be a possibility for creative theological development, both politically and ecologically, but it brings problems of its own. In our time a kingly image seems contrived, perhaps unintelligible. It is also problematic when viewed from a feminist perspective. Some would argue that it is the key metaphor of patriarchy. In contrast the image "spaceship earth," recently given currency by a number of ecological thinkers, is intelligible in terms of contemporary experience and seems to be free of sexist implications, but it brings with it the liabilities of its technological and authoritarian implications. Is our world best thought of as a machine?

Fourth, in regard to the nature-history question and to the problem of finding the best root-metaphor, is the debate between those who would uphold the concept that nature has intrinsic value before God, and those who would eschew that idea as either unintelligible or wrong-headed. Does nature have its own integrity, worth and goodness, as humanity does? Or is the human species the only one in the cosmos that has rights, the only creature that has intrinsic worth, goodness and integrity in the eyes of God? If we opt for the view that nature has intrinsic worth, how do we protect the biblical emphasis on human rights? (For example, a wilderness area may have to be flooded in order to provide electric power for a slum.) If, on the other hand, we opt for the view that nature has *no* intrinsic value before God, apart from its relationship with humanity, how is the relationship between humanity and nature to be defined? How is nature to be anything but the slave of the human master? How, then, are we to avoid all the ecological problems inherent in the exploitative, domineering anthropocentrism of modern Western culture?

IV

Fifth, perhaps the most difficult theological question of all is the issue of our understanding of God as it relates to sexual dualism. This issue has been sharpened in recent years by such liberation theologians as Rosemary Ruether. Among political and ecological theologians the issue has been largely bypassed or ignored.

The classical diety of Western theology has been depicted as a patriarchal ruler. This is the God who performs "mighty acts," who creates the world *ex nihilo* at the very beginning, and who remains – in the popular theological imagination, if not in explicit theological doctrine – the Wholly Other God, the transcendent God of power. Symbolically and politically, this God has functioned to oppress women. In the modern period the classical Western deity more and more took on the garb of the One who ultimately validates scientific and industrial progress, including not only much that was truly progressive, but also the industrial rape of nature and, ultimately, through a variety of corporate structures, the oppression of the poor and the dispossessed.

Originally, however, from the perspective of the Exodus story and the prophets, the "God who acts" motif entailed the liberation of the oppressed and the renewal of the earth. It seems, then, that the "Male Sky God" imagery of the West has incorporated both negative and positive aspects.

Female theological imagery also has both positive and negative connotations. Female imagery has sometimes functioned to validate a markedly positive attitude toward women (for example, the young Psyche, the image of a liberated woman, or Artemis, the free, assertive huntress). Female imagery has also functioned to create and sustain a vital and sensitive relationship to the world of nature (especially in connection with the archaic Earth Goddess imagery). But female theological imagery has had its darker sides. On occasion it has encouraged a turning away from the challenges of historical existence, especially the life of the city (one thinks of the *Bacchae),* and a turning toward the stable and unchanging – sometimes orgiastic and destructive – rhythms of nature. This movement has meant a turning toward political stasis and a certain ruthless acceptance of social inequities as eternally ordained by the Deity.

Male motifs can function to encourage political liberation, but they can also encourage the rape of women and of the earth, and the oppression of the poor. Female motifs can encourage positive approaches toward women and nature, but these motifs can also bring with them the tendency to undercut the struggle for social justice in the city. The question, then, in this theological era "After the Death of God the Father" (Mary Daly) is this: How are we to draw on the positive political and ecological aspects of the male and female motifs, while rejecting the negative tendencies of each? Is some kind of synthesis, or advance beyond, the ancient female-male theological dichotomy possible?

V

All these are complex areas for research and reflection. They will require a concerted effort by theologians who take both ecology and justice seriously, and who are prompted by a sense of urgency that will allow them to struggle creatively and resolutely with the deeper issues – if not in perfect harmony, at least with a sense of solidarity.

"We seek to overcome the deadly Leviathan of the Pentagon of Power," Rosemary Ruether has written, "transforming its power into manna to feed the hungry of the earth. The revolution of the feminine revolts against the denatured Babel of concrete and steel that stifles the living soil."[1] Is not this, in brief, the challenge before all of us today, whether our interests are primarily ecological or political, whether we are Jews or Greeks, males or females, First World or Third World?

Note

1. *Liberation Theology* [Paulist, 1972], pp. 125 f.

6

The Dynamics of the Future: Reflections on the Earth Process

Thomas Berry

OUR CONTEMPORARY WORLD IS AWAKENING ONCE AGAIN TO THE REALITY and wonder of the earth. Hardly anything is more important for the future of man. The human venture depends absolutely on this quality of awe and reverence and joy in the earth and all that lives and grows upon the earth; for man himself is among these living things. As soon as man isolates himself from these currents of life and from the profound mood that these engender within him, then the most basic satisfactions of human existence are diminished, for all the products of his machines cannot evoke in man that total commitment to life from the subconscious regions of his being that is needed to sustain the life process and to carry it on into a hazardous future. How man feels about himself and about the earth process, these are questions of utmost urgency, not only because of the inherent difficulty that we face in moving on into the future but also because of the idea presented by some of a disposable earth, the idea that man will soon have used up the earth and its energies and must find a way of colonizing another planetary body if he is to survive. According to this view, earth is no longer a manifestation of divine power or spiritual presence; it is simply a deposit of natural resources that are rapidly being consumed as the planet twirls its way through space. This leads to a certain fear lest the continents become slag heaps amid oceans of refuse. While this description of the earth at some future moment is extreme, it does indicate the severity of the challenge that confronts us. But since even in this view the exhaustion of the planet surely will not take place tomorrow, some centuries remain for an adjustment to take place. If this cannot be achieved then the consequences of our plunder economy, what is known as "industry," clearly seems to be leading to a tragic situation. The fairest of the planets could soon be in a fatal condition. Our discussion, then, turns on the question of death and life, not of an individual or a nation, not even of the human species, but the death of the planet itself as a dwelling place for the higher forms of life.

The entire past of man, the very meaning of the earth process, are involved in this question. Also involved is the question of the human energies needed to shape an alternative and humanly desirable future for man upon earth. If an answer is to be given, then, it must begin with the observation that the earth process itself is the manifestation of a vast amount of energy. In the sequence of earth mutations great stores of energy have been created that now exist within the earth, not only as fossil fuels but as forces within the very structure of matter. Yet the fossil fuels, which came into existence over a vast period of some millions of years, are now being consumed in a matter of decades. Waste materials mount to a volume almost beyond our capacity for effective disposal. Fumes from our engines rise above the atmosphere to form a film of residue that may some day affect the entire planet. If such a film is formed it will filter the sunlight and may even cause extensive alteration in the quality and quantity of the light and heat that reach the earth's surface. If such things ever took place then it would seem that by bringing man into existence the earth would have produced the instrument of its own destruction. We are forced to ask: Is this the meaning of man, that he should have the high honor of wasting the earth? Must we define man in terms of his destructive impact upon the splendors of a globe that once sailed so graciously through the sky and its clouds and storms, a globe that brought forth valleys filled with flowers and adorned by streams flowing down from the awesome mountains, a globe filled with the song of birds and movement of animals that romped over its surface, a globe that, finally, after some four billion years' preparation, brought forth man and in this manner awakened to consciousness of itself? This earth-human consciousness sings full expression of itself in Beethoven's *Ode to Joy*. This same consciousness as expressed in man enters into the play of the universe, with his gorgeous rituals and with a wonder and worship of the entire process. Thus we have two visions, the vision of awakening joy in the beginning, the vision of impending destruction in the end.

Here we should be mindful that this peril of the earth is not the first peril that the earth and living things upon the earth have endured. The earth has struggled its way into being amidst an amazing sequence of destructive forces that have broken loose upon it. A long sequence of cataclysmic events shaped the continents; the various forms of life have engaged in a continuing struggle for survival. Indeed, the greater number of species that have lived upon the earth disappeared prior to the modern period. The earth itself gropes toward its own realization. It has never achieved that state of equilibrium that we envisage in our minds, either in its structural being or in its biological forms. But if the present danger to the planet is not its first peril, it is the first that has been produced with the conscious intrusion of earth's own intelligence into the most intimate functioning of the earth process. This is something radically different from the seismic convulsions, the advance of glaciers, the sequence of species. It is the exploitation of energies in a definitive form; it is the turn from the storing of energies to the burning off of energies that cannot be replaced. This difficulty has happened because of man's need to fuel the vast machinery that he has created. This industrial machinery, spread over the earth, has established a technosphere that is incompatible with the biosphere. Its energy demands are such that it threatens to consume the resources of the earth; which then, presumably, would itself be disposed of, along with the living things upon the earth and the technosphere itself.

But even while we recognize the difficulty of adjusting the technosphere and the biosphere to each other, we must note that the human community can hardly do without the industrial production, commercial distribution, and consumer economy that now exist throughout the various continents of the earth. The basic difficulty, it seems, is that men have so far worked within the micro-dimensions of the industrial technological process. When the inventors were playing around with the first internal combustion engines they had no idea that such a little thing fueled on a little oil from the earth could possibly endanger the planet or adversely affect the forms of life. Those who were using insecticides saw only the immediate effects of what they were doing, and these immediate effects were a wonderful gain and support for the human venture. So with the entire adventure of man as he began to manipulate the forces of earth with greater and greater skills. If a little machine was such a blessing then a greater machine must be a greater blessing, until a certain machine mania eventuates and the larger effects begin to manifest themselves. By this time a process had been initiated that can neither be halted nor reversed. Thus the need of man to think through the larger dimensions of whatever he does and the need to discern the larger patterns of reality from any possible dysfunction. Earth-sickness is a difficult thing to cure. As Professor René Dubos has noted concerning the medical practice that preserves the life of man individually: if only this is practiced without attention to the major health issue of the human community and the sequence of generations, then medical practice itself could bring about a debilitation of the human species. Not only those administering the industrial order and men in the various professions, but also scientists themselves, due to the analytical nature of their study, have too frequently avoided discussion or investigation of the larger implications of what they were doing. This they discarded as being too "philosophical," as "non-scientific," or as not the essential direction that their investigation should take. Thus science has tended to work within limits too narrow and too exclusive. Scientists no less than the rest of us were victimized by a kind of mind fixation, almost a trance state, that failed to recognize impending difficulties until recently, when scientists along with the other professions begin to assess the human and earthly significance of what they are doing.

Periods in the Earth Process

Having stated our basic problem in this way, we might turn to our inquiry concerning the dynamics of the future by indicating the distinctive periods affecting the earth process in the beginning of the higher civilizations some five thousand years ago.

During the first period the human order was intimately associated with the physical and biological earth processes. Mankind lived in an ocean of energy in which the physical and psychic forms of energy were intimately related. Men found the meaning of their own existence in response to the energies about them. These man perceived as divine forces supporting him with an abundance of their products. During this period the physical energies of the earth and its resources were little affected. As specifically human energies were awakened and utilized in harmony with the earth process there was little disturbance of the integral earth process. There was even a certain benefit in its new capacity to bring forth grain and other fruits under human cultivation. This is a period when there was a dominance of the unconscious depths of the human psyche, when the great visions took place. The feeling of identity with the earth was at its height. The response of man to the earth process was immediate. Earth was experienced as the Great Mother, heaven as a comprehensive providence. The ultimate mystery of things was venerated with special forms of worship. This is the age of the gods as was seen by Giambattista Vico in his *New Science of the Nature of the Nations*. Much of mankind's great poetry was written at this time.

During this period also human energies were stored up in such abundance that all later ages have found in this period the most profound support for the course of human affairs. Despite all the changes that have taken place in identifying the human quality of life, this age still keeps its basic normative value. Men have a deep feeling for this age when the interior of man had a special sensitivity for the earth process. The sequence of the seasons was celebrated with a variety of festival that contributed much of the charm and fascination of life and evoked much of the cultural creativity associated with this age. Man had a feeling for the cosmic dimensions of his own being. Even beyond the cosmic there was communion with the world of the sacred, that benign presence guiding and supporting all things in heaven and on earth. It was the period of the great symbolisms. Mythical narratives were created that provided man with a revelation of the deepest realities of the universe. It is difficult to describe the power that flows from this period and which has supplied almost limitless energies for sustaining a human mode of being. Both the volume and the variety of the cultural formations of this period remain an astounding witness to its greatness. Even now the energies that emanate from this period increase rather than diminish. The further man advances into the future the more he understands and appreciates these primordial intuitions of the human mind and the overwhelming power of these imaginative visions. It is impossible to imagine what man would be apart from this first period when the dynamics of the earth took such a leap in the forms and magnitude of its expression.

The Second Period

The second period of the dynamics of the earth is the period when the reason of man took control and released vast physical energies to the advancement of man but frequently to the detriment of the earth. With science as an aid the machinery of exploitation was established. Man considered himself fortunate to escape the rhythms of the physical universe. As his understanding of the earth processes increased he took more command of the world as an objective reality containing a vast amount of material resources awaiting "development." This was the age of individual and collective consciousness, as opposed to the feeling awareness of the unconscious realms of man's being that were concerned with the world of the absolute more than with the world of time and which were expressed in myth and symbol rather than in philosophical or scientific language. In this period human reason achieved wonders in liberating man from many of the burdens that he had formerly borne. Rational understanding penetrated into the mysteries of the universe with a different technique and with a different mode of understanding from that of the earlier period. Then after some centuries of probing into the structure and functioning of the earth, science revealed a supreme mystery, that the earth is more cosmogenesis than cosmos. It discovered the time dimension, the developmental nature of the universe. The earth is in a state of movement and transformation rather than in a state of fixed equilibrium. From this it follows that man, as part of the earth, is himself undergoing constant transformation into himself. Neither the earth nor man is yet completely given to itself. Each day is similar to the preceding day, but yet it is different, unique, beyond repetition. The whole earth and all its parts are becoming; this is the fascination of living in time, if it is also a tension and responsibility. Man's adaptation to this discovery of time and continuing transformation is something that has not yet come about. Adjustment to the discoveries of science must be dealt with by science and its technologies, but not without the insights and visions of a different order that will also determine the future of man and the earth.

But while this period of rational inquiry into the functioning of the world had its divine side, it also had its demonic aspect. This was manifested first in its denunciation of past ways of knowing as various forms of ignorance and inadequacy; thus it became alienated from the past. If much of the past was inadequate to the reality of things, much of the human vision of the past was irreplaceable by other modes of knowing. Nor could the energies that flowed into the human order from this earlier period be replaced by the more rational efforts of man's conscious mind. Thus the distortion of the human that was often associated with the new period that moved from a medieval scholasticism through the Renaissance and Reformation into the enlightenment period of the French *philosophes* to the positivism of Comte and Spencer and Huxley from which science is only now becoming liberated.

A second defective aspect of the new period was the plundering of the earth's resources that we have already mentioned. This had the effect not simply of causing needless damage to the physical aspect of the earth; it caused even greater damage to the entire mode of thinking about the earth. Man in this period lost his intimacy with the earth. From subject the earth became object. From a healing source of aesthetic delight and joy of a higher, even sacred nature, the earth became a treasure of natural resources to be utilized by man. The earth was no longer a voice speaking to man and lifting him up to the world of the infinite and eternal. Its rivers were for carrying away refuse, not for contemplation.

A third difficulty with this age of the rational and the secular was the alienation of man from himself. Alienation from the past and alienation from the earth necessarily led to the alienation of man from himself and a decline in the human quality of life. The ancient mystique was gone, the mystique of the earth, of man, of history, of future expectation. The consequent human mood found expression in the literature of the absurd, in social unrest, in an educational impasse. Yet man never knew more about any of these things than at this time. This is the great paradox. The modern period is wonderfully in contact with all these areas of the real, and yet so distant. Man knows so much of the past and yet is not adequately nourished by the past; he knows so much about the earth and yet he finds himself at odds with the earth; he knows so much about himself and yet is so profoundly alienated from himself.

The consequence of this has been a feeling of meaninglessness which has caused man's inherent drive toward fulfillment of the earth process to weaken. This was the growing anxiety of Teilhard de Chardin toward the end of his life, that man's attachment to the earth and to the fulfillment of the historical evolutionary process would be weakened. He saw this as the basic problem of human energetics. This fulfillment of the earth process, this growing toward unity, this centration of man upon himself, this final attainment of the ultrahuman mode of being, all this required enormous human energies that must be evoked from the depths of man's being and from a commitment to the values of the earth process itself. At the end of this second period then, mankind witnesses the crisis of hope – not hope in the theological sense, but hope in the earthly sense of commitment to the future of the earth, of man, of the human community.

The Third Period

But even before the second phase of the dynamics of the earth ends, a third phase is begun, the recovery of man from the threefold alienation that we have mentioned. Primarily it is a recovery of man's own deeper self, the recovery of those psychic energies that have consistently dwindled in recent centuries. This third phase is brought into being by a spontaneous adjustment of the former inadequate perspectives of the human intelligence, and also in reaction to man's recent experience of the limitations in the available physical energies needed to fuel the machinery that serves the insatiable needs of contemporary society. This third phase must provide a new type of energy to support human existence throughout the ages to come.

While there can be some discussion of the extent and availability of the energies of the earth and the ability of man to dispose of the waste materials that result from use of these energies, there can be less discussion of the need for human energies on a vast scale, including the courage and the intelligence needed to carry out the grand designs of the earth's future. No amount of physical energy can supply the energies needed in the will to live and to expand the human mode of being. The primary shift now taking place in emphasis is from the external world to the internal world, from physical forces to the psychic energies of the earth. This involves an understanding and development of the psychic depths of the unconscious, a new awareness of the unity of the psychic and the physical as two phases of the single earth process, a recovery of symbolism as the main instrument for evoking these energies in an effective manner, a renewal of the sacred meaning of the earth, a new mystique of science and technology and their integration in an integral human way of being, knowing and acting.

Everywhere we perceive a new awareness of the psychic quality of the real. This we find emphasized in the later writings of Teilhard de Chardin: "However, it may well be, perhaps, that this contradiction is a warning to our minds that we must completely reverse the way in which we see things. We still persist in regarding the physical as constituting the 'true' phenomenon in the universe, and the psychic as a sort of epiphenomenon. However, as suspected (if I understand them correctly) by such coolly objective minds as Louis de Broglie and Leon Brillouin, surely, if we really wish to unify the real, we should completely reverse the values – that is, we should consider the whole of thermodynamics as an unstable and ephemeral by-effect of the concentration on itself of what we call 'consciousness' or 'spirit' " (*Activation of Energy*, p. 393). We find similar statements in the writings of Carl Jung: "The psyche is the world's pivot: not only is it the one great condition for the existence of a world at all, it is also an intervention in the existing natural order, and no one can say with certainty where this intervention will finally end" (*Works,* vol. VIII, 217).

This new awareness of the psychic structure of reality brings us to a new experience of subjectivity and the release of powers and experiences that take place within the deeper self of man. Once self-alienation is overcome then joy emerges in new dimensions along with the boundless energies that are contained in the human personality. These are attested to by all those who work directly with the interior processes of the human. Fields of energy never before appreciated emerge into being and become available for dynamizing man's activities. As regards these fields of energy there is a difference between the physical energy and psychic energy. The use of physical energy frequently leads to sterility of the matter once the energy is extracted; it also leads to waste products that often enough are dangerous to the life process. In contrast with this dissipation by use, psychic energies are increased by use and by participation. It has often been noted that material things are diminished by the number who share in them while immaterial realities are increased by the number who share in them and by the use made of them. Truth, understanding, joy, poetry, music – these are increased by the number who share in them as the light of truth is reflected back and forth from one person to another. Joy is increased by being shared. A completely individual joy is hardly of the human order. It needs to be shared. In the sharing of joy the radiance is increased and a greater range of human experience is established. This amounts to almost pure creation; for the joy of one is not diminished but intensified, and a new source of human energy is created.

A Strengthening of Symbolism

Along with a new appreciation of the psychic as a dimension of the earth, and a feeling for the psychic and the physical as complementary dimensions of each other, there is also a strengthening of the ancient symbolisms of the human community since it is in and through its symbols that the deeper experiences of the self express themselves. Through symbols those interior energies are released that sustain the human venture and the entire civilizational process. Ultimately these are symbols of the earth and its transformations. Much of the failure men have experienced in their struggle to achieve a satisfactory mode of human existence during these past few centuries is due to the loss of those primordial symbols that have fostered the human process through the centuries. Without these symbols it is not possible for the conscious rational mind and the deeper feelings and intuitions of the self to communicate with each other. The emotions and imagination are also alienated from the functional life of the individual and from the humanization process upon which the human community depends in its local as well as in its global dimensions. When these symbols are rendered ineffective in the established society they inevitably turn into destructive channels of expression. One of our greatest sources of assurance that the future is entering on a constructive phase of human endeavor is the widespread renewal of the symbolic traditions of the past and the ability manifested in adapting these symbols to the realistic modern context. Rather than symbols removing mankind from the realities of life it is through symbols that man establishes his most vital contact with the realities of life. The greatest single force in this renewal of the symbols of the human community is Carl Jung. He has made a contribution of unmeasured significance to the dynamics of the future in his work. The doctrine of archetypes that he has set forth enables these symbols to attain a systematic presentation and exposition.

The Force of Will

The next force that needs to be mentioned, to indicate wherein mankind must place its hopes for the future, is the force of will. This subject is not adequately dealt with either speculatively or practically in recent times. The best presentation in a realistic context is probably that found in the teachings of Don Juan as communicated through the books of Carlos Castaneda. The ideal of the warrior as someone with will is presented there in all the starkness found in the desert fathers or in the Japanese samurai. That part of the psyche designated as "will" has been manifested especially in the creative moments of mankind, but never before have such demands been made on the will as are being made at present and which will be made in the future. Schopenhauer is the philosopher most distinguished by his emphasis on will as the determinant of the real. But this has shown up again in the work of Teilhard de Chardin. He saw quite clearly that when man carried his scientific investigation into the origin and functioning of the world and became consciously aware of the evolutionary process, man must thenceforth consciously *will* the further stages of this evolutionary process which until then had come about by the spontaneities of the earth rather than by the deliberate will of man. A new stage in the dynamics of the earth was reached. Man passed over a threshold. Almost immediately this responsibility became too much for man to carry. Thus the type of historical pessimism that set in with the work of Oswald Spengler in *The Decline of the West*. Thus too the existentialist anxiety that has marked the mid-twentieth century. We live now in a moment of indecision, as a person carrying the world in his hands and afraid of tripping over his own feet and letting the world fall to its destruction.

But while this peril is a cause for concern it is also a cause for advancing consciousness, since the powers that man has recently assumed have brought about a state of profound reflection on the mystery of the earth. Responsible men no longer think of the world simply as a collection of "natural resources." They realize that the earth is an awesome mystery, ultimately as fragile as man himself is fragile, and that man must tread carefully over the earth's surface lest harm come to it. But man's responsibility to the earth is not simply that of preserving the earth and establishing an equilibrium of forces upon the earth, it is the task of leading the earth on through its next series of transformations which must eventuate as the future unfolds before us. The difficulty is that while man unknowingly was carried through the evolutionary process in former centuries, the time has come when man must lead and guide the evolutionary process. As Teilhard once wrote: "To my mind, what is our prime concern in connection with the ultra-evolution of man is not to know how, for perhaps hundreds of thousands of years to come, we are going to feed an ever growing population and fuel machines that are becoming ever more complicated and voracious. It will be to discover how man can maintain and increase, without check, throughout these vast periods of time, a passionate will not only to subsist but to press on: as we said, without that will every physical or chemical force we dispose of would remain heartbreakingly idle in our hands" (*Activation of Energy,* p. 370).

For will to succeed in this task of shaping the future with the ease and excitement, the human satisfaction, the cultural achievement and human magnificence that is indicated, something more than the will of the phenomenal ego must be functioning. The deeper self of man, the entire libido, must be functioning. The individual will can function in this capacity only through its union with the human community. Even beyond this union with the human community must be union with the earth process. Only the earth can adequately will the earth. If man successfully wills the future it will be because the will of the earth itself is manifested in and through him, not because he has determined the future of the earth with some rational empirical faculty.

Recovery of the Sacred

In this future-oriented process there is the recovery of the sacred and its tremendous psychic dynamism. One of the most serious defects of the recent secular period of man's development has been the loss of the sacred. While the sacred can never be recovered precisely in the form in which it existed in prior centuries, it can be recovered in the mystique and mystery of the earth. There are many reasons for this exclusive commitment to a scientific and secular life orientation in the past. It was in part due to the effort to quiet the devastating social and political conflicts that emerged out of the sectarian diversity of religious convictions. But it was also in part due to the decline of religious authenticity itself. For all of these reasons the former religious energy in the society has been diminished. Rather than resolving the problems of the sacred the solutions were set aside, with an awareness that these could not be solved until a later stage of man's development. Yet a substantial element of life was lost. An integral educational experience was no longer possible. Cultivation of the most profound instincts in man was neglected. Thus the emergence of a superficial humanist ideal that could not support any ultimate life meaning or provide the needed dynamic in relating the individual human personality to the society or to the earth process. A renewed sense of the sacred is now emerging as a most dynamic source for the energy needed for creation of the future. Spiritual disciplines are once again being practiced throughout the world. For some the ultimate mystery of things is experienced in the depth of the inner self; for some this mystery is found in the human community; for others in the earth process. Yet in each instance the threefold experience seems to be present. A way is being found whereby each human person becomes heir to the total religious heritage of the human community. Within this context the religious antagonisms of the past can be overcome, the particular traditions can be renewed, and the sacred can appear once again in the midst of human affairs to dynamize and sustain the efforts men make to create the world of the future.

We must feel that we are supported by that same power that brought the earth into being, that power that spun the galaxies out into space, that lit the sun and brought the moon into its orbit. That earth power by which the historical sequence of living forms grew up out of the earth until it came to consciousness in man, that same force that brought man through those millions of years of wandering as a hunter and food gatherer, that same force that led man to the establishment of his cities and that inspired the thinkers, artists and poets of the ages, those same earthly and historical forces themselves are all present, indeed the entire force of the ages is present and we might feel their impact at this time and understand that we are not isolated out in the chill of space with the burden of the future upon us and without the aid of any other power than that of our limited rational processes.

The important thing to achieve back of the biosphere, the noosphere, the technosphere, is the human sphere which includes all of these, for man is the pervading presence in all. He is by definition that reality in which the whole earth has its being. He is himself the mystical quality of the earth, the unifying principle, the integration of the various tensions and polarities of the material and the spiritual, the physical and the psychic, the natural and the manufactured, the intuitive and the scientific, the technological and the spiritual. He is the unity in which all these inhere and achieve their meaning, fulfillment, their reality, their salvation. In this sense man functions on the earth as the pervading logos. He is not simply the microcosmos. More than this, he is the true macrocosmos. The physical world is the microcosmos. Or we might say that the physical world is the *macro-anthropos,* the cosmic person, the *Mahapurusha* (in the term of India's traditions).

This being so there is need to be tender with the earth, for the suffering of the earth is the suffering of man, exploitation of the earth is exploitation of the human, elimination of the aesthetic splendors of the earth is the diminishment of man. To serve man by tearing the mountains apart, and losing their wonder and awesome qualities for some mineral resources within them, may very well be the destruction of a great range of psychic experience that is urgently needed by man.

If the ancient rituals whereby man communicated with the earth and fostered its productivity no longer seem effective, and if recent efforts to establish psychic rapport between man and the plant world are somewhat exaggerated, these do express something rather profound as regards the fruitfulness of the earth and man's reverence for the earth. It would be philosophically unrealistic, historically inaccurate, and scientifically unwarranted to say that man and the earth do not exist in an intimate and reciprocal emotional relationship. This emotional-aesthetic relationship of man with the entire cosmic order was perhaps best expressed in the ancient Navaho parting invocation:

> Go in beauty, beauty before you, beauty behind you, beauty to your right, beauty to your left, beauty above you, beauty beneath you. Go in beauty. In beauty all is finished.

This constitutes the dynamics of the human, or rather the human dynamics of the universe, whether in days gone by or in days to come. And this is what is most significant. It is not exactly that we are lacking in the dynamic forces needed to create the world of the future. We live immersed in a sea of energy beyond all comprehension. As Don Juan tells us, "The desert oozes power." But this power in an ultimate sense is ours not by domination but by invocation.

7

The Biblical Vision
of the Ecological Crisis

Rosemary Radford Ruether

We need to recover an understanding of ecojustice in which the enmity
or harmony of nature with humanity is part of the human historical
drama of good and evil.

TWO DECADES AGO IT WAS COMMON TO SPEAK OF THE NEED FOR
economic "development" among "backward" nations. The assumption behind this language was that Western-style industrialization was the model
of progress, and that all nations could be judged by how far they had
come along on that road. Poor nations were poor because they were at
some retarded stage of this evolutionary road of development. They
needed economic assistance from more "developed" nations to help them
"take off" faster.

Movements of Dissent

In the mid-'60s there were two major movements of dissent from
this model of "developmentalism." One of them occurred primarily
among social thinkers in the Third World, especially Latin America, who
began to reject the idea of development for that of liberation. They con-
tended that poor countries were poor not because they were "undeveloped," but because they were misdeveloped. They were the underside of a
process in which, for five centuries, Western colonizing countries had
stripped the colonized countries of their wealth, using cheap or slave labor, in order to build up the wealth which now underlies Western capitalism. One could not overcome this pattern of misdevelopment by a method
of "assistance" that merely continues and deepens the pattern of pillage
and dependency which created the poverty in the first place.

A few years after this critique of development from a Third World
standpoint, a second dissenting movement appeared, primarily among social thinkers in advanced industrial countries. This movement focused on
the issue of modern industrialized societies' ecological disharmony with
the carrying capacities of the natural environment. It dealt with such is-

sues as air, water and soil pollution; the increasing depletion of finite resources, including minerals and fossil fuels; and the population explosion.

This dissent found dramatic expression in the Club of Rome's report
on *Limits to Growth,* which demonstrated that indefinite expansion of
Western-style industrialization was, in fact, impossible. This system, dependent on a small affluent minority using a disproportionate share of the
world's natural resources, was fast depleting the base upon which it
rested: nonrenewable resources. To expand this type of industrialization
would simply accelerate the impending debacle; instead, we must stop developing and try to stabilize the economic system and population where
they are.

These two critiques of development – the Third World liberation
perspective and the First World ecological perspective – soon appeared to
be in considerable conflict with each other. The liberation viewpoint
stressed pulling control over the natural resources of poor countries out
from under Western power so that the developmental process could continue under autonomous, socialist political systems. The First World ecological viewpoint often sounded, whether consciously or not, as though it
were delivering bad news to the hopes of poor countries. Stabilizing the
world as it is seemed to suggest stabilizing its unjust relationships. The
First World, having developed advanced industry at the expense of the labor and resources of the Third World, was now saying: "Sorry, the good-
ies have just run out. There's not enough left for you to embark on the
same path." Population alarmists sounded as though Third World populations were to be the primary "targets" for reduction. Social justice and
the ecological balance of humanity with the environment were in conflict.
If one chose ecology, it was necessary to give up the dream of more
equal distribution of goods.

Religious Responses

In the late 60s there rose a spate of what might be called theological or religious responses to the ecological crisis, again primarily in advanced industrial countries. Two major tendencies predominated among
such writers. One trend, represented by books such as Theodore Roszak's
Where the Wasteland Ends, saw the ecological crisis in terms of the entire
Western Judeo-Christian reality principle. Tracing the roots of this false
reality principle to the Hebrew Bible itself, Roszak, among others, considered the heart of the ecological crisis to be the biblical injunction to
conquer and subdue the earth and have dominion over it. The earth and
its nonhuman inhabitants are regarded as possessions or property given to
"man" for "his" possession. "Man" exempts "himself" (and I use the male
generic advisedly) from the community of nature, setting himself above

and outside it somewhat as God "himself" is seen as sovereign over it. Humanity is God's agent in this process of reducing the autonomy of nature and subjugating it to the dominion of God and God's representative, man.

For Roszak and others, this conquest-and-dominion approach turned nature into a subjugated object and denied divine presence in it. Humanity could no longer stand in rapt contemplation before nature or enter into worshipful relations with it. A sense of ecstatic kinship between humanity and nature was destroyed. The divinities were driven out, and the rape of the earth began. In order to reverse the ecological crisis, therefore, we must go back to the root error of consciousness from which it derives. We must recover the religions of ecstatic kinship in nature that preceded and were destroyed by biblical religion. We must reimmerse God and humanity in nature, so that we can once again interact with nature as our spiritual kin, rather than as an enemy to be conquered or an object to be dominated. Only when we recover ancient animism's I-Thou relationship with nature, rather than the I-It relation of Western religion, can we recover the root principle of harmony with nature that was destroyed by biblical religion and its secular stepchildren.

This neoanimist approach to the ecological crisis was persuasive, evoking themes of Western reaction to industrialism and technological rationality that began at least as far back as the romanticism of the early 19th century. But many voices quickly spoke up in defense of biblical faith. A variety of writers took exception to romantic neoanimism as the answer, contending that biblical faith in relation to nature had been misunderstood. Most of the writers in this camp tended to come up with the "stewardship" model. Biblical faith does not mandate the exploitation of the earth, but rather commands us to be good stewards, conserving earth's goods for generations yet to come. In general, these writers did implicitly concede Roszak's point that biblical faith rejects any mystical or animist interaction with nature. Nature must be regarded as an object, not as a subject. It is our possession, but we must possess it in a thrifty rather than a profligate way.

Economic Considerations

One problem with both of these Western religious responses to the ecological crisis: there was very little recognition that this crisis took place within a particular economic system. The critique of the Third World liberationists was not accorded much attention or built into these responses. The ecological crisis was regarded primarily as a crisis between "man" and "nature," rather than as a crisis resulting from the way in which a particular exploitative relationship between classes, races and nations used natural resources.

The Protestant "stewardship" approach suggested a conservationist model of ecology. We should conserve resources, but without much acknowledgment that they had been unjustly used within the system that was being conserved. The countercultural approach, on the other hand, did tend to be critical of Western industrialism, but in a romantic, primitivist way. It idealized agricultural and handicraft economies but had little message for the victims of poverty who had already been displaced from that world of the preindustrial village. Thus it has little to say to the concerns of Third World economic justice, except to suggest that the inroads of Western industrialism should be resisted by turning back the clock.

Is there a third approach that has been overlooked by both the nature mystics and the puritan conservationists? Both of these views seem to me inadequate to provide a vision of the true character of the crisis and its solution. We cannot return to the Eden of the preindustrial village. However much those societies may possess elements of wisdom, these elements must be recovered by building a new society that also incorporates modern technological development. The countercultural approach never suggests ways of grappling with and changing the existing system. Its message remains at the level of dropping out into the preindustrial farm – an option which, ironically, usually depends on having an independent income!

The stewardship approach, with its mandate of thrift within the present system, rather than a recognition of that system's injustice, lacks a vision of a new and different economic order. Both the romantic and the conservationist approaches never deal with the question of ecojustice; namely, the reordering of access to and use of natural resources within a just economy. How can ecological harmony become part of a system of economic justice?

Misinterpretations of Scripture

To find a theology and/or spirituality of ecojustice, I would suggest that, in fact, our best foundation lies precisely in the Hebrew Bible – that same biblical vision which, anachronistically, the romantics have scapegoated as the problem and which the conservationists have interpreted too narrowly and unperceptively. Isaiah 24 offers one of the most eloquent statements of this biblical vision that is found particularly in the prophets of the Hebrew Scriptures. The puritan conservationists have too readily accepted a 19th century theology that sets history against nature – a theology which is basically western European rather than biblical. The biblical vision is far more "animistic" than they have been willing to concede.

In Scripture, nature itself operates as a powerful medium of God's presence or absence. Hills leap for joy and rivers clap their hands in God's presence. Or, conversely, nature grows hostile and barren as a medium of divine wrath.

The romantics, on the other hand, have blamed Scripture for styles of thought about nature that developed in quite different circles. The concept of nature as evil and alien to humanity began basically in late apocalyptic and gnostic thought in the Christian era. The divine was driven out of nature not to turn nature into a technological instrument, but rather to make it the habitation of the devil; the religious "man" should shun it and flee from it in order to save "his" soul for a higher spiritual realm outside of and against the body and the visible, created world. Christianity and certainly Judaism objected to this concept as a denial of the goodness of God's creation, though Christianity became highly infected by this negative view of nature throughout its first few centuries, and that influence continued to be felt until well into the 17th century.

The new naturalism and science of the 17th century initially had the effect of restoring the vision of nature as good, orderly and benign – the arena of the manifestation of God's divine reason, rather than of the devil's malice. But this Deist view of nature (as the manifestation of *divine* reason) was soon replaced by a Cartesian world view that set *human* reason outside and above nature. It is this technological approach – treating nature as an object to be reduced to human control – that is the heart of modern exploitation, but it does not properly correspond to any of the earlier religious visions of nature. Any recovery of an appropriate religious vision, moreover, must be one that does not merely ignore these subsequent developments, but that allows us to review and critique where we have gone wrong in our relationship to God's good gift of the earth. In my opinion, it is precisely the vision of the Hebrew prophets that provides at least the germ of that critical and prophetic vision.

A Covenantal Vision

The prophetic vision neither treats nature in a romantic way nor reduces it to a mere object of human use. Rather, it recognizes that human interaction with nature has made nature itself historical. In relation to humanity, nature no longer exists "naturally," for it has become part of the human social drama, interacting with humankind as a vehicle of historical judgment and a sign of historical hope. Humanity as a part of creation is not outside of nature but within it. But this is the case because nature itself is part of the covenant between God and creation. By this covenantal view, nature's responses to human use or abuse become an ethical sign. The erosion of the soil in areas that have been abused for their mineral wealth, the pollution of air where poor people live, are not just facts of nature; what we have is an ethical judgment on the exploitation of natural resources by the rich at the expense of the poor. It is no accident that nature is most devastated where poor people live.

When human beings break their covenant with society by exploiting the labor of the worker and refusing to do anything about the social costs of production – i.e., poisoned air and water – the covenant of creation is violated. Poverty, social oppression, war and violence in society, and the polluted, barren, hostile face of nature – both express this violation of the covenant. The two are profoundly linked together in the biblical vision as parts of one covenant, so that, more and more, the disasters of nature become less a purely natural fact and increasingly become a social fact. The prophetic text of Isaiah 24 vividly portrays this link between social and natural hostility in the broken order of creation:

> Behold, the Lord will lay waste the earth and make it desolate,
> and he will twist its surface and scatter its inhabitants. . . .
> The earth shall be utterly laid waste and utterly despoiled; . . .
> The earth mourns and withers, the world languishes and withers; . . .
> The earth lies polluted under its inhabitants;
> for they have transgressed the laws, violated the statutes, broken the
> everlasting covenant.
> Therefore a curse devours the earth,
> and its inhabitants suffer for their guilt; . . .
> The city of chaos is broken down,
> every house is shut up so that none can enter. . . .
> Desolation is left in the city, the gates are battered into ruins.
>
> [Isa. 24:1, 3, 4-5, 10, 12]

But this tale of desolation in society and nature is not the end of the prophetic vision. When humanity mends its relation to God, the result must be expressed not in contemplative flight from the earth but rather in the rectifying of the covenant of creation. The restoration of just relations between peoples restores peace to society and, at the same time, heals nature's enmity. Just, peaceful societies in which people are not exploited also create peaceful, harmonious and beautiful natural environments. This outcome is the striking dimension of the biblical vision. The Peaceable Kingdom is one where nature experiences the loss of hostility between animal and animal, and between human and animal. The wolf dwells with the lamb, the leopard lies down with the kid, and the little child shall lead them.

> They shall not hurt or destroy in all my holy mountain, for the earth
> shall be full of the knowledge of the Lord. [Is. 11:9].

The biblical dream grows as lush as a fertility religion in its description of the flowering of nature in the reconciled kingdom of God's Shalom.

The wilderness and the dry land shall be glad, the desert shall rejoice and blossom;
Like the crocus it shall blossom abundantly, and rejoice with joy and singing.

[Is. 35:1-2]

"The tree bears its fruit, the fig trees and vine give their full yield. . . . Rejoice in the Lord, for he has given early rain . . . The threshing floors shall be full of grain, the vats shall overflow with wine and oil."

[Joel 2:22-24]

"Behold the days are coming," says the Lord, "when the plowman will overtake the reaper and the treader of grapes him who sows the seed: the mountains shall drip sweet wine, and all the hills shall flow with it." [Amos 9:13]

In the biblical view, the raping of nature and the exploitation of people in society are profoundly understood as part of one reality, creating disaster in both. We look not to the past but to a new future, brought about by social repentance and conversion to divine commandments, so that the covenant of creation can be rectified and God's Shalom brought to nature and society. Just as the fact of nature and society grows hostile through injustice, so it will be restored to harmony through righteousness. The biblical understanding of nature, therefore, inheres in a human ethical vision, a vision of ecojustice, in which the enmity or harmony of nature with humanity is part of the human historical drama of good and evil. This is indeed the sort of ecological theology we need today, not one of either romance or conservationism, but rather an ecological theology of ethical, social seriousness, through which we understand our human responsibility for ecological destruction and its deep links with the struggle to create a just and peaceful social order.

8

Epilogue

Carolyn Merchant

THE MECHANISTIC VIEW OF NATURE, DEVELOPED BY THE SEVENTEENTH-century natural philosophers and based on a Western mathematical tradition going back to Plato, is still dominant in science today. This view assumes that nature can be divided into parts and that the parts can be rearranged to create other species of being. "Facts" or information bits can be extracted from the environmental context and rearranged according to a set of rules based on logical and mathematical operations. The results can then be tested and verified by resubmitting them to nature, the ultimate judge of their validity. Mathematical formalism provides the criterion for rationality and certainty, nature the criterion for empirical validity and acceptance or rejection of the theory.

The work of historians and philosophers of science notwithstanding, it is widely assumed by the scientific community that modern science is objective, value-free, and context-free knowledge of the external world. To the extent to which the sciences can be reduced to this mechanistic mathematical model, the more legitimate they become as sciences. Thus the reductionist hierarchy of the validity of the sciences first proposed in the nineteenth century by French positivist philosopher August Comte is still widely assumed by intellectuals, the most mathematical and highly theoretical sciences occupying the most revered position.

The mechanistic approach to nature is as fundamental to the twentieth-century revolution in physics as it was to classical Newtonian science, culminating in the nineteenth-century unification of mechanics, thermodynamics, and electromagnetic theory. Twentieth-century physics still views the world in terms of fundamental particles – electrons, protons, neutrons, mesons, muons, pions, taus, thetas, sigmas, pis, and so on. The search for the ultimate unifying particle, the quark, continues to engage the efforts of the best theoretical physicists.

Mathematical formalism isolates the elements of a given quantum mechanical problem, places them in a lattice-like matrix, and rearranges them through a mathematical function called an *operator.* Systems theory extracts possibly relevant information bits from the environmental context and stores them in a computer memory for later use. But since it cannot store an infinite number of "facts," it must select a finite number of potentially relevant pieces of data according to a theory or set of rules governing the selection process. For any given solution, this mechanistic approach very likely excludes some potentially relevant factors.

Systems theorists claim for themselves a holistic outlook, because they believe that they are taking into account the ways in which all the parts in a given system affect the whole. Yet the formalism of the calculus of probabilities excludes the possibility of mathematizing the gestalt – that is, the ways in which each part at any given instant take their meaning from the whole. The more open, adaptive, organic, and complex the system, the less successful is the formalism. It is most successful when applied to closed, artificial, precisely defined, relatively simple systems. Mechanistic assumptions about nature push us increasingly in the direction of artificial environments, mechanized control over more and more aspects of human life, and a loss of the quality of life itself.

In the social sphere, the mechanistic model helps to guide technological and industrial development. In *The Technological Society,* Jacques Ellul discussed the techniques of economics and the mechanistic organization of specialties inherent in and entailed by the machines and mathematical methods themselves. The calculating machine, punch card machine, microfilm, and computer transform statistical methods and administrative organization into specialized agencies centered around one or more statistical categories.

Econometric models and stochastics are used to operate on statistical data in order to analyze, compare, and predict. In social applications, attempts to predict public reaction through the calculus of probabilities may make a public informed of its conformation to a trend act in the inverse manner.

> But the public, by so reacting falls under the influence of a new prediction which is completely determinable. . . . It must be assumed, however, that one remains within the framework of rational behavior. The system works all the better when it deals with people who are better integrated into the mass . . . whose consciousness is partially paralyzed, who lend themselves willingly to statistical observations and systematization.[1]

Such attempts to reduce human behavior to statistical probabilities and to condition it by such psychological techniques as those developed by B. F. Skinner are manifestations of the pervasiveness of the mechanistic mode of thought developed by the seventeenth-century scientists.

Holism was proposed as a philosophical alternative to mechanism by J. C. Smuts in his book *Holism and Evolution (1926),* in which he attempted to define the essential characteristics of holism and to differentiate it from nineteenth-century mechanism. He attempts to show that

> Taking a plant or animal as a type of whole, we notice the fundamental holistic characters as a unity of parts which is so close and intense as to be more than a sum of its parts; which not only gives a particular conformation or structure to the parts but so relates and determines them in their synthesis that their functions are altered; the synthesis affects and determines the parts so that they function toward the "whole"; and the whole and the parts therefore reciprocally influence and determine each other and appear more or less to merge their individual characters.[2]

Smuts saw a continuum of relationships among parts from simple physical mixtures and chemical compounds to organisms and minds in which the unity among parts was affected and changed by the synthesis. "Holism is a process of creative synthesis; the resulting wholes are not static, but dynamic, evolutionary, creative. . . . The explanation of nature can therefore not be purely mechanical; and the mechanistic concept of nature has its place and justification only in the wider setting of holism."

The most important example of holism today is provided by the science of ecology. Although ecology is a relatively new science, its philosophy of nature, holism, is not. Historically, holistic presuppositions about nature have been assumed by communities of people who have succeeded in living in equilibrium with their environments. The idea of cyclical processes, of the interconnectedness of all things, and the assumption that nature is active and alive are fundamental to the history of human thought. No element of an interlocking cycle can be removed without the collapse of the cycle. The parts themselves thus take their meaning from the whole. Each particular part is defined by and dependent on the total context. The cycle itself is a dynamic interactive relationship of all its parts, and process is a dialectical relation between part and whole. Ecology necessarily must consider the complexities and the totality. It cannot isolate the parts into simplified systems that can be studied in a laboratory, because such isolation distorts the whole.

External forces and stresses on a balanced ecosystem, whether natural or man made, can make some parts of the cycle act faster than the systems' own natural oscillations. Depending on the strength of the external disturbance, the metabolic and reproductive reaction rates of the slowest parts of the cycle, and the complexity of the system, it may or may not be able to absorb the stresses without collapsing.[3] At various times in history, civilizations which have put too much external stress on their environments have caused long-term or irrevocable alterations.

By pointing up the essential role of every part of an ecosystem, that if one part is removed the system is weakened and loses stability, ecology has moved in the direction of the leveling of value hierarchies. Each part contributes equal value to the healthy functioning of the whole. All living things, as integral parts of a viable ecosystem, thus have rights. The necessity of protecting the ecosystem from collapse due to the extinction of vital members was one argument for the passage of the Endangered Species Act of 1973. The movement toward egalitarianism manifested in the democratic revolutions of the eighteenth century, the extension of citizens' rights to blacks, and finally, voting rights to women was thus carried a step further. Endangered species became equal to the Army Corps of Engineers: the sail darter had to have a legal hearing before the Tellico Dam could be approved, the Furbish lousewort could block construction of the Dickey-Lincoln Dam in Maine, the red-cockaded woodpecker must be considered in Texas timber management, and the El Segundo Blue Butterfly in California airport expansion.

The conjunction of conservation and ecology movements with women's rights and liberation has moved in the direction of reversing both the subjugation of nature and women. In the late nineteenth and early twentieth centuries, the strong feminist movement in the United States begun in 1842 pressed for women's suffrage first in the individual states and then in the nation. Women activists also formed conservation committees in the many women's organizations that were part of the Federation of Women's Clubs established in 1890. They supported the preservationist movement for national, state, and city parks and wilderness areas led by John Muir and Frederick Law Olmsted, eventually splitting away from the managerial, utilitarian wing headed by Gifford Pinchot and Theodore Roosevelt.[4]

Today the conjunction of the women's movement with the ecology movement again brings the issue of liberation into focus. Mainstream women's groups such as the League of Women Voters took an early lead in studying and pressing for clean air and water legislation. Socialist-feminist and "science for the people" groups worked toward revolutionizing economic structures in a direction that would equalize female and male work options and reform a capitalist system that creates profits at the expense of nature and working people.

The March 1979 accident at the Three-Mile Island nuclear reactor near Harrisburg, Pennsylvania, epitomized the problems of the "death of nature" that have become apparent since the Scientific Revolution. The manipulation of nuclear processes in an effort to control and harness nature through technology backfired into disaster. The long-range economic interests and public image of the power company and the reactor's designer were set above the immediate safety of the people and the health of the earth. The hidden effects of radioactive emissions, which by concentrating in the food chain could lead to an increase in cancers over the next several years, were initially downplayed by those charged with responsibility for regulating atomic power.

Three-Mile Island is a recent symbol of the earth's sickness caused by radioactive wastes, pesticides, plastics, photochemical smog, and fluorocarbons. The pollution "of her purest streams" has been supported since the Scientific Revolution by an ideology of "power over nature," an ontology of interchangeable atomic and human parts, and a methodology of "penetration" into her innermost secrets. The sick earth, "yea dead, yea putrified," can probably in the long run be restored to health only by a reversal of mainstream values and a revolution in economic priorities. In this sense, the world must once again be turned upside down.

As natural resources and energy supplies diminish in the future, it will become essential to examine alternatives of all kinds so that, by adopting new social styles, the quality of the environment can be sustained. Decentralization, nonhierarchical forms of organization, recycling of wastes, simpler living styles involving less-polluting "soft" technologies, and labor-intensive rather than capital-intensive economic methods are possibilities only beginning to be explored.[5] The future distribution of energy and resources among communities should be based on the integration of human and natural ecosystems. Such a restructuring of priorities may be crucial if people and nature are to survive.

Notes

1. Jacques Ellul, *The Technological Society,* trans. J. Wilkinson (New York: Random House, 1964), pp. 163 ff., quotation on p. 163; B. F. Skinner, *Beyond Freedom and Dignity* (New York: Random House, 1971). See also B. F. Skinner, *Walden Two* (New York: Macmillan, 1972; first published 1948). For a philosophical critique of systems theory, see Hubert Dreyfus, *What Computers Can't Do* (New York: Harper & Row, 1972), especially p. 170.

2. J. C. Smuts, *Holism and Evolution* (New York: Macmillan, 1926), pp. 86, 87. On holism in the biological sciences, see Arthur Koestler, "Beyond Holism and Reductionism: The Concept of the Holon," in *Beyond Reductionism: New Perspectives in the Life Sciences,* ed. A. Koestler and J. R. Smythies (Boston: Beacon Press, 1969).

3. On ecological cycles, see Barry Commoner, *The Closing Circle: Nature, Man, and Technology* (New York; Bantam Books, 1971), Chap. 2.

4. Samuel P. Hays, *Conservation and the Gospel of Efficiency: The Progressive Conservation Movement, 1890-1920* (Cambridge, Mass.: Harvard University Press, 1959), pp. 142-43.

5. Murray Bookchin, "Ecology and Revolutionary Thought," in *Post-Scarcity Anarchism* (San Francisco: Ramparts Press, 1971), pp. 57-82, and M. Bookchin, "Toward an Ecological Solution" (Berkeley, Cal.: Ecology Center Reprint, n. d.). See also Victor Ferkiss, *Technological Man* (New York: New American Library, 1969), Chap. 9, pp. 205-11; Theodore Roszak, *Where the Wasteland Ends* (Garden City, N.Y.: Doubleday, 1973), pp. 367-71; Paul Goodman and Percival Goodman, *Communitas.* 2nd ed., rev. (New York: Vintage, 1960); Paul Goodman, *People or Personnel* (New York: Random House, 1965); E. F. Schumacher, *Small is Beautiful: Economics as if People Mattered* (New York: Harper & Row, 1973); Ernest Callenbach, *Ecotopia* (Berkeley, Cal.: Banyan Tree Books, 1976).

Part II

Further Conversation

9

Toward an Ecological-Feminist Theology of Nature

Rosemary Radford Ruether

AN ECOLOGICAL-FEMINIST THEOLOGY OF NATURE MUST RETHINK THE WHOLE Western theological tradition of the hierarchical chain of being and chain of command. This theology must question the hierarchy of human over nonhuman nature as a relationship of ontological and moral value. It must challenge the right of the human to treat the nonhuman as private property and material wealth to be exploited. It must unmask the structures of social domination, male over female, owner over worker that mediate this domination of nonhuman nature. Finally, it must question the model of hierarchy that starts with nonmaterial spirit (God) as the source of the chain of being and continues down to nonspiritual "matter" as the bottom of the chain of being and the most inferior, valueless, and dominated point in the chain of command.

The God/ess who is primal Matrix, the ground of being-new being, is neither stifling immanence nor rootless transcendence. Spirit and matter are not dichotomized but are the inside and outside of the same thing. When we proceed to the inward depths of consciousness or probe beneath the surface of visible things to the electromagnetic field that is the ground of atomic and molecular structure, the visible disappears. Matter itself dissolves into energy. Energy, organized in patterns and relationships, is the basis for what we experience as visible things. It becomes impossible anymore to dichotomize material and spiritual energy. Consciousness comes to be seen as the most intense and complex form of the inwardness of material energy itself as it bursts forth at that evolutionary level where matter is organized in the most complex and intensive way – the central nervous system and cortex of the human brain.

If we follow Teilhard de Chardin's interpretation of evolution, the radial energy of matter develops along the lines of increasing complexity and centralization. At certain "boiling points" of life energy, there is a critical leap to a new stage of being, from minerals to plant life, from plant life to animate life, moving through increasing stages of intelligence until the breakthrough to self-conscious intelligence.[1]

It becomes evident that one can no longer make the dichotomy between nature and history. Nature itself is historical. The universe is a great being that is born, grows, and presumably will die. Critical moments of transformation appear at stages of the universe's growth, bringing into being new possibilities. These were latent in what existed before and yet represent something new, something that could not simply be expected from the preexisting forms of being. Nature contains transcendence and freedom, as well as necessity. The change from mineral being to plant life, from plant life to animate life, and then to self-conscious intelligence is not just quantitative, but qualitative transformation. At each stage a qualitatively new dimension of life comes into being.

So far the evolutionary view of matter and radial energy in Teilhard de Chardin and others could lead simply to a new version of the chain of being. The chain of being has been laid on its side, so to speak. But this view still preserves the same presuppositions of the superiority of the "higher" over the "lower" forms and hence the domination of the "highest" form – namely, the human – over the rest solely for human self-interest. Indeed, Teilhard does not question the racist assumptions that white Western development is the privileged line of human development that has a right to control and reshape the rest of humanity.[2] This hierarchicalism of evolutionary theory has to be modified by several considerations.

We come to recognize the continuity of human consciousness with the radial energy of matter throughout the universe. Our intelligence is a special, intense form of this radial energy, but it is not without continuity with other forms; it is the self-conscious or "thinking dimension" of the radial energy of matter. We must respond to a "thou-ness" in all beings. This is not romanticism or an anthropomorphic animism that sees "dryads in trees," although there is truth in the animist view. The spirit in plants or animals is not anthropomorphic but biomorphic to its own forms of life. We respond not just as "I to it," but as "I to thou," to the spirit, the life energy that lies in every being in its own form of existence. The "brotherhood of man" needs to be widened to embrace not only women but also the whole community of life.

The more complex forms of life represent critical breakthroughs to new stages of existence that give them qualitatively more mobility and freedom for response. But they are radically dependent on all the stages of life that go before them and that continue to underlie their own existence. The plant can happily carry out its processes of photosynthesis without human beings, but we cannot exist without the photosynthesis of plants. The more complex forms of life are not the source and foundation of the less complex forms, just the opposite. An animal depends on a whole ecological community of life processes of plants, insects, other animals, water, air, and soil that underlie its existence. Still more, human beings cannot live without the whole ecological community that supports and makes possible our existence.

The privilege of intelligence, then, is not a privilege to alienate and dominate the world without concern for the welfare of all other forms of life. On the contrary, it is the responsibility to become the caretaker and cultivator of the welfare of the whole ecological community upon which our own existence depends. By what right are we the caretakers of nature when nonhuman nature takes care of its own processes very well and, in most cases, better without us? Human self-consciousness carries with it a danger that exists in no other form of creaturely life. Nonhuman creatures, to be sure, eat and are eaten by others. There is violence and bloodshed in nature, but it takes place within its own built-in balances. If one creature rapidly and drastically increases its population, it kills off its own life-support system and so dies off until it reaches a population back in balance with its ecological community.

Humans alone perpetuate their evolutionary advances primarily through cultural-social means. We don't grow our clothes on our bodies or our tools in the nails at the ends of our hands; we create these as artifacts. So we can continually change and develop them as part of our technology. More than that, we have the ability to create dysfunctional relationships with the earth, with our ecological community, and with each other and to preserve them socially. We alone can "sin." We alone can disrupt and distort the balances of nature and force the price for this distortion on less fortunate humans, as well as the nonhuman community. We cannot do this forever. Finally, the universe will create inversions, under the weight of human distortion and oppression, that will undermine the whole human life-support system. But we may be able to bring the earth down with us in our downfall. We may destroy much of the work of evolutionary development back to the most primary level of minerals and photosynthesis, and leave even this deeply poisoned against the production of life. We are the rogue elephant of nature.

Thus we have not so much the privilege of intelligence, viewed as something above and against nonhuman nature, but the responsibility and necessity to convert our intelligence to the earth. We need to learn how to use intelligence to mend the distortions we have created and how to convert intelligence into an instrument that can cultivate the harmonies and balances of the ecological community and bring these to a refinement. We can turn the desert wilderness or the jungle into the garden. But we need to do that not simply by bulldozing what is and ignoring all other needs but our own, but by understanding the integrity of the existing ecological community and learning to build our niche in that community in harmony with the rest. We do this out of a genuine recognition of our interdependence. We cannot violate the ecological community without ultimately destroying our own life-support system. The notion of dominating the universe from a position of autonomy is an illusion of alienated consciousness. We have only two real options: either to learn to use our intelligence to become *servants* of the survival and cultivation of nature or to lose our own life-support system in an increasingly poisoned earth.

This conversion of our intelligence to the earth will demand a new form of human intelligence. The dominant white Western male rationality has been based on linear, dichotomized thought patterns that divide reality into dualisms: one is good and the other bad, one superior and the other inferior, one should dominate and the other should be eliminated or suppressed. The biological base of these patterns is specialization in left-brain, rational functions in a way that suppresses the right-brain, relational sense. This one-sided brain development seems more dominant in males than in females, possibly because of later verbal development in males.[3]

This biological tendency has been exaggerated by socialization into dominant and subordinate social roles. Dominant social roles exaggerate linear, dichotomized thinking and prevent the development of culture that would correct this bias by integrating the relational side. Women and other subordinate groups, moreover, have had their rational capacities suppressed through denial of education and leadership experience and so tend to be perceived as having primarily intuitive and affective patterns of thought. Thus socialization in power and powerlessness distorts integration further and creates what appears to be dichotomized personality cultures of men and women, that is, masculinity and femininity.

What we must now realize is that the patterns of rationality of left-brain specialization are, in many ways, ecologically dysfunctional. Far from this rationality being the mental counterpart of "natural law," it screens out much of reality as "irrelevant" to science and reduces scientific knowledge to a narrow spectrum fitted to dominance and control. But the systems it sets up are ecologically dysfunctional because they fail to see the larger relational patterns within which particular "facts" stand. This rationality tends toward monolithic systems of use of nature. Linear thinking, for example, directs agriculture, or even decorative planting, toward long rows of the same plant. This magnifies the plants' vulnerability to disease. Humans then compensate with chemical sprays, which in turn send a ripple effect of poisons through the whole ecological system. Nature, by contrast, diffuses and intersperses plants, so that each balances and corrects the vulnerabilities of the other. The inability to see the forest for the trees is typical of linear thinking.

Linear thinking simplifies, dichotomizes, focuses on parts, and fails to see the larger relationality and interdependence. Ecological thinking demands a different kind of rationality, one that integrates left-brain linear thought and right-brain spatial and relational thought. One has to disrupt the linear concept of order to create a different kind of order that is truly the way nature "orders," that is, balances and harmonizes, but that appears very "disorderly" to the linear, rational mind. One observes a meadow with many kinds of plants and insects balancing each other, each with their ecological niches, and then one learns to plant for human use in a way that imitates these same principles, in a more simplified and selective fashion. Converting our minds to the earth means understanding the more diffuse and relational logic of natural harmony. We learn to fit human ecology into its relation to nonhuman ecology in a way that maximizes the welfare of the whole rather than undermining and subverting (polluting) the life system.

Converting our minds to the earth cannot happen without converting our minds to each other, since the distorted and ecologically dysfunctional relationships appear necessary, yet they actually support the profits of the few against the many. There can be no ecological ethic simply as a new relation of "man" and "nature." Any ecological ethic must always take into account the structures of social domination and exploitation that mediate domination of nature and prevent concern for the welfare of the whole community in favor of the immediate advantage of the dominant class, race, and sex. An ecological ethic must always be an ethic of ecojustice that recognizes the interconnection of social domination and domination of nature.

Nonhuman nature, in this sense, is not just a "natural fact" to which we can "return" by rejecting human culture. Nature is a product not only of natural evolution but of human historical development. It partakes of the evils and distortions of human development. There is virtually no place on the planet where one can go to find "nature untouched by human hands." Even if humans have not been there before, their influence has been carried by winds, water, and soil, birds, insects, and animals who bear within their beings the poisoning effects of human rapine of the globe. Nature, in this sense, can be seen as "fallen," not that it is evil itself but in that it has been marred and distorted by human misdevelopment. The remaking of our relation with nature and with each other, then, is a historical project and struggle of re-creation.

Nature will never be the same as it would have been without human intervention. Although we need to remake the earth in a way that converts our minds to nature's logic of ecological harmony, this will necessarily be a new synthesis, a new creation in which human nature and nonhuman nature become friends in the creating of a livable and sustainable cosmos.

Notes

1. Pierre Teilhard de Chardin, *The Phenomenon of Man*, Harper & Row, New York, 1959, pp. 53-74.

2. *Ibid.*, pp. 209-210.

3. Sally P. Springer and Georg Deutsch, *Left Brain, Right Brain*, Freeman, San Francisco, 1981, pp. 121-130.

10

Split Culture

Susan Griffin

WE WHO ARE BORN INTO THIS CIVILIZATION HAVE INHERITED A HABIT OF mind. We are divided against ourselves. We no longer feel ourselves to be a part of this earth. We regard our fellow creatures as enemies. And, very young, we even learn to disown a part of our own being. We come to believe that we do not know what we know. We grow used to ignoring the evidence of our own experience, what we hear or see, what we feel in our own bodies. We come into maturity keeping secrets. But we forget this secret knowledge and feel instead only a vague shame, a sense that perhaps we are not who we say we are. Yet we have learned well to pretend that what is true is not true. In some places the sky is perpetually gray, and the air is filled with a putrid smell. Forests we loved as children disappear. The waters we once swam are forbidden to us now because they are poisoned. We remember there was a sweet taste to fruit, that there used to be more birds. But we do not read these perceptions as signs of our own peril.

Long ago we gave up ourselves. Now, if we are dying by increments, we have ceased to be aware of this death. How can we know our own death if we do not know our own existence? We have traded our real existence, our real feelings for a delusion. Instead of fighting for our lives, we bend all our efforts to defend delusion. We deny all evidence at hand that this civilization, which has shaped our minds, is also destroying the earth.

The dividedness of our minds is etched into our language. To us, the word *thought* means an activity separate from feeling, just as the word *mind* suggests a place apart from the body and from the rhythms of the earth. We do not use the word *animal to* describe human qualities. Our word *spirit* rises in our imaginations above the earth as if we believed that holiness exists in an inverse proportion to gravity. The circumstance of our birth is common to us; we are all of woman born. But we have a word *race* which suggests to us that human beings belong to different categories of virtue by birth. Through the words *masculine and feminine,* which we use to designate two alien and alienated poles of human behavior, we make our sexuality a source of separation. We divide ourselves and all that we know along an invisible borderline between what we call Nature and what we believe is superior to Nature.

Now we find ourselves moving almost without recourse toward a war that will destroy all of our lives. And were this not true, we have learned that the way we live has damaged the atmosphere, our bodies, even our genetic heritage so severely that perhaps we cannot save ourselves. We are at the edge of death, and yet, like one who contemplates suicide, we are our own enemies. We think with the very mind that has brought disaster on us. And this mind, taught and trained by this civilization, does not know itself. This is a mind in exile from its own wisdom.

According to this worldview – a view whose assumptions are so widely accepted by this civilization that we do not even think of it as an ideology – there is a hierarchy to existence. God and the angels, things pure in spirit and devoid of any material content, come first. Everything earthly is corrupt. But among the corrupt, human beings are of the highest spiritual order, more significant, valuable, and trustworthy than animals, or certainly trees or, of course, tomatoes, and obviously more intelligent than mountains, or oceans, or particles of sand. Among human beings, a similar order exists. Those of the human species who belong to what is thought of as the white race, and those who are part of the masculine gender, are at the top of this hierarchy. Various glosses on this fundamental belief place the rest of us in different descending orders.

We have learned of the scientific revolution that it was a victory over the irrational, over magical thought that led to the Inquisition and the witch burnings. And we do not commonly associate the philosophy of St. Augustine about men and women with the scientific worldview because we are accustomed to thinking that science and religion are at opposite positions in a polemic that expressed itself in the trial of Galileo. Despite the fact that Galileo recanted to the church, we no longer believe the world was literally created in seven days, nor do we place the earth at the center of the solar system.

But what we have not considered is that a civilization may suffer a great transformation in its institutions and its philosophy – power can shift from church to state, and the authority for knowledge from priest to scientist – and yet still retain, in a new guise and a new language, the essence of the old point of view. Such is the case with the scientific revolution, so that many assumptions, methods, and even questions we take to be scientific, actually partake of the same paradigm that in an earlier age we described as Christian.

Let us look at Newton's *Optics* for an example. Before Newton's work on optics, many different ideas about vision were believed, including the notion that a ray of light emanated from the human eye and illuminated the world. Through observation and experiment, Newton concluded that color is not a property of the eye nor the property of any object but is instead produced by the retina, sensitive to light refracted at different angles. This and like discoveries in the seventeenth and eighteenth centuries fell into a philosophical doctrine that was taken to be an experimentally proven vision of the true nature of the world. The scientific point of view argued that we cannot trust our senses, that we are deceived by the appearance of the material world, that color is a form of illusion, that color is simply a figment of our minds and does not exist.[1]

Thus if religion told us that the earth was a corrupt place, that our true home was heaven, that sensual feeling was not to be trusted and could lead us to hell and damnation, science did not in essence contradict that doctrine. For science, too, told us not to trust our senses, that matter is deceptive, and that we are alien to our surroundings. If, then, religion told us that our own senses could not be trusted and that therefore we must bow to scripture and the authority of the priest, now science tells us that we must bow to the truth of objective experimental data and the authority of scientific experts. In both systems, not only are we alienated from a world that is described as deceiving us; we are also alienated from our own capacity to see and hear, to taste and touch, to know and describe our own experience.

Such is the strength of this old way of thinking – that the earth and what is natural in ourselves is not to be trusted – that it hardly occurs to us that there is another way to interpret Newton's discovery; we have confused his discovery with our old paradigmatic vision.

For indeed one can make a very different interpretation of Newton's observations of the nature of optics. Instead of believing we are deceived by matter or our senses, instead of deciding that color does not exist, we can assert, since we do experience color, that in our experience of color we have entered into a union with what we perceive. That together with matter we create color. That our sense of color is indeed evidence of a profound, sensual, and emotional connection we have with all that is part of this earth. That the joy color gives us is perhaps part of the balance of the universe.

There is another example of how the old paradigm affects what we take to be impartial science, from Francis Bacon's argument that science ought to proceed by experimentation. It must be close to self-evident, one can object here, that scientific experimentation is a movement toward respect of the material world. Before the idea of experiment, the nature of the material world was not even considered worthy of observation. Speculation and deductive reason were the sources of truth. I must digress for a moment to point out that if one is part of Nature oneself, speculation, especially when it involves self-reflection, *is* a kind of experiment. And perhaps this is not really a digression. For indeed, what is missing in Bacon's idea of scientific experiment is any self-reflection. He assumes that a superior objectivity, a state of emotional and physical detachment, can belong to the scientist who performs an experiment.

In different ages, both religion and science have been the focus of our hopes and the arbiters of what we call truth. Because they have expressed the consciousness of a whole civilization, both institutions also carry with them and epitomize, in their ideas and traditions, the troubled conflict, the dividedness, of our consciousness. Both institutions within Western civilization have been shaped by and have deepened our alienation from this earth.

If the church once offered the denigration of incarnate life as a solution to the human condition, now science offers us the control of matter as our rescue. But what can be wrong with cultivating either the human spirit or the soil we live on? Human creativity is a part of Nature, but rather we think of ourselves as working against Nature. The paradigm that tells us we are apart from and above this earth is not simply an intellectual response to Nature. It is instead a deeply fearful attitude. And the fear that lies under this thought, like all fear, turns into rage.

The pursuit of scientific knowledge in our civilization is beset by an emotional dilemma. In order to control Nature, we must know Nature. But just as we are seeking to know, there is a knowledge we fear. We are afraid to remember what we, in our bodies and in our feelings, still know, but what, in our fragmented, civilized consciousness we have been persuaded to forget. That, like the forests we destroy, or the rivers we try to tame, *we* are Nature.

The discovery of the solar system, of gravitational law, of evolution, of the microscopic world of the cell, of the genetic information that is part of matter, of the nature of light, and of the continuum between matter and energy, should transform consciousness so that we in this civilization might begin to regard the human condition with humility rather than arrogance. The thinkers who made what we call the scientific revolution had begun to discover a vast matrix of natural order, a very large wisdom whose boundaries we cannot even imagine. Just as the Earth is not the center of the solar system, so the biosphere is not centered on the human species nor circumscribed by human culture. We are dependent on the universe around us not only to breathe and eat, but even to keep our feet on the ground. For we do this not at will but because we exist in a field of energy. All that we do is shaped by and partakes of that field. And our perceptions and what we experience as real depend upon the nature and movements of matter and light. Not only are we mortal, but the very human form suffers a slow change over generations. Between my arm and the air, between the movements of a flame and what we call the solid mass of wood, there is no boundary.

But we have come to rely upon another image of ourselves: as discrete static beings. And we have learned to think that we must take control of our environment in order to survive. We believe that it is a cultural order, the order we have willed, and not natural order, the order of which we are a part, that makes us safe. Thus, if the discoveries of modern science have given us the means to manipulate Nature, they have also terrified us. And this is why, in the fourteenth century, when science began to challenge our old idea of who we are, the witch burnings began. The slave trade began in the sixteenth century at the height of this revolution in thought. And in the twentieth century, when science again questioned the old notion that we are above Nature, the Nazi Holocaust and now the nuclear holocaust have commenced.

But in separating Nature from culture within himself, the man who believes this delusion has split his own needs and desires from his intelligence and from all meaning. Thus his own desires return to him as meaningless, as cruel and senseless violations. Out of the lost fragments of his own psyche, he has created a monstrous image to contain his own self-loathing. Thus the pornographer creates out of his own sexual desires a meeting between two bodies that is without emotion, without any deep or soulful connection. And when he invents a woman, a pornographic heroine, he gives her a body without a spirit, without any sensibility, without a significant consciousness. She is like the dead matter, the brute matter, of scientific theory.

And the modern mind invents the same image of Nature itself. Matter is dead. A forest has no spiritual life. When Reagan was governor of California, he said in response to ecologists who were trying to preserve the great coastal forests, "If you have seen one tree you have seen them all." Believing a mountain to have no inner reason, no sacredness unto itself, the modern technologist takes coal out of the soil simply by cutting away half of the face of the mountain. Suddenly the whole of the mountain begins to erode. Chemicals from this erosion enter the streams in an unnatural balance. Trees, plants, fish, animals die. The countryside, once breathtakingly beautiful, begins to look like a place of devastation. He transforms the mountain into what he believed the mountain to be.

In the same way, society transforms those who have become symbols of Nature into objects of degradation. If a woman is a symbol of Nature wherever she is pictured as submissive or wherever she is disempowered in the social order, we can believe that culture has a supernatural power over Nature. If the Jew, who we imagine plots against us, is stripped of all civil rights, we can believe that we have control over natural power. Even those of us who suffer materially and psychologically from this delusory system of control have been educated to feel a false sense of safety from it.

Yet indeed none of us are safe. Now our lives are, every one of us, endangered by this delusion. For the delusion itself cannot rest. It is like the hungry tiger of our fearful dreams: devouring.

When the technologist destroys the mountain, he must feel, momentarily, a false sense of triumph. Like the explorers of an earlier age, he has conquered this piece of earth. He has wrested from her what he wanted. He has beaten her. And yet now, as he looks on the devastation he has caused, he cannot help but see there an image of his own inner life. His soul has been robbed by this theft. The death he sees before him must at one and the same time remind him of the part of himself he has murdered and his own inevitable mortality which, in the very act of controlling Nature, he has tried to deny.

The very images and avenues that express our power over Nature take us back to our own memory and knowledge of Nature's power both inside and outside of ourselves. Therefore our delusion demands that we gain a greater control over Nature. We must escalate our efforts. We must improve our technology.

One can see the dimensions of this madness more clearly in the development of the nuclear power industry. At each turning point, when a piece of human technology was seen to fail, the architects of this industry never questioned the fundamental premise that we are meant to make use of the energy inside the atom by splitting matter apart. Instead, another technological solution was offered. And each technological solution has in turn posed a greater danger.

Repeatedly one reads in the newspapers that an error in the design of a nuclear power plant has been covered over by the men who build and operate the plants. In many cases the economic motivation for such a denial is clear. To design the plant properly would take many more millions of dollars. But even given this economic motive, one wonders why these men, who often live in the area of the plant and work there every day, are not afraid for their own lives or the lives of their families. But the answer is that they rely for a feeling of safety not on rational information about natural law, but on the delusion that culture, through technology or any other means, can control Nature.

The mind that invents a delusion of power over Nature in order to feel safe is afraid of fear itself. And the more this mind learns to rely on delusion, the less tolerance this mind has for any betrayal of that delusion. For we must remember that this mind has denied that it itself is a thing of Nature. It has begun to identify not only its own survival, but its own existence with culture. The mind believes that it exists because what it thinks is true. Therefore, to contradict delusion is to threaten the mind's very existence. And the ideas, words, numbers, concepts have become more real to this mind than material reality.

Thus when this mind is threatened by a material danger, it does not respond rationally. For this mind has lost touch with material reality. It is a mind possessed by madness, by a hallucinated idea of its own power. We can see such a mind at work in Stalin, during the period of Soviet industrialization. In this period, the Soviet Union as a nation faced the grave material danger of hunger and starvation. And yet, as a solution, Stalin chose to destroy real and operating farms before the new, sanctioned way of farming was functioning. Issac Deutscher writes vividly of this cast of mind, "The whole experiment seemed to be a piece of prodigious insanity, in which all the rules of logic and principles of economics were turned upside down. It was as if a whole nation had suddenly abandoned and destroyed its houses and huts which, though obsolete and decaying, existed in reality, and moved lock, stock, and barrel, into some illusory buildings."

But what is essential to understand about this mind is that it is in a panic. It will go to any lengths to defend its delusory idea of reality. Those who opposed Stalin's plans for collectivization were sent to prison camps or murdered.

And the extent to which a belief in ideas over reality is a part of this century was predicted by George Orwell in his novel, *1984,* through the humorous but now distressingly accurate parody of a governmental slogan he invented, "Peace is War." Thus today it is actually presented as a rational argument that a buildup in arms, or a "preventative" invasion of another country, is the best way to keep peace.

We all understand economic motivation as fundamental to human nature. And yet we are making a mistake if we believe that this is the only motivation. For economics touch upon reality. It would, after all, be of no economic profit to anyone living to destroy the earth. Such a destruction could only be seen as profitable by a madman. But it is madness and the motivations of madness that I am describing here.

It is only when we understand how economic motivation can be shaped and changed by this madness that we can begin to see the real danger that our culture's state of delusion poses for us. Let us take the slave trade for an example. There is an obvious economic profit to be gained by adventurers from the sale of other human beings. And yet we must question whether simply self-interest leads naturally to such a violation of other beings. Is it not a soul already distorted that can consider enslaving another human being?

Self-interest, the desire to survive, is simply part of flesh, an emotion that arises in us by virtue of our material existence, by virtue even of our love for life and for this earth. But early in childhood we are taught that our survival depends on a freedom from natural power. We are taught that we live not through the understanding of Nature but through the manipulation of Nature.

If one studies the definitions of liberty in the *Oxford English Dictionary* one sees that liberty, first defined as an "exemption or release from captivity, bondage or slavery," later becomes "the faculty or power to do as one likes," and then becomes "an unrestrained use of or access to" – as in "to take liberties with a wench" – and finally, liberty means "at one's power or disposal."

Like the Inquisition and the witch burnings, the slave trade began at the time of the scientific revolution, in the sixteenth century. This revolution threatened to change the old worldview that men ordered Nature and replaced it with an understanding of a natural law to which we are all subject. The delusion that we are free from natural law was endangered. But that freedom could be regained symbolically by enslaving a people whom this culture conceived of as symbols of Nature. At this time and through the nineteenth century it was both a scientific and a general belief that Africans were closer to Nature than white men and women. In the nineteenth century, after evolutionary theory, scientists argued that Africans had descended more directly from primates.

That the slave trade was not motivated by simple economic self-interest becomes more clear when one studies the conditions that had to be endured by the men, women, and children taken into captivity on the slave ships. So many died during these trips across the water, not only from disease and exposure to the elements, but also from the brutality of the slave traders. Had these men valued their cargo from a simple economic motive they might have taken more care to preserve these lives. But, instead, an unwonted measure of cruelty entered their acts.

Ruth and Jacob Weldon, an African couple who experienced a slave passage, recorded an incident of a child of nine months who was flogged continuously for refusing to eat. Because this beating failed to move the child to eat, the captain ordered that "the child be placed feet first into a pot of boiling water. After trying other torturous methods with no success, the captain dropped the child and caused its death. Not deriving enough satisfaction from this sadistic act, he then commanded the mother to throw the body of the child overboard. The mother refused but she was beaten until she submitted."

That Bell Hooks called this behavior sadistic is entirely fitting. Clearly, to murder a child in order to get that child to eat is not rational behavior. Rather, the motive lay elsewhere, with the desire to inflict cruelty for its own sake. But why is it that a slave trader should be cruel to a black child? Because of his blackness this child became, in the insane mind of this civilization, and in the mind of this captain, a symbol of natural power. And the infancy of the boy would remind this man of his own infancy, of his own memory of vulnerability, of his own naturalness. Thus, at one and the same time, he could show his power over Nature, and punish his own vulnerable child, the child within him who was still part of Nature. Underneath his hatred and his cruelty existed a profound self-hatred.

Each time that the child refused to do as he ordered, he was, in an undiscovered region of his own soul, terrified. For this could only mean that he was losing his power, and therefore that his whole existence was being threatened. In this way, the captain could believe that he murdered a nine-month-old child in defense of himself. And if a part of him suffered with that child, he could punish his own compassion, and compassion itself, by forcing the child's mother to throw the child overboard. For such a compassion is also dangerous to this mind, since compassion brings us back to our own capacity to feel.

The same blend of economic and symbolic motivation inspired the Holocaust. At the time of Hitler's rise to power, Germany suffered from a terrible economic depression. And at the same time the old paradigmatic view of man at the center of the universe was again being threatened by scientific discovery. The Nazi Party identified the Jew as responsible for the economic privation. But what is the emotional experience of economic poverty? It is not simply the absence of money that is felt, but the absence of food, or shelter, or safety. Poverty, or even economic insecurity, places us at the mercy of Nature. We become afraid of loss, of suffering, of death. In its delusion of power over Nature, the European mind had made the Jew the symbol of Nature. Frightened by economic insecurity and by a changing worldview, the Nazi stripped the Jew of civil rights and of the right to own possessions, and the Holocaust began.

We can recognize in Hitler's madness a self-portrait of this civilization that has shaped our minds. Today modem science makes the same attempt to control procreation through genetic engineering. And in an article by Rosalie Bertell (in *Reclaim the Earth)*, one reads that radiation causes genetic mutation and sterility. Thus civilization continues to rage at procreation. And today we also share with the Nazi mind a plan for a final solution to the problem of Nature. This solution is to destroy Nature and replace Nature with a record of her destruction. One sees this pattern again and again in history. Despite the fact that the Third Reich attempted to hide the existence of concentration camps from international scrutiny, the atrocities committed in them were carefully documented by the SS *(Schutzstaffel,* a quasi military unit of the Nazi party). Hitler used to watch films in his private rooms of men and women being murdered and tortured.

Today US military strategists have developed a new plan for winning a nuclear war. They argue that the winner of a nuclear war will be the side that has kept the best record of destruction, the side that knows the most about what has taken place. Hence intelligence-gathering devices are being prepared for launching into space, where these machines will not be destroyed. These men have actually confused their own physical survival with the survival of information.

It is in the nature of the deluded mind to choose to preserve its delusion over its own life. When the German armies were faltering on the Russian Front, Hitler diverted troop and supply trains from that crucial battle in order to carry women, men and children to Auschwitz to their deaths. He imagined his war against the Jew to be more important. And this was the real war in which his mind was engaged – a war, in fact, with himself. For Hitler's personal hatred for the Jew was a covert hatred of a part of himself.

This is also true of our civilization as a whole. We do not know ourselves. We try to deny what we know. We try to break the heart and the spirit of Nature, which is our own heart and our own spirit. We are possessed by an illness created by our minds, an illness that resembles sado-masochism, schizophrenia, paranoia – all the forms of the troubled soul. We are divided from our selves. We punish ourselves. We are terrified of what we know and who we are. And finally, we belong to a civilization bent upon suicide, secretly committed to destroying Nature and destroying the self that is Nature.

But we each have another secret too, a secret knowledge of wholeness. The schemata of memory exclude our memory of childhood. We do not think we still know what it was to be a child, untaught by culture to be divided from ourselves. Yet within each of us, in our bodies, that memory still exists. Our own breath reminds us of that knowledge, of a time when we were curious, when we let Nature speak to us and in us.

There exists a culture that is not alienated from Nature but expresses Nature. The mind is a physical place. The mind is made up of tissue and blood, of cells and atoms, and possesses all the knowledge of the cell, all the balance of the atom. Human language is shaped to the human mouth, made by and for the tongue, made up of sounds that can be heard by the ear. And there is to the earth and the structure of matter a kind of resonance. We were meant to hear one another, to feel. Our sexual feelings, our capacity for joy and pleasure, our love of beauty, move us toward a love that binds us to an existence. If there is a sound wave anywhere on this earth, if there is the sound of weeping or of laughter, this reaches my ears, reaches your ears. We are connected not only by the fact of our dependency on this biosphere and our participation in one field of matter and energy, in which no boundary exists between my skin and the air and you, but also by what we know and what we feel. Our own knowledge, if we can once again possess it, is as vast as existence.

I am a woman born in and shaped by this civilization, with the mind of this civilization, but also with the mind and body of a woman, with human experience. Suffering grief in my own life, I have felt all the impulses that are part of my culture in my own soul. In my resistance to pain and change, I have felt the will toward self-annihilation. And still the singing in my body daily returns me to a love of this earth. I know that by a slow practice, if I am to survive, I must learn to listen to this song.

Notes

1. "I cannot sufficiently admire the eminence of those men's wits, that have received and held it to be true, and with the sprightliness of their judgments offered such violence to their own senses, so that they have been able to prefer that which their reason dictated to them, to that which sensible experiments represented most manifestly to the contrary. . . . I cannot find any bounds for my admiration, how that reason in Aristarchus and Copernicus, to commit such a rape on their senses, as in despite thereof to make herself mistress of credulity." (From Galileo's *Dialogues Concerning the Two Great Systems of the World,* Vol. 1, as cited in E. A. Burtt, The *Metaphysical Foundations of Modern Science,* New York, 1954.)

11

Feminism and Ecology: Making Connections

Karen J. Warren

The current feminist debate over ecology raises important and timely issues about the theoretical adequacy of the four leading versions of feminism – liberal feminism. traditional Marxist feminism, radical feminism, and socialist feminism. In this paper I present a minimal condition account of ecological feminism, or *eco-feminism*. I argue that if eco-feminism is true or at least plausible, then each of the four leading versions of feminism is inadequate, incomplete, or problematic as a theoretical grounding for eco-feminism. I conclude that, if eco-feminism is to be taken seriously, then a transformative feminism is needed that will move us beyond the four familiar feminist frameworks and make an eco-feminist perspective central to feminist theory and practice.

Introduction

In *New Woman/New Earth,* Rosemary Ruether writes:

Women must see that there can be no liberation for them and no solution to the ecological crisis within a society whose fundamental model of relationships continues to be one of domination. They must unite the demands of the women's movement with those of the ecological movement to envision a radical reshaping of the basic socioeconomic relations and the underlying values of this society.[1]

According to Ruether, the women's movement and the ecology movement are intimately connected. The demands of both require "transforming that worldview which underlies domination and replacing it with an alternative value system."[2] Recent writings by feminists Elizabeth Dodson Gray, Susan Griffin, Mary Daly, Carolyn Merchant, Joan Griscom, Ynestra King, and Ariel Kay Salleh, underscore Ruether's basic point: ecology is a feminist issue.[3]

Why is this so? Feminists who debate the ecology issue agree that there are important connections between the oppression of women and the oppression of nature,[4] but they disagree about both the nature of those connections and whether those connections are "potentially liberating or simply a rationale for the continued subordination of women."[5] Stated slightly differently, while many feminists agree that ecology is a feminist issue, they disagree about the nature and desirability of "ecological feminism," or *eco-feminism*.

This disagreement is to be expected. Just as there is not one version of feminism, there is not one version of eco-feminism. The varieties of eco-feminism reflect not only differences in the analysis of the woman/nature connection, but also differences on such fundamental issues as the nature of and solutions to women's oppression, the theory of human nature, and the conceptions of freedom, equality, and epistemology on which the various feminist theories depend.

In order to accommodate the varieties of eco-feminist perspectives, it is important to provide a minimal condition account of eco-feminism which captures the basic claims to which all eco-feminists are committed. As I use the term, *eco-feminism* is a position based on the following claims: (i) there are important connections between the oppression of women and the oppression of nature; (ii) understanding the nature of these connections is necessary to any adequate understanding of the oppression of women and the oppression of nature; (iii) feminist theory and practice must include an ecological perspective; and (iv) solutions to ecological problems must include a feminist perspective.[6]

Suppose that eco-feminism is true or at least plausible. To what extent do the four leading versions of feminism – liberal feminism, traditional Marxist feminism, radical feminism, and socialist feminism – capture or make a place for eco-feminism? To answer this question is to determine the extent to which the leading versions of feminism constitute an adequate theoretical grounding for eco-feminism .

My primary aim in this paper is to assess the adequacy of the four leading versions of feminism from the perspective of eco-feminism. I argue that while each may provide important insights into the oppression of women and nature, nonetheless, in its present form and taken by itself, each is inadequate, incomplete, or at least sufficiently problematic as a theoretical grounding for eco-feminism. I conclude by suggesting that if eco-feminism is to be taken seriously, then what is needed is a new "transformative" feminism, one which moves us beyond the current debate over the four leading versions of feminism and makes an eco-feminist perspective central to feminist theory and practice.

Two qualifications on the scope of the paper are in order. First, eco-feminism is a relatively new movement. In some cases, the leading versions of feminism have not, in fact, articulated a position on ecology or on the nature of the connection between the oppression of women and the oppression of nature. As such, in some cases, the ecological implications attributed in this paper to a given feminist theory are only hypothetical:

they are suppositions about what such feminist accounts *might* be like, given what is known of the more general tenets of those feminist positions, rather than accounts of viewpoints actually stated.

Second, I provide neither a defense of eco-feminism nor a defense of a "transformative feminism." Rather, on the assumption that eco-feminism is true or plausible, I attempt to clarify the extent to which the four leading versions of feminism are problematic as a theoretical basis for eco-feminism. The concluding discussion of a transformative feminism is intended mainly to be suggestive of possible directions to pursue which will both expand upon the insights of current feminisms and include eco-feminism as an integral aspect of feminist theory and practice.

Eco-feminism and Patriarchal Conceptual Frameworks

Eco-feminists take as their central project the unpacking of the connections between the twin oppressions of women and nature. Central to this project is a critique of the sort of thinking which sanctions that oppression. One way to understand this critique is to talk about conceptual frameworks.

Underlying eco-feminism is the view that, whether we know it or not, each of us operates out of a socially constructed mind set or *conceptual framework*, i.e., a set of beliefs, values, attitudes, and assumptions which shape, reflect, and explain our view of ourselves and our world. A conceptual framework is influenced by such factors as sex-gender, race, class, age, sexual preference, religion, and nationality. A *patriarchal conceptual framework* is one which takes traditionally male-identified beliefs, values, attitudes, and assumptions as the only, or the standard, or the superior ones; it gives higher status or prestige to what has been traditionally identified as "male" than to what has been traditionally identified as "female."

A patriarchal conceptual framework is characterized by *value-hierarchical thinking*. In the words of eco-feminist Elizabeth Dodson Gray, such thinking "is a perception of diversity which is so organized by a spatial metaphor (Up-and-Down) that greater value is always attributed to that which is higher."[7] It puts men "up" and women "down," culture "up" and nature "down," minds "up" and bodies "down."

Such patriarchal value-hierarchical thinking gives rise to *a logic of domination*, i.e., a value-hierarchical way of thinking which explains, justifies, and maintains the subordination of an "inferior" group by a "superior" group on the grounds of the (alleged) inferiority or superiority of the respective group. By attributing greater value to that which is higher, the up-down organization of perceptions, mediated by a logic of domination, serves to legitimate inequality "when, in fact, prior to the metaphor of Up-Down one would have said only that there existed diversity."[8]

Eco-feminists assume that patriarchal value-hierarchical thinking supports the sort of "either-or" thinking which generates *normative dualisms,* i.e., thinking in which the disjunctive terms (or sides of the dualism) are seen as exclusive (rather than inclusive) and oppositional (rather than complementary), and where higher value or superiority is attributed to one disjunct (or, side of the dualism) than the other. It, thereby, conceptually separates as opposites aspects of reality that in fact are inseparable or complementary; e.g., it opposes human to nonhuman, mind to body, self to other, reason to emotion.[9]

According to eco-feminism, then, the connections between the oppression of women and the oppression of nature ultimately are *conceptual:* they are embedded in a patriarchal conceptual framework and reflect a logic of domination which functions to explain, justify, and maintain the subordination of both women and nature. Eco-feminism, therefore, encourages us to think ourselves out of "patriarchal conceptual traps,"[10] by *reconceptualizing* ourselves and our relation to the nonhuman natural world in nonpatriarchal ways.

What makes a critique of patriarchal conceptual frameworks distinctively "eco-feminist" has to do with the interconnections among the four minimal condition claims of eco-feminism. First, and most obviously, the critique is used to show that there are important connections between the oppression of women and the oppression of nature (condition [i]). Second, by understanding how a patriarchal conceptual framework sanctions the oppression of both women and nature (condition [ii]), eco-feminists are in a position to show why "naturism" (i.e., the domination of nature) ought to be included among the systems of oppression maintained by patriarchy. This opens the door for showing how, in Sheila Collins' words,

> Racism, sexism, class exploitation, and ecological destruction are four
> interlocking pillars upon which the structure of patriarchy rests.[11]

Third, the critique of patriarchal conceptual frameworks is grounded in familiar ecological principles: everything is interconnected with everything else; all parts of an ecosystem have equal value; there is no free lunch; "nature knows best"; healthy, balanced ecosystems must maintain diversity; there is unity in diversity.[12] This grounding is the basis for the uniquely eco-feminist position that an adequate feminist theory and practice embrace an ecological perspective (condition [iii]). Fourth, the critique goes two ways: not only must a proper feminist theory and practice reflect an ecological perspective (condition [iii]); the ecological movement must embrace a feminist perspective (condition [iv]). Otherwise, the ecological movement will fail to make the conceptual connections between the oppression of women and the oppression of nature (and to link these to other systems of oppression), and will risk utilizing strategies and implementing solutions which contribute to the continued subordination of women.

The stakes are high. If eco-feminism is correct, then a feminist debate over ecology is much deeper and more basic to both the feminist and ecology movements than traditional construals of feminism or ecology might have us believe. What is at stake is not only the success of the feminist and ecology movements, but the theoretical adequacy of feminism itself.

An Eco-Feminist Critique of the Four Leading Versions of Feminism

Feminism traditionally has been construed as the movement to end the oppression of women. All feminists agree that the oppression of women (i.e., the unequal and unjust status of women) exists, is wrong, and ought to be changed. But feminists disagree markedly about how to understand that oppression and how to bring about the necessary changes.

In her book *Feminist Politics and Human Nature,* Alison Jaggar offers an extensive analysis of the four leading versions of feminism and the key respects in which these theories differ. In what follows, I use Jaggar's analysis as the basis for my account of the eco-feminist critique of the leading versions of feminism.

Liberal Feminism

Liberal feminism emanates from the classical liberal tradition that idealizes a society in which autonomous individuals are provided maximal freedom to pursue their own interests. Liberal feminists trace the oppression of women to the lack of equal legal rights and unfair disadvantages in the public domain. Hence, the liberation of women requires the elimination of those legal and social constraints that prevent women from exercising their right of self-determination.

Liberal feminism endorses a highly individualistic conception of human nature. Humans are essentially separate, rational agents engaged in competition to maximize their own interests. The "mental" capacity to reason, i.e., the capacity to act in accordance with objective principles and to be consistent in the pursuit of ends, is what grounds the basic, essential, and equal dignity of all individuals. Basic human properties (e.g., rationality, autonomy, dignity) are ascribed to individuals independent of any historical or social context, and moral consideration is due humans on the basis of these distinctive human properties.

Because humans are conceived as essentially separate rational agents, a liberal feminist epistemology construes the attainment of knowledge as an individual project. The liberal feminist epistemological goal is to formulate value-neutral, intersubjectively verifiable, and universalizable rules that enable any rational agent to attain knowledge "under a veil of ignorance." Both genuine knowledge and "the moral point of view" express the impartial point of view of the rational, detached observer.

There are two sorts of ecological implications of liberal feminism. Both are generated within a liberal framework that applies traditional moral and legal categories to nonhumans. They are liberal feminist insofar as the ecological perspective is based on the same sorts of considerations that liberal feminists have appealed to traditionally in arguments for equal rights, equal opportunities or fair consideration for women.

The first ecological implication draws the line of moral considerability at humans, separating humans from nonhumans and basing any claims to moral consideration for nonhumans either on the alleged rights or interests of humans, or on the consequences of such consideration for human well-being. Liberal feminists who do (or might) take this stance justify such practices as legal protection of endangered species, restrictions on the use of animals in laboratory research, or support for the appropriate technology, anti-nuclear, and peace movements on the grounds that they are mandated by consideration of the rights, interests, or well-being of present or future generations of humans (including women, mothers, and children).

The second extends the line of moral considerability to qualified nonhumans on the grounds that they, like women (or humans), are deserving of moral consideration in their own right: they are rational, sentient, interest carriers, or right holders.[13] According to this second sort of ecological stance, responsible environmental practices toward nonhumans are justified on the grounds that individual nonhumans share certain morally relevant characteristics with humans in virtue of which they are deserving of protection or moral consideration.

From an eco-feminist perspective, both sorts of ecological implications are inadequate or at least seriously problematic. First, both basically keep intact a patriarchal conceptual framework characterized by value-hierarchical thinking and oppositional normative dualisms: humans over and against nature, the "mind" (or "rational") over and against the "body" (or the "nonrational"). As such, although liberal feminist ecological concerns may expand the traditional ethical framework to include moral and legal consideration of qualified nonhumans, or even to include the instrumental value of ecosystemic well-being for human welfare, they will be unacceptable to eco-feminists.

Second, the extreme individualism of a liberal feminist ecological perspective conflicts with the eco-feminist emphasis on the independent value of the integrity, diversity, and stability of ecosystems, and on the ecological themes of interconnectedness, unity in diversity, and equal value to all parts of the human-nature system. It also conflicts with "ecological ethics" per se. Ecological ethics are holistic, not individualistic; they take the value and well-being of a species, community, or ecosystem, and not merely of particular individuals, let alone human individuals, as basic. For eco-feminists, an ecological ethics based on a "web-like" view of relationships among all life forms conflicts with the hierarchical rules- and individual rights-based ethics of the liberal ethical tradition.

The eco-feminist critique of hierarchical rights- and rules-based ethical models reflects current feminist scholarship on ethics and moral reasoning. For example, in her recent book *In A Different Voice*, psychologist Carol Gilligan compares highly individualized and hierarchical rules- and rights-oriented ethics (embedded in the liberal tradition) with web-like and contextual ethics of care and reciprocal responsibility.[14] She argues that the two ethical orientations reflect important differences in moral reasoning between men and women, and on such basic issues as the conception of the self, morality, and conflict resolution. In her article "Moral Revolution," philosopher Kathryn Pyne Addelson argues that there is a bias in "our world view" by the near exclusion of women from the domain of intellectual pursuits, "a bias that requires a revolutionary change in ethics to remedy."[15] According to Addelson:

> It is a bias that allows moral problems to be defined from the top of various hierarchies of authority in such a way that the existence of the authority is concealed, and so the existence of alternative definitions that might challenge that authority and radically change our social organization is also concealed.[16]

Addelson's criticism of traditional ethics is at the same time a criticism of liberal feminism: the liberal feminist ethical tradition (what Addelson calls "the Judith Thomson tradition") assumes that defining moral problems from the top of the hierarchy is the "official" or "correct" or "legitimate" point of view;[17] it does not notice that "dominant-subordinate social structures are *creators* of inequality."[18] By contrast, what Addelson calls "the Jane tradition" uses the perceptions and power of a subordinate group – women – "to eliminate dominant-subordinate structures through the creation of new social forms which do not have that structure."[19] The women of the Jane tradition, unlike those of the Thomson tradition, challenge the patriarchal conceptual framework which defines "our" world view, how things "really are," and how things "ought to be," and which assumes the superiority of the hierarchical rules- and rights-approach to ethics.

Whatever else the strengths and weaknesses of the Gilligan and Addelson accounts of alternative ethical frameworks, their contributions to a discussion of eco-feminism are noteworthy. Each provides important reasons for being suspicious of approaches to feminism, ethics, or ecological concerns based on a patriarchal conceptual framework. To the extent that the ecological implications of liberal feminism do so, they perpetuate the sort of thinking and bias which, according to Gilligan and Addelson, fails to pay adequate attention to other values (e.g., care, friendship, reciprocity in relationships) and to the epistemological and moral point of view of a subordinate group in our society: women. The Gilligan and Addelson accounts thereby provide the sorts of reasons eco-feminists offer for rejecting a liberal feminist ecology.

Traditional Marxist Feminism

Traditional Marxist feminism views the oppression of women, like the oppression of workers, as a direct result of the institution of class society and, under capitalism, of private property. The specific oppression of women is due to the sexual division of labor whereby women are excluded from the public realm of production and occupy dependent economic positions in the traditional monogamous family. Thus, the liberation of women requires that the traditional family be dissolved as an economic (though not necessarily as a social) unit. As Engels states in a much quoted sentence, "The first condition of the liberation of the wife is to bring the whole female sex into public industry."[20] Since women's oppression is a class oppression, women's liberation will be a class movement accomplished together with male workers by overthrowing capitalism.

For traditional Marxist feminists (like traditional Marxists generally), the essential human activity is not pure thought or reason (as liberals assume) but conscious and productive activity – *praxis*. Praxis is conscious physical labor directed at transforming the material world to meet human needs. Humans are distinguished from nonhumans by their ability to consciously and purposefully transform their environment to meet their material needs through the activity of praxis.[21]

Since human nature is developed historically and socially through praxis, human nature is not a fixed or immutable condition. Furthermore, since human nature is understood in terms of praxis, humans are only truly free when they engage in productive activity which extends beyond the satisfaction of basic survival needs. For traditional Marxist feminists, women will be free when they are economically independent and when their work expresses the full development of human productive activity (or praxis), rather than the coercion of economic necessity.

A Marxist feminist epistemology is a radical departure from that of liberal feminism. Since humans are viewed as necessarily existing in dialectical relationship with each other, knowledge is viewed as a social construction; it is part of the basic shared human activity of praxis. The development of knowledge is not an individual undertaking, and there is no value-neutral knowledge accessible to some impartial, detached observer.

For traditional Marxist feminists, "all forms of knowledge are historically determined by the prevailing mode of production."[22]

In *Marx and Engels on Ecology,* Howard L. Parsons discusses four general sorts of ecological criticisms which have been raised against traditional Marxism:

> Marx, Engels, and Marxism, generally have been criticized for certain alleged positions on ecological matters: (1) they have pitted man against nature; (2) they have anthropocentrically denied the values of external nature; (3) they have overstressed the conflicts in nature and have understressed its harmony; and (4) they have denied basic human values.[23]

These criticisms rest on such Marxist claims as "nature is man's inorganic body," man is "the real conscious master of Nature," and "the purely natural material in which *no* human labor is objectified . . . has no value."[24] The alleged criticisms are that since such claims emphasize the use value of the natural world in the production of economic goods (e.g., food, clothing, shelter), the transformation of nature to meet human material needs in the essential human activity of praxis, and the domination, mastery, or control of nature "by man," Marxism is not a suitable basis for an ecological ethic.[25]

Whether traditional Marxism can overcome these objections is being rigorously debated; it is beyond the scope of this paper to discuss that issue here. Nonetheless, it is important to indicate what the particular challenges are for traditional Marxist feminism from an eco-feminist perspective.

First, given the primacy of class in the traditional Marxist feminist account of oppression and liberation, a Marxist feminist must reconcile traditional Marxist claims about nature with a political vision that does not pit men and women, as one class, over and against nature. Otherwise, the sort of patriarchal conceptual framework which traditionally has sanctioned the exploitation of nature will survive relatively unscathed, even if women get elevated to equal status with men (but against nature).

Second, traditional Marxists argue that environmental problems under capitalism will continue as long as the means of production (i.e., the raw materials, land, energy resources) and forces of production (i.e., the factories, machinery, skills) are used to support environmental research and development in the interest of expanding capital. Marxist feminists must show that a liberating or appropriate technology and science, based on ecological principles, could help protect and preserve, rather than exploit, nature.

Perhaps the most significant challenge to a plausible Marxist eco-feminism, however, lies in a third area of difficulty, viz., its general failure to take seriously gender as a constitutive category of social reality.

This "gender blindness" in traditional Marxist analyses of women's oppression serves to distort, rather than clarify, the nature of women's oppression. Since eco-feminism assumes that the connections between the oppression of women and the oppression of nature have to do with sex-gender systems, a "gender blind" traditional Marxist feminism will be hard pressed to make visible those connections.

Radical Feminism

Radical feminism departs from both liberal feminism and traditional Marxist feminism by rooting women's oppression in reproductive biology and a sex gender system. According to radical feminists, patriarchy (i.e., the systematic domination by men) oppresses women in sex-specific ways by defining women as beings whose primary functions are either to bear and raise children (i.e., to be mothers) or to satisfy male sexual desires (i.e., to be sex objects). Since the oppression of women is based on "male control of women's fertility and women's sexuality," the liberation of women is to "end male control of women's bodies" by dismantling patriarchy.[26] Women will be free when no longer bound by the constraints of compulsory heterosexuality and compulsory child-bearing and child-rearing roles.

Insofar as there is one radical feminist conception of human nature,[27] it is that humans are essentially embodied. We are not (as the Cartesian philosophical tradition might have us suppose) bodiless minds, i.e., "mental" or thinking beings whose essential nature exists independently from our own or others' physical, emotional, or sexual existence. By taking women's bodies, and, in particular, women's reproductive biology, as indispensable to women's nature, radical feminism brings child-bearing and child-rearing functions into the political arena. It makes women's sex politically significant. It is in this way that for the radical feminist, "the personal is (profoundly) political."

A radical feminist epistemology self-consciously explores strategies (e.g., consciousness-raising processes) to correct the distortions of patriarchal ideology. It emphasizes a variety of sources of reliable knowledge (e.g., intuition, feelings, spiritual or mystical experiences) and the integration of women's felt mystical/intuitive/spiritual experiences into feminist theory and epistemology. Challenging the traditional "political versus spiritual" dichotomy, many radical feminists support a "politics of women's spirituality" which makes a spiritual ingredient necessary to any adequate feminist political theory.[28]

Radical feminists have had the most to say about eco-feminism. Taking up the question "Are women closer to nature than men?" some radical feminists (e.g., so-called "nature feminists," Mary Daly, Susan Griffin, Starhawk) have answered "yes." They applaud the close connections between women and nature, and urge women to celebrate our bodies, rejoice in our place in the community of inanimate and animate beings, and seek symbols that can transform our spiritual consciousness so as to be more in tune with nature. Other radical feminists answer "no"; they criticize nature feminists for regressing to harmful patriarchal sex-role stereotyping which feeds the prejudice that women have specifically female or womanly interests in preventing pollution, nurturing animals, or saving the planet.[29]

Even though to date eco-feminism has tended to be associated with radical feminism, there are noteworthy worries about radical feminism from an eco-feminist perspective. First, since radical feminism generally pays little attention to the historical and material features of women's oppression (including the relevance of race, class, ethnic, and national background), it insufficiently articulates the extent to which women's oppression is grounded in concrete and diverse social structures. In this respect, it lacks the sort of theoretical leverage needed to reveal the interconnections between the oppression of nature and women, on the one hand, and other forms of oppression (e.g., racism, classism).

Second, it mystifies women's experiences to locate women closer to nature than men, just as it underplays important aspects of the oppression of women to deny the connection of women with nature, for the truth is that women, like men, are both connected to nature and separate from it, natural and cultural beings. Insofar as radical feminism comes down in favor of one side or the other of the nature-culture dualism – by locating women either on the nature or on the culture side – it mistakenly perpetuates the sort of oppositional, dualistic thinking for which patriarchal conceptual frameworks are criticized.

This last point raises a conceptual and methodological worry about radical feminism as a grounding of eco-feminist concerns; the worry has to do with framing the feminist debate over ecology in terms of the question, "Are women closer to nature than men?"[30] In order for the question to be meaningfully raised, one must presuppose the legitimacy of the nature-culture dualism. The idea that one group of persons is, or is not, closer to nature than another group assumes the very nature-culture split that eco-feminism denies. As Joan Griscom puts it, "the question itself is flawed."[31] She argues:

> Since we are all part of nature, and since all of us, biology and culture
> alike, is part of nature, the question ultimately makes no sense.[32]

It is "unwitting complicity"[33] in the patriarchal mind set that accounts for the question being raised at all. Insofar as radical feminism engages in such complicity, its approach to the feminist debate over ecology is methodologically suspect and conceptually flawed.

Socialist Feminism

Socialist feminism attempts to integrate the insights of traditional Marxist feminism with those of radical feminism by making domination by class and by sex gender fundamental to women's oppression. The socialist feminist program applies the historical materialist method of traditional Marxism to issues of sex and gender made visible by radical feminists.[34] By widening the Marxist notions of praxis and production to include procreation and child rearing, socialist feminists argue that the economic system and sex-gender system are dialectically reinforced in historically specific ways.[35] Thus, for socialist feminists, the liberation of women requires the end of both capitalism and patriarchy.

The socialist feminist view of human nature is that humans are created historically and culturally through the dialectical interrelation of human biology, physical environment, and society.[36] Since contemporary society consists of groups of individuals defined by age, sex, class, race, nationality, and ethnic background, each of these is included in the conception of human nature. Differences between men and women are viewed as social constructions, not pre-social or biological givens. For the socialist feminist, even if human biology is in some sense determined, it is nonetheless also socially conditioned. As Jaggar puts it, "Biology is 'gendered' as well as sexed."[37] In this respect, according to Jaggar,

> The goal of socialist feminism is to abolish the social relations that constitute humans not only as workers and capitalists but also as women and men. . . . the ideal of socialist feminism is that women (and men) will disappear as socially constructed categories.[38]

Like traditional Marxist feminists, socialist feminists view knowledge as a social construction; like radical feminists, they claim that women, as a subordinate group, have a "special epistemological standpoint that makes possible a view of the world that is unavailable to capitalist or to working class men."[39] This "standpoint of women," as Jaggar calls it, is historical materialist as well as sex-gendered; it is constructed from and accounts for the felt experiences of women of different ages, classes, races, and ethnic and national backgrounds.[40]

Since socialist feminism is an attempt to wed the insights of traditional Marxist feminism and radical feminism, it might seem that it would provide the most promising theoretical framework for eco-feminist concerns. In fact, however, many socialist feminists have been quite guarded in their enthusiasm for ecological matters.[41] This is understandable. The Marxist side of their politics makes them suspicious of a radical feminist grounding of ecological concerns in women's spiritual or sex-gender-based connection with nature.

Some socialist feminists have attempted to make a place for eco-feminist concerns by interpreting the Marxist attitude of domination over nature as "the psychological result of a certain mode of organizing production."[42] They argue that what is needed are new modes of conceptualizing and organizing production which allow for both reproductive freedom for women and recognition of the independent value of nonhuman nature. From an eco-feminist perspective, such a reconceptualization of traditional Marxist views is necessary if women are not to be brought into public production with men over and against nature.

The attractiveness of socialist feminism from an eco-feminist perspective lies in its emphasis on the importance of factors in addition to sex gender and class for an understanding of the social construction of reality and the interconnections among various systems of oppression. But, as is, it is incomplete. From an eco-feminist perspective, insofar as socialist feminism does not explicitly address the systematic oppression of nature, it fails to give an account of one of the "four interlocking pillars upon which the structure of patriarchy rests" – sexism, racism, classism, *and* naturism.

Transformative Feminism

So far I have argued that, from an eco-feminist perspective, there are good reasons to worry about the adequacy of each of the four leading versions of feminism as a theoretical grounding for eco-feminism. If this view is correct, what, then, is needed?

If one takes seriously eco-feminist claims about the nature and importance of the connections between the oppression of women and the oppression of nature, then I think what is needed is an integrative and transformative feminism, one that moves us beyond the current debate over the four leading versions of feminism and makes a responsible ecological perspective central to feminist theory and practice. In what follows, I offer a few suggestions about how such a transformative feminism might be developed.

First, a transformative feminism would expand upon the traditional conception of feminism as "the movement to end women's oppression" by recognizing and making explicit the interconnections between all systems of oppression. In this regard, a transformative feminism would be informed by the conception of feminism which has been advanced by many black feminists and Third World feminists articulating the needs and concerns of black women and women in development. These feminists have argued that because of the basic connections between sexist oppression and other forms of systematized oppression, feminism, properly understood, is a movement to end *all* forms of oppression.[43]

Socialist feminism has opened the door for such a transformative feminism by acknowledging the structural interconnections between sexism, racism, and classism; eco-feminism contributes insights about the important connections between the oppression of women and the oppression of nature. A transformative feminism would build on these insights to develop a more expansive and complete feminism, one which ties the liberation of women to the elimination of all systems of oppression.

Second, a transformative feminism must provide a central theoretical place for the diversity of women's experiences, even if this means abandoning the project of attempting to formulate one overarching feminist theory or one woman's voice.[44] This is in accordance with the basic goal of any theory. As Evelyn Fox Keller puts it:

> The essential goal of theory in general I take to be to represent our experience of the world in as comprehensive and inclusive a way as possible; in that effort we seek a maximal intersubjectivity.[45]

A transformative feminism would acknowledge the social construction of knowledge and a conception of epistemology that takes seriously the felt experiences of women as a subordinate group – however different those experiences may be. As a related point, it would be a call to oppressed groups to collectively assert *for themselves* their felt experiences, needs, and distinctiveness. In this respect, it would reflect a commitment to what Iris Young calls "a politics of difference," viz., one that asserts the value and specificity of group difference in political theory and practice.[46]

Third, a transformative feminism would involve a rejection of a logic of domination and the patriarchal conceptual framework which gives rise to it. By showing how systems of oppression are rooted in this common conceptual framework, it would address the conceptual and structural interconnections among all forms of domination. In this way, it would encourage feminists concerned with ecology to join allegiance with those seeking to end oppression by race and class. Otherwise, feminist concerns over ecology would degenerate into a largely white middle-class movement. As Rosemary Ruether warns:

> The ethic of reconciliation with the earth has yet to break out of its snug corners of affluence and find meaningful cohesion with the revolution of insurgent people.[47]

The promise of a transformative feminism requires making connections with "the revolution of insurgent people."

Fourth, a transformative feminism would involve a rethinking of what it is to be human, especially as the conception of human nature becomes informed by a nonpatriarchal conception of the interconnections between human and nonhuman nature. This would involve a psychological restructuring of our attitudes and beliefs about ourselves and "our world" (including the nonhuman world), and a philosophical rethinking of the notion of the self such that we see ourselves as both co-members of an ecological community and yet different from other members of it.

Fifth, a transformative feminism would involve recasting traditional ethical concerns to make a central place for values (e.g., care, friendship, reciprocity in relationships, appropriate trust, diversity) underplayed or lost in traditional, particularly modern and contemporary, philosophical construals of ethics. It would include nonhierarchical models of morality and conflict resolution (e.g., consensual decision making and mediation) and involve a rethinking of the "moral point of view" in light of the social and historical context of human nature.

Sixth, a transformative feminism would involve challenging patriarchal bias in technology research and analysis and the use of appropriate science and technologies, i.e., those brought into the service of preserving, rather than destroying, the Earth.[48] Only then would the eco-feminist reconceptualization of the relationship between human and nonhuman nature come around full circle.

Conclusion

In this paper I have argued that from the perspective of eco-feminism, the four leading versions of feminism are inadequate, incomplete, or seriously problematic as a theoretical grounding of eco-feminist concerns. I have suggested that if eco-feminism is correct, then what is needed is a "transformative feminism." The adequacy of such a transformative feminism would depend on how accurately it captures and systematizes the points of view of women as oppressed persons, the insights of eco-feminism, and the interconnections between all systems of oppression.

When one describes a lake by looking down at it from above, or by only skimming across its surface, one gets a limited and partial view of the nature of the lake. It is only when one dives deep and looks at the lake from the bottom up that one sees the diversity and richness of the various life forms and processes that constitute the lake.

So, too, it is with feminist theorizing. It is only when we dive deep and conceptualize reality from the various points of view of women of different ages, classes, races, ethnic and national backgrounds, however different those experiences may be, that our feminist theories will see the diversity and richness of those points of view. It is only when we dive deep and see the interconnections between various systems of oppression that our feminist theories will hold much water. A transformative feminism has the potential to make these connections. It has the potential for making the connections between feminism and ecology from the bottom up.

Notes

1. Rosemary Radford Ruether, *New Woman/New Earth: Sexist Ideologies and Human Liberation* (New York: The Seabury Press, 1975), p. 204.

2. *Ibid.*

3. Elizabeth Dodson Gray, *Green Paradise Lost* (Wellesley, Mass.: Roundtable Press, 1981), and *Patriarchy As A Conceptual Trap* (Wellesley, Mass.: Roundtable Press, 1982); Susan Griffin, *Women and Nature* (New York: Harper and Row, 1978); Mary Daly, *Gyn/Ecology: The Meta-Ethics of Radical Feminism* (Boston: Beacon Press, 1978): Carolyn Merchant, *The Death of Nature: Women, Ecology, and the Scientific Revolution (New* York: Harper and Row, 1983), and "Earthcare: Women and the Environmental Movement," *Environment* 23 (1981): 2-13, 38-40; Joan L. Griscom, "On Healing the Nature/History Split in Feminist Thought," *Heresies #13: Feminism and Ecology* 4 (1981): 4-9; Ynestra King, "Feminism and the Revolt of Nature," *Heresies #13: Feminism and Ecology* 4 (1981): 12-16, and "The Eco-feminist Imperative," in Leonie Caldecott and Stephanie Leland, eds, *Reclaim the Earth: Women Speak Out for Life on Earth* (London: The Women's Press, 1983; pp. 12-16, and "Toward an Ecological Feminism and a Feminist Ecology," in Joan Rothschild, ed., *Machina Ex Dea: Feminist Perspectives on Technology* (New York: Pergamon Press, 1983), pp. 118-29; Ariel Kay Salleh, "Deeper than Deep Ecology: The Eco-Feminist Connection," *Environmental Ethics* 3 (1984): 339-45.

4. Although more traditional uses of the term *oppression* refer to domination or subordination of humans by humans, eco-feminists use the expression "oppression of nature" to refer to the domination or subordination of nonhuman nature by humans.

5. Ynestra King, "Feminism and the Revolt of Nature," p. 12.

6. The minimal condition account given here does not, by itself, specify what counts as a "feminist perspective," an "ecological perspective," "feminist theory and practice" or "solutions to ecological problems." Nor does it specify whether a "science of ecology" must reflect a commitment to gender ideologies or in some sense be a "feminist science." Questions about the meaning, scope, and application of conditions (i) to (iv) are deliberately left open.

7. Elizabeth Dodson Gray, *Green Paradise Lost,* p. 20.

8. *Ibid.*

9. Alison M. Jaggar, *Feminist Politics and Human Nature* (Totowah N.J.: Rowman and Allanheld, 1983), p. 96. Joyce Trebilcot argues that "In feminism, there is a movement toward the elimination of all dualisms" because dualisms not only function evaluatively (to justify the "superior's" power over the "inferior") and epistemologically (they determine perceptions); they also function to determine in part the conception or meaning of the things related. Joyce Trebilcot, "Conceiving Women: Notes on the Logic of Feminism," in Marilyn Pearsall, ed., *Women and Values: Readings in Recent Feminist Philosophy* (Belmont, Calif.: Wadsworth Publishing Co., 1986), pp. 358-63.

10. Elizabeth Dodson Gray describes a "conceptual trap" as "a set of outmoded beliefs" and "a way of thinking that is like a room which – once inside – you cannot imagine a world outside." Gray, *Patriarchy as a Conceptual Trap*, pp. 16-17.

11. Sheila D. Collins, *A Different Heaven and Earth* (Valley Forge: Judson Press, 1974), p. 161. I take it that this account is compatible with there being other "pillars" on which patriarchal structures rest (e.g., "imperialism" in capitalist patriarchal structures).

12. See the discussions of eco-feminism given by King, "Toward an Ecological Feminism and a Feminist Ecology"; Don E. Marietta, Jr., "Environmentalism, Feminism, and the Future of American Society," *The Humanist* 44 (1984): 15-18, 30; Merchant, "Earthcare: Women and the Environmental Movement."

13. For example, consider animal liberationism. According to Tom Regan's rights-based version of animal liberationism, individual nonhuman animals have moral rights against humans which impose on us obligations to treat them in certain ways. Tom Regan, *All That Dwell Therein: Essays on Animal Rights and Environmental Ethics* (Berkeley: University of California Press, 1982). According to Peter Singer's utilitarian-based version, our obligations to nonhuman animals are grounded in their capacity to feel pain and pleasure; failure to acknowledge that animals and other sentient nonhumans deserve moral consideration is just "speciesism," akin to racism, sexism, and classism, i.e., the view that humans are morally superior to animals. Peter Singer, *Animal Liberation* (New York: New York Review/Random House, 1975). Both Regan and Singer's versions of animal liberation extend traditional liberal ethical concerns to individual nonhumans on the basis of certain morally relevant characteristics they allegedly share with humans.

14. Carol Gilligan. *In a Different Voice* (Cambridge, Mass.: Harvard University Press, 1982).

15. Kathryn Pyne Addelson, "Moral Revolution," in *Women and Values*, p. 306.

16. *Ibid.*, p. 307.

17. *Ibid.*

18. *Ibid.*, p. 306.

19. *Ibid.*

20. Frederick Engels, *The Origin of the Family, Private Property and the State* (New York: International Publishers, 1972), pp. 137-38.

21. For example, Marx writes "Men can be distinguished from animals by consciousness, by religion or by anything else you like. They themselves begin to distinguish themselves from animals as soon as they begin to *produce* their means of subsistence, a step which is conditioned by their physical organization." Karl Marx and Frederick Engels, *The German Ideology*, ed. with an introduction by C. J. Arthur (New York: International Publishers, 1970), p. 42.

22. Jaggar, *Feminist Politics and Human Nature*, p. 358.

23. *Marx and Engels* on *Ecology*, ed. Howard L. Parsons (Westport, Conn.: Greenwood Press, 1977), p. 35. Parsons defends Marx, Engels, and Marxism against each of these criticisms.

24. *Ibid.*, pp. 133-141, and 122.

25. For recent discussions of problems for an environmentally attractive interpretation of traditional Marxist doctrine, see Val Routley, "On Karl Marx as an Environmental Hero," *Environmental Ethics,* 3 (1981): 237-44; Hwa Yol Jung, "Marxism, Ecology, and Technology," *Environmental Ethics* 5 (1983): 169-71; Charles Tolman, "Karl Marx, Alienation, and the Mastery of Nature." *Environmental Ethics* 3 (1981): 63-74. For a defense of a Marxian ecological ethic, see Donald C. Lee, "On the Marxian View of the Relationship between Man and Nature." *Environmental Ethics* 2 (1980): 3-16, and "Toward a Marxian Ecological Ethic: A Response to Two Critics." *Environmental Ethics* 4 (1982): 339-43; Howard L. Parsons, *Marx and Engels on Ecology.*

26. Jaggar, *Feminist Politics and Human Nature,* p. 266.

27. Jaggar identifies four radical feminist conceptions of human nature. *Ibid.,* pp. 11-12, 85-105 .

28. See Charlene Spretnak, "Introduction," in Charlene Spretnak, ed., *The Politics of Women's Spirituality* (New York: Doubleday, 1982), p. xxx, n. 20.

29. For a discussion of these two radical feminist positions, see Ynestra King, "Feminism and the Revolt of Nature."

30. Sherry B. Ortner was one of the first to address this question in her article, "Is Female to Male As Nature is to Culture?" in Michelle Rosaldo and Louise Lamphere, eds., *Woman, Culture, and Society* (Stanford: Stanford University Press, 1974), pp. 67-87.

31. Griscom, "On Healing the Nature/Culture Split in Feminist Thought," p. 9.

32. *Ibid.*

33. The phrase "unwitting complicity" is from Ynestra King. "Feminism and the Revolt Against Nature," p. 15.

34. Jaggar, *Feminist Politics and Human Nature,* p. 124.

35. *Ibid.,* p. 129

36. *Ibid.,* p. 125.

37. *Ibid.,* p. 126.

38. *Ibid.,* p. 132.

39. *Ibid.,* p. 126

40. According to Jaggar, a "standpoint" is "a position in society from which certain features of reality come into prominence and from which others are obscured" (*ibid.,* p. 382). The "standpoint of women" is "that perspective which reveals women's true interests and this standpoint is reached only through scientific and political struggle. Those who construct the standpoint of women must begin from women's experience as women describe it, but they must go beyond that experience theoretically and ultimately may require that women's experiences be redescribed" (*ibid.,* p. 384).

41. For example, in her otherwise thorough treatment of socialist feminism in *Feminist Politics and Human Nature,* Alison Jaggar explicitly addresses the issue of the connection between socialist feminism and ecology in less than one

full page (pp. 306-07). From an eco-feminist perspective, such a limited treatment of the feminism-ecology connection leaves the incorrect impression that ecology is not, or is not a very important, feminist issue. Furthermore, this (what might be called "ecology blindness") reinforces oppositional thinking which separates discussions of political philosophy from the life sciences (e.g., ecology) and discussions of human nature from non-human nature. From an eco-feminist perspective, it thereby reinforces the mistaken view that an adequate feminist political theory can be articulated without incorporation of an ecological perspective, and that an adequate theory of human nature can be articulated without essential reference to nonhuman nature.

42. *Ibid.,* p. 306.

43. See, e.g., Bell Hooks, *Feminist Theory: From Margin to Center* (Boston: South End Press, 1984), pp. 17-31: "The Combahee River Collective Statement," in Barbara Smith, ed., *Home Girls: A Black Feminist Anthology* (New York: Kitchen Table Women of Color Press, 1983), p. 272; Gita Sen and Caren Gowen, *Development, Crisis and Alternative Visions: Third World Women's Perspectives* (New Dehli: DAWN, 1985), p. 13.

44. For an account of reasons to be wary of attempts to articulate "the women's voice," see Maria Lugones and Elizabeth V. Spelman "Have We Got a Theory for You! Feminist Theory, Cultural Imperialism and the Woman's Voice," *Women's Studies International Forum* 6 (1983): 573-81.

45. Evelyn Fox Keller, "Women, Science, and Popular Mythology," in Joan Rothschild, ed., *Machine Ex Dea: Feminist Perspectives on Technology* (New York: Pergamon Press, 1983), p. 134.

46. Iris Marion Young, "Elements of a Politics of Difference," read at the Second Annual North American Society for Social Philosophy, Colorado Springs, August 1985.

47. Rosemary Radford Ruether, "Mother Earth and the Megamachine," in Carol Christ and Judith Plaskow, eds., *Woman-Spirit Rising: A Feminist Reader in Religion* (San Francisco: Harper and Row, 1979), p. 51.

48. For a discussion of a variety of feminist perspectives on science and technology, see Rothschild, ed., *Machina Ex Dea:* see also Judy Smith, *Something Old, Something New, Something Borrowed, Something Due* (Missoula, Mont.: Women and Technology Network, 1980).

12

Feminism, Deep Ecology, and Environmental Ethics

Michael E. Zimmerman

Deep ecologists have criticized reform environmentalists for not being sufficiently radical in their attempts to curb human exploitation of the nonhuman world. Eco-feminists, however, maintain that deep ecologists, too, are not sufficiently radical, for they have neglected the crucial role played by patriarchalism in shaping the cultural categories responsible for Western humanity's domination of Nature. According to eco-feminists, only by replacing those categories – including atomism, hierarchalism, dualism, and androcentrism – can humanity learn to dwell in harmony with nonhuman beings. After reviewing the eco-feminist critique both of reform environmentalism and of deep ecology, I sketch a critical dialogue between eco-feminism and deep ecology.

. . . from the similitude of the thoughts and passions of one man to the thoughts and passions of another, whosoever looketh into himself, and considereth what he doth when he does think, opine, reason, hope, fear, etc., and upon what grounds: he shall thereby read and know what are the thoughts and passions of all other men upon like occasions.

Thomas Hobbes[1]

. . . to demand that our human interpretations and values should be universal and perhaps constitutive values is one of the hereditary madnesses of human pride. . . . As if a world would still remain over after one deducted the perspective!
Friedrich Nietzsche[2]

The patriarchal self-deception about the origins of consciousness ends logically in the destruction of the Earth.   Rosemary Radford Reuther[3]

Introduction

In this essay, I examine the feminist contention that both reform environmentalism and deep ecology are inadequate means for ending the human domination of nature, because both approaches ignore the decisive phenomena of patriarchalism and androcentrism. For example, one of the most important of the reform movements in environmental ethics urges us to "extend" rights to nonhuman beings in order to protect them from human abuse.[4] For many feminists, however, the concept of rights is so bound up with a masculinist interpretation of self and reality that it cannot serve to end the exploitation of nature that arises from that interpretation. At first glance, deep ecology would appear to be in agreement with the feminist critique of reformist environmental ethics. Deep ecology maintains that the humanity-nature relation cannot be transformed by moral "extensionism" or any other variety of reformism.[5] Instead, this transformation can only begin with the elimination of the anthropocentric world view that portrays humanity itself as the source of all value and that depicts nature solely as raw material for human purposes. Feminists claim, however, that deep ecology obscures the crucial issue by talking about *human*-centeredness, instead of about male-centeredness *(androcentrism).*[6] A truly "deep" ecology would have to be informed by the insights of eco-feminists, who link the male domination of nature with the male domination of woman. As Ariel Kay Salleh remarks, in deep ecology

> There is a concerted effort to rethink Western metaphysics, epistemology, and ethics . . ., but this "rethink" remains an idealism closed in on itself because it fails to face up to the uncomfortable psychosexual origins of our culture and its crisis. . . . Sadly, from the eco-feminist point of view, deep ecology is simply another self-congratulatory reformist move: the transvaluation of values it claims for itself is quite peripheral. . . . [T]he deep ecology movement will not truly happen until men are brave enough to rediscover and to love the woman inside themselves.[7]

In what follows I first present a brief account of the feminist explanation for the male domination of nature and woman. This account provides a context helpful for seeing why feminists are dissatisfied with the programs that some males have offered for healing the humanity-nature relationship. I then discuss, in turn, feminist critiques of the reformist "moral extensionism" and of deep ecology. Finally, I offer some critical reflections about some aspects of the feminist critique of deep ecology.

The Feminist Critique of the Domination of Nature

Contemporary feminism is a complex movement, with its share of disagreement about the origins, nature, and importance of patriarchy and androcentrism.[8] Most feminists would agree, however, that a major source of contemporary social and environmental ills is the fact that patriarchal culture has, on the one hand repressed and devalued female experience and, on the other hand, has both absolutized and universalized male experience. The opening citations offer differing attitudes toward the male's universalization of his own experience. Hobbes, in a manner typical of male thinkers throughout history, presumes that *his* experience of self, other, and reality is true for *all* people, Nietzsche reveals his attunement to the idea that the power motives inherent in such claims allow a person to make one's own way of thinking the absolute truth, and Rosemary Radford Reuther concludes that the unwarranted universalization of masculinist categories has led, over the millennia, to lopsided practices that are responsible for the domination of nature (and woman). Ending this male domination could have dramatic consequences. According to Virginia Held, "If feminists can succeed not only in making visible but also in keeping within our awareness the aspects of 'mankind' that have been obscured and misrepresented by taking the 'human' to be the masculine, virtually all existing thought may be turned on its head."[9] So long as patriarchally raised men fear and hate women, and so long as men conceive of nature as female, men will continue in their attempts to deny what they consider to be the feminine/natural within themselves and to control what they regard as the feminine/natural outside themselves.

Marilyn French offers the following account of the origin of the male aversion to woman and nature.[10] Thousands of years ago, men gradually began to define the male as truly human, in contrast with the female, who was portrayed as being only partly human insofar as she was so closely identified with natural processes (birth, lactation, child rearing. menstrual cycles, etc.). The discovery by men of their role in pregnancy may also have enabled them to conceive of women no longer as a miraculous source of life from within themselves, but instead as mere carriers and nourishers of the seed implanted in them by men. The experience of being able to create something with so little personal involvement may have, in turn, led men to conceive of God as a transcendent, nonnatural, "male" source of power. This God replaced the Goddess who had emphasized pleasure, affiliation, mutual caring, harmony between nature and humanity. The idea of God emphasized power, hierarchy, independence, and dualism between nature and males. According to French, the rise of the transcendent, male power-god symbolizes the beginning of the human worship of power. She summarizes her views in the following way:

> Patriarchy is an ideology founded on the assumption that man is distinct from the animal and superior to it. The basis for this superiority is man's contact with a higher power/knowledge called god, reason, or control. The reason for man's existence is to shed all animal residue and realize fully his "divine" nature, the part that seems unlike any part owned by animals – mind, spirit, or control. In the process of achieving this, man has attempted to subdue nature both outside and inside himself; he has created a substitute environment in which he appears to be no longer dependent upon nature. The aim of the most influential human minds has been to create an entirely factitious world, a world dominated by man, the one creature in control of his own destiny. This world, if complete, would be *entirely* in man's control . . . . and man

himself would have eradicated or concealed his basic bodily and emotional bonds to nature.[11]

The male's conception of himself as essentially cultural, nonfemale, nonnatural, immortal, and transcendent, as opposed to the essentially natural, noncultural, mortal woman, has continued in various guises for several thousand years.[12] Carolyn Merchant maintains, however, that the patriarchal view of nature as fearsome, threatening, wild, and uncontrollable was tempered for a long time by the alternative vision of Mother Nature: bounteous, kind, life-giving. But with the coming of the modern age, the motherly dimension of nature was eclipsed by the fearsome vision of a wild woman who must be known (Bacon) in order to be controlled. It is probably no accident that the great witchcraft trials raged during the time Europe was making the transition to a mechanistic world view. About this transition, Merchant remarks that

> The metaphor of the earth as a nurturing mother was gradually to vanish as a dominate image as the Scientific Revolution proceeded to mechanize and rationalize the world view. The second image, nature as disorder, called forth an important modern idea, that of power over nature. Two new ideas, those of mechanism and of the domination and mastery of nature, became core concepts of the modern world. . . . As Western culture became increasingly mechanized in the 1600s, the female earth and virgin earth were subdued by the machine.[13]

At the basis of man's attempt to control nature is what has been called "the God project": the quest to become divine, immortal, incorruptible.[14] The drive for such immortality may be said to motivate both the technological domination of nature as well as the nuclear arms race, either of which may result in the destruction of the Earth.[15] Men at war project death and evil onto the enemy: both sides are under the illusion that by killing the enemy, they will have eradicated both mortality and wickedness. Paradoxically, male humanity's effort to deny death and to control all things seems to hasten the death of all things. Rosemary Radford Reuther writes that

> It is not extreme to see this [self-destructive] denouement as inherent in the fundamental patriarchal revolution of consciousness that sought to deny that the spiritual component of humanity was a dimension of the maternal matrix of being. . . . Patriarchal religion split apart from the dialectical unities of mother religion into absolute dualism, elevating a male-identified consciousness to transcendent apriority. Fundamentally this is rooted in an effort to deny one's own mortality, to identify essential (male) humanity with a transcendent divine sphere beyond the matrix of coming-to-be-and-passing-away.[16]

While Judaeo-Christian scripture sometimes accords nature goodness insofar as it is a creature of God, more often these scriptures assert the absolute difference between God and creation.[17] Genesis tells us that only humans are made "in the image of God" and, hence, are given dominion over the rest of creation. In the patriarchal culture of Jews and Christians, this idea of human dominion over creation was conceived as *male* dominion. In early modern times, the view of the special status of humanity in general, and males in particular, was secularized. Today, even nonreligious modern people take it for granted that there is a natural hierarchy at the top of which stands humankind.[18] Modern Western humanity presumes that only humans are the source of truth, value, and meaning; nature is merely an object whose sole value lies in its usefulness for man. Nature must be channeled and repressed for the purpose of human control, security, and survival. In industrial society, men are trained and disciplined in ways that repress the "useless" and "counterproductive" aspects of nature at work in them, including feelings, emotions, and other "womanly" sensibilities. Power over the human organism is a crucial ingredient of the technological domination of the rest of nature.[19]

The technological project is closely linked to the scientific revolution initiated by thinkers such as Descartes. Descartes' extreme rationalism and his subject-object dualism are the products of an extremely masculinist view of self and reality, a view that is shared by many males in modern society. Cut off from their feelings, men become isolated, rigid, overly rational, and committed to abstract principles at the expense of concrete personal relationships. As a result of their attachment to abstract doctrines, males have developed highly rationalistic moral philosophies. Such philosophies include little or no role for *caring* and *feeling* as preconditions for ethics, including the ethic concerning humanity's relation to nature. Marti Kheel notes:

> What seems to be lacking in much of the literature in environmental ethics (and in ethics in general) is the open admission that we cannot even begin to talk about the issue of ethics unless we admit that we *care* (*or feel something*). And it is here that the emphasis of many feminists on personal experience and emotion has much to offer in the way of reformulating our traditional notion of ethics.[20]

Feminists maintain that most modern moral theory is linked to the very androcentric-patriarchal way of thinking that is responsible for the domination of nature. The rationalistic subject-object dualism is mirrored in the abstract, calculative, rational, and atomistic ethical systems that have arisen to govern competition among men after the death of their biblical God. Such systems lack the relational-intuitive sensibility that feminists maintain is required for the new *ethos* in which the nature-humanity dualism is overcome. The doctrine of "the natural rights of man" is allegedly an example of such an androcentric ethical system. In recent years, a number of environmental philosophers have attempted to "extend" rights to nonhuman beings, in order to protect those beings from human abuse. In the next section, I examine the feminist contention that such moral reformism cannot heal the nature-humanity dualism, since the concept of "rights" is linked to the rationalistic-atomistic metaphysics that has led to the domination of nature.

The Feminist Critique of the "Natural Rights of Man"

It has been argued that moral philosophers attempting to "expand" prevailing moral categories to "cover" the cases of animals or plants are analogous to the "normal scientists" trying to shore up the prevailing paradigm in the face of anomalies (cf. Kuhn).[21] In the face of the anomalous moral issues involved in the human exploitation of nature, however, refinements of the existing ethical paradigms will not be of much help. What is needed, we are told, is a "paradigm shift" that produces a nonandrocentric framework in which nature will appear as something other than an object to be dominated. Such a shift is *not* involved in the efforts by some reformers to "extend" rights to nonhuman beings in order to protect them from human abuse.

Natural rights theory is a typical example of a masculinist moral system, i.e., a system based on a male way of perceiving self, other, and nature.[22] The fundamental claims of natural rights theory are: that humans are endowed with certain inalienable rights, including life, liberty, and property; that humans are morally prohibited from interfering with another person's rights so long as that person does not interfere with legitimate rights of their own; and that humans have a right to defend their rights against those who would attempt wrongfully to deprive them of their rights. Natural rights theorists tend to restrict rights (and moral standing) to human beings, and they portray nonhuman beings as being virtually devoid of intrinsic worth. Locke argued that labor ontologically transforms natural things; they go from being valueless entities to valuable ones when human labor is mixed with them.[23] The fact that Locke is one of the founders of liberal capitalism, and that his labor theory of value was very influential on Karl Marx, helps to explain why both capitalism and communism treat nature primarily as an object for human use.[24]

Feminists are not alone in criticizing the doctrine of natural rights, but they maintain that only the feminist critique enables us to grasp both the origins and impact of the atomistic and egoist self-understanding lying at the base of the "rights of man." The doctrine of natural rights, we are told, is androcentric, hierarchical, dualistic, atomistic, and abstract. It is *androcentric* because its conception of human beings is based on a masculinist experience which excludes (and implicitly negates) female experience; it is *hierarchical* because it gives preference to male experience, and also because it portrays humans as radically more important than any other sort of beings; it is *dualistic* because of its distinction between humans (rational, intrinsically valuable, rights-possessing) and nonhumans (nonrational, instrumentally valuable, rights-lacking); it is atomistic because its portrayal of human beings (as separate egos) is consistent with the *atomistic* metaphysics of modern science; and it is *abstract* because conflicts about rights are resolved in rationalistic and impersonal terms that ignore both the feelings and the particular traits/needs of the individuals involved. Founders of the doctrine of natural rights were men who presupposed that the male experience of self, world, and morality was universal. According to Naomi Scheman, this view is perpetuated by the way in which males are raised within patriarchal structure:

> The view of a separate, autonomous, sharply individuated self embedded in liberal political and economic ideology and in the individualist philosophies of mind can be seen as a defensive reification of the process of ego development in males raised by women in a patriarchal society. Patriarchal family structure tends to produce men of whom these political and philosophical views seem factually descriptive and who are, moreover, deeply motivated to accept the truth of those views as the truth about themselves.[25]

The idea of the self as an isolated ego competing with other egos for scarce resources was most forcibly articulated by Hobbes. Later, this idea was reinforced by Darwin's evolutionary doctrine, which itself seems to reflect his own experience of competitive, egoistical social relations in nineteenth-century England.[26] Thus, the theory that competitive behavior is "natural" and "necessary" seems based at least in part on the fact that Darwin saw nature through the framework of competitive social categories. It has been argued that the "state of nature" was neither so bellicose nor so male-dominated as Hobbes and Darwin would have had us believe.[27] So long as people conceive of themselves as isolated, autonomous egos, who are only externally related to others and to nature, they inevitably tend to see life in terms of scarcity and competition. When people conceive of themselves as internally related to others and to nature, however, they tend to see life in terms of bounty, not scarcity, cooperation, not aggressive competition.

The isolationist-competitive view of human nature, then, reflects not a fact about human nature, but instead the experience of men raised in a patriarchal culture. Feminists argue that liberal political philosophers can adhere to a doctrine of the isolated, independent male ego because they presuppose that *women at home* will continue to knit together the social fabric on which the competing male egos depend.[28] Scheman maintains that

> men have been free to imagine themselves as self-defining only because women have held the intimate social world together, in part by

seeing ourselves as inseparable from it. The norms of personhood, which liberals would strive to make as genuinely universal as they now only pretend to be, depend in fact on their not being so – just what we should expect from an ideology.[29]

From the masculinist perspective, the self appears not to be constituted by relationships with others, but instead is a self-contained entity which constitutes temporary, external relationships with other self-contained entities. If a relationship is terminated (that is, if a contract is ended or broken), the self-contained self is not changed, since the relationship is wholly external. According to Nancy Chodorow, a leading proponent of the psychological school called "object-relations" theory, this male view of the self as an isolated ego stems from early childhood relations between son and mother.[30] At first, the little boy identifies himself with his mother; later, however, he discovers that he is sexually differentiated from her. Seeking to gain his own sexual identity, the boy experiences his own withdrawal from his mother as abandonment. Experiencing profound anger and grief because of this perceived abandonment, he subsequently fears, mistrusts, and hates women. Moreover, he tends to define himself in a negative way as *not female*. His fear and anger lead him to want to dominate both the woman (mother image) within himself and the woman outside of him. As he grows up, he shields himself from his feelings, which overwhelmed him during the trauma of separation, and he defines himself as radically separate from others: he is hesitant to involve himself once again in relationship, since his most important relationship ended in such pain. Because "mother" was originally identified with all of reality, boys and men tend to regard as "female" the undifferentiated natural background against which individual entities stand out. Mother Nature, then, appears as a threatening, unpredictable force from which a man must differentiate himself and which he must control.

Because girls maintain their sense of identity with their mothers for a much longer time than do boys, their sense of self is bound up with relationship. Many women claim that they do not experience themselves as radically separate, self-contained egos, but instead as a network of personal relationships. These relationships are not external, but internal and constitutive of the "self." If a relationship is removed or disrupted, the "self" is inevitably affected. Hence, the notion of fending only for "oneself" does not have the same persuasiveness for many women as it tends to have for men, who conceive of themselves as essentially unrelated to others. Caring for others is, for a woman, difficult to distinguish from caring for herself. If men often have difficulty in relating to others, women often have difficulty in assuming their own identity. Carol Gilligan has postulated that the differing senses of self possessed by males and females lead to differences both in moral perception and moral decision making.[31] Hence, the male preoccupation with "rights" can be related to the male sense of being an isolated ego competing with other egos for ostensibly scarce resources.

When social atomism was being developed in the seventeenth century, it reflected the scientific trend to conceive of material reality atomistically. Hobbes, for example, explicitly modeled his philosophical anthropology on mechanistic-atomistic scientific principles. Most other thinkers, however, were less strong-minded than Hobbes; partly because they clung to religious ideas about man's immortal soul, they hesitated to reduce man to the state of a mere machine. Thus, they employed Cartesian dualism to distinguish "rational" humanity from "extended" material reality. This dualism allowed them to depict nature as a mere thing without intrinsic value, since nature lacks mind or soul. The doctrine that human beings are intrinsically valuable because they alone possess an immortal soul is based on ingredients drawn from the Greek and Judaeo-Christian traditions. Even after the decline of Greek metaphysics and the Judaeo-Christian tradition, modern people continue to maintain that human beings are somehow "special."

This continuing sense of human specialness played an important role in the development of modern moral and legal philosophy, which is notoriously anthropocentric. Hugo Grotius, for example, transformed the Roman doctrine of *jus naturae* (natural right or law) so that it no longer applied to all creatures, but only to rational, self-interested creatures capable of entering into contracts.[32] Plants and animals, lacking such capacity, were said not to have any rights. Kant, moreover, argued that animals lack moral standing because they are not rational; we are prohibited from abusing them only because such practices may encourage humans to abuse each other.

In part, these changes in moral and legal philosophy stemmed from the modern scientific view that the universe is without meaning or purpose, that it is composed of externally related atoms, and that the atomistic human ego is the source of purpose, value, and meaning. Today, however, many scientists no longer view reality as being constituted by individual, isolated, externally related entities, but instead as a network of internal relationships.[33] It is, then, an example of what Whitehead called "misplaced concreteness" to define an animal apart from the environment (air, land, trees, food chains, predators, etc.) that constitutes its "niche." Nothing is separate; all is connected internally. Internal relations are such that they constitute the "reality" of the thing in question; if you alter the relationships, you alter the thing, since it does not exist apart from those relationships. Humanity, too, is an aspect of the fabric of life on Earth; we are not apart. Hence, the emergence of self-conscious human beings can be interpreted as an event by which nature can observe and evaluate *itself*.

The fact-value distinction so important for modern science and philosophy may be undermined by the realization that the universe itself generates novelty, purpose, and diversity. The current dialogue between science and theology reflects the growing trend to regard categories such as "meaning" and "purpose" not as anthropomorphic projections, but instead as ingredients in the cosmos.[34] Furthermore, the subject-object dualism lying at the base of the fact-value dichotomy is now being overcome by significant changes in the idea of what constitutes scientific research. The masculinist conception of science as an abstract and rationalistic quest for the universal ignores the fact that the quest for understanding must involve moods and feelings that disclose crucial aspects of the particular and unique.[35] Androcentric thinking denigrates feelings by asserting that they lack the persuasiveness and universality of conclusions arrived at by way of rational argumentation. Supposedly, rational calculation alone can serve as the proper guide for the ego in its quest for survival in the harsh, competitive world. From this viewpoint, the only limits to humanity's use of nature are *prudential* ones. Before our enormous industrial activity causes the biosphere to collapse, market mechanisms and technological innovations will lead self-interested human beings to adjust their behavior in order to preserve the conditions needed for human life. Yet the purely prudential and self-interested calculations at work in the exploitation of the nonhuman world can go forward smoothly only so long as one does not allow oneself to *feel* the consequences those calculations have for life on Earth – human as well as nonhuman.[36]

In summary, while many feminists acknowledge that the concept of human rights reveals a genuine concern for respecting the interests of other individuals, many feminists are critical of the concept because it is based on masculinist experience that is wrongly universalized and because it fails to include moral categories that arise from a feminine experience of self and world. The experience of relatedness reported by many women gives rise to a morality of caring for the concrete needs of those with whom one is related. This sense of concrete relationship and kinship extends to the natural world as well. Hence, feminists argue that the domination of nature is a masculinist project, one rooted in man's disassociation from the natural world. The doctrine of natural rights is unsuitable for establishing a nondomineering relation between humanity and nature because it (1) is androcentric, (2) regards nonhuman beings as having only instrumental value, (3) is hierarchical, (4) is dualistic, (5) is atomistic, (6) adheres to abstract ethical principles that overemphasize the importance of the isolated individual, (7) denies the importance of feeling for informing moral behavior, and (8) fails to see the essential relatedness of human life with the biosphere that gave us birth. Hence, environmental ethicists who hope to protect nature by "extending" rights to nonhuman beings are part of a reform movement that cannot succeed.

Before concluding this section, some critical observations are in order. After having gone through the phase of seeking to dissolve differences between men and women, many feminists began to affirm those differences – and to conclude that woman is better than man.[37] Hence, some feminists have praised relatedness and feelings at the expense of allegedly "masculinist" traits of individuality and rationality. But other feminists warn that this move runs the risk of simply reaffirming traditional views that women are "feelers," while men are "thinkers." Affirmation of such views is rooted in "essentialist" doctrines of the differences between men and women. Feminists opposed to such essentialism argue that reasoning and feeling are *human* capabilities that do not belong exclusively to one sex or the other. In a non-patriarchal society, human beings would presumably manifest a healthy interplay between emotion and thinking – and moral issues would be informed by both as well. Yet, the notion that a healthy human being would be androgynous, that is, a "combination" of traits currently described as "male" or "female" is problematic insofar as that notion maintains the dualism between male and female. At this stage in human history, we are still groping to understand what it would mean to be a mature man or woman in a nonpatriarchal society.[38]

In any event, many feminists are cautious about simply rejecting the morality of rights and replacing it with a morality of feelings. According to Carole Pateman, for example, some feminists have argued that "since 'justice' is the work of men and an aspect of the domination of women, women should reject it totally and remark their lives on the basis of love, sentiment, and personal relations."[39] Pateman counters by arguing that the liberal concepts of rights, justice, and the individual help guide the dialectic that goes on "between the particular or personal and the universal or political. . . ."[40]

Carol Gilligan has also suggested that a morality of compassion based on the feminine sense of relatedness is complementary with the morality of justice based on the masculine sense of separateness. By overemphasizing interrelatedness, feminists run the risk of leaving no categories for conceiving of people as individuals, or for making moral choices when faced with conflicts between individuals. As Jane Flax notes, "Women, in part because of their own history as daughters, have problems with differentiation and the development of a true self and reciprocal relations."[41]

Overemphasizing internal relatedness can also be a problem when it comes to environmental ethics. Marti Kheel warns of the danger of a kind of environmental totalitarianism that sacrifices the individual for the good of the whole. Kheel insists that while individuals are not radically separate, but instead are internally related "knots" within the fabric of reality, these knots are intrinsically important:

> A vision of nature that perceives value both in the individual and in the whole of which it is a part is a vision that entails a reclaiming of the term *holism* from those for whom it signifies a new form of hierarchy (namely, a valuing of the whole over the individual). Such a vision asks us to abandon the dualistic way of thinking that sees value as inherently exclusive (i.e., they believe that the value of the whole cannot also be the value of the individual).[42]

Thinkers such as Pateman and Kheel help justify the conclusion that the doctrine of natural rights may be useful if applied in a nonpatriarchal, nonatomistic view of humanity and nature, i.e., a view which emphasizes both the essential interrelatedness of all things and the concrete character of the relations between individual "knots" in the cosmic whole. However, so long as natural rights theory presupposes that possessors of rights must be self-interested, rational agents capable of fulfilling the "duties" corresponding to rights; and moreover, so long as natural rights theory clings to metaphysical atomism and egoism, then natural rights theory will not be very useful in correcting current moral problems in the humanity-nature relationship. The reformist impulse behind the extension of rights to nonhuman beings must transform itself into a profound critique of the metaphysical and epistemological presuppositions of patriarchal culture. These androcentric and anthropocentric presuppositions blind us to the fact that human beings are not radically separate from nature, but instead are manifestations of it. We tend to assign rights to those beings which possess attributes (such as consciousness or awareness) resembling our own, for we assume that our attributes are the measure for the rest of reality. A more humble humanity, attuned to the internal relatedness of all things, would presumably respect all things as ingredients in a social cosmos.

Radical Feminism and Deep Ecology

Deep ecology or radical environmentalism claims that environmental pollution, extinction of countless species of plants and animals, clear-cutting of rain forests, overpopulation, genetic engineering, and similar modern practices and problems are symptoms of the real disease: anthropocentrism. By regarding themselves as radically separate from and superior to the rest of nature, modern human beings have increasingly exploited nonhuman reality. Most environmentally concerned people seek to reform current practices in order to avoid disaster for humanity. Clearly, these reformists remain anthropocentric in their orientation. They justify preserving wilderness areas, for example, because such areas are aesthetically pleasing to humans or recreationally valuable. According to deep ecologists, reformism is important in the short run, but for the long run what is needed is radical change in humankind's understanding of its place in nature. We must learn "to let beings be," i.e., to dwell in harmony with the living fabric of the biosphere, of which we are but one strand. Deep ecologists insist that talk of "letting beings be" does not call for human passivity. Instead, it suggests human activity which fulfills itself in communal, creative ways that are not dependent on a constantly increasing material living standard. Acquisitive modern society is based on metaphysical-epistemological categories such as anthropocentrism, atomism, hierarchalism, dualism, and mechanism. The ethical basis of that society is also human-centered. Deep ecologists frequently contrast themselves with so-called New Agers, who – following thinkers such as Teilhard de Chardin and Buckminster Fuller – regard humankind as the species which has evolved to the point of guiding subsequent evolution on planet Earth. New Agers suggest that science and technology can provide humankind with more efficient, less polluting methods for producing goods, so that a higher standard of living for all humankind is consistent with the well-being of the biosphere. Deep ecologists reply that humankind has only a self-proclaimed right to become the evolutionary managers of Earth.

Not surprisingly, deep ecology is a controversial view. Some regard it as utopian and naive; others as promoting a kind of fascism/totalitarianism that would sacrifice human life for the "good" of the biosphere; still others argue that it remains anthropocentric since it still regards human beings as different from all other forms of life.[43] While other animals are to be allowed to fulfill their "evolutionary destinies," humanity is supposed to curb its own "destiny," if that destiny happens to involve extinguishing and dominating other forms of life. Deep ecologists counter by saying that many critics of the movement misunderstand it, mostly because of their anthropocentric biases.[44] The feminist critics of deep ecology, however, have a different basis.

At first glance, deep ecology may seem to be in almost complete agreement with the feminist view that abstract, dualistic, atomistic, and hierarchial categories are responsible for the domination of nature. A new *ethos,* according to deep ecologists, is required for humans to dwell appropriately on Earth. Moreover, deep ecologists – like feminists – have been critical of reformist attempts to extend modern moral categories to "protect" nonhuman beings from human abuse. Feminist critics of deep ecology, however, assert that it speaks of a gender-neutral "anthropocentrism" as the root of the domination of nature, when in fact *androcentrism* is the real root. Only the interpretive lens of androcentrism enables us to understand the origin and scope of dualistic, atomistic, hierarchical, and mechanistic categories. Deep ecologists are still only reformists: they want to improve the humanity-nature relationship without taking the radical step of eliminating both man's domination of woman (including the woman inside of each man) and the culturally enforced self-denigration of woman. Moreover, since deep ecology was formulated almost exclusively by men, and since men under patriarchy allegedly think in distorted ways, the similarity between the principles of deep ecology and what we might call eco-feminism may be largely superficial.

In her article "Deeper than Deep Ecology: The Eco-Feminist Connection," Ariel Salleh makes a number of specific criticisms of deep ecology, especially certain works by Arne Naess and Bill Devall.[45] First, deep ecologists often use sexist language, as for example when they speak unself-consciously of the need for improving "man's relation with nature." Use of such language reveals that deep ecologists have not acknowledged the basic social inequality between men and women. Salleh argues that "The master-slave role which marks man's relation with nature is replicated in man's relation with woman." Deep ecologists argue that artificial control of population is a necessary means for developing a new relation with nature. Here, deep ecologists seem to preach the same gospel as other men before them: controlling female reproductive processes by technical means will solve problems allegedly caused by a natural process. Deep ecologists use highly rationalistic arguments that betray their ongoing commitment to masculinist-scientistic modes of thought. Because their experience is deformed by masculinist modes of thought, male deep ecologists should consult women who are more in tune with the natural world than are men, and who are open to the experience of reality in an alternative way. Solutions proposed by deep ecologists are naive, according to Salleh, insofar as they are offered outside of the context of the critique of patriarchalism. For example, when deep ecologists call for decentralizing society, they ignore the fact that patriarchal culture has always favored hierarchy and centralization – and that unless patriarchal consciousness is abandoned, schemes for decentralization are hopeless. Despite their good intentions, then, deep ecologists exhibit a pervasive masculinist bias that works against their aims. Salleh says that

> In arguing for an eco-phenomenology, [Bill] Devall certainly attempts to bypass this ideological noose [mechanistic metaphysics] – "Let us think like a mountain," he says – but again, the analysis here rests on what is called "a gestalt of person-in-nature": a conceptual effort, a grim intellectual determination "to care"; "to show reverence" for Earth's household and "to let" nature follow "its separate" evolutionary path.[46]

Salleh concludes that deep ecologists are males who, damaged by patriarchy, are seeking to heal themselves:

> Watts, Snyder, Devall, all want education for the spiritual development of "personhood." This is the self-estranged male reaching for the original androgynous natural unity within himself. The deep ecology movement is very much a spiritual search for people in a barren secular age;

but how much of this quest for self-realization is driven by ego and will? If, on the one hand, the search seems to be stuck at an abstract cognitive level, on the other, it may be led full circle and sabotaged by the ancient compulsion to fabricate perfectability. Men's ungrounded restless search for the alienated Other part of themselves has led to a society where not life itself, but "change," bigger and better, whiter than white, has become the consumptive end. . . . But the deep ecology movement will not truly happen until men are brave enough to redis-cover and to love the woman inside themselves. And we women, too, have to be allowed to love what we are, if we are to make a better world.[47]

Salleh's critique is, in my opinion, only partly accurate, and her ac-cusatory tone may limit her audience as much as the misogyny of a great deal of systematic thinking diminishes its applicability. It may well be, of course, that men – especially those men who are seeking to move beyond the constricted categories of modern manhood – need to experience the righteous anger of women who have for so long experienced the repres-siveness of patriarchal society. Salleh is right, moreover, in saying that most deep ecologists continue to write in the technical-rationalistic style that gives their work some measure of credibility within patriarchy. Yet feminists themselves are familiar with the problem of discovering their own "voice." And Salleh herself uses a style of writing and argumenta-tion that does not seem radically different from that of deep ecologists such as Devall or Naess. The fact is that in order to gain a hearing within "establishment" journals and presses, authors (male and female alike) must conform to traditional linguistic forms, even though those forms may be aligned with patriarchal social structures.

It is not surprising, of course, to hear that deep ecologists tend to write in ways that are called masculinist, since this is how men and women alike are socialized to write. Is it not possible, however, that de-spite such a writing style, and despite how they've been socialized, male deep ecologists may in fact open to their own feelings and to their relat-edness to nature in ways that evade the effects of patriarchy? What to women might appear as a clumsy, obviously male way of speaking might be for the male speaker an expression of a genuine sense of kinship with nature, including the nature within him.

Is it not too sweeping a generalization to say that women are more attuned to nature than are men? Not for Salleh, who claims that deep ecologists are attuned to nature only in a manner distorted by patriarchal culture, and that their masculinist forms of speaking and writing are signs of that distorted experience. She asserts that such distorted experience oc-curs because deep ecologists are out of touch with the woman within them. Is the term *woman* meant to refer to the feelings, emotions, and relational sensibility with which many men are out of touch? Yet to conceive of such traits as "feminine" seems to suggest an essentialist and/or genetic doctrine of the differences between men and women: that man is thinker, woman is feeler. Is such a doctrine consistent with the conviction of many feminists that men and women alike are distorted products of the psychological, social, and cultural practices of patriarchy? If we humans are essentially or naturally dichotomized by sex-linked traits (reason vs. feeling), then there is no real point in trying to change human cultural practices. In recent years, a number of feminists have favored such an essentialist view and have concluded that woman is better than man.

This variety of essentialist feminism often rejects reason, science, technology, abstraction, individuation, hierarchy, and so on, as the bitter fruits of patriarchal culture. Other feminists, however, argue that such categories and practices are not intrinsically evil; instead, they become destructive when utilized in a one-sided culture such as patriarchy. The fact that these categories arose within the history of patriarchy does *not* mean that truly liberated women should eschew them entirely in order to avoid being "infected" with patriarchalism. Great scientists report that their work is not merely rational and deductive, but involves insight into particular relationships and concrete events. Modern science has gone astray by its pretense to pure objectivity and rationality. Contemporary feminist criticism may help bring about a change in our understanding of the nature of scientific inquiry. Modern science and technology are potentially liberating, but have been misdirected because of the patriarchal view that nature (including human nature) must be exploited to enhance power and security. When social categories change, feminists argue, the technological domination of nature will change accordingly.

The fact that all people tend to be distorted under patriarchal culture leads to another observation about Salleh's critique of deep ecology. If deep ecologists cannot get to the heart of the matter because their experience is too deeply distorted by patriarchy, cannot we say something analogous about women? How can authentic female experience and self-expression be possible under patriarchy? And what can be meant by the concept of "authentic" female experience? Leaving aside essentialist arguments, we would have to conclude that authentic experience cannot be identical with "natural" experience, since human experience is always culturally mediated. Would authentic female experience be that formed by a feminist culture? But what then of authentic male experience? Would it be possible in such a culture? Or must there be two separate cultures, male and female, for members of the two sexes to become truly human? If patriarchy is an interpretive framework, is feminism itself not another such framework? Does feminism pretend to provide a nondistorted, impartial way of interpreting experience? Are feminists raised under patriarchy motivated by their own version of the power drive that is essential to patriarchy?

To such questions, feminists might reply in a two-fold way. First, the quest to articulate feminine experience is motivated by the conviction that many women experience self and world in a way differently than is reported by men. Women want and need to validate the fact that there is *another mode* of experience. Such validation is important, even if the experience of women is distorted by patriarchy. Second, this validation makes possible the next stage of development: the search not simply for authentic female experience, but for authentic *human* experience. Required for such experience are cultural arrangements and categories compatible with the development of people who are aware both of their own uniqueness, and of their profound relationships with other people and the rest of the natural world. Cultural practices, then, not genetic differences, are responsible for the current differentiation between "masculine" and "feminine" experience. Ultimately, then, feminism seeks to liberate women and men alike from the distorted mode of existence necessitated under patriarchy. Authentic human existence would inevitably transform the current exploitative treatment of nature.

Critics of feminism, however, regard as disingenuous the claim that the real motive of feminism is to liberate *all* people. Such critics contend that feminists have their own power agenda. Feminists make patriarchy responsible for too much; they portray men as the villains of world history, even though some feminists try to temper this portrayal by saying that *individual* men are not to blame, since they have been socialized to behave in a domineering and destructive way. Further, radical feminism accuses men of projecting unwanted traits onto women and nature. Yet projection is surely not something in which men alone engage. What traits, then, are women projecting onto men? And what benefits accrue to women through projecting such traits? Do women split off from themselves and project onto men violence, aggressiveness, selfishness, greed, anger, hostility, death hating, nature fearing, individuality, and responsibility? And as a result of bearing these projected traits, do men behave much more violently, selfishly, etc., than they would if these projected traits were withdrawn by women? If women do project these traits, one benefit gained would be for them to regard themselves as peaceful, charitable, concerned about others, compassionate, emotional, in harmony with nature, loving, thoughtful, and more truly human. But can such positive, "good" characteristics belong only to one sex? In searching for their own "voice," are feminists willing to acknowledge their own "dark side," which is all too easily projected onto men? And do they realize that men, too, are the victims of patriarchy, that they lack a real "voice" of their own, apart from the impersonal voice that they have assumed in the process of having to split off their own feelings? While benefiting from the material well-being and technological progress made possible by masculinist science and industry, do women rid themselves of responsibility for the negative side effects of such progress by attributing them to rapacious male behavior? Feminists can say that patriarchal categories are the problem, and that changing those categories according to feminist principles will bring about an end to the domination of woman and nature. Yet there is no assurance that new forms of domination and power will not arise in the process.

By way of reply, many feminists acknowledge that individual men turn out as they do as a result of ancient child-rearing and socialization processes that they themselves did not choose, that women must own up to what they project onto men, that women have their own fears about mortality and have their own resentment against nature, and that the feminist critique of patriarchy must engage in searching self-criticism. Feminists would remind critics, however, of the danger involved in *blaming the victim* for her present condition. For example, in medieval China mothers were responsible for enforcing upon their daughters the tribal practice of foot binding. It is wrong to conclude, however, that women were responsible for this practice, since they were part of a patriarchal culture which *expected* them to behave in this way. Moreover, the fact that women tend to split off from themselves and to project "masculine" traits onto men tends to *disempower* women, and is encouraged by men. Women suffer from being the "second sex." Finally, feminists insist that they are not interested in instituting new forms of control and domination, but instead are seeking to design a participatory process that empowers women and men alike. At present, many people find it difficult to imagine an alternative to a society based on hierarchy and control, since this is the only sort of society we have known for centuries. Human imagination, courage, commitment, and lots of time will be necessary to bring to fruition the dream of a process-oriented society.

To the extent that some women have been less socialized by the atomistic, dualistic, hierarchical categories that-when employed under patriarchy – appear to be responsible for much ill-treatment of nature and woman, it is plausible to suggest that those women are in a better position than most men to help reconstruct the humanity-nature relation in light of their ongoing sensitivity toward and involvement with their own bodies and the rest of nature. We must be careful, however, not to fall prey to the sex-based stereotyping that has been so crucial to maintaining patriarchy. Men and women are both capable of becoming more open to and at harmony with the natural world. Deep ecologists and eco-feminists need to unite in reconstructing Western humanity's current attitudes toward nature.

Conclusion

It will be a long time before the majority of people are centered, integrated, and capable of profound relationships with other people and the rest of the natural world. Patriarchalism, androcentrism, and anthropocentrism will die hard. In the meantime, we are making use of norms and following cultural practices that threaten the future of life on Earth. Hence, "reform environmentalism" must be promoted at the same time that evolutionary changes in consciousness go forward. And we must make use of the available moral doctrines, including human rights, to protect people from being exploited in this currently competitive world, even as we are in the process of developing nonpatriarchal categories. Respecting the worth of every human being – female and male – is a crucial stage in the development of respect for the worth of nonhuman beings. Thus, feminism and deep ecology are consistent with those programs aimed at transforming human life, since only such transformation can lead to a renewal of the humanity-nature relationship.

When we realize that philosophers are highly aware people, and that even they have a difficult time in discovering the prejudices at work in their most basic concepts, we may despair about the possibility of a cultural transformation of the sort necessary both to spare the Earth and humankind from environmental disaster. Presently, most philosophers take environmental ethics even less seriously than they take feminism. Feminism at least has the advantage of concerning itself with human beings, while environmental philosophy asks people to take seriously the possibility that humans have moral obligations toward *merely natural things!* Yet eco-feminism and deep ecology insist that human beings are not radically separate from nature; that the fulfillment of our own humanity is profoundly linked with learning to appreciate the nature within us and without. In light of such appreciation, we might make use of the idea that nature has "rights," so long as we do not speak of rights in the technical sense used by moral philosophers, but instead in a general way to suggest that all things have intrinsic worth that we are called on to respect. Currently, however, the prospects are not bright that humanity will quickly move toward an appreciation of the humanity-nature relation that is consistent with eco-feminism. Indeed, it can be argued that until human beings learn to respect each other, until the "rights of humanity" become widespread, there is not much chance that human beings will learn to respect nonhuman reality in a way that tempers the human domination of nature.

If highly educated, self-conscious, self-critical philosophers have difficulty in discovering their negative attitudes toward woman and nature, does this mean that less educated women and men will have an even more difficult time? Or do patriarchal-anthropocentric modes of thought become even more deeply entrenched in the process of education? Are we foolish in expecting *philosophers* to wake up? Are people who are supposedly less well educated more open to alternative modes of thinking and experiencing than those who are the academically trained? But isn't almost everyone "educated" into the dominant paradigm? Is education not simply another social vehicle – along with industry, hospitals, asylums, police academies, military training camps, television, radio, and so on – responsible for inculcating women and men alike in the prevailing patriarchal paradigm? When we consider how entrenched these mind- and body-shaping social institutions are, we may despair about the possibility of a real shift in human existence.

Nevertheless, we may take hope from the global awakening of the quest for the feminine voice that can temper the one-sidedness of the masculine voice. If humans are in fact an inseparable ingredient in the matrix of life on Earth, could it be that the Earth is at work in us now, awakening us to the dangers created by our one-sided thinking? We cannot know what the results of this awakening might be, nor can we currently specify precisely the kinds of categories that emerge as consciousness moves beyond its patriarchal phase into a new, more fully encompassing human phase. Trying to imagine a different kind of humanity-nature relationship, one that goes beyond merely prudential concerns about destroying the biosphere, is very difficult for those of us whose understanding of "mankind" and nature are so fixed by the prevailing masculinist categories. It is possible, however, that the dualistic, hierarchical, atomistic, and abstract epistemology, metaphysics, and ethics that have led to the present exploitation of nature, of woman, and of humanity in general may be tempered by nondualistic, communitarian, relational, and particularized categories that make possible a more appropriate mode of dwelling on Earth. If and when that time arises, the very field called "environmental ethics" will presumably have long since disappeared.

Notes

1. Thomas Hobbes, *Leviathan.* Introduction, in Edwin A. Burtt, ed., *The English Philosophers from Bacon to Mill* (New York: Modern Library), p. 130.

2. Friedrich Nietzsche, *The Will to Power* trans. Walter Kaufmann and R. J. Hollingdale (New York: Vintage Books, 1968), p. 305, secs. 565 and 567.

3. Rosemary Radford Reuther, *New Woman, New Earth: Sexist Ideologies and Human Liberation* (New York: Seabury Press, 1975), p. 195.

4. Examples of such efforts include Christopher D. Stone, *Should Trees Have Standing? Toward Legal Rights for Natural Objects* (Los Altos: William Kaufmann, 1974); Peter Singer, *Animal Liberation* (New York: New York Review, 1975); Joel Feinberg, "The Rights of Animals and Unborn Generations," in *Philosophy and Environmental Crisis,* ed. William T. Blackstone (Athens: University of Georgia Press, 1974).

5. Some important works on deep ecology include: Arne Naess, "The Shallow and the Deep, Long Range Ecology Movement," *Inquiry* 16 (1973): 95-100; Arne Naess, "The Arrogance of Anti-humanism?" *Ecophilosophy* 6 (1984); Naess, "Identification as a Source of Deep Ecological Attitudes," in *Deep Ecology,* ed. Michael Tobias (San Diego: Avant Books, 1984); George Sessions, "Shallow and Deep Ecology: A Review of the Philosophical Literature," in *Ecological Consciousness: Essays from* the *Earthday X Colloquium,* ed. Robert C. Schultz and J. Donald Hughes (Washington, D.C.: University Press of America, 1981); Sessions, "Ecological Consciousness and Paradigm Change," in *Deep Ecology;* William B. Devall, "The Deep Ecology Movement," *Natural Resources Journal* 20 (1980): 299-322; Bill Devall and George Sessions, *Deep Ecology: Living as If Nature Mattered* (Salt Lake City: Peregrine Smith Books, 1985); Warwick Fox, "Deep Ecology: Toward a New Philosophy for our Time?" *The Ecologist* 14 (1984): 194-204; Alan Drengson, *Shifting Paradigms: From Technocrat to Planetary Person* (Victoria, B.C.: LightStar Press, 1983); Michael E. Zimmerman, "Toward a Heideggerean *Ethos* for Radical Environmentalism," *Environmental Ethics* 5 (1983): 99-131; Murray Bookchin, *The Ecology of Freedom: The Emergence and Dissolution of Hierarchy* (Palo Alto: Cheshire Books, 1982). Fritjof Capra and Charlene Spretnak, in *The Green Movement: The Global Promise* (New York: Dutton, 1984), provide a synthesis of deep ecology and radical feminism which can be called eco-feminism. In his book, *The Turning Point: Science. Society, and the Rising Culture* (New York: Bantam Books, 1982), Fritjof Capra argues that the decline of patriarchy is one of the three crucial changes that will usher in a new era of improved relations between humanity and the natural world.

6. For bibliographical help on the woman-nature relationship, cf. Jane Yett, "Women and their Environment: A Bibliography for Research and Teaching," *Environmental Review* 8 (1984): 86-94. Significant contributions to the literature include: Marti Kheel, "The Liberation of Nature: A Circular Affair," *Environmental Ethics* 7 (1985): 135-149; Ynestra King. "Toward an Ecological Feminism and a Feminist Ecology," in Joan Rothschild, ed., *Machina Ex Dea: Feminist Perspectives on Technology* (New York: Pergamon Press, 1983); Carolyn Merchant, *The Death of Nature: Women, Ecology and the Scientific Revolution* (New York: Harper & Row, 1980); Annette Kolodny, *The Lay of the Land: Metaphor as History in American Life and Letters* (Chapel Hill: University of North Carolina Press, 1975); Kolodny, *The Land Before Her* (Chapel Hill: University of North Carolina Press, 1983); Brian Easlea, *Science and Sexual Oppression: Patriarchy's Confrontation with Woman and Nature* (London: Weidenfeld and Nicholson, 1981); Elizabeth Dodson Gray, *Green Paradise Lost* (Wellesley, Mass.: Roundtable Press, 1979).

7. Ariel Kay Salleh, "Deeper than Deep Ecology: The Eco-Feminist Connection," *Environmental Ethics* 6 (1984): 339-45.

8. In *Feminist Politics and Human Nature* (Totowa, N.J.: Rowman & Allanheld, 1983), Alison M. Jaggar provides an insightful account of four major schools of feminism: liberal, traditional Marxist, radical, and socialist. Jaggar favors the Marxist approach. Radical feminists maintain that socialist, Marxist, and liberal feminists make use of masculinist political ideologies. A change of

class structure, or the extension of rights to women, cannot solve the problems created by patriarchal consciousness. Other very helpful analyses of the history of modern feminism can be found in Hester Eisenstein, *Contemporary Feminist Thought* (Boston: G. K. Hall & Co., 1983): and Hester Eisenstein and Alice Jardine, eds., *The Future of Difference* (New Brunswick: Rutgers University Press, 1985).

9. Virginia Held, "Feminism and Epistemology: Recent Work on the connection between Gender and Knowledge," *Philosophy and Public Affairs* 14 (1985): 296-307. For a thoughtful critical discussion of the radical feminist critique of masculinist epistemology, cf. Lorraine B. Code, Is the Sex of the Knower Epistemologically Significant?" *Metaphilosophy* 12 (1981): 267-76.

10. Marilyn French, *Beyond Power: Women, Men, and Morality* (New York: Summit Books, 1985). According to Ellen Messer-Davidow (personal communication), "Feminist anthropologists point out that some peoples do not align male/female and culture/nature, a construct of the Enlightenment . . ., but use generations, language proficiency, or residence (clearing and bush) as constructs to organize their cultures." The male/female, culture/language relationship, then, is apparently not as universal as French seems to think. For an insightful treatment, from a male perspective, of the love-hate relation men have with women, cf. Wolfgang Lederer, *The Fear of Women* (New York: Harcourt, Brace Jovanovich, 1968).

11. French, *Beyond Power,* p. 341.

12. On the patriarchal attitude toward nature, cf. Sherry B. Ortner, "Is Female to Male as Nature is to Culture," in Michelle Rosaldo and Louise Lamphere, eds., *Woman, Culture, and Society* (Stanford: Stanford University Press, 1974); and Joan Bamberger, "The Myth of Matriarchy: Why Men Rule in Primitive Society," in *Woman, Culture, and Society.*

13. Carolyn Merchant, *The Death of Nature,* p. 2. Cf. also Brian Easlea. *Witch-Hunting, Magic and the New Philosophy* (Atlantic Highlands, N.J.: Humanities Press, 1980): and Mary Daly, *Gyn/Ecology* (Boston: Beacon Press, 1978).

14. Cf. Reuther, *New Woman, New Earth;* also cf. Ken Wilber, *The Atman Project* (Wheaton, Ill.: Quest Books, 1980); Wilber, *Up From Eden: A Transpersonal View of Evolution* (Boulder, Colo.: Shambhala, 1981).

15. Cf. Michael E. Zimmerman, "Humanism, Ontology, and the Nuclear Arms Race," *Research in Philosophy and Technology* 6 (1983): 151-72; Zimmerman, "Anthropocentric Humanism and the Arms Race," *Nuclear War: Philosophical Perspectives,* ed. Michael Fox and Leo Groarke (New York: Peter Lang Publishers, 1985).

16. Reuther, *New Woman, New Earth,* pp. 154 ff.

17. The pioneering essay criticizing the environmental consequences of the Judaeo-Christian tradition is Lynn White, Jr., "The Historical Roots of our Ecologic Crisis," *Science* 155 (1967): 1203-07. Cf. also David Crownfield, "The Curse of Abel," *North American Review,* Summer, 1973, pp. 58-63. Cf. Mary Daly's famous feminist critique of patriarchal Christianity, *Beyond God the Father* (Boston: Beacon Press, 1973); also Reuther, *New Woman, New Earth.* In defense of the Judaeo-Christian tradition, cf. Loren Wilkinson,

Earthkeeping: Christian Stewardship of Natural Resources (Grand Rapids: Eerdman's, 1980); Wesley Granberg-Michaelson, *A Worldly Spirituality: The Call to Redeem the Earth* (New York: Harper & Row, 1985). Cf. also the work done by Vincent Rossi and his colleagues of The Eleventh Commandment Fellowship, P.O. Box 14606, San Francisco, CA 94114. The "eleventh commandment" reads: "The Earth is the Lord's and the Fullness thereof: Thou shalt not despoil the Earth, nor destroy the Life thereon."

18. Cf. William Leiss, *The Domination of Nature* (Boston: Beacon Press, 1972).

19. Concerning the idea that modern technology shapes both human body and mind to its purposes, cf. the work of members of the Frankfurt Critical School, such as Max Horkheimer, Theodor Adorno, and Herbert Marcuse; more recently, cf. the work of Michel Foucault; also cf. David Michael Levin, "The Body Politic: Political Economy and the Human Body," *Human Studies* 8 (1985): 235-78.

20. Kheel, "The Liberation of Nature," pp. 143-44.

21. Cf. Thomas Kuhn, *The Structure of Scientific Revolutions* (Chicago: University of Chicago Press, 1970).

22. For a review of criticisms of natural rights, cf. Michael E. Zimmerman, "The Crisis of Natural Rights and the Search for a Non-Anthropocentric Basis for Moral Behavior," *The Journal of Value Inquiry* 19 (1985): 43-53. Notable critiques include: Alasdair McIntyre, *After Virtue* (Notre Dame: University of Notre Dame Press, 1981); Charles Taylor, "Atomism," in his *Philosophy and the Human Sciences, Philosophical Perspectives,* vol. 2 (Cambridge: Cambridge University Press, 1985); H. J. McCloskey, "Rights," *Philosophical Quarterly,* 15 (1966): 115-27; H. J. McCloskey, "Moral Rights and Animals," *Inquiry* 22 (1979): 23-25. Cf. also Tom Regan's critical response to McCloskey, "McCloskey on Why Animals Cannot Have Rights," *Philosophical Quarterly* 26 (1976): 251-57. And cf. my essay, "The Crisis of Natural Rights" and Joel Feinberg, "The Rights of Animals and Unborn Generations," *Philosophy and Environmental Crisis,* ed. William T. Blackstone (Athens: The University of Georgia Press, 1974), pp. 43-68. Also cf. Kenneth. E. Goodpaster, "On Being Morally Considerable," *Journal of Philosophy* 75 (1978): 308-25. Goodpaster maintains that Feinberg mistakenly restricts rights to individual animals, and insists that entire bioregions can be said to have an interest of their own, too. Cf. also Christopher D. Stone, *Should Trees Have Standing? Toward Legal Rights for Natural Objects* (Los Altos, California: William Kaufmann, 1974), along with John Rodman's critique of Stone in John Rodman's incisive essay, "The Liberation of Nature?" *Inquiry* 20 (1977): 83-131. For a critique of the "natural rights" approach to environmental ethics, cf. J. Baird Callicott's review of Tom Regan, *The Case for Animal Rights, Environmental Ethics* 7 (1985): 365-72. Finally, cf. Kenneth E. Goodpaster, "From Egoism to Environmentalism," in *Ethics and the Problems of the 21st Century,* ed. Kenneth E. Goodpaster and K. M. Sayre (Notre Dame: Notre Dame University Press).

23. John Locke, *An Essay Concerning the True Original, Extent and End of Civil Government,* in Burtt, *The English Philosophers from Hobbes to Mill,* pp. 419-420: "For it is labor indeed that puts the difference of value on every-

thing. . . . Nature and the earth furnished only the almost worthless materials as in themselves." Cf. Lorenne M. G. Clark, "Women and Locke: Who Owns the Apples in the Garden of Eden?" in *The Sexism of Social and Political Theory: Women and Reproduction from Plato to Nietzsche,* ed. Lorenne M. G. Clark and Lynda Lange (Toronto: The University of Toronto Press, 1979). Ellen Messer-Davidow (personal communication) has argued that "Locke is not guilty of dualism . . . because he does not divide beings into two categories. Instead of only humans and animals or only males and females, he recognizes several categories: animals, women, men, children, various socioeconomic classes, and people who do not have full use of their faculties (his terms: idiots, etc.). In other words, . . . Locke does not construct living beings in rigid dichotomies. He distinguishes not two but several categories."

24. On the Marxist treatment of nature, cf. Michael E. Zimmerman, "Marx and Heidegger on the Technological Domination of Nature," *Philosophy Today* 23 (1979): 99-112; Kostas Axelos, *Alienation, Praxis, and Techne in the thought of Karl Marx,* trans. Ronald Bruzina (Austin: University of Texas Press, 1976); Alfred Schmidt, *The Concept of Nature in Marx,* trans. Ben Fowkes (London: New Left Books, 1971); Albrecht Wellmer, *The Critical Theory of Society,* trans. John Cumming (New York: Herder & Herder, 1971).

25. Naomi Scheman, "Individualism and the Objects of Psychology," in *Discovering Reality: Feminist Perspectives on Epistemology, Metaphysics, Methodology, and Philosophy of Science,* ed. Sandra Harding and Merrill Hintikka (Boston: D. Reidel Publishing Company, 1983), p. 234.

26. Cf. Ruth Hubbard, "Have Only Men Evolved?" in *Discovering Reality.* For a nonfeminist criticism of the circularity of Darwin's reasoning about "natural" competition, cf. Jeremy Rifkin, *Algeny* (New York: Penguin Books, 1984).

27. Michael Gross and Mary Beth Averill, "Evolution and Patriarchal Myths of Scarcity and Competition," *Discovering Reality,* p. 72. Cf. Jane Flax, "Political Philosophy and the Patriarchal Unconscious," in *Discovering Reality,* for an insightful account of how Hobbes' competitive view of human nature is rooted in a masculinist philosophical anthropology.

28. On the antagonism between family and society, personal and public relationships, cf. Carole Pateman, "'The Disorder of Women': Women, Love, and the Sense of Justice," *Ethics* 90 (1980): 20-34.

29. Naomi Scheman, "Individualism and the Objects of Psychology," in *Discovering Reality.*

30. On object-relations theory, cf. Nancy Chodorow, *The Reproduction of Mothering* (Berkeley: University of California Press, 1978); Chodorow, "Family Structure and the Feminine Personality," in *Woman, Culture, and Society;* Dorothy Dinnerstein, *The Mermaid and the Minotaur: Sexual Arrangements and the Human Malaise* (New York: Harper & Row, 1976); Flax, "Political Philosophy and the Political Unconscious." For a critical exchange on object-relations theory, cf. Judith Lorber, Rose Laub Coser, Alice S. Rossi, and Nancy Chodorow, "On *The Reproduction of Mothering:* A Methodological Debate," *Signs* 6 (1981): 482-514.

31. Carol Gilligan, *In a Different Voice: Psychological Theory and Women's Development* (Cambridge: Harvard University Press, 1982). For an appraisal of the moral development approach to ethical issues, cf. the essays in the special issue of *Ethics,* vol. 92 (April 1982).

32. Cf. John Rodman, "Animal Justice: The Counter-Revolution in Natural Right and Law," *Inquiry* 22 (1979): 3-22.

33. Cf. John P. Briggs and F. David Peat, *Looking Glass Universe: The Emerging Science of Wholeness* (New York: Simon and Schuster, 1984); Nick Herbert, *Quantum Reality: Beyond the New Physics* (Garden City, N.Y.: Anchor/Doubleday, 1985); John Briggin, *In Search of Shroedinger's Cat: Quantum Physics and Reality* (New York: Bantam Books, 1984); Paul Davies, *Other Worlds: Space, Superspace and the Quantum Universe* (New York: Simon and Schuster, 1980); Fritjof Capra, *The Tao of Physics* (New York: Bantam Books, 1982); Roger S. Jones, *Physics as Metaphor* (New York: New American Library, 1982); Charles Birch and John B. Cobb, Jr., *The Liberation of Life* (Cambridge: Cambridge University Press, 1981). For a feminist approach to the new physics, cf. Robin Morgan, *The Anatomy of Freedom: Feminism, Physics, and Global Politics* (Garden City, N.Y.: Anchor/Doubleday, 1982), especially the chapter called "The New Physics of Meta-Politics," and Marti Kheel, "The Liberation of Nature: A Circular Affair." For a deep ecological approach to the new physics, cf. J. Baird Callicott, "Intrinsic Value, Quantum Theory, and Environmental Ethics," *Environmental Ethics* 7 (1985): 257-75.

34. Cf. A. R. Peacocke, *Creation and the World of Science* (Oxford: Oxford University Press, 1979).

35. On the importance of feeling as a mode of disclosure in such realms as physical science, cf. Evelyn Fox Keller, *A Feeling for the Organism: The Life and Work of Barbra McClintock* (New York: W. H. Freeman and Company, 1983); *Reflections on Gender and Science* (New Haven: Yale University Press, 1985); "Feminism and Science," in *The Signs Reader: Women, Gender, and Scholarship,* ed. Elizabeth Abel and Emily K. Abel (Chicago: University of Chicago Press, 1983); "Gender and Science," *Discovering Reality;* "Women, Science, and Popular Mythology," *Dea Ex Machina.*

36. There have been male philosophers who have emphasized the importance of feeling and sentiment in moral theory. David Hume is the most important example. Concerning the value of Hume's thought for environmental ethics, cf. J. Baird Callicott, "Elements of an Environmental Ethic," *Environmental Ethics* I (1979): 71-81; Callicott, "Hume's Is/Ought Dichotomy and the Relation of Ecology of Leopold's Land Ethic," *Environmental Ethics* 4 (1982): 163-74.

37. On this shift in the feminist movement, cf. Eisenstein, *Contemporary Feminist Thought,* and Eisenstein and Jardine, eds., *The Future of Difference.*

38. My thanks to Kathryn Carter for conversations that helped to clarify these issues.

39. Carole Pateman, "'The Disorder of Women': Women, Love, and the Sense of Justice," *Ethics* 91 (1980): 33.

40. *Ibid.*

41. Flax, "Political Philosophy and the Patriarchal Unconscious," *Discovering Reality.*

42. Kheel, "The Liberation of Nature," p. 140.

43. Cf. Richard Watson, "A Critique of Anti-Anthropocentric Biocentrism," *Environmental Ethics* 5 (1983): 245-56; "Eco-Ethics: Challenging the Underlying Dogmas of Environmentalism," *Whole Earth Review,* March 1985, pp. 5-13.

44. Warwick Fox has written a brilliant reply to Richard Sylvan's essay, "A Critique of Deep Ecology," *Discussion Papers in Environmental Philosophy,* no. 12, Philosophy Department, RSSS, Australian National University, 1985. Fox's paper, *Approaching Deep Ecology: A Response to Richard Sylvan's Critique of Deep Ecology* (University of Tasmania: Environmental Studies Occasional Paper, no. 20, 1986), shows how Sylvan − like other critics of deep ecology − misrepresents and fails to take seriously the concepts of deep ecology. Cf. also Arne Naess, "A Defense of the Deep Ecology Movement," *Environmental Ethics* 6 (1984): 265-70.

45. Salleh, "Deeper than Deep Ecology." The essays she criticizes are Arne Naess, "The Shallow and the Deep, Long Range Ecology Movement," and Bill Devall, "The Deep Ecology Movement."

46. Salleh, "Deeper than Deep Ecology," p. 344.

47. *Ibid.,* pp. 344-45.

13

The Ecology of Feminism and the Feminism of Ecology

Ynestra King

[Woman] became the embodiment of the biological function, the image of nature, the subjugation of which constituted that civilization's title to fame. For millennia men dreamed of acquiring absolute mastery over nature, of converting the cosmos into one immense hunting ground. It was to this that the idea of man was geared in a male-dominated society. This was the significance of reason, his prouded boast.
– Horkheimer and Adorno, *Dialectic of Enlightenment*[1]

ALL HUMAN BEINGS ARE NATURAL BEINGS. THAT MAY SEEM LIKE AN obvious fact, yet we live in a culture that is founded on the repudiation and domination of nature. This has a special significance for women because, in patriarchal thought, women are believed to be closer to nature than men. This gives women a particular stake in ending the domination of nature – in healing the alienation between human and nonhuman nature. This is also the ultimate goal of the ecology movement, but the ecology movement is not necessarily feminist.

For the most part, ecologists, with their concern for nonhuman nature, have yet to understand that they have a particular stake in ending the domination of women. They do not understand that a central reason for woman's oppression is her association with the despised nature they are so concerned about. The hatred of women and the hatred of nature are intimately connected and mutually reinforcing. Starting with this premise, this article explores why feminism and ecology need each other, and suggests the beginnings of a theory of ecological feminism: ecofeminism.

What Is Ecology?

Ecological science concerns itself with the interrelationships among all forms of life. It aims to harmonize nature, human and nonhuman. It is an integrative science in an age of fragmentation and specialization. It is also a critical science which grounds and necessitates a critique of our existing society. It is a reconstructive science in that it suggests directions for reconstructing human society in harmony with the natural environment.

Social ecologists are asking how we might survive on the planet and develop systems of food and energy production, architecture, and ways of life that will allow human beings to fulfill our material needs and live in harmony with nonhuman nature. This work has led to a social critique by biologists and to an exploration of biology and ecology by social thinkers. The perspective that self-consciously attempts to integrate both biological and social aspects of the relationship between human beings and their environment is known as *social ecology*. This perspective, developed primarily by Murray Bookchin,[2] to whom I am indebted for my understanding of social ecology, has embodied the anarchist critique that links domination and hierarchy in human society to the despoliation of nonhuman nature. While this analysis is useful, social ecology without feminism is incomplete.

Feminism grounds this critique of domination by identifying the prototype of other forms of domination: that of man over woman. Potentially, feminism creates a concrete global community of interests among particularly life-oriented people of the world: women. Feminist analysis supplies the theory, program, and process without which the radical potential of social ecology remains blunted. Ecofeminism develops the connections between ecology and feminism that social ecology needs in order to reach its own avowed goal of creating a free and ecological way of life.

What are these connections? Social ecology challenges the dualistic belief that nature and culture are separate and opposed. Ecofeminism finds misogyny at the root of that opposition. Ecofeminist principles are based on the following beliefs:

1. The building of Western industrial civilization in opposition to nature interacts dialectically with and reinforces the subjugation of women, because women are believed to be closer to nature. Therefore, ecofeminists take on the life-struggles of all of nature as our own.

2. Life on earth is an interconnected web, not a hierarchy. There is no natural hierarchy; human hierarchy is projected onto nature and then used to justify social domination. Therefore, ecofeminist theory seeks to show the connections between all forms of domination, including the domination of nonhuman nature, and ecofeminist practice is necessarily antihierarchical.

3. A healthy, balanced ecosystem, including human and nonhuman inhabitants, must maintain diversity. Ecologically, environmental simplification is as significant a problem as environmental pollution. Biological simplification, i.e., the wiping out of whole spe-

cies, corresponds to reducing human diversity into faceless workers, or to the homogenization of taste and culture through mass
consumer markets. Social life and natural life are literally simplified to the inorganic for the convenience of market society.
Therefore we need a decentralized global movement that is
founded on common interests yet celebrates diversity and opposes
all forms of domination and violence. Potentially, ecofeminism is
such a movement.

4. The survival of the species necessitates a renewed understanding
   of our relationship to nature, of our own bodily nature, and of
   nonhuman nature around us; it necessitates a challenging of the
   nature-culture dualism and a corresponding radical restructuring
   of human society according to feminist and ecological principles.
   Adrienne Rich says, "When we speak of transformation we speak
   more accurately out of the vision of a process which will leave
   neither surfaces nor depths unchanged, which enters society at
   the most essential level of the subjugation of women and nature
   by men. . . . "[3]

The ecology movement, in theory and practice, attempts to speak
for nature – the "other" that has no voice and is not conceived of subjec-
tively in our civilization. Feminism represents the refusal of the original
"other" in patriarchal human society to remain silent or to be the "other"
any longer. Its challenge of social domination extends beyond sex to social domination of all kinds, because the domination of sex, race, and
class and the domination of nature are mutually reinforcing. Women are
the "others" in human society, who have been silent in public and who
now speak through the feminist movement.

Women, Nature and Culture: The Ecofeminist Position

In the project of building Western industrial civilization, nature became something to be dominated, overcome, made to serve the needs of
men. She was stripped of her magical powers and properties and was reduced to "natural resources" to be exploited by human beings to fulfill
human needs and purposes which were defined in opposition to nature
(see Merchant, who interprets the scientific revolution as the death of nature, and argues that it had a particularly detrimental effect on women.)[4]
A dualistic Christianity had become ascendant with the earlier demise of
old goddess religions, paganism, and animistic belief systems.[5] With the
disenchantment of nature came the conditions for unchecked scientific exploration and technological exploitation.[6] We bear the consequences today
of beliefs in unlimited control over nature and in science's ability to
solve any problem, as nuclear power plants are built without provisions

for waste disposal, and satellites are sent into space without provision for retrieval.

In this way, nature became "other," something essentially different from the dominant, to be objectified and subordinated. Women, who are identified with nature, have been similarly objectified and subordinated in patriarchal society. Women and nature, in this sense, are the original "others." Simone de Beauvoir has clarified this connection. For de Beauvoir, "transcendence" is the work of culture, it is the work of men. It is the process of overcoming immanence, a process of culture-building that is based on the increasing domination of nature. It is enterprise. "Immanence," symbolized by women, is that which calls men back, that which reminds man of what he wants to forget. It is his own link to nature that he must forget and overcome to achieve manhood and transcendence:

> Man seeks in woman the Other as Nature and as his fellow being. But we know what ambivalent feelings Nature inspires in man. He exploits her, but she crushes him, he is born of her and dies in her; she is the source of his being and the realm that he subjugates to his will; Nature is a vein of gross material in which the soul is imprisoned, and she is the supreme reality; she is contingence and Idea, the finite and the whole; she is what opposes the Spirit, and the Spirit itself. Now ally, now enemy, she appears as the dark chaos from whence life wells up, as this life itself, and as the over-yonder toward which life tends. Woman sums up Nature as Mother, Wife, and Idea; these forms now mingle and now conflict, and each of them wears a double visage.[7]

For de Beauvoir, patriarchal civilization is about the denial of men's mortality – of which women and nature are incessant reminders. Women's powers of procreation are distinguished from the powers of creation – the accomplishments through the vehicles of culture by which men achieve immortality. And yet this transcendence over women and nature can never be total: thus the ambivalence, the lack of self without other, the dependence of the self on the other both materially and emotionally. Thus develops a love-hate fetishization of women's bodies, which finds its ultimate manifestation in the sadomasochistic, pornographic displays of women as objects to be subdued, humiliated, and raped – the visual enactment of these fears and desires. (See Griffin, *Pornography and Silence,* for a full development of the relationship between nature-hating, women-hating, and pornography.)[8]

An important contribution of de Beauvoir's work is to show that men seek to dominate women and nature for reasons that are not simply economic. They do so as well for psychological reasons that involve a denial of a part of themselves, as do other male culture-making activities. The process begins with beating the tenderness and empathy out of small boys and directing their natural human curiosity and joy in affecting the world around them into arrogant attitudes and destructive paths.

For men raised in woman-hating cultures, the fact that they are born
of women and are dependent upon nonhuman nature for existence is
frightening. The process of objectification, of the making of women and
nature into "others" to be appropriated and dominated, is based on a profound forgetting by men. They forget that they were born of women,
were dependent on women in their early helpless years, and are dependent on nonhuman nature all their lives, which allows first for objectification and then for domination. "The loss of memory is a transcendental
condition for science. All objectification is a forgetting."[9]

But the denied part of men is never fully obliterated. The memory
remains in the knowledge of mortality and the fear of women's power. A
basic fragility of gender identity exists that surfaces when received truths
about women and men are challenged and the sexes depart from their
"natural" roles. Opposition to the not-very-radical Equal Rights Amend-
ment can be partially explained on these grounds. More threatening are
homosexuality and the gay liberation movement, because they name a
more radical truth – that sexual orientation is not indelible, nor is it naturally heterosexual. Lesbianism, particularly, which suggests that women
who possess this repudiated primordial power can be self-sufficient, reminds men that they may not be needed. Men are forced into remembering their own dependence on women to support and mediate the construction of their private reality and their public civilization. Again there is the
need to repress memory and oppress women.

The recognition of the connections between women and nature and
of woman's bridge-like position between nature and culture poses three
possible directions for feminism. One direction is the integration of
women into the world of culture and production by severing the woman-
nature connection. Writes anthropologist Sherry Ortner, "Ultimately, both
men and women can and must be equally involved in projects of creativity and transcendence. Only then will women be seen as aligned with culture, in culture's ongoing dialectic with nature."[10] This position does not
question nature-culture dualism itself, and it is the position taken by most
socialist-feminists (see King, "Feminism and the Revolt of Nature")[11]
and by de Beauvoir and Ortner, despite their insights into the connections
between women and nature. They see the severance of the woman-nature
connection as a condition of women's liberation.

Other feminists have reinforced the woman-nature connection:
woman and nature, the spiritual and intuitive, versus man and the culture
of patriarchal rationality.[12] This position also does not necessarily question nature-culture dualism or recognize that women's ecological sensitivity and life orientation is a socialized perspective that could be socialized
right out of us depending on our day-to-day lives. There is no reason to
believe that women placed in positions of patriarchal power will act any
differently from men, or that we can bring about a feminist revolution

without consciously understanding history and without confronting the existing economic and political power structures.

Ecofeminism suggests a third direction: a recognition that although the nature-culture dualism is a product of culture, we can nonetheless *consciously choose* not to sever the woman-nature connection by joining male culture. Rather, we can use it as a vantage point for creating a different kind of culture and politics that would integrate intuitive, spiritual, and rational forms of knowledge, embracing both science and magic insofar as they enable us to transform the nature-culture distinction and to envision and create a free, ecological society.

Ecofeminism and the Intersection of Feminism and Ecology

The implications of a culture based on the devaluation of life-giving and the celebration of life-taking are profound for ecology and for women. This fact about our culture links the theories and politics of the ecology movement with those of the feminist movement. Adrienne Rich has written:

> We have been perceived for too many centuries as pure Nature, exploited and raped like the earth and the solar system; small wonder if we now long to become Culture: pure spirit, mind. Yet it is precisely this culture and its political institutions which have split us off from itself. In so doing it has also split itself off from life, becoming the death culture of quantification, abstraction, and the will to power which has reached its most refined destructiveness in this century. It is this culture and politics of abstraction which women are talking of changing, of bringing into accountability in human terms.[13]

The way to ground a feminist critique of "this culture and politics of abstraction" is with a self-conscious ecological perspective that we apply to all theories and strategies, in the way that we are learning to apply race and class factors to every phase of feminist analysis.

Similarly, ecology requires a feminist perspective. Without a thorough feminist analysis of social domination that reveals the interconnected roots of misogyny and hatred of nature, ecology remains an abstraction: it is incomplete. If male ecological scientists and social ecologists fail to deal with misogyny – the deepest manifestation of nature-hating in their own lives – they are not living the ecological lives or creating the ecological society they claim.

The goals of harmonizing humanity and nonhuman nature, at both the experiential and theoretical levels, cannot be attained without the radical vision and understanding available from feminism. The twin concerns of ecofeminism – human liberation and our relationship to nonhuman nature – open the way to developing a set of ethics required for decision-

making about technology. Technology signifies the tools that human beings use to interact with nature, including everything from the digging
stick to nuclear bombs.

Ecofeminism also contributes an understanding of the connections
between the domination of persons and the domination of nonhuman nature. Ecological science tells us that there is no hierarchy in nature itself,
but rather a hierarchy in human society that is projected onto nature.
Ecofeminism draws on feminist theory which asserts that the domination
of woman was the original domination in human society, from which all
other hierarchies – of rank, class, and political power – flow. Building on
this unmasking of the ideology of a natural hierarchy of persons,
ecofeminism uses its ecological perspective to develop the position that
there is no hierarchy in nature: among persons, between persons and the
rest of the natural world, or among the many forms of nonhuman nature.
We live on the earth with millions of species, only one of which is the
human species. Yet the human species in its patriarchal form is the only
species which holds a conscious belief that it is entitled to dominion over
the other species, and over the planet. Paradoxically, the human species is
utterly dependent on nonhuman nature. We could not live without the rest
of nature; it *could* live without us.

Ecofeminism draws on another basic principle of ecological science
– unity in diversity – and develops it politically. Diversity in nature is
necessary, and enriching. One of the major effects of industrial technology, capitalist or socialist, is environmental simplification. Many species
are simply being wiped out, never to be seen on the earth again. In human society, commodity capitalism is intentionally simplifying human
community and culture so that the same products can be marketed anywhere to anyone. The prospect is for all of us to be alike, with identical
needs and desires, around the globe: Coca Cola in China, blue jeans in
Russia, and American rock music virtually everywhere.

Few peoples of the earth have not had their lives touched and
changed to some degree by the technology of industrialization.
Ecofeminism as a social movement resists this social simplification
through supporting the rich diversity of women the world over, and seeking a oneness in that diversity. Politically, ecofeminism opposes the ways
that differences can separate women from each other, through the oppressions of class, privilege, sexuality, and race.

The special message of ecofeminism is that when women suffer
through both social domination and the domination of nature, most of life
on this planet suffers and is threatened as well. It is significant that feminism and ecology as social movements have emerged now, as nature's revolt against domination plays itself out in human history and in nonhuman nature at the same time. As we face slow environmental poisoning
and the resulting environmental simplification, or the possible unleashing

of our nuclear arsenals, we can hope that the prospect of the extinction of life on the planet will provide a universal impetus to social change. Ecofeminism supports utopian visions of harmonious, diverse, decentralized communities, using only those technologies based on ecological principles, as the only practical solution for the continuation of life on earth.

Visions and politics are joined as an ecofeminist culture and politics begin to emerge. Ecofeminists are taking direct action to effect changes that are immediate and personal as well as long-term and structural. Direct actions include learning holistic health and alternate ecological technologies, living in communities that explore old and new forms of spirituality which celebrate all life as diverse expressions of nature, considering the ecological consequences of our lifestyles and personal habits, and participating in creative public forms of resistance, including nonviolent civil disobedience.

Toward an Ecofeminist Praxis: Feminist Antimilitarism

Theory never converts simply or easily into practice: in fact, theory often lags behind practice, attempting to articulate the understanding behind things people are already doing. *Praxis* is the unity of thought and action, or theory and practice. Many of the women who founded the feminist antimilitarist movement in Europe and the United States share the ecofeminist perspective I have articulated. I believe that the movement as I will briefly describe it here grows out of such an understanding. For the last three years I have been personally involved in the ecofeminist antimilitarist movement, so the following is a firsthand account of one example of our praxis.

The connections between violence against women, a militarized culture, and the development and deployment of nuclear weapons have long been evident to pacifist feminists.[14] Ecofeminists like myself, whose concerns with all of life stem from an understanding of the connections between misogyny and the destruction of nature, began to see militarism and the death-courting weapons industry as the most immediate threat to continued life on the planet, while the ecological effects of other modern technologies pose a more long-term threat. In this manner militarism has become a central issue for most ecofeminists. Along with this development, many of us accepted the analysis of violence made by pacifist feminists and, therefore, began to see nonviolent direct action and resistance as the basis of our political practice.

The ecofeminist analysis of militarism is concerned with the militarization of culture and the economic priorities reflected by our enormous "defense" budgets and dwindling social services budgets. The level of weaponry and the militaristic economic priorities are products of patriarchal culture that speak violence at every level. Our freedom and our lives are threatened, even if there is no war and none of the nuclear weapons are ever used. We have tried to make clear the particular ways that women suffer from war-making – as spoils to victorious armies, as refugees, as disabled and older women and single mothers who are dependent on dwindling social services. We connect the fear of nuclear annihilation with women's fear of male violence in our everyday lives.

For ecofeminists, military technology reflects a pervasive cultural and political situation. It is connected with rape, genocide, and imperialism, with starvation and homelessness, with the poisoning of the environment, and with the fearful lives of the world's peoples – especially those of women. Military and state power hierarchies join and reinforce each other through military technology. Particularly as shaped by ecofeminism, the feminist anti-militarist movement in the United States and Europe is a movement against a monstrously destructive technology and set of power relationships embodied in militarism.

Actions have been organized at the Pentagon in the United States and at military installations in Europe. The Women's Pentagon Action, originally conceived at an ecofeminist conference which I and others organized, has taken place at the Pentagon twice so far, on November 16 and 17, 1980, and November 15 and 16, 1981. It included about two thousand women the first year, and more than twice that the second. I took part in planning both actions and we took care to make the actions reflect *all* aspects of our politics. Intentionally there were no speakers, no leaders; the action sought to emphasize the connections between the military issue and other ecofeminist issues.

The themes of the Women's Pentagon Action have carried over into other actions our group has participated in, including those organized by others. At the June 12-14, 1982 disarmament demonstrations in New York City, the group's march contingent proclaimed the theme: "A feminist world is a nuclear free zone," the slogan hanging beneath a huge globe held aloft. Other banners told of visions for a feminist future, and members wore bibs that read "War is man-made," "Stop the violence in our lives," and "Disarm the patriarchy." There have been similar actions, drawing inspiration from the original Women's Pentagon Actions, elsewhere in the United States and in Europe. In California, the Bohemian Club, a male-only playground for corporate, government, and military elite, was the site of a demonstration by women who surrounded the club, enacting a life-affirming protest ritual (see Starhawk).[15] In England on December 12, 1982, thirty thousand women surrounded a US military installation, weaving into the fence baby clothes, scarves, poems and other personal-life symbols. At one point, spontaneously, the word *freedom* rose from the lips of the women and was heard round and round the base.

Three thousand women nonviolently blocked the entrances to the base on December 13 (see Fisher).[16]

The politics being created by these actions draw on women's culture: embodying what is best in women's life-oriented socialization, building on women's difference, organizing antihierarchically in small groups in visually and emotionally imaginative ways, and seeking an integration of issues.

These actions exemplify ecofeminism. While technocratic experts (including feminists) argue the merits and demerits of weapons systems, ecofeminism approaches the disarmament issues on an intimate and moral level. Ecofeminism holds that a personalized, decentralized life-affirming culture and politics of direct action are crucially needed to stop the arms race and transform the world's priorities. Because such weaponry does not exist apart from a contempt for women and all of nature, the issue of disarmament and threat of nuclear war is a feminist issue. It is the ultimate human issue, and the ultimate ecological issue. And so ecology, feminism, and liberation for all of nature, including ourselves, are joined.

Notes

1. Max Horkheimer and Theodor W. Adorno, *Dialectic of Enlightenment*, Seabury Press, New York, 1972, p. 248.

2. Murray Bookchin, *The Ecology of Freedom: The Emergence and Dissolution of Hierarchy*, Cheshire Books, Palo Alto, 1982.

3. Adrienne Rich, *On Lies, Secrets, and Silence*, W. W. Norton, New York, 1979, p. 248.

4. Carolyn Merchant, *The Death of Nature: Women, Ecology, and the Scientific Revolution*, Harper & Row, New York, 1980.

5. Rosemary Radford Reuther, *New Woman/New Earth: Sexist Ideologies and Human Liberation*, Seabury Press, New York, 1975.

6. Merchant, *op.cit.*

7. Simone de Beauvoir, *The Second Sex*, Modern Library, Random House, New York, 1968, p. 144.

8. Susan Griffin, *Pornography and Silence: "Culture's" Revenge against Nature*, Harper & Row, New York, 1981.

9. Horkheimer, *op.cit.*, p. 230.

10. Sherry B. Ortner, "Is Female to Male as Nature is to Culture?" *Woman, Culture and Society*, Michele Zimbalist Rosaldo and Louis Lamphere, eds., Stanford University Press, Stanford, 1974, p. 87.

11. Ynestra King, "Feminism and The Revolt of Nature," *Heresies* 13: 12-16, Fall 1981.

12. Many such feminists call themselves ecofeminists. Some of them cite Susan Griffin's *Woman and Nature* (Harper & Row, San Francisco, 1978) as the source of their understanding of the deep connections between women and na-

ture, and their politics. *Woman and Nature* is an inspirational poetic work with political implications. It explores the terrain of our deepest naturalness, but I do not read it as a delineation of a set of politics. To use Griffin's work in this way is to make it into something it was not intended to be. In personal conversation and in her more politically explicit works such as *Pornography and Silence* (1981), Griffin is antidualistic, struggling to bridge the false oppositions of nature and culture, passion and reason. Both science and poetry are deeply intuitive processes. Another work often cited by ecofeminists is Mary Daly's *Gyn/ecology* (1978). Daly, a theologian/philosopher, is also an inspirational thinker, but she is a genuinely dualistic thinker, reversing the "truths" of patriarchal theology. While I have learned a great deal from Daly, my perspective differs from hers in that I believe that any truly ecological politics, including ecological feminism, must be ultimately antidualistic.

13. Adrienne Rich, *Of Woman Born,* W.W. Norton, New York, 1976, p. 285.

14. Barbara Deming, *We Cannot Live Without Our Lives,* Grossman, New York, 1974.

15. Starhawk, *Dreaming the Dark: Magic, Sex and Politics,* Beacon Press, Boston, 1982, p. 168.

16. Berenice Fisher, "Women Ignite English Movement," *Womanews,* Feb. 1983.

Other Sources

Daly, Mary. *Gyn/ecology: The Metaethics of Radical Feminism.* Boston: Beacon Press, 1978.

Griffin, Susan. *Woman and Nature.* New York: Harper & Row, 1978.

King, Ynestra. "All is Connectedness: Scenes from the Women's Pentagon Action USA." In *Keeping the Peace: A Women's Peace Handbook,* Lynne Johnes, ed., London: The Women's Press, 1983.

14

Development, Ecology, and Women

Vandana Shiva

Development As a New Project of Western Patriarchy

"Development" was to have been a postcolonial project, a choice for accepting a model of progress in which the entire world remade itself on the model of the colonizing modern West, without having to undergo the subjugation and exploitation that colonialism entailed. The assumption was that western style progress was possible for all. Development, as the improved well-being of all, was thus equated with the westernization of economic categories – of needs, of productivity, of growth. Concepts and categories about economic development and natural resource utilization that had emerged in the specific context of industrialization and capitalist growth in a center of colonial power were raised to the level of universal assumptions and applicability in the entirely different context of basic needs satisfaction for the people of the newly independent Third World countries.

Yet, as Rosa Luxemberg has pointed out, early industrial development in western Europe necessitated the permanent occupation of the colonies by the colonial powers and the destruction of the local "natural economy."[1] According to her, colonialism is a constant necessary condition for capitalist growth: without colonies, capital accumulation would grind to a halt. "Development" – as capital accumulation and the commercialization of the economy for the generation of "surplus" and profits – thus involved the reproduction not merely of a particular form of creation of wealth, but also of the associated creation of poverty and dispossession. A replication of economic development based on commercialization of resource use for commodity production in the newly independent countries created the internal colonies.[2]

Development was thus reduced to a continuation of the process of colonization. It became an extension of the project of wealth creation in modern western patriarchy's economic vision, which was based on the exploitation or exclusion of women (of the West and non-West), on the exploitation and degradation of nature, and on the exploitation and erosion of other cultures. "Development" could not but entail destruction for women, nature, and subjugated cultures, which is why, throughout the

161

Third World, women, peasants, and tribals are struggling for liberation from "development" just as they earlier struggled for liberation from colonialism.

The United Nations Decade for Women (1975-1985) was based on the assumption that the improvement of women's economic position would automatically flow from an expansion and diffusion of the development process. Yet, by the end of the Decade, it was becoming clear that development itself was the problem. Insufficient and inadequate "participation" in "development" was not the cause of women's increasing underdevelopment. It was, rather, their enforced but asymmetric participation in it, by which they bore the costs but were excluded from the benefits, that was responsible. Development exclusivity and dispossession aggravated and deepened the colonial processes of ecological degradation and the loss of political control over nature's sustenance base. Economic growth was a new colonialism, draining resources away from those who needed them most. The discontinuity lay in the fact that it was now new national elites, not colonial powers, that masterminded the exploitation on grounds of "national interest" and growing GNPs, and it was accomplished with more powerful technologies of appropriation and destruction.

Ester Boserup[3] has documented how women's impoverishment increased during colonial rule, pointing out those rulers who spent centuries subjugating and crippling their own women into de-skilled, de-intellectualized appendages, disfavored the women of the colonies on matters of access to land, technology, and employment. The economic and political processes of colonial underdevelopment bore the clear mark of modern western patriarchy, and while large numbers of women and men were impoverished by these processes, women tended to lose more. The privatization of land for revenue generation displaced women more critically, eroding their traditional land-use rights. The expansion of cash crops undermined food production, and women were often left with meager resources to feed and care for children, the aged, and the infirm, when men migrated or were conscripted into forced labor by the colonizers. As a collective document by women activists, organizers and researchers stated at the end of the UN Decade for Women, "The almost uniform conclusion of the Decade's research is that, with a few exceptions, women's relative access to economic resources, incomes and employment has worsened, their burden of work has increased, and their relative and even absolute health, nutritional and educational status has declined."[4]

Women's displacement from productive activity by the expansion of development was rooted largely in the manner in which development projects appropriated or destroyed the natural resource base used for sustenance and survival. It destroyed women's productivity both by removing land, water, and forests from their management and control, as well as through the ecological destruction of these resources, impairing nature's productivity and renewability. While gender subordination and patriarchy are the oldest of oppressions, they have taken on new and more violent forms through the project of development. Patriarchal categories which understand destruction as "production" and regeneration of life as "passivity" have generated a crisis of survival. Passivity, as an assumed category of the "nature" of nature and women, denies the activity of nature and life. Fragmentation and uniformity as assumed categories of progress and development destroy the living forces which arise from relationships within the "web of life" and the diversity in the elements and patterns of these relationships.

The economic biases and values against nature, women, and indigenous peoples are captured in this typical analysis of the "unproductiveness" of traditional natural societies:

> Production is achieved through human and animal, rather than mechanical, power. Most agriculture is unproductive; human or animal manure may be used but chemical fertilizers and pesticides are unknown. . . . For the masses, these conditions mean poverty.[5]

The assumptions are evident: nature is unproductive; organic agriculture based on nature's cycles of renewability spells poverty; women and tribal and peasant societies embedded in nature are similarly unproductive, not because it has been demonstrated that in cooperation they produce *less* goods and services for needs, but because it is assumed that "production" takes place only when mediated by technologies for commodity production, even when such technologies destroy life. A stable and clean river is not a productive resource in this view: it needs to be "developed" with dams in order to become so. Women, sharing the river as a commons to satisfy the water needs of their families and society are not involved in productive labor; when substituted by the engineering man, water management and water use become productive activities. Natural forests remain unproductive until they are developed into monoculture plantations of commercial species. Development is thus equivalent to maldevelopment, a development bereft of the feminine, the conservation, the ecological principle. The neglect of nature's work in renewing herself, and women's work in producing sustenance in the form of basic, vital needs is an essential part of the paradigm of maldevelopment, which sees all work that does not produce profits and capital as non- or unproductive work. As Maria Mies has pointed out, this concept of surplus has a patriarchal bias because, from the point of view of nature and women, it is not based on material surplus produced *over and above* the requirements of the community: it is stolen and appropriated through violent modes from nature (who needs a share of her produce to reproduce herself) and from women (who need a share of nature's produce to produce sustenance and ensure survival).[6]

From the perspective of Third World women, productivity is a measure of producing life and sustenance; that this kind of productivity has been rendered invisible does not reduce its centrality to survival – it merely reflects the domination of modern patriarchal economic categories which see only profits, not life.

Maldevelopment As the Death of the Feminine Principle

In this analysis, maldevelopment becomes a new source of male-female inequality. 'Modernization' has been associated with the introduction of new forms of dominance. Alice Schlegel has shown that under conditions of subsistence, the interdependence and complementarity of the separate male and female domains of work is the characteristic mode, based on diversity, not inequality.[7] Maldevelopment militates against this equality in diversity, and superimposes the ideologically constructed category of western technological man as a uniform measure of the worth of classes, cultures, and genders. Dominant modes of perception based on reductionism, duality, and linearity are unable to cope with equality in diversity, with forms and activities that are significant and valid, even though different. The reductionist mind superimposes the roles and forms of power of western male-oriented concepts on women, all nonwestern peoples, and even on nature, rendering all three "deficient," and in need of "development." Diversity, and unity and harmony in diversity, become epistemologically unattainable in the context of maldevelopment, which then becomes synonymous with women's underdevelopment (increasing sexist domination), and nature's depletion (deepening ecological crises). Commodities have grown, but nature has shrunk. The poverty crisis of the South arises from the growing scarcity of water, food, fodder, and fuel, associated with increasing maldevelopment and ecological destruction. This poverty crisis touches women most severely, first because they are the poorest among the poor, and then because, with nature, they are the primary sustainers of society.

Maldevelopment is the violation of the integrity of organic, interconnected, interdependent systems, that sets in motion a process of exploitation, inequality, injustice, and violence. It is blind to the fact that a recognition of nature's harmony and action to maintain it are preconditions for distributive justice. This is why Mahatma Gandhi said, "There is enough in the world for everyone's need, but not for some people's greed."

Maldevelopment is maldevelopment in thought and action. In practice, this fragmented, reductionist, dualist perspective violates the integrity and harmony of humankind in nature, and the harmony between men and women. It ruptures the cooperative unity of masculine and feminine, and places man, shorn of the feminine principle, above nature and women, and separated from both. The violence to nature as symptomatized by the ecological crisis, and the violence to women, as symptomatized by their subjugation and exploitation, arise from this subjugation of the feminine principle. I want to argue that what is currently called development is essentially maldevelopment, based on the introduction or accentuation of the domination of man over nature and women. In it, both are viewed as the "other," the passive nonself. Activity, productivity, and creativity which were associated with the feminine principle, are expropriated as qualities of nature and women, and transformed into the exclusive qualities of man. Nature and women are turned into passive objects, to be used and exploited for the uncontrolled and uncontrollable desires of alienated man. From being the creators and sustainers of life, nature and women are reduced to being "resources" in the fragmented, antilife model of maldevelopment.

Two Kinds of Growth, Two Kinds of Productivity

Maldevelopment is usually called "economic growth," measured by the Gross National Product. Porritt, a leading ecologist, has this to say of GNP:

> *Gross* National Product – for once a word is being used correctly. Even conventional economists admit that the hey-day of GNP is over for the simple reason that as a measure of progress, it's more or less useless. GNP measures the lot, all the goods and services produced in the money economy. Many of these goods and services are not beneficial to people, but rather a measure of just how much is going wrong; increased spending on crime, on pollution, on the many human casualties of our society, increased spending because of waste or planned obsolescence, increased spending because of growing bureaucracies: it's all counted.[8]

The problem with GNP is that it measures some costs as benefits (e.g., pollution control) and fails to measure other costs completely. Among these hidden costs are the new burdens created by ecological devastation, costs that are invariably heavier for women, both in the North and South. It is hardly surprising, therefore, that as GNP rises, it does not necessarily mean that either wealth or welfare increase proportionately. I would argue that GNP is increasingly becoming a measure of how real wealth – the wealth of nature and that produced by women for sustaining life – is rapidly decreasing. When commodity production as the prime economic activity is introduced as development, it destroys the potential of nature and women to produce life and goods and services for basic needs. More commodities and more cash mean less life – in nature (through ecological destruction) and in society (through denial of basic needs). Women are devalued, first, because their work cooperates with nature's processes and, second, because work which satisfies needs and ensures sustenance is devalued in general. Precisely because more growth in maldevelopment has meant less sustenance of life-support systems, it is now imperative to recover the feminine principle as the basis for development which conserves and is ecological. Feminism as ecology, and ecology as the revival of *Prakriti* – the source of all life – become the decentered powers of political and economic transformation and restructuring.

This involves, first, a recognition that categories of "productivity" and growth which have been taken to be positive, progressive and universal are, in reality, restricted patriarchal categories. When viewed from the point of view of nature's productivity and growth, and women's production of sustenance, they are found to be ecologically destructive and a source of gender inequality. It is no accident that the modern, efficient, productive technologies created within the context of growth in market economic terms are associated with heavy ecological costs, borne largely by women. The resource and energy-intensive production processes they give rise to demand ever-increasing withdrawals from the ecosystem. These withdrawals disrupt essential ecological processes and convert renewable resources into nonrenewable ones. A forest, for example, provides inexhaustible supplies of diverse biomass over time if its capital stock is maintained and it is harvested on a sustained yield basis. The heavy and uncontrolled demand for industrial and commercial wood, however, requires the continuous overfelling of trees which exceeds the regenerative capacity of the forest ecosystem, and eventually converts the forests into nonrenewable resources. Women's work in the collection of water, fodder, and fuel is thus rendered more energy- and time-consuming. (In Garhwal, for example, I have seen women who originally collected fodder and fuel in a few hours, now traveling long distances by truck to collect grass and leaves in a task that might take up to two days.) Sometimes the damage to nature's intrinsic regenerative capacity is impaired not by overexploitation of a particular resource but, indirectly, by damage caused to other related natural resources through ecological processes. Thus the excessive overfelling of trees in the catchment areas of streams and rivers destroys not only forest resources, but also renewable supplies of water, through hydrological destabilization. Resource intensive industries disrupt essential ecological processes not only by their excessive demands for raw material, but by their pollution of air and water and soil. Often such destruction is caused by the resource demands of nonvital industrial products.

In spite of severe ecological crises, this paradigm continues to operate because, for the North and for the elites of the South, resources continue to be available, even now. The lack of recognition of nature's processes for survival *as factors in the process of economic development* shrouds the political issues arising from resource transfer and resource destruction, and creates an ideological weapon for increased control over natural resources in the conventionally employed notion of productivity. All other costs of the economic process consequently become invisible. The forces which contribute to the increased "productivity" of a modern farmer or factory worker, for instance, come from the increased use of natural resources. Lovins has described this as the amount of "slave" labor presently at work in the world.[9] According to him, each person on earth, on an average, possesses the equivalent of about 50 slaves, each working a 40-hour week. Humankind's global energy conversion from all sources (wood, fossil fuel, hydroelectric power, nuclear) is currently more than 20 times the energy content of the food necessary to feed the present world population at the FAO (Food and Agriculture Organization of the United Nations) standard diet of 3,600 calories per day. The "productivity" of the western male compared to women or Third World peasants is not intrinsically superior; it is based on inequalities in the distribution of this "slave" labor. The average inhabitant of the United States, for example, has 250 times more "slaves" than the average Nigerian. If Americans were short of 249 of those 250 "slaves," one wonders how efficient they would prove themselves to be?

It is these resource and energy intensive processes of production which divert resources away from survival, and hence from women. What patriarchy sees as productive work is, in ecological terms, highly destructive production. The second law of thermodynamics predicts that resource intensive and resource wasteful economic development must become a threat to the survival of the human species in the long run. Political struggles based on ecology in industrially advanced countries are rooted in this conflict between *long term survival options* and *short term over-production and over-consumption*. Political struggles of women, peasants, and tribals based on ecology in countries like India are far more acute and urgent since they are rooted in the *immediate threat to the options for survival* for the vast majority of the people, *posed by resource intensive and resource wasteful economic growth* for the benefit of a minority.

In the market economy, the organizing principle for natural resource use is the maximization of profits and capital accumulation. Nature and human needs are managed through market mechanisms. Demands for natural resources are restricted to those demands registering on the market; the ideology of development is in large part based on a vision of bringing all natural resources into the market economy for commodity production. When these resources are already being used by nature to maintain her production of renewable resources and by women for sustenance and livelihood, their diversion to the market economy generates a scarcity condition for ecological stability and creates new forms of poverty for women.

Two Kinds of Poverty

In a book entitled *Poverty: the Wealth of the People,* an African writer draws a distinction between poverty as subsistence, and misery as deprivation. It is useful to separate a cultural conception of subsistence living as poverty from the material experience of poverty that is a result of dispossession and deprivation.

Culturally perceived poverty need not be real material poverty: subsistence economies which satisfy basic needs through self-provisioning are not poor in the sense of being deprived. Yet the ideology of development declares them so because they do not participate overwhelmingly in the market economy, and do not consume commodities produced for and distributed through the market *even though they might be satisfying those needs through self-provisioning mechanisms.* People are perceived as poor if they eat millet (grown by women) rather than commercially produced and distributed processed foods sold by global agribusiness. They are seen as poor if they live in self-built housing made from natural material like bamboo and mud rather than in cement houses. They are seen as poor if they wear handmade garments of natural fiber rather than synthetics. Subsistence, as culturally perceived poverty, does not necessarily imply a low physical quality of life. On the contrary, millet is nutritionally far superior to processed foods; houses built with local materials are far superior, being better adapted to the local climate and ecology; natural fibers are preferable to manufactured fibers in most cases, and certainly more affordable.

This cultural perception of prudent subsistence living as poverty has provided the legitimization for the development process as removing poverty. As a culturally biased project, it destroys wholesome and sustainable lifestyles and creates real material poverty, or misery, by the denial of survival needs themselves, through the diversion of resources to resource intensive commodity production. Cash crop production and food processing take land and water resources away from sustenance needs, and exclude increasingly large numbers of people from their entitlements to food. At no point has the global marketing of agricultural commodities been assessed against the background of the new conditions of scarcity and poverty that it has induced. This new poverty, moreover, is no longer cultural and relative: it is absolute, threatening the very survival of millions on this planet.

The economic system based on the patriarchal concept of productivity was created for the very specific historical and political phenomenon of colonialism. In it, the input for which efficiency of use had to be maximized in the production centers of Europe, was industrial labor. For colonial interest, therefore, it was rational to improve the labor resource *even at the cost of wasteful use of nature's wealth.* This rationalization has, however, been illegitimately universalized to all contexts and interest groups. And, on the plea of increasing productivity, labor-reducing technologies have been introduced in situations where labor is abundant and cheap, and resource-demanding technologies have been introduced where resources are scarce and already fully utilized for the production of sustenance. Traditional economies with a stable ecology have shared with industrially advanced affluent economies the ability to use natural resources to satisfy basic vital needs. The former differ from the latter in two essential ways. First, the same needs are satisfied in industrial societies through longer technological chains requiring higher energy and resource inputs and excluding large numbers without purchasing power. And second, affluence generates new and artificial needs requiring the increased production of industrial goods and services. Traditional economies are not advanced in the matter of nonvital needs satisfaction, but as far as the satisfaction of basic and vital needs is concerned, they are often what Marshall Sahlins has called "the original affluent society." The needs of the Amazonian tribes are more than satisfied by the rich rainforest; their poverty begins with its destruction. The story is the same for the Gonds of Bastar in India or the Penans of Sarawak in Malaysia.

Thus economies based on indigenous technologies are viewed as "backward" and "unproductive." Poverty, as the denial of basic needs, is not necessarily associated with the existence of traditional technologies, and its removal is not necessarily an outcome of the growth of modern ones. On the contrary, the destruction of ecologically sound traditional technologies, often created and used by women, along with the destruction of their material base is generally believed to be responsible for the "feminization" of poverty in societies which have had to bear the costs of resource destruction.

The contemporary poverty of the Afar nomad is not rooted in the inadequacies of traditional nomadic life, but in the *diversion of the productive pastureland of the Awash Valley.* The erosion of the resource base for survival is increasingly being caused by the demand for resources by the market economy, dominated by global forces. The creation of inequality through economic activity which is ecologically disruptive arises in two ways. First, inequalities in the distribution of privileges make for unequal access to natural resources – these include privileges of both a political and economic nature. Second, resource intensive production processes have access to subsidized raw material on which a substantial number of people, especially from the less privileged economic groups, depend for their survival. The consumption of such industrial raw material is determined purely by market forces, and not by considerations of the social or ecological requirements placed on them. The costs of resource destruction are externalized and unequally divided among various economic groups in society, but are borne largely by women and those who satisfy their basic material needs directly from nature, simply because they have no purchasing power to register their demands on the goods and services provided by the modern production system. Gustavo Esteva has called development a permanent war waged by its promoters and suffered by its victims.[10]

The paradox and crisis of development arises from the mistaken identification of culturally perceived poverty with real material poverty, and the mistaken identification of the growth of commodity production as better satisfaction of basic needs. In actual fact, there is less water, less fertile soil, less genetic wealth as a result of the development process. Since these natural resources are the basis of nature's economy and women's survival economy, their scarcity is impoverishing women and marginalized peoples in an unprecedented manner. Their new impoverishment lies in the fact that resources which supported their survival were absorbed into the market economy while they themselves were excluded and displaced by it.

The old assumption that, with the development process, the availability of goods and services will automatically be increased and poverty will be removed, is now under serious challenge from women's ecology movements in the Third World, even while it continues to guide development thinking in centers of patriarchal power. Survival is based on the assumption of the sanctity of life; maldevelopment is based on the assumption of the sacredness of "development." Gustavo Esteva asserts that the sacredness of development has to be refuted because it threatens survival itself. "My people are tired of development," he says, "they just want to live."[11]

The recovery of the feminine principle allows a transcendence and transformation of these patriarchal foundations of maldevelopment. It allows a redefinition of growth and productivity as categories linked to the production, not the destruction, of life. It is thus simultaneously an ecological and a feminist political project which legitimizes the way of knowing and being that creates wealth by enhancing life and diversity, and which delegitimizes the knowledge and practice of a culture of death as the basis for capital accumulation.

Endnotes

1. Rosa Luxemberg, *The Accumulation of Capital,* Routledge and Kegan Paul, London, 1951.

2. An elaboration of how "development" transfers resources from the poor to the well-endowed is contained in J. Bandyopadhyay and V. Shiva, "Political Economy of Technological Polarisations" in *Economic and Political Weekly,* Vol. XVIII, 1982, pp. 1827-32; and J. Bandyopadyay and V. Shiva, "Political Economy of Ecology Movements," in *Economic and Political Weekly.*

3. Ester Boserup, *Women's Role in Economic Development,* Allen and Unwin, London, 1970.

4. DAWN, *Development Crisis and Alternative Visions: Third World Women's Perspective,* Christian Michelsen Institute, Bergen, 1985, p. 21.

5. M. George Foster, *Traditional Societies and Technological Change,* Allied Publishers, Delhi, 1973.

6. Maria Mies, *Patriarchy and Accumulation on a World Scale,* Zed Books, London, 1986.

7. Alice Schlegel, ed., *Sexual Stratification: A Cross-Cultural Study,* Columbia University Press, New York, 1977.

8. Jonathan Porritt, *Seeing Green,* Blackwell, Oxford, 1984.

9. A. Lovins, cited in S. R. Eyre, *The Real Wealth of Nations,* Edward Arnold, London, 1978.

10. Gustavo Esteva, "Regenerating People's Space," in *Towards a Just World Peace: Perspective From Social Movements,* S. N. Mendlowitz and R. B. J. Walker, Butterworths and Committee for a Just World Peace, London, 1987.

11. Esteva, *op. cit.*

15

The Power and the Promise
of Ecological Feminism

Karen J. Warren

Ecological feminism is the position that there are important connections – historical, symbolic, theoretical – between the domination of women and the domination of nonhuman nature. I argue that because the conceptual connections between the dual dominations of women and nature are located in an oppressive patriarchal conceptual framework characterized by a logic of domination, (1) the logic of traditional feminism requires the expansion of feminism to include ecological feminism and (2) ecological feminism provides a framework for developing a distinctively feminist environmental ethic. I conclude that any feminist theory and any environmental ethic which fails to take seriously the interconnected dominations of women and nature is simply inadequate.

Introduction

Ecological feminism (ecofeminism) has begun to receive a fair amount of attention lately as an alternative feminism and environmental ethic.[1] Since Francoise d'Eaubonne introduced the term *ecofeminisme* in 1974 to bring attention to women's potential for bringing about an ecological revolution,[2] the term has been used in a variety of ways. As I use the term in this paper, ecological feminism is the position that there are important connections – historical, experiential, symbolic, theoretical – between the domination of women and the domination of nature, an understanding of which is crucial to both feminism and environmental ethics. I argue that the promise and power of ecological feminism is that *it provides a distinctive framework both for reconceiving feminism and for developing an environmental ethic which takes seriously connections between the domination of women and the domination of nature.* I do so by discussing the nature of a feminist ethic and the ways in which ecofeminism provides a feminist and environmental ethic. I conclude that any feminist theory *and* any environmental ethic which fail to take seriously the twin and interconnected dominations of women and nature are at best incomplete and at worst simply inadequate.

Feminism, Ecological Feminism, and Conceptual Frameworks

Whatever else it is, feminism is at least the movement to end sexist oppression. It involves the elimination of any and all factors that contribute to the continued and systematic domination or subordination of women. While feminists disagree about the nature of and solutions to the subordination of women, all feminists agree that sexist oppression exists, is wrong, and must be abolished.

A "feminist issue" is any issue that contributes in some way to understanding the oppression of women. Equal rights, comparable pay for comparable work, and food production are feminist issues wherever and whenever an understanding of them contributes to an understanding of the continued exploitation or subjugation of women. Carrying water and searching for firewood are feminist issues wherever and whenever women's primary responsibility for these tasks contributes to their lack of full participation in decision making, income producing, or high status positions engaged in by men. What counts as a feminist issue, then, depends largely on context, particularly the historical and material conditions of women's lives.

Environmental degradation and exploitation are feminist issues because an understanding of them contributes to an understanding of the oppression of women. In India, for example, both deforestation and reforestation through the introduction of a monoculture species tree (e.g., eucalyptus) intended for commercial production are feminist issues because the loss of indigenous forests and multiple species of trees has drastically affected rural Indian women's ability to maintain a subsistence household. Indigenous forests provide a variety of trees for food, fuel, fodder, household utensils, dyes, medicines, and income-generating uses, while monoculture-species forests do not.[3] Although I do not argue for this claim here, a look at the global impact of environmental degradation on women's lives suggests important respects in which environmental degradation is a feminist issue.

Feminist philosophers claim that some of the most important feminist issues are *conceptual* ones: these issues concern how one conceptualizes such mainstay philosophical notions as reason and rationality, ethics, and what it is to be human. Ecofeminists extend this feminist philosophical concern to nature. They argue that, ultimately, some of the most important connections between the domination of women and the domination of nature are conceptual. To see this, consider the nature of conceptual frameworks.

A *conceptual framework is* a set of *basic* beliefs, values, attitudes, and assumptions which shape and reflect how one views oneself and one's world. It is a socially constructed lens through which we perceive ourselves and others. It is affected by such factors as gender, race, class, age, affectional orientation, nationality, and religious background.

Some conceptual frameworks are oppressive. An *oppressive conceptual framework is* one that explains, justifies, and maintains relationships of domination and subordination. When an oppressive conceptual framework is *patriarchal,* it explains, justifies, and maintains the subordination of women by men.

I have argued elsewhere that there are three significant features of oppressive conceptual frameworks: (1) value-hierarchical thinking, i.e., "up-down" thinking which places higher value, status, or prestige on what is "up" rather than on what is "down"; (2) value dualisms, i.e., disjunctive pairs in which the disjuncts are seen as oppositional (rather than as complementary) and exclusive (rather than as inclusive), and which place higher value (status, prestige) on one disjunct rather than the other (e.g., dualisms which give higher value or status to that which has historically been identified as "mind," "reason," and "male" than to that which has historically been identified as "body," "emotion," and "female"); and (3) logic of domination, i.e., a structure of argumentation which leads to a justification of subordination.[4]

The third feature of oppressive conceptual frameworks is the most significant. A logic of domination is not *just* a logical structure. It also involves a substantive value system, since an ethical premise is needed to permit or sanction the "just" subordination of that which is subordinate. This justification typically is given on grounds of some alleged characteristic (e.g., rationality) which the dominant (e.g., men) have and the subordinate (e.g., women) lack.

Contrary to what many feminists and ecofeminists have said or suggested, there may be nothing *inherently* problematic about "hierarchical thinking" or even "value-hierarchical thinking" in contexts other than contexts of oppression. Hierarchical thinking is important in daily living for classifying data, comparing information, and organizing material. Taxonomies (e.g., plant taxonomies) and biological nomenclature seem to require *some* form of "hierarchical thinking." Even "value-hierarchical thinking" may be quite acceptable in certain contexts. (The same may be said of "value dualisms" in non-oppressive contexts.) For example, suppose it is true that what is unique about humans is our conscious capacity to radically reshape our social environments (or "societies"), as Murray Bookchin suggests.[5] Then one could truthfully say that humans are better equipped to radically reshape their environments than are rocks or plants – a "value-hierarchical" way of speaking.

The problem is not simply *that* value-hierarchical thinking and value dualisms are used, but *the way* in which each has been used *in oppressive conceptual frameworks* to establish inferiority and to justify subordination.[6] It is the logic of domination, *coupled with* value-hierarchical thinking and value dualisms, which "justifies" subordination. What is explanatorily basic, then, about the nature of oppressive conceptual frameworks is the logic of domination.

For ecofeminism, that a logic of domination is explanatorily basic is important for at least three reasons. First, without a logic of domination, a description of similarities and differences would be just that – a description of similarities and differences. Consider the claim, "Humans are different from plants and rocks in that humans can (and plants and rocks cannot) consciously and radically reshape the communities in which they live; humans are similar to plants and rocks in that they are both members of an ecological community." Even if humans are "better" than plants and rocks with respect to the conscious ability of humans to radically transform communities, one does not *thereby* get any *morally* relevant distinction between humans and nonhumans, or an argument for the domination of plants and rocks by humans. To get *those* conclusions one needs to add at least two powerful assumptions, viz., (A2) and (A4) in argument A below:

(A1) Humans do, and plants and rocks do not, have the capacity to consciously and radically change the community in which they live.

(A2) Whatever has the capacity to consciously and radically change the community in which it lives is morally superior to whatever lacks this capacity.

(A3) Thus, humans are morally superior to plants and rocks.

(A4) For any X and Y. if X is morally superior to Y, then X is morally justified in subordinating Y.

(A5) Thus, humans are morally justified in subordinating plants and rocks.

Without the two assumptions that *humans are morally superior* to (at least some) nonhumans, (A2), and that *superiority justifies subordination,* (A4), all one has is some difference between humans and some nonhumans. This is true *even if* that difference is given in terms of superiority. Thus, it is the logic of domination, (A4), which is the bottom line in ecofeminist discussions of oppression.

Second, ecofeminists argue that, at least in Western societies, the oppressive conceptual framework which sanctions the twin dominations of women and nature is a patriarchal one characterized by all three features of an oppressive conceptual framework. Many ecofeminists claim that, historically, within at least the dominant Western culture, a patriarchal conceptual framework has sanctioned the following argument B:

(B1) Women are identified with nature and the realm of the physical; men are identified with the "human" and the realm of the mental.

(B2) Whatever is identified with nature and the realm of the physical is inferior to ("below") whatever is identified with the "human" and the realm of the mental; or, conversely, the latter is superior to ("above") the former.

(B3) Thus, women are inferior to ("below") men; or, conversely, men are superior to ("above") women.

(B4) For any X and Y, if X is superior to Y, then X is justified in subordinating Y.

(B5) Thus, men are justified in subordinating women.

If sound, argument B establishes *patriarchy*, i.e., the conclusion given at (B5) that the systematic domination of women by men is justified. But according to ecofeminists, (B5) is justified by just those three features of an oppressive conceptual framework identified earlier: value-hierarchical thinking, the assumption at (B2); value dualisms, the assumed dualism of the mental and the physical at (B1) and the assumed inferiority of the physical vis-à-vis the mental at (B2); and a logic of domination, the assumption at (B4), the same as the previous premise (A4). Hence, according to ecofeminists, insofar as an oppressive patriarchal conceptual framework has functioned historically (within at least dominant Western culture) to sanction the twin dominations of women and nature (argument B), both argument B and the patriarchal conceptual framework, from whence it comes, ought to be rejected.

Of course, the preceding does not identify which premises of B are false. What is the status of premises (B1) and (B2)? Most, if not all, feminists claim that (B1), and many ecofeminists claim that (B2), have been assumed or asserted within the dominant Western philosophical and intellectual tradition.[7] As such, these feminists assert as a matter of historical fact, that the dominant Western philosophical tradition has assumed the truth of (B1) and (B2). Ecofeminists, however, either deny (B2) or do not affirm (B2). Furthermore, because some ecofeminists are anxious to deny any ahistorical identification of women with nature, some ecofeminists deny (B1) when (B1) is used to support anything other than a strictly historical claim about what has been asserted or assumed to be true within patriarchal culture – e.g., when (B1) is used to assert that women properly are identified with the realm of nature and the physical.[8] Thus, from an ecofeminist perspective, (B1) and (B2) are properly viewed as problematic though historically sanctioned claims: they are problematic precisely because of the way they have functioned historically in a patriarchal conceptual framework and culture to sanction the dominations of women and nature.

What *all* ecofeminists agree about, then, is the way in which *the logic of domination* has functioned historically within patriarchy to sustain and justify the twin dominations of women and nature.[9] Since *all* feminists (and not just ecofeminists) oppose patriarchy, the conclusion given at (B5), all feminists (including ecofeminists) must oppose at least the logic of domination, premise (B4), on which argument B rests – whatever the truth-value status of (B1) and (B2) *outside of* a patriarchal context.

That *all* feminists must oppose the logic of domination shows the breadth and depth of the ecofeminist critique of B: it is a critique not only of the three assumptions on which this argument for the domination of women and nature rests, viz., the assumptions at (B1), (B2), and (B4); it is also a critique of patriarchal conceptual frameworks generally, i.e., of those oppressive conceptual frameworks which put men "up" and women "down," allege some way in which women are morally inferior to men, and use that alleged difference to justify the subordination of women by men. Therefore, ecofeminism is necessary to *any* feminist critique of patriarchy, and, hence, necessary to feminism (a point I discuss again later).

Third, ecofeminism clarifies why the logic of domination, and any conceptual framework which gives rise to it, must be abolished in order both to make possible a meaningful notion of difference which does not breed domination and to prevent feminism from becoming a "support" movement based primarily on shared experiences. In contemporary society, there is no one "woman's voice," no *woman* (or *human*) *simpliciter:* every woman (or human) is a woman (or human) of some race, class, age, affectional orientation, marital status, regional or national background, and so forth. Because there are no "monolithic experiences" that all women share, feminism must be a "solidarity movement" based on shared beliefs and interests rather than a "unity in sameness" movement based on shared experiences and shared victimization.[10] In the words of Maria Lugones, "Unity – not to be confused with solidarity – is understood as conceptually tied to domination."[11]

Ecofeminists insist that the sort of logic of domination used to justify the domination of humans by gender, racial or ethnic, or class status is also used to justify the domination of nature. Because eliminating a logic of domination is part of a feminist critique – whether a critique of patriarchy, white supremacist culture, or imperialism – ecofeminists insist that *naturism* is properly viewed as an integral part of any feminist solidarity movement to end sexist oppression and the logic of domination which conceptually grounds it.

Ecofeminism Reconceives Feminism

The discussion so far has focused on some of the oppressive conceptual features of patriarchy. As I use the phrase, the "logic of traditional feminism" refers to the location of the conceptual roots of sexist oppression, at least in Western societies, in an oppressive patriarchal conceptual framework characterized by a logic of domination. Insofar as other systems of oppression (e.g., racism, classism, ageism, heterosexism) are also conceptually maintained by a logic of domination, appeal to the logic of traditional feminism ultimately locates the basic conceptual interconnections among *all* systems of oppression in the logic of domination. It thereby explains at a *conceptual* level why the eradication of sexist oppression requires the eradication of the other forms of oppression.[12] It is by clarifying this conceptual connection between systems of oppression that a movement to end sexist oppression – traditionally the special turf of feminist theory and practice – leads to a reconceiving of feminism as *a movement to end all forms of oppression.*

Suppose one agrees that the logic of traditional feminism requires the expansion of feminism to include other social systems of domination (e.g., racism and classism). What warrants the inclusion of nature in these "social systems of domination"? Why must the logic of traditional feminism include the abolition of "naturism" (i.e., the domination or oppression of nonhuman nature) among the "isms" feminism must confront? The conceptual justification for expanding feminism to include ecofeminism is twofold. One basis has already been suggested: by showing that the conceptual connections between the dual dominations of women and nature are located in an oppressive and, at least in Western societies, patriarchal conceptual framework characterized by a logic of domination, ecofeminism explains how and why feminism, conceived as a movement to end sexist oppression, must be expanded and reconceived as also a movement to end naturism. This is made explicit by the following argument C:

(C1) Feminism is a movement to end sexism.

(C2) But Sexism is conceptually linked with naturism (through an oppressive conceptual framework characterized by a logic of domination).

(C3) Thus, Feminism is (also) a movement to end naturism.

Because, ultimately, these connections between sexism and naturism are conceptual embedded in an oppressive conceptual framework – the logic of traditional feminism leads to the embracement of ecological feminism.[13]

The other justification for reconceiving feminism to include ecofeminism has to do with the concepts of gender and nature. Just as conceptions of gender are socially constructed, so are conceptions of nature. Of course, the claim that women and nature are social constructions does not require anyone to deny that there are actual humans and actual trees, rivers, and plants. It simply implies that *how* women and nature are conceived is a matter of historical and social reality. These conceptions vary cross-culturally and by historical time period. As a result, any discussion of the "oppression or domination of nature" involves reference to historically specific forms of social domination of nonhuman nature by humans, just as discussion of the "domination of women" refers to historically specific forms of social domination of women by men. Although I do not argue for it here, an ecofeminist defense of the historical connections between the dominations of women and of nature, claims (B1) and (B2) in argument B, involves showing that within patriarchy the feminization of nature and the naturalization of women have been crucial to the historically successful subordinations of both.[14]

If ecofeminism promises to reconceive traditional feminism in ways which include naturism as a legitimate feminist issue, does ecofeminism also promise to reconceive environmental ethics in ways which are feminist? I think so. This is the subject of the remainder of the paper.

Climbing from Ecofeminism to Environmental Ethics

Many feminists and some environmental ethicists have begun to explore the use of first-person narrative as a way of raising philosophically germane issues in ethics often lost or underplayed in mainstream philosophical ethics. Why is this so? What is it about narrative which makes it a significant resource for theory and practice in feminism and environmental ethics? Even if appeal to first-person narrative is a helpful literary device for describing ineffable experience or a legitimate social science methodology for documenting personal and social history, how is first-person narrative a valuable vehicle of argumentation for ethical decision making and theory building? One fruitful way to begin answering these questions is to ask them of a particular first-person narrative.

Consider the following first-person narrative about rock climbing:

> For my very first rock climbing experience, I chose a somewhat private spot, away from other climbers and on-lookers. After studying "the chimney," I focused all my energy on making it to the top. I climbed with intense determination, using whatever strength and skills I had to accomplish this challenging feat. By midway I was exhausted and anxious. I couldn't see what to do next – where to put my hands or feet. Growing increasingly more weary as I clung somewhat desperately to the rock, I made a move. It didn't work. I fell. There I was, dangling midair above the rocky ground below, frightened but terribly relieved that the belay rope had held me. I knew I was safe. I took a look up at

the climb that remained. I was determined to make it to the top. With renewed confidence and concentration, I finished the climb to the top.

On my second day of climbing, I rappelled down about 200 feet from the top of the Palisades at Lake Superior to just a few feet above the water level. I could see no one – not my belayer, not the other climbers, no one. I unhooked slowly from the rappel rope and took a deep cleansing breath. I looked all around me – really looked – and listened. I heard a cacophony of voices – birds, trickles of water on the rock before me, waves lapping against the rocks below. I closed my eyes and began to feel the rock with my hands – the cracks and crannies, the raised lichen and mosses, the almost imperceptible nubs that might provide a resting place for my fingers and toes when I began to climb. At that moment I was bathed in serenity. I began to talk to the rock in an almost inaudible, child-like way, as if the rock were my friend. I felt an overwhelming sense of gratitude for what it offered me – a chance to know myself and the rock differently, to appreciate unforeseen miracles like the tiny flowers growing in the even tinier cracks in the rock's surface, and to come to know a sense of *being in relationship* with the natural environment. It felt as if the rock and I were silent conversational partners in a longstanding friendship. I realized then that I had come to care about this cliff which was so different from me, so unmovable and invincible, independent and seemingly indifferent to my presence. I wanted to be with the rock as I climbed. Gone was the determination to conquer the rock, to forcefully impose my will on it; I wanted simply to work respectfully with the rock as I climbed. And as I climbed, that is what I felt. I felt myself *caring* for this rock and feeling thankful that climbing provided the opportunity for me to know it and myself in this new way.

There are at least four reasons why use of such a first-person narrative is important to feminism and environmental ethics. First, such a narrative gives voice to a felt sensitivity often lacking in traditional analytical ethical discourse, viz., a sensitivity to conceiving of oneself as fundamentally "in relationship with" others, including the nonhuman environment. It is a modality which *takes relationships themselves seriously*. It thereby stands in contrast to a strictly reductionist modality that takes relationships seriously only or primarily because of the nature of the *relators* or parties to those relationships (e.g., relators conceived as moral agents, right holders, interest carriers, or sentient beings). In the rock-climbing narrative above, it is the climber's relationship with the rock she climbs which takes on special significance – which is itself a locus of value – in addition to whatever moral status or moral considerability she or the rock or any other parties to the relationship may also have.[15]

Second, such a first-person narrative gives expression to a variety of ethical attitudes and behaviors often overlooked or underplayed in mainstream Western ethics, e.g., the difference in attitudes and behaviors toward a rock when one is "making it to the top" and when one thinks of oneself as "friends with" or "caring about" the rock one climbs.[16] These different attitudes and behaviors suggest an ethically germane contrast between two different types of relationship humans or climbers may have toward a rock: an imposed conqueror-type relationship, and an emergent caring-type relationship. This contrast grows out of, and is faithful to, felt, lived experience.

The difference between conquering and caring attitudes and behaviors in relation to the natural environment provides a third reason why the use of first-person narrative is important to feminism and environmental ethics: it provides a way of conceiving of ethics and ethical meaning as *emerging out of* particular situations moral agents find themselves in, rather than as being *imposed on* those situations (e.g., as a derivation or instantiation of some predetermined abstract principle or rule). This emergent feature of narrative centralizes the importance of *voice*. When a multiplicity of cross-cultural *voices* are centralized, narrative is able to give expression to a range of attitudes, values, beliefs, and behaviors which may be overlooked or silenced by imposed ethical meaning and theory. As a reflection of and on felt, lived experiences, the use of narrative in ethics provides a stance from which ethical discourse can be held accountable to the historical, material, and social realities in which moral subjects find themselves.

Lastly, and for our purposes perhaps most importantly, the use of narrative has argumentative significance. Jim Cheney calls attention to this feature of narrative when he claims, "To contextualize ethical deliberation is, in some sense, to provide a narrative or story, from which the solution to the ethical dilemma emerges as the fitting conclusion."[17] Narrative has argumentative force by suggesting *what counts* as an appropriate conclusion to an ethical situation. One ethical conclusion suggested by the climbing narrative is that what counts as a proper ethical attitude toward mountains and rocks is an attitude of respect and care (whatever that turns out to be or involve), not one of domination and conquest.

In an essay entitled "In and Out of Harm's Way: Arrogance and Love," feminist philosopher Marilyn Frye distinguishes between "arrogant" and "loving" perception as one way of getting at this difference in the ethical attitudes of care and conquest.[18] Frye writes:

> The loving eye is a contrary of the arrogant eye.
>
> The loving eye knows the independence of the other. It is the eye of a seer who knows that nature is indifferent. It is the eye of one who knows that to know the seen, one must consult something other than one's own will and interests and fears and imagination. One must look at the thing. One must look and listen and check and question.
>
> The loving eye is one that pays a certain sort of attention. This attention can require a discipline but *not* a self-denial. The discipline is one of self-knowledge, knowledge of the scope and boundary of the self. . . .

In particular, it is a matter of being able to tell one's own interests
from those of others and of knowing where one's self leaves off and
another begins. . . .

The loving eye does not make the object of perception into something
edible, does not try to assimilate it, does not reduce it to the size of the
seer's desire, fear and imagination, and hence does not have to sim-
plify. It knows the complexity of the other as something which will
forever present new things to be known. The science of the loving eye
would favor The Complexity Theory of Truth [in contrast to The Sim-
plicity Theory of Truth] and presuppose The Endless Interestingness of
the Universe.[19]

According to Frye, the loving eye is not an invasive, coercive eye which
annexes others to itself, but one which "knows the complexity of the other
as something which will forever present new things to be known."

When one climbs a rock as a conqueror, one climbs with an arrogant eye. When one climbs with a loving eye, one constantly "must look
and listen and check and question." One recognizes the rock as something
very different, something perhaps totally indifferent to one's own presence, and finds in that difference joyous occasion for celebration. One
knows "the boundary of the self," where the self – the "I," the climber –
leaves off and the rock begins. There is no fusion of two into one, but a
complement of two entities *acknowledged* as separate, different, independent, yet *in relationship;* they are in relationship *if only* because the
loving eye is perceiving it, responding to it, noticing it, attending to it.

An ecofeminist perspective about both women and nature involves
this shift in attitude from "arrogant perception" to "loving perception" of
the nonhuman world. Arrogant perception of nonhumans by humans presupposes and maintains *sameness* in such a way that it expands the moral
community to those beings who are thought to resemble (be like, similar
to, or the same as) humans in some morally significant way. Any environmental movement or ethic based on arrogant perception builds a moral
hierarchy of beings and assumes some common denominator of moral
considerability in virtue of which like beings deserve similar treatment or
moral consideration and unlike beings do not. Such environmental ethics
are or generate a "unity in sameness." In contrast, "loving perception"
presupposes and maintains *difference* – a distinction between the self and
other, between human and at least some nonhumans – in such a way that
perception of the other as other *is* an expression of love for one
who/which is recognized at the outset as independent, dissimilar, different. As Maria Lugones says, in loving perception, "Love is seen not as
fusion and erasure of difference but as incompatible with them."[20] "Unity
in sameness" alone is an *erasure of difference.*

"Loving perception" of the nonhuman natural world is an attempt to
understand what it means *for humans* to care about the nonhuman world,

a world *acknowledged* as being independent, different, perhaps even indifferent to humans. Humans *are* different from rocks in important ways, even if they are also both members of some ecological community. A moral community based on loving perception of oneself *in relationship with* a rock, or with the natural environment as a whole, is one which acknowledges and respects difference, whatever "sameness" also exists.[21] The limits of loving perception are determined only by the limits of one's (e.g., a person's, a community's) ability to respond lovingly (or with appropriate care, trust, or friendship) – whether it is to other humans or to the nonhuman world and elements of it.[22]

If what I have said so far is correct, then there are very different ways to climb a mountain and *how* one climbs it and *how* one narrates the experience of climbing it matter ethically. If one climbs with "arrogant perception," with an attitude of "conquer and control," one keeps intact the very sorts of thinking that characterize a logic of domination and an oppressive conceptual framework. Since the oppressive conceptual framework which sanctions the domination of nature is a patriarchal one, one also thereby keeps intact, even if unwittingly, a patriarchal conceptual framework. Because the dismantling of patriarchal conceptual frameworks is a feminist issue, *how* one climbs a mountain and *how* one narrates – or tells the story – about the experience of climbing also are *feminist issues*. In this way, ecofeminism makes visible why, at a conceptual level, environmental ethics is a feminist issue. I turn now to a consideration of ecofeminism as a distinctively feminist and environmental ethic.

Ecofeminism as a Feminist and Environmental Ethic

A feminist ethic involves a twofold commitment to critique male bias in ethics wherever it occurs, and to develop ethics which are not male-biased. Sometimes this involves articulation of values (e.g., values of care, appropriate trust, kinship, friendship) often lost or underplayed in mainstream ethics.[23] Sometimes it involves engaging in theory building by pioneering in new directions or by revamping old theories in gender sensitive ways. What makes the critiques of old theories or conceptualizations of new ones "feminist" is that they emerge out of sex-gender analyses and reflect whatever those analyses reveal about gendered experience and gendered social reality.

As I conceive feminist ethics in the pre-feminist present, it rejects attempts to conceive of ethical theory in terms of necessary and sufficient conditions, because it assumes that there is no essence (in the sense of some transhistorical, universal, absolute abstraction) of feminist ethics. While attempts to formulate joint necessary and sufficient conditions of a feminist ethic are unfruitful, nonetheless, there are some necessary conditions, what I prefer to call "boundary conditions," of a feminist ethic. These boundary conditions clarify some of the minimal conditions of a feminist ethic without suggesting that feminist ethics has some ahistorical essence. They are like the boundaries of a quilt or collage. They delimit the territory of the piece without dictating what the interior, the design, the actual pattern of the piece looks like. Because the actual design of the quilt emerges from the multiplicity of voices of women in a cross-cultural context, the design will change over time. It is not something static.

What are some of the boundary conditions of a feminist ethic? First, nothing can become part of a feminist ethic – can be part of the quilt – that promotes sexism, racism, classism, or any other "isms" of social domination. Of course, people may disagree about what counts as a sexist act, racist attitude, classist behavior. What counts as sexism, racism, or classism may vary cross-culturally. Still, because a feminist ethic aims at eliminating sexism and sexist bias, and (as I have already shown) sexism is intimately connected in conceptualization and in practice to racism, classism, and naturism, a feminist ethic must be anti-sexist, anti-racist, anti-classist, anti-naturist and opposed to any "ism" which presupposes or advances a logic of domination.

Second, a feminist ethic is a *contextualist* ethic. A contextualist ethic is one which sees ethical discourse and practice as emerging from the voices of people located in different historical circumstances. A contextualist ethic is properly viewed as a *collage* or *mosaic*, a *tapestry* of voices that emerges out of felt experiences. Like any collage or mosaic, the point is not to have *one picture* based on a unity of voices, but a *pattern* which emerges out of the very different voices of people located in different circumstances. When a contextualist ethic is *feminist*, it gives central place to the voices of women.

Third, since a feminist ethic gives central significance to the diversity of women's voices, a feminist ethic must be structurally pluralistic rather than unitary or reductionistic. It rejects the assumption that there is "one voice" in terms of which ethical values, beliefs, attitudes, and conduct can be assessed.

Fourth, a feminist ethic reconceives ethical theory as theory in process which will change over time. Like all theory, a feminist ethic is based on some generalizations.[24] Nevertheless, the generalizations associated with it are themselves a pattern of voices within which the different voices emerging out of concrete and alternative descriptions of ethical situations have meaning. The coherence of a feminist theory so conceived is given within a historical and conceptual context, i.e., within a set of historical, socioeconomic circumstances (including circumstances of race, class, age, and affectional orientation) and within a set of basic beliefs, values, attitudes, and assumptions about the world.

Fifth, because a feminist ethic is contextualist, structurally pluralistic, and "in-process," one way to evaluate the claims of a feminist ethic is in terms of their *inclusiveness:* those claims (voices, patterns of voices) are morally and epistemologically favored (preferred, better, less partial, less biased) which are more inclusive of the felt experiences and perspectives of oppressed persons. The condition of inclusiveness requires and ensures that the diverse voices of women (as oppressed persons) will be given legitimacy in ethical theory building. It thereby helps to minimize empirical bias, e.g., bias rising from faulty or false generalizations based on stereotyping, too small a sample size, or a skewed sample. It does so by ensuring that any generalizations which are made about ethics and ethical decision making include – indeed cohere with – the patterned voices of women.[25]

Sixth, a feminist ethic makes no attempt to provide an "objective" point of view, since it assumes that in contemporary culture there really is no such point of view. As such, it does not claim to be "unbiased" in the sense of "value-neutral" or "objective." However, it does assume that whatever bias it has as an ethic centralizing the voices of oppressed persons is a *better bias* – "better" because it is more inclusive and therefore less partial – than those which exclude those voices.[26]

Seventh, a feminist ethic provides a central place for values typically unnoticed, underplayed, or misrepresented in traditional ethics, e.g., values of care, love, friendship, and appropriate trust.[27] Again, it need not do this at the exclusion of considerations of rights, rules, or utility. There may be many contexts in which talk of rights or of utility is useful or appropriate. For instance, in contracts or property relationships, talk of rights may be useful and appropriate. In deciding what is cost-effective or advantageous to the most people, talk of utility may be useful and appropriate. In a feminist *qua* contextualist ethic, whether or not such talk is useful or appropriate depends on the context; *other values* (e.g., values of care, trust, friendship) are *not* viewed as reducible to or captured solely in terms of such talk.[28]

Eighth, a feminist ethic also involves a reconception of what it is to be human and what it is for humans to engage in ethical decision making, since it rejects as either meaningless or currently untenable any gender-free or gender-neutral description of humans, ethics, and ethical decision making. It thereby rejects what Alison Jaggar calls "abstract individualism," i.e., the position that it is possible to identify a human essence or human nature that exists independently of any particular historical context.[29] Humans and human moral conduct are properly understood essentially (and not merely accidentally) in terms of networks or webs of historical and concrete relationships.

All the props are now in place for seeing how ecofeminism provides the framework for a distinctively feminist and environmental ethic. It is a feminism that critiques male bias wherever it occurs in ethics (including environmental ethics) and aims at providing an ethic (including an environmental ethic) which is not male biased – and it does so in a way that satisfies the preliminary boundary conditions of a feminist ethic.

First, ecofeminism is quintessentially anti-naturist. Its anti-naturism consists in the rejection of any way of thinking about or acting toward nonhuman nature that reflects a logic, values, or attitude of domination. Its anti-naturist, anti-sexist, anti-racist, anti-classist (and so forth, for all other "isms" of social domination) stance forms the outer boundary of the quilt: nothing gets on the quilt which is naturist, sexist, racist, classist, and so forth.

Second, ecofeminism is a contextualist ethic. It involves a shift *from* a conception of ethics as primarily a matter of rights, rules, or principles predetermined and applied in specific cases to entities viewed as competitors in the contest of moral standing, *to* a conception of ethics as growing out of what Jim Cheney calls "defining relationships," i.e., relationships conceived in some sense as defining who one is.[30] As a contextualist ethic, it is not that rights, or rules, or principles are *not* relevant or important. Clearly they are in certain contexts and for certain purposes.[31] It is just that what *makes* them relevant or important is that those to whom they apply are entities *in relationship with* others.

Ecofeminism also involves an ethical shift *from* granting moral consideration to nonhumans *exclusively* on the grounds of some similarity they share with humans (e.g., rationality, interests, moral agency, sentiency, right-holder status) *to* "a highly contextual account to see clearly what a human being is and what the nonhuman world might be, morally speaking, *for* human beings."[32] For an ecofeminist, *how* a moral agent is in relationship to another becomes of central significance, not simply *that* a moral agent is a moral agent or is bound by rights, duties, virtue, or utility to act in a certain way.

Third, ecofeminism is structurally pluralistic in that it presupposes and maintains difference – difference among humans as well as between humans and at least some elements of nonhuman nature. Thus, while ecofeminism denies the "nature/culture" split, it affirms that humans are both members of an ecological community (in some respects) and different from it (in other respects). Ecofeminism's attention to relationships and community is not, therefore, an erasure of difference but a respectful acknowledgement of it.

Fourth, ecofeminism reconceives theory as theory in process. It focuses on patterns of meaning which emerge, for instance, from the storytelling and first-person narratives of women (and others) who deplore the twin dominations of women and nature. The use of narrative is one way to ensure that the content of the ethic – the pattern of the quilt – may/will change over time, as the historical and material realities of women's lives change and as more is learned about women-nature connections and the destruction of the nonhuman world.[33]

Fifth, ecofeminism is inclusivist. It emerges from the voices of women who experience the harmful domination of nature and the way that domination is tied to their domination as women. It emerges from listening to the voices of indigenous peoples such as Native Americans who have been dislocated from their land and have witnessed the attendant undermining of such values as appropriate reciprocity, sharing, and kinship that characterize traditional Indian culture. It emerges from listening to voices of those who, like Nathan Hare, critique traditional approaches to environmental ethics as white and bourgeois, and as failing to address issues of "black ecology" and the "ecology" of the inner city and urban spaces.[34] it also emerges out of the voices of Chipko women who see the destruction of "earth, soil, and water" as intimately connected with their own inability to survive economically.[35] With its emphasis on inclusivity and difference, ecofeminism provides a framework for recognizing that what counts as ecology and what counts as appropriate conduct toward both human and nonhuman environments is largely a matter of context.

Sixth, as a feminism, ecofeminism makes no attempt to provide an "objective" point of view. It is a social ecology. It recognizes the twin dominations of women and nature as social problems rooted both in very concrete, historical, socioeconomic circumstances and in oppressive patriarchal conceptual frameworks which maintain and sanction these circumstances.

Seventh, ecofeminism makes a central place for values of care, love, friendship, trust, and appropriate reciprocity – values that presuppose that our relationships to others are central to our understanding of who we are.[36] It thereby gives voice to the sensitivity that in climbing a mountain, one is doing something in relationship with an "other," an "other" whom one can come to care about and treat respectfully.

Lastly, an ecofeminist ethic involves a reconception of what it means to be human, and in what human ethical behavior consists. Ecofeminism denies abstract individualism. Humans are who we are in large part by virtue of the historical and social contexts and the relationships we are in, including our relationships with nonhuman nature. Relationships are not something extrinsic to who we are, not an "add on" feature of human nature; they play an essential role in shaping what it is to be human. Relationships of humans to the nonhuman environment are, in part, constitutive of what it is to be a human.

By making visible the interconnections among the dominations of women and nature, ecofeminism shows that both are feminist issues and that explicit acknowledgement of both is vital to any responsible environmental ethic. Feminism *must* embrace ecological feminism if it is to end the domination of women because the domination of women is tied conceptually and historically to the domination of nature.

A responsible environmental ethic also *must* embrace feminism. Otherwise, even the seemingly most revolutionary, liberational, and holistic ecological ethic will fail to take seriously the interconnected dominations of nature and women that are so much a part of the historical legacy and conceptual framework that sanctions the exploitation of nonhuman nature. Failure to make visible these interconnected, twin dominations results in an inaccurate account of how it is that nature has been and continues to be dominated and exploited and produces an environmental ethic that lacks the depth necessary to be truly *inclusive* of the realities of persons who at least in dominant Western culture have been intimately tied with that exploitation, viz., women. Whatever else can be said in favor of such holistic ethics, a failure to make visible ecofeminist insights into the common denominators of the twin oppressions of women and nature is to perpetuate, rather than overcome, the source of that oppression.

This last point deserves further attention. It may be objected that as long as the end result is "the same" – the development of an environmental ethic which does not emerge out of or reinforce an oppressive conceptual framework – it does not matter whether that ethic (or the ethic endorsed in getting there) is feminist or not. Hence, it simply is *not* the case that any adequate environmental ethic must be feminist. My argument, in contrast, has been that it *does* matter, and for three important reasons. First, there is the scholarly issue of accurately representing historical reality, and that, ecofeminists claim, requires acknowledging the historical feminization of nature and naturalization of women as part of the exploitation of nature. Second, I have shown that the conceptual connections between the domination of women and the domination of nature are located in an oppressive and, at least in Western societies, patriarchal conceptual framework characterized by a logic of domination. Thus, I have shown that failure to notice the nature of this connection leaves at best an incomplete, inaccurate, and partial account of what is required of a conceptually adequate environmental ethic. An ethic which *does not* acknowledge this is simply *not* the same as one that does, whatever else the similarities between them. Third, the claim that, in contemporary culture, one can have an adequate environmental ethic which is *not* feminist assumes that, in contemporary culture, the label *feminist* does not add anything crucial to the nature or description of environmental ethics. I have shown that at least in contemporary culture this is false, for the word *feminist* currently helps to clarify just *how* the domination of nature is conceptually linked to patriarchy and, hence, how the liberation of nature is conceptually linked to the termination of patriarchy. Thus, because it has critical bite in contemporary culture, it serves as an important reminder that in contemporary sex-gendered, raced, classed, and naturist culture, an unlabeled position functions as a privileged and "unmarked" position. That is, without the addition of the word *feminist,* one presents environmental ethics as if it has no bias, including male-gender bias, which is just what ecofeminists deny: failure to notice the connections between the twin oppressions of women and nature *is* male-gender bias.

One of the goals of feminism is the eradication of all oppressive sex-gender (and related race, class, age, affectional preference) categories and the creation of a world in which *difference does not breed domination* – say, the world of 4001. If in 4001 an "adequate environmental ethic" is a "feminist environmental ethic," the word *feminist* may then be redundant and unnecessary. However, this is *not* 4001, and in terms of the current historical and conceptual reality the dominations of nature and of women are intimately connected. Failure to notice or make visible that connection in 1990 perpetuates the mistaken (and privileged) view that "environmental ethics" is *not* a feminist issue, and that *feminist* adds nothing to environmental ethics.[37]

Conclusion

I have argued in this paper that ecofeminism provides a framework for a distinctively feminist and environmental ethic. Ecofeminism grows out of the felt and theorized about connections between the domination of women and the domination of nature. As a contextualist ethic, ecofeminism refocuses environmental ethics on what nature might mean, morally speaking, *for* humans, and on how the relational attitudes of humans to others – humans as well as nonhumans – sculpt both what it is to be human and the nature and ground of human responsibilities to the nonhuman environment. Part of what this refocusing does is to take seriously the voices of women and other oppressed persons in the construction of that ethic.

A Sioux elder once told me a story about his son. He sent his seven-year-old son to live with the child's grandparents on a Sioux reservation so that he could "learn the Indian ways." Part of what the grandparents taught the son was how to hunt the four leggeds of the forest. As I heard the story, the boy was taught, "to shoot your four-legged brother in his hind area, slowing it down but not killing it. Then, take the four legged's head in your hands, and look into his eyes. The eyes are where all the suffering is. Look into your brother's eyes and feel his pain. Then, take your knife and cut the four-legged under his chin, here, on his neck, so that he dies quickly. And as you do, ask your brother, the four-legged, for forgiveness for what you do. Offer also a prayer of thanks to your four-legged kin for offering his body to you just now, when you need food to eat and clothing to wear. And promise the four-legged that you

will put yourself back into the earth when you die, to become nourishment for the earth, and for the sister flowers, and for the brother deer. It
is appropriate that you should offer this blessing for the four-legged and,
in due time, reciprocate in turn with your body in this way, as the four-
legged gives life to you for your survival." As I reflect upon that story, I
am struck by the power of the environmental ethic that grows out of and
takes seriously narrative, context, and such values and relational attitudes
as care, loving perception, and appropriate reciprocity, and doing what is
appropriate in a given situation – however that notion of appropriateness
eventually gets filled out. I am also struck by what one is able to see,
once one begins to explore some of the historical and conceptual connections between the dominations of women and of nature. A *re-conceiving*
and *re-visioning* of both feminism and environmental ethics, is, I think,
the power and promise of ecofeminism.

Endnotes

1. Explicit ecological feminist literature includes works from a variety of schol-
arly perspectives and sources. Some of these works are Leonie Caldecott and
Stephanie Leland, eds., *Reclaim the Earth: Women Speak Out for Life on
Earth* (London: The Women's Press, 1983); Jim Cheney, "Eco-Feminism and
Deep Ecology," *Environmental Ethics* 9 (1987): 115-45; Andrée Collard with
Joyce Contrucci, *Rape of the Wild: Man's Violence against Animals and the
Earth* (Bloomington: Indiana University Press, 1988); Katherine Davies, "His-
torical Associations: Women and the Natural World," *Women & Environments*
9, no. 2 (Spring 1987): 4-6; Sharon Doubiago, "Deeper than Deep Ecology:
Men Must Become Feminists," in *The New Catalyst Quarterly*, no. 10 (Winter
1987/88): 10-11; Brian Easlea, *Science and Sexual Oppression: Patriarchy's
Confrontation with Women and Nature* (London: Weidenfeld & Nicholson,
1981); Elizabeth Dodson Gray, *Green Paradise Lost* (Wellesley, Mass.:
Roundtable Press, 1979); Susan Griffin, *Women and Nature: The Roaring Inside Her* (San Francisco: Harper and Row, 1978); Joan L. Griscom, "On Healing the Nature/History Split in Feminist Thought," in *Heresies #13: Feminism
and Ecology* 4, no. 1 (1981): 4-9; Ynestra King, "The Ecology of Feminism
and the Feminism of Ecology," in *Healing Our Wounds: The Power of Ecological Feminism*, ed. Judith Plant (Boston: New Society Publishers, 1989),
pp. 18-28; "The Eco-feminist Imperative," in *Reclaim the Earth*, ed. Caldecott
and Leland (London: The Women's Press, 1983). pp. 12-16, "Feminism and
the Revolt of Nature," in *Heresies #13: Feminism and Ecology* 4, no. I (1981):
12-16, and "What is Ecofeminism?" *The Nation* 12 December 1987; Marti
Kheel, "Animal Liberation Is A Feminist Issue," *The New Catalyst Quarterly*,
no. 10 (Winter 1987-88): 8-9; Carolyn Merchant, *The Death of Nature:
Women, Ecology, and the Scientific Revolution* (San Francisco, Harper and
Row, 1980); Patrick Murphy, ed., "Feminism, Ecology, and the Future of the
Humanities," special issue of *Studies in the Humanities* 15, no. 2 (December
1988); Abby Peterson and Carolyn Merchant, "Peace with the Earth: Women
and the Environmental Movement in Sweden," *Women's Studies International*

Forum 9, no. 5-6. (1986): 465-79; Judith Plant, "Searching for Common Ground: Ecofeminism and Bioregionalism," in *The New Catalyst Quarterly*, no. 10 (Winter 1987/88): 6-7; Judith Plant, ed., *Healing Our Wounds: The Power of Ecological Feminism* (Boston: New Society Publishers, 1989); Val Plumwood, "Ecofeminism: An Overview and Discussion of Positions and Arguments," *Australasian Journal Of Philosophy*, Supplement to vol. 64 (June 1986): 120-37; Rosemary Radford Ruether, *New Woman/New Earth: Sexist Ideologies & Human Liberation* (New York: Seabury Press, 1975); Kirkpatrick Sale, "Ecofeminism – A New Perspective," *The Nation*, (26 September 1987): 302-05; Ariel Kay Salleh, "Deeper than Deep Ecology: The Eco-Feminist Connection," *Environmental Ethics* 6 (1984): 339-45, and "Epistemology and the Metaphors of Production: An Eco-Feminist Reading of Critical Theory," in *Studies in the Humanities* 15 (1988): 130-39; Vandana Shiva, *Staying Alive: Women, Ecology and Development* (London: Zed Books, 1988); Charlene Spretnak, "Ecofeminism: Our Roots and Flowering," *The Elmswood Newsletter*, Winter Solstice 1988; Karen J. Warren, "Feminism and Ecology: Making Connections," *Environmental Ethics* 9 (1987): 3-21; "Toward an Ecofeminist Ethic," *Studies in the Humanities* 15 (1988): 140-156; Miriam Wyman, "Explorations of Ecofeminism," *Women & Environments* (Spring 1987): 6-7; Iris Young, "'Feminism and Ecology' and 'Women and Life on Earth: Eco-Feminism in the 80's'," *Environmental Ethics* 5 (1983): 173-80; Michael Zimmerman, "Feminism, Deep Ecology, and Environmental Ethics," *Environmental Ethics* 9 (1987): 21-44.

2. Francoise d'Eaubonne, *Le Feminisme ou la Mort* (Paris: Pierre Horay, 1974), pp. 213-52.

3. I discuss this in my paper, "Toward An Ecofeminist Ethic."

4. The account offered here is a revision of the account given earlier in my paper "Feminism and Ecology: Making Connections." I have changed the account to be about "oppressive" rather than strictly "patriarchal" conceptual frameworks in order to leave open the possibility that there may be some patriarchal conceptual frameworks (e.g., in non-Western cultures) which are *not* properly characterized as based on value dualisms.

5. Murray Bookshin, "Social Ecology versus 'Deep Ecology'," in *Green Perspectives: Newsletter of the Green Program Project*, no. 4-5 (Summer 1987): 9.

6. It may be that in contemporary Western society, which is so thoroughly structured by categories of gender, race, class, age, and affectional orientation, that there simply is no meaningful notion of "value-hierarchical thinking" which does not function in an oppressive context. For purposes of this paper, I leave that question open.

7. Many feminists who argue for the historical point that claims (B1) and (B2) have been asserted or assumed to be true within the dominant Western philosophical tradition do so by discussion of that tradition's conceptions of reason, rationality, and science. For a sampling of the sorts of claims made within that context, see "Reason, Rationality, and Gender," ed. Nancy Tuana and Karen J. Warren, a special issue of the American Philosophical Association's *Newsletter on Feminism and Philosophy* 88, no. 2 (March 1989): 17-71. Ecofeminists who claim that (B2) has been assumed to be true within the dominant Western

philosophical tradition include: Gray, *Green Paradise Lost;* Griffin, *Woman and Nature: The Roaring Inside Her;* Merchant, *The Death of Nature;* Ruether, *New Woman/New Earth.* For a discussion of some of these ecofeminist historical accounts, see Plumwood, "Ecofeminism." While I agree that the historical connection between the domination of women and the domination of nature is a crucial one, I do not argue for that claim here.

8. Ecofeminists who deny (B1) when (B1) is offered as anything other than a true, descriptive, historical claim about patriarchal culture often do so on grounds that an objectionable sort of biological determinism, or at least harmful female sex-gender stereotypes, underlie (B1). For a discussion of this "split" among those ecofeminists ("nature feminists") who assert and those ecofeminists ("social feminists") who deny (B1) as anything other than a true historical claim about how women are described in patriarchal culture, see Griscom, "On Healing the Nature/History Split."

9. I make no attempt here to defend the historically sanctioned truth of these premises.

10. See, e.g., Bell Hooks, *Feminist Theory: From Margin to Center* (Boston: South End Press, 1984), pp. 51-52.

11. Maria Lugones, "Playfulness, 'World-Travelling,' and Loving Perception," *Hypatia 2,* no. 2 (Summer 1987): 3.

12. At an *experiential* level, some women are "women of color," poor, old, lesbian, Jewish, and physically challenged. Thus, if feminism is going to liberate these women, it also needs to end the racism, classism, heterosexism, anti-Semitism, and discrimination against the handicapped that is constitutive of their oppression as black, or Latina, or poor, or older, or lesbian. or Jewish, or physically challenged women.

13. This same sort of reasoning shows that feminism is also a movement to end racism, classism, age-ism, heterosexism and other "isms," which are based in oppressive conceptual frameworks characterized by a logic of domination. However, there is an important caveat: ecofeminism is *not* compatible with all feminisms and all environmentalisms. For a discussion of this point, see my article, "Feminism and Ecology: Making Connections." What it *is* compatible with is the minimal condition characterization of feminism as a movement to end sexism that is accepted by all contemporary feminisms (liberal, traditional Marxist, radical, socialist, Blacks and non-Western).

14. See, e.g., Gray, *Green Paradise Lost;* Griffin, *Women and Nature;* Merchant, *The Death of Nature;* and Ruether, *New Woman/New Earth.*

15. Suppose, as I think is the case, that a necessary condition for the existence of a moral relationship is that at least one party to the relationship is a moral being (leaving open for our purposes what counts as a "moral being"). If this is so, then the Mona Lisa cannot properly be said to have or stand in a moral relationship with the wall on which she hangs, and a wolf cannot have or properly be said to have or stand in a moral relationship with a moose. Such a necessary-condition account leaves open the question whether *both* parties to the relationship must be moral beings. My point here is simply that however one resolves *that* question, recognition of the relationships themselves as a lo-

cus of value is a recognition of a source of value that is different from and not reducible to the values of the "moral beings" in those relationships.

16. It is interesting to note that the image of being friends with the Earth is one which cytogeneticist Barbara McClintock uses when she describes the importance of having "a feeling for the organism," "listening to the material [in this case the corn plant]," in one's work as a scientist. See Evelyn Fox Keller, "Women, Science, and Popular Mythology," in *Machina Ex Dea: Feminist Perspectives on Technology,* ed. Joan Rothschild (New York: Pergamon Press, 1983), and Evelyn Fox Keller, *A Feeling For the Organism: The Life and Work of Barbara McClintock* (San Francisco: W. H. Freeman, 1983).

17. Cheney, "Eco-Feminism and Deep Ecology," 144.

18. Marilyn Frye, "In and Out of Harm's Way: Arrogance and Love," *The Politics of Reality* (Trumansburg, New York: The Crossing Press, 1983), pp. 66-72.

19. *Ibid.,* pp. 75-76.

20. Maria Lugones, "Playfulness," p. 3.

21. Cheney makes a similar point in "Eco-Feminism and Deep Ecology," p. 140.

22. *Ibid.,* p. 138.

23. This account of a feminist ethic draws on my paper "Toward an Ecofeminist Ethic."

24. Marilyn Frye makes this point in her illuminating paper, "The Possibility of Feminist Theory," read at the American Philosophical Association Central Division Meetings in Chicago, 29 April-1 May 1986. My discussion of feminist theory is inspired largely by that paper and by Kathryn Addelson's paper "Moral Revolution," in *Women and Values: Reading in Recent Feminist Philosophy,* ed. Marilyn Pearsall (Belmont, Calif.: Wadsworth Publishing Co., 1986), pp. 291-309.

25. Notice that the standard of inclusiveness does not exclude the voices of men. It is just that those voices must cohere with the voices of women.

26. For a more in-depth discussion of the notions of impartiality and bias, see my paper, "Critical Thinking and Feminism," *Informal Logic* 10, no. 1 (Winter 1988): 31-44.

27. The burgeoning literature on these values is noteworthy. See, e.g., Carol Gilligan, *In a Different Voice: Psychological Theories and Women's Development* (Cambridge: Harvard University Press, 1982); *Mapping the Moral Domain: A Contribution of Women's Thinking to Psychological Theory and Education,* ed. Carol Gilligan, Janie Victoria Ward, and Jill McLean Taylor, with Betty Bardige (Cambridge: Harvard University Press, 1988); Nel Noddings, *Caring: A Feminine Approach to Ethics and Moral Education* (Berkeley: University of California Press, 1984); Maria Lugones and Elizabeth V. Spelman, "Have We Got a Theory for You! Feminist Theory, Cultural Imperialism, and the Women's Voice," *Women's Studies International Forum* 6 (1983): 573-81; Maria Lugones, "Playfulness"; Annette C. Baier, "What Do Women Want in A Moral Theory?" *Nous* 19 (1985): 53-63.

28. Jim Cheney would claim that our fundamental relationships to one another as moral agents are not as moral agents to rights holders, and that whatever rights a person properly may be said to have are relationally defined rights, not rights possessed by atomistic individuals conceived as Robinson Crusoes who do not exist essentially in relation to others. On this view, even rights talk itself is properly conceived as growing out of a relational ethic, not vice versa.

29. Alison Jaggar, *Feminist Politics and Human Nature* (Totowa, N.J.: Rowman and Allanheld, 1980), pp. 42-44.

30. Henry West has pointed out that the expression "defining relations" is ambiguous. According to West, "the 'defining' as Cheney uses it is an adjective, not a principle – it is not that ethics defines relationships; it is that ethics grows out of conceiving of the relationships that one is in as defining what the individual is."

31. For example, in relationships involving contracts or promises, those relationships might be correctly described as that of moral agent to rights holders. In relationships involving mere property, those relationships might be correctly described as that of moral agent to objects having only instrumental value, "relationships of instrumentality." In comments on an earlier draft of this paper, West suggested that possessive individualism, for instance, might be recast in such a way that an individual is defined by his or her property relationships.

32. Cheney, "Eco-Feminism and Deep Ecology," p. 144.

33. One might object that such permission for change opens the door for environmental exploitation. This is not the case. An ecofeminist ethic is anti-naturist. Hence, the unjust domination and exploitation of nature is a "boundary condition" of the ethic; no such actions are sanctioned or justified on ecofeminist grounds. What it *does* leave open is some leeway about what counts as domination and exploitation. This, I think, is a strength of the ethic, not a weakness, since it acknowledges that *that* issue cannot be resolved in any practical way in the abstract, independent of a historical and social context.

34. Nathan Hare, "Black Ecology," in *Environmental Ethics,* ed. K. S. Shrader-Frechette (Pacific Grove, Calif.: Boxwood Press, 1981), pp. 229-36.

35. For an ecofeminist discussion of the Chipko movement, see my "Toward an Ecofeminist Ethic," and Shiva's *Staying Alive.*

36. See Cheney, "Eco-Feminism and Deep Ecology," p. 122.

37. I offer the same sort of reply to critics of ecofeminism such as Warwick Fox who suggest that for the sort of ecofeminism I defend. the word *feminist* does not add anything significant to environmental ethics and, consequently, that an ecofeminist like myself might as well call herself a deep ecologist. He asks: "Why doesn't she just call it [i.e., Warren's vision of a transformative feminism] deep ecology? Why specifically attach the label *feminist* to it . . .'?" (Warwick Fox, "The Deep Ecology-Ecofeminism Debate and Its Parallels," *Environmental Ethics* 11, no. 1 [1989]: 14, n. 22). Whatever the important similarities between deep ecology and ecofeminism (or, specifically, my version of ecofeminism) – and, indeed. there are many – it is precisely my point

here that the word *feminist* does add something significant to the conception of environmental ethics, and that any environmental ethic (including deep ecology) that fails to make explicit the different kinds of interconnections among the domination of nature and the domination of women will be, from a feminist (and ecofeminist) perspective such as mine, inadequate.

16

Ecology, Feminism, and Theology

Mary Ann Hinsdale

TWENTY YEARS AGO "EARTH DAY" WAS RIDICULED AS A "HIPPIE FAD." TODAY, one can read almost daily accounts in the newspaper of air and water pollution, acid rain, global warming, destruction of the rain forests, and disposal problems concerning toxic waste. Indeed, environmental destruction is no longer confined to the "accidents" of an irresponsible technological society, but has even become a military strategy (witness the napalming of Vietnamese jungles and the deliberate oil spills in the Persian Gulf war).

Both the ecology and the feminist movements represent social movements which, over the last thirty years, have been intent on addressing the environmental crisis. Though not specifically "religious," I believe both movements, especially as they have intersected in the "ecofeminist" movement, offer some challenging perspectives for reflecting on the traditional Christian doctrines of creation and redemption. If, as some have claimed, it is Christianity's anthropocentric bias which is responsible for the consequent subjection and domination of nature, and that it therefore deserves a major share of the blame for today's ecological crisis,[1] perhaps Christian theology ought to re-examine the foundation of these doctrines. This article will summarize some of the major insights from contemporary ecological and feminist theory and suggest what might be helpful in them for articulating a theology which is both faithful to the Christian gospel and responsive to the critical needs of our world at the end of the twentieth century.

I. Defining Ecology

Etymologically, "ecology" refers to the study of the *oikos*, or the home. As a science, it is concerned with the study of the interrelationships of organisms in their home or environment. As a philosophy, it is concerned with "the loving pursuit and realization of the wisdom of dwelling in harmony with one's place."[2] There are a variety of philosophical approaches to ecology, but one can distinguish generally between the *reformist* approaches, which seek an environmental ethic, and more *radical* critiques, which raise questions concerning the very philosophical foundations of Western industrial society and seek to develop new visions, new ecologically-informed ways of understanding that include practical living.

The differences between these two approaches can be observed in the use of the terms "environmentalism" and "ecology," which are not synonymous. In 1972, the Norwegian philosopher, Arne Naess, wrote of "deep" and "shallow" ecology to bring further precision to this distinction. Environmentalists accept the anthropocentric view that nature exists solely to serve human ends and purposes. Such an instrumentalist view of humans as separate from their environment, and of conservation based not on nature's own sake but on its value to humans, Naess called "shallow ecology."[3]

"Deep ecology," on the other hand, professes two "ultimate norms": 1) *self-realization,* which goes beyond the modern Western self, defined as an isolated ego striving for hedonistic gratification, to an identification which includes the nonhuman world; and 2) *biocentric equality,* which holds that "all organisms and entities in the ecosphere, parts of the interrelated whole, are equal in intrinsic worth."[4]

Thus, for example, animal rights – insofar as it is merely an ethical extension of human rights to nonhumans – along with other reformist positions such as "resource conservation" and "limits to growth," established along ethical hierarchies, are ultimately considered anthropocentric and "shallow."[5] While deep ecologists use such vocabulary as "rights" and "obligations," their use differs from the technical philosophical theories attached to them by the supposition of an ecological egalitarianism, which is "an intuition" experienced, not "an ethical theory to be defended by rational argument."[6] For Naess, the essence of deep ecology is:

> to keep asking more searching questions about human life, society, and Nature as in the Western philosophical tradition of Socrates . . . "we ask why and how, where others do not. For instance, ecology as a science does not ask what kind of a society would be the best for maintaining a particular ecosystem – that is considered a question for value theory, for politics, for ethics." Thus deep ecology goes beyond the so-called factual scientific level to the level of self and Earth wisdom.[7]

II. The Feminist Critique

Feminism is also characterized by a spectrum of positions. Although feminist philosopher Rosemarie Tong discusses no fewer than seven varieties (liberal, Marxist, radical, psychoanalytic, socialist, existentialist and postmodern), philosopher Alison Jaggar prefers simply four: liberal, Marxist, radical and socialist.[8] Feminist theologians have also come to recognize the pluralism within feminism and have sometimes used the designations of "reformist" or "radical" to refer to them.[9] Though some have recently backed away from the tensions such categorization has caused,[10] the definite differences among feminist scholars in religion, for example in the distinction between feminist theologians and *thea*logians (goddess feminists), do make some kind of designation seem appropriate. One that is becoming more widely used is the distinction between "biblical" and "post-biblical" feminists. "Biblical" feminists are those who do not find the *essential* message of the Bible to be oppressive, but nevertheless engage in interpretation which aims at critiquing oppressive texts, recovering, and even reconstructing them.[11] "Post-biblical" feminists are those who reject the Bible and Christianity and Judaism as inherently incompatible with women's achievement of full personhood.

Neither Tong nor Jaggar discusses religious feminism. This is regrettable because both biblical and post-biblical feminists often show little awareness that different conceptions of human nature, epistemology and political theory also characterize their positions.[12] For example, until recently few biblical feminists who focused on women being able to receive "equal rights" (or "equal rites") in the church were conscious that their feminism takes a *liberal* political stance. Likewise, post-biblical feminists dealing with the goddess and women's spirituality failed to recognize that their *radical* feminist stance, with its essentialist and universalizing tendencies, often perpetuated a "false consciousness" concerning "women's experience" – too often only the experience of "white, middle-class, heterosexual" women. The realization that both biblical and post-biblical feminism needs to acknowledge what feminist philosophers call "standpoint consciousness" is becoming a more sound characteristic of religious feminist scholarship.[13]

III. The Ecofeminist Movement

Feminists have extended their critique of domination on the basis of sex to include domination of nature as well. Françoise d'Eaubonne, coining the word *eco-feminisme* to describe this more holistic understanding of liberation, argued in 1974 that when the fate of the human species and of the planet is at stake, "no male-led 'revolution' will counteract the horrors of overpopulation and destruction of natural resources."[14] Ecofeminism as a movement, the strength of which is that "it did not emerge solely in the halls of academia, or the mind of one person or even one culture,"[15] gained impetus when the meltdown at Three Mile Island prompted women in the United States to come together *en masse* to explore the connections between feminism, ecology and militarism and to share their visions for life on earth.[16] For ecofeminism the key category of analysis is "nature," particularly the interrelated dominations of nature and of women. Though it is not a religious movement *per se*, it is interesting that ecofeminists often cite the thought of a theologian, Rosemary Ruether, as foundational for their own:

> Women must see that there can be no liberation for them and no solution to the ecological crisis within a society whose fundamental model of relationships continues to be one of domination. They must unite the demands of the women's movement with those of the ecological movement to envision a radical reshaping of the basic socioeconomic relations and the underlying values of this society.[17]

Though just as within feminism, there are differences in ecofeminism; all ecofeminists *agree* that there are important connections between the oppression of nature (naturism) and the oppression of women (sexism). They are likewise in harmony in viewing the patriarchal conceptual framework, which gives rise to value-hierarchical thinking, as responsible for a logic of domination. Furthermore, since the connections between the oppression of women and nature are basically conceptual, they believe what is necessary is a reconceptualization. Finally, ecofeminists in general agree that familiar ecological principles, derived from Barry Commoner's "laws of ecology," ground their critique of the patriarchal framework:

- life is an interconnected web, not a hierarchy
- all parts of the ecosystem have equal value
- there is no free lunch
- nature knows best
- healthy systems maintain diversity
- unity in diversity[18]

What ecofeminists *disagree* about is the nature of the connections between women and nature and whether such connections are potentially liberating or reinforcing of the inferior and subordinate position of women. Here ecofeminists are conscious that the "standpoint consciousness" which categorizes feminist theory – liberal, radical, or socialist – will also affect one's position concerning the domination of nature/women.[19]

Liberal feminism, sometimes called "equal rights" feminism, "idealizes a society in which autonomous individuals are provided maximal freedom to pursue their own interests."[20] The liberation of women requires the elimination of those legal and social constraints that prevent women from exercising their right of self-determination. Though such questioning of "natural" roles or destinies has worked *for* women and other dehumanized peoples, Ynestra King argues that liberal feminism, with its individualist, rationalist, utilitarian bias, is the least able appropriately to address ecology, because it is by and large a white middle-class movement, concerned with the extension of male power and privilege to women like themselves, not the fate of women as a whole.[21] To the extent that they address ecological concerns, liberal feminists will be 'environmentalists' rather than ecologists, "basing any claims to moral consideration for nonhumans either on the alleged rights or interests of humans, or on the consequences of such consideration for human well-being."[22] Ecofeminists like King and Warren believe that liberal feminism leads women into absurdly unsisterly positions, like supporting the draft and maintaining women's contract credibility in surrogate motherhood cases (which denies the natural mother any right to her child). In short, with regard to a view of nature and women's connectedness to it, liberal feminism's position involves the rationalization and, ultimately, the domination of nature.[23]

Radical feminism embraces the view that the biologically based ideology of women being closer to nature is the root cause of domination of women by men. Concerned with the essential embodiedness of human nature, radical (or "cultural") feminism finds the woman/nature connection potentially emancipatory, taking women's bodies (particularly the childbearing and childrearing functions) into the political arena. Such feminists celebrate the life experience of the female ghetto and emphasize "women's ways of knowing" which involves intuition, caring, feelings, spiritual or mystical experiences and the integration of these experiences into feminist theory and epistemology. Some radical/cultural feminists advocate a separate women's culture.

Ecofeminism has been most often associated with radical feminism, though recently a critique of radical/cultural feminism has emerged from within ecofeminism. There is concern that the eclectic potpourri of beliefs and practices which comprise what is known as the "feminist spirituality movement" tends to mystify women's experience and pays little attention to the historical and material features of women's oppression. Radical feminism tends to ignore race and class issues and fails to see the extent to which women's oppression is grounded in concrete diverse social structures. It also perpetuates dualistic, hierarchical thinking, since it comes down in favor of one side of the nature/culture dualism.

> The truth is that nature is itself. It is neither male human nor female human. That should be obvious. But unfortunately it is not. The ground we walk upon is not 'Mother Earth'; it is living soil with a chemistry and biology of its own which we must come to understand and respect.[24]

Socialist feminism is the attempt to integrate the insights of traditional Marxist feminism with those of radical feminism by making domination by class and gender fundamental to women's oppression. Socialist feminists point out how the economic system and the sex/gender system are reinforced in historically specific ways. Differences between men and women are social constructions, not biologically given. Capitalism is a result of patriarchy; women's liberation requires the end of both.[25]

What is problematic for ecofeminists, however, is that while "socialist feminists have articulated a strong economic and class analysis, they have not sufficiently addressed the domination of nature. . . . Socialist feminists have addressed . . . domination between persons, but they have not seriously attended to the domination of either nonhuman nature or inner nature."[26] Neither have the socialist feminists recognized (as the radical feminists have) that there is a female political imagination which manifests itself in the political practice of a feminism of difference. They "forget that no revolution in human history has succeeded without a strong cultural foundation and a utopian vision emerging from the life experience of the revolutionary subjects."[27]

IV. Ecofeminist Solutions

In summary, then, ecofeminists believe that socialist feminists and radical (nature) feminists each have something the other needs. Socialists emphasize history and disregard nature and biology; radical feminists emphasize nature and disregard history and social structures. Ecofeminists, however, are about the "organic forging of a genuinely antidualistic, or dialectical, theory and praxis," which seeks to enter history, to interpret the historical significance of *the fact* that women have been positioned at the dividing line where the organic emerges into the social. "The domination of nature originates in society and therefore must be resolved in society. Therefore, the embodied woman as social historical agent, rather than product of natural law is the subject of ecofeminism."[28]

Ecofeminists are thus convinced that practice does not wait for theory; it comes out of the imperatives of history. They believe that women are the revolutionary bearers of this antidualistic potential that does not sever the woman/nature connection, but uses it as a vantage point for creating a different kind of culture and politics that would integrate intuitive, spiritual and rational knowledge, so as to transform the nature/culture distinction and to envision and create a free ecological society. The best summary of the movement's current thinking is Karen Warren's program of "transformative feminism."[29] Such a responsible ecological perspective central to feminist theory and practice would:

1) recognize and make explicit the interconnections between all systems of oppression;

2) provide a central theoretical place for the diversity of women's experience, even if this meant abandoning the project of attempting to formulate one overarching feminist theory;

3) reject the logic of domination and the patriarchal conceptual framework and address the conceptual and structural interconnections among all forms of domination, by making connections with the revolution of insurgent people;

4) rethink what it means to be human (which involves a rethinking of the notion of the self, such that we see ourselves as co-members of an ecological community and yet different from other members of it);

5) recast traditional ethical concerns to make a central place for values such as care, friendship, and reciprocity in relationships;

6) challenge patriarchal bias in technology research, while promoting the use of appropriate technology.

What do these insights imply for theology and the church? With reference to the Christian tradition in particular, which has historically been accused—with good reason— of bearing a major part of the responsibility for the domination and ruination of nature, what are the implications for a renewed Christian understanding of creation and redemption?

V. Implications for a Theology of Creation

This examination of the deep ecology and ecofeminist movements suggests several possible themes by which Christian theology might rethink its teaching on creation and redemption.

1. First, both deep ecology and ecofeminism would urge a reinterpretation of the divine command to "subdue the earth" in Genesis 1:26-28[30] which goes beyond the contemporary theological solutions which speak of "stewardship" – a position which remains essentially anthropocentric – and stresses an *ecocentric* interdependence.[31] In its notion of "self-realization," deep ecology stresses the fundamental interdependence of humans not only with traditionally accepted aspects of "the self" (family and loved ones), but with the environment as whole. Both deep ecology and ecofeminism argue that if human beings *are* nature, then to use the theological vocabulary of "the order of creation" for purposes of differentiation is basically "anthropocentric" and perpetuates value-hierarchical thinking.

Of course, the phrase "the order of creation" is also used in another sense, to indicate the material world which first had to "be there" in order that redemption might be accomplished. The early church insisted on the doctrine of *creatio ex nihilo* in order to combat the dangerous consequences of maintaining the eternity of matter. Here the main question is not simply one of cosmology, but of soteriology: the creation created by God gives matter an authentic ontological place in the world as something "good." Yet the fundamental distinction remains between the Creator and the created. According to ecofeminism and deep ecology, humanity and nature may indeed be one. Neither, however, is "divine."

2. Deep ecology's stress on biocentrism is not only problematic for Christianity.[32] Ecofeminists also see problems in maintaining absolutely *no* differentiation between conscious human nature and non-sentient nature. To say there are "no boundaries" among life forms, and thus, no intrinsic differences, could result in saying there is no difference between a virus and a human being who is invaded by this virus. To avoid such problems, ecofeminists suggest thinking about interdependence using the category of *relationship*. Process theologians are developing theologies of nature along this line which enable one to recognize the goodness of creation in such a way that one may recognize degrees of intrinsic value relative to the experiential richness and self-concern of an organism.[33]

3. Since they are not primarily religious movements, it is not clear whether deep ecology or ecofeminism would regard Christianity's distinction between creator/creature as fostering relationships of domination.[34] In fact, although ecofeminism especially decries the interlocking oppressions (sexism, racism, classism, heterosexism and naturism), it offers no account for their existence. No theory of "the Fall" or of the existence of "evil" explains from where such oppressions come. If the answer is that they are created by humans, the implication is that humans are somehow more responsible for domination (more than the animals, the forests, rocks, or soil). But in a web of interrelated beings, why are humans more responsible? Perhaps ecofeminism can also learn something from Christian theology.

Matthew Fox, for one, has given us a contemporary recovery of two competing traditions within Christianity: the Fall/Redemption and Creation-centered traditions. The one is an inheritance from Augustine; the other from Irenaeus. In Fox's categories, ecofeminism stresses an Irenaean approach. Nature is not "fallen" but in process of growth; it is becoming. The deutero-Pauline theology on which Irenaeus drew does not stress redemption as a buying back, but as a coming to fullness (*pleroma*), a "bringing together in harmony" (*anakephalaiosis*). The question remains whether ecofeminism attends sufficiently to the reality of evil and destruction – often rampant in nature. Still, its posture seems more consonant with an Irenaean theology of redemption.[35]

Other possibilities for a renewed Christian doctrine of nature in harmony with ecofeminist insights would be to recover the biblical notions of jubilee and *sophia* or the Jewish notion of *shabbat*, all of which emphasize the integrity and celebration of creation.[36] After all, the biblical tradition makes it clear that the crown of creation is *not*, as is frequently misunderstood, the human being, but the sabbath.[37]

4. It is probably no accident that where ecofeminist and deep ecological ideas are finding most resonance in contemporary theology is among theologians who are engaged in a complete rethinking, not only of specific doctrines which seem to have relevance for ecology – the doctrines of God, creation, and redemption – but of the whole perspective from which one does theology. The most creative attempts in this regard are emerging from process and feminist theologians such as John Cobb, Jay McDaniel, Sallie McFague, Lois Daly and Grace Jantzen.[38]

These theologians are not interested merely in fashioning a new "theology of" creation or redemption, but are concerned to offer a perspective from which all theological topics should ultimately be rethought. They cause us to ask whether it is time to speak of "the hermeneutical privilege of nature/the earth," much as we have learned from liberation theologies to speak of the "preferential option" or hermeneutical privilege of the poor. John Cobb observes that fashioning a more ecological "theology of nature" must not simply be

> a new way of speaking of "doctrines of". . . . We are not trying only to spell out what traditional theology implies about nature. Instead, we want to see the whole of theology influenced and reconceived in light of what we are learning about nature."[39]

From this brief sketch, it is quite apparent that both deep ecology and ecofeminism present challenges and opportunities for theology, especially the traditional doctrines of creation and redemption and the articulation of a more adequate theology of nature. To undertake such a dialogue will not only be exciting, but crucial to the survival of both nature and theology.

Notes

1. Lynn White's essay is probably the most often quoted critique of Christian theology's anti-environmental stance: "The Historical Roots of Our Ecological Crisis," *Science* 155 (1967) 1203-07.

2. Donald Edward Davis, *ECOphilosophy. A Field Guide to the Literature* (San Pedro: R. and R. Miles, 1989) xii. Carolyn Merchant, ("Earthcare, Women and the Environment Movement." *Environment* 23 [June, 1981] 7) notes that the first to link the home and environment was Ellen Swallow, the first woman student at MIT. As an instructor in sanitary chemisty and nutrition, she developed in 1892 a science of environmental quality, which she called "ecology," concerned with industrial health, water and air quality, transportation, and nutrition. See also, Robert Clark, *Ellen Swallow: The Woman Who Founded Ecology* (Chicago: Follett, 1973).

3. Arne Naess, "The Shallow and the Deep, Long-Range Ecology Movements: A Summary." *Inquiry* 16 (1973) 95-100. See also George Sessions, "The Deep Ecology Movement: A Review," *Environmental Review* 11 (1987) 116; and

Warwick Fox, "Deep Ecology: A New Philosophy of Our Time?" *The Ecologist* 14 (1984) 104-200.

4. Bill Devall and George Sessions, *Deep Ecology* (Salt Lake City: Gribbs Smith, 1985) 67.

5. Sessions, "The Deep Ecology Movement," 116.

6. A. Naess, "Intuition, Intrinsic Value and Deep Ecology. A Reply to Warwick Fox," *The Ecologist* 14 (1984) 201-03. For a statement of the eight principles of "deep ecology" see the 1984 summary of George Sessions and Arne Naess in Duvall and Sessions, *Deep Ecology*, 70. For a Christian critique of these principles see John B. Cobb and H. Daly, eds. *For the Common Good* (Boston: Beacon, 1990).

7. Duvall and Sessions, *Deep Ecology*, 65. For an account of the mechanistic world view of modern science, which sanctioned the exploitation of nature, unrestrained commercial expansion, and a new socio-economic order that subordinated women, see Carolyn Merchant, *The Death of Nature: Women, Ecology and the Scientific Revolution* (San Francisco: Harper and Row, 1980).

8. Rosemarie Tong, *Feminist Thought: A Comprehensive Introduction* (Boulder, CO: Westview Press, 1989); Alison Jaggar, *Feminist Politics and Human Nature* (Totowa, N.J.: Rowman and Littlefield, 1988).

9. See Carol P. Christ and Judith Plaskow, eds., *Womanspirit Rising* (San Francisco: Harper and Row, 1979) 1-16. For a discussion of the variety of feminist positions and their import for church, see Marcia Bunge, "Feminism in Different Voices: Resources for the Church," *Word and World* 8/4 (1988) 321-26.

10. E.g., Judith Plaskow and Carol Christ, *Weaving the Visions: New Patterns in Feminist Spirituality* (San Francisco: Harper and Row, 1989).

11. Probably the most advanced discussion of feminist biblical hermeneutics is that of Elisabeth Schüssler Fiorenza in her works *In Memory of Her* (New York: Crossroad, 1983) and *Bread Not Stone* (Boston: Beacon, 1984).

12. Rosemary Ruether, Elisabeth Schüssler Fiorenza and Carter Heyward are notable exceptions.

13. See Mary Potter-Engel and Susan Brooks Thistlethwaite, eds., *Lift Every Voice: Constructing Christian Theologies From the Underside* (San Francisco: Harper and Row, 1989).

14. Françoise d'Eaubonne, *Le Feminisme où la mort* (Paris: Pierre Horay, 1974) 213-52; cited in Mary Daly, *Gyn/Ecology: The Metaethics of Radical Feminism* (Boston: Beacon, 1978) 9.

15. Judith Plant, *Healing the Wounds: The Promise of Ecofeminism* (Toronto: Between the Lines, 1989) 257.

16. Leonie Caldecott and Stephanie Leland, eds., *Reclaim the Earth: Women Speak Out for Life on Earth* (London: The Women's Press, 1983) 6. For other chronicles of ecofeminist events and projects during the 1980's, see Ynestra King, *What Is Ecofeminism?* (New York: Ecofeminist Resources, 1989) esp. "Ecological Feminism," 38-43; and Merchant, "Earthcare," 6-13; 38-40.

17. Rosemary Ruether, *New Women, New Earth: Sexist Ideologies and Human Liberation* (New York: Seabury, 1975) 204.

18. See Ynestra King, "The Ecology of Feminism and Feminism of Ecology," *What Is Ecofeminism?*, 26-27; and Merchant, "Earthcare," 10-11.

19. For this view, see Karen J. Warren, "Feminism and Ecology: Making the Connections," *Environmental Ethics* 9 (1989) 3-20. See also, Carolyn Merchant, "Ecofeminism and Feminist Theory," in Irene Diamond and Gloria Orenstein (eds) *Reweaving the World: The Emergence of Ecofeminism* (San Francisco: Sierra Club, 1990).

20. Warren, "Feminism and Ecology," 8.

21. King, *What Is Ecofeminism?*, 119.

22. Warren, "Feminism and Ecology," 9.

23. King, *What Is Ecofeminism?*, 119-20.

24. Elizabeth Dodson Gray, "The Nature of Our Cultural Assumptions," *Daughters of Sarah* (May/June, 1990) 9.

25. Warren, "Feminism and Ecology," 16-17.

26. King, *What Is Ecofeminism?*, 128.

27. *Ibid.*, 129.

28. *Ibid.*, 129-34.

29. Warren, "Ecology and Feminism," 17-20.

30. See for this Jürgen Moltman's remarks in his essay in *God in Creation* (San Francisco: Harper and Row, 1985) 29-33.

31. Many deep ecologists now use the term *ecocentricism* in order to dispel the notion that biocentricsm was limited only to living beings.

32. See the remarks by John Cobb in John B. Cobb and Herman Daly, *For the Common Good: Redirecting the Economy Toward Community, the Environment and a Sustainable Future.* (Boston: Beacon, 1989).

33. See, for example, Jay McDaniel's discussion in *Of God and Pelicans. A Theology of Reverence for Life.* (Louisville: John Knox, 1989) 51-84.

34. Radical feminism, such as that espoused by Mary Daly, has long seen the male Father/God as the primordial instance of patriarchal dualism and domination.

35. See Matthew Fox, *Original Blessing* (Sante Fe, NM: Bear and Co. 1983).

36. On "jubilee" see Sharon H. Ringe, *Jesus, Liberation, and the Biblical Jubilee: Images for Ethics and Christology* (Philadelphia: Fortress, 1985); Karen Lebacqz, *Justice in an Unjust World* (Minneapolis: Augsburg, 1987), 122-60; and Arthur Waskow, "Both the Land and Society Need Rest," *Compass* (July, 1990) 51 and also "From Compassion to Jubilee," *Tikkun* 5 (1990) 78-81.

37. Moltmann, *God in Creation*, 31.

38. In addition to the works already mentioned see the World Council of Churches' sub-unit on Church and Society report, edited by Charles Birch,

William Eakin and Jay McDaniel, *Liberating Life: Contemporary Approaches to Ecological Theology* (Maryknoll, NY: Orbis, 1990).

39. John Cobb, "The Role of Theology of Nature," in Birch, Eakin, McDaniel, *Liberating Life*, 263.

17

Ecofeminism and Panentheism

Ivone Gebaras
Interviewed by Mary Judith Ress

You talk of three phases of feminist theology. Could you summarize each phase for us?

First, these phases are not necessarily chronological, but often are mixed together in a given country or group, depending on the historical circumstances and the level of awareness in each. Also, I would like to say that I have only been working in feminist theology since about 1980, when I started asking myself the questions theologians such as Dorothee Solle, Rosemary Radford Reuther and Mary Daly (in her earlier stage) were asking. I found that those questions were as valid in Latin America as they were in the United States and Europe.

The first phase, which began about twenty years ago, is what I call the discovery by women that we are oppressed historical subjects. We discovered our oppression in the Bible, in theology, in our churches. I stress that this discovery came from the secular feminist movement and *not* from within our churches, which are patriarchal constructs.

In this phase, we rediscovered the many women in the Bible and reclaimed them as key actors in the history of liberation: Sarah and Hagar, Miriam, Ruth, Esther, Judith. Mary, of course. Magdalene and the women at the empty tomb.

This was a real step forward, but it was not enough. In this phase, we tended to overvalue the feminine. We fell into the patriarchal trap of underlining all the domestic qualities associated with women: our role as mothers, our double-duty work day, etc. We held up the beautiful Judith, who by her beauty seduced Holifernes, only to slay him and thus save her people – without ever questioning the violent, patriarchal framework in which Judith is presented.

Also in this phase, there was a certain desire to "get even." We tended to think we were the "good" gender, the martyrs – and at the same time some of us began to think we were superior to poor, weak men.

In the second phase, which I call the "feminization of theological concepts," we began to rediscover the submerged feminine expressions of God in the Bible. We discovered God's "maternal" face in texts such as

Isaiah 49. We also gained a voice in decision-making in our churches; professional women, academics, and leaders of grassroots organizations were invited to participate so that the "women's perspective" would be present. And this made our male counterparts happy; in the case of liberation theologians, this is what they had been working toward – the inclusion of women theologians within their ranks.

But while we began to criticize patriarchy within the Bible, within theology, we didn't criticize the concept of God, Father Almighty, all powerful, omnipotent, Being-unto-himself who out of his goodness created everything, heaven and Earth, men and women. We didn't notice that the story we were presented was a power struggle between God and humanity – and that every time humanity deviated from God's will, a "catastrophe" occurred because we had broken with God, we had gone against God's will. Our image of ourselves was of *fallen beings.* And the only way we could be saved was for God to send His son, who was also God, to rescue us from our original sin.

But who decided what was God's will, which has throughout history favored the rich, the white race, the male? Our religious leaders, who said they were more capable of discovering what was God's will for us.

Even more insidiously, we were told and came to believe that we were God's chosen people, and in God's name Christianity took on a messianic, missionary triumphalism: we were superior to all other peoples and all other religious expressions that had developed through the ages.

Liberation theology asks the question: "How to speak of God in the face of hunger, injustice, misery, dictatorship, the destruction of entire peoples?" It offers a more collective understanding of God and stresses the social nature of sin. God becomes the God of life and of justice who has a preferential love for the poor. But liberation theology has not changed the patriarchal anthropology and cosmology upon which Christianity is based. Liberation theology, like the first and second phases of feminist theology, did not challenge the underlying patriarchal structure of Christianity itself.

And what you call "holistic ecofeminism," the third phase, would offer a new anthropology and cosmology for Christianity?

The great challenge is whether Christianity will be flexible enough to change the foundations of its anthropology and cosmology to respond to holistic ecofeminism. I think it can. And I think it must, because today we are experiencing a world-wide institutional crisis where the old religious sanctions and admonitions are simply exhausted. Nobody listens to them anymore.

What then is "holistic ecofeminism?" It doesn't sound very Latin American!

No, what I call holistic ecofeminism or critical feminism comes out of a worldwide critique of modernity. It comes from a growing suspicion that the sciences, both social and physical, may not have the solutions to carry us into a safe, more life-giving future. But let us be clear here: this thinking is not a Latin American native flower – just as, if we are honest, liberation theology is not native, but was highly influenced by European thinking. Both have been given different shades and hues by Latin Americans, but let us not fall into a naive nationalism when speaking of theologies! And here, besides the feminist theologians I mentioned before, I must recognize the influence of people like Teilhard de Chardin, Fritjof Capra, Thomas Berry, Brian Swimme, among others.

Holistic ecofeminism questions a theology that sees God as above all things. God has always been used by both the left and the right to justify particular political programs. There simply is no pure God!

There is also a growing suspicion that the age-old conviction that "redemption comes through suffering" might not be true. There is growing dissatisfaction with liberation theology. The promise of a new society founded upon justice and equality just hasn't happened. We are tired of the struggle, which is often violent and which promises our liberation at the end. All we have seen is destruction and death, never victory. So we are suspicious of this approach, tired of yet another document. Analysis on the political and economic situation of our people is very important, but it is not everything!

Instead, we look at the air, the water, the Earth. We look at all the garbage surrounding us, and we sense deep within ourselves that our planet is not just a place – it is our own body. Ecofeminism proposes a new relationship with the Earth and with the entire cosmos.

For me, "holistic ecofeminism" has a double purpose. First is the fundamental concern for the oppressed – the voiceless of history – who when they are born are *de facto* excluded from the chance to live a full life because of their economic situation. It is the poor who are the greatest consumers of patriarchal religion because of the consolation it provides! They are caught in a vicious circle here, but for me it is absolutely key to avoid distancing myself from these voiceless ones. Second is the commitment to put an end to patriarchy in all its forms.

But what are you proposing when you say we must change the anthropological basis upon which Christianity is built?

I suggest that we must first change our image of men and women within the cosmos. And when we change that image, our image of God changes. Any image of God is nothing more than the image of the experience or the understanding we have of ourselves. We must re-situate the human within – not above – the cosmos. This is diametrically opposed to a Christian anthropology that insists humanity is "Lord of Creation" ordered by the Creator to "increase and dominate the Earth." In the current anthropology, the human's right to dominate, control, and possess has been legitimatized by the Creator and thus becomes part of human nature, pre-established – and therefore impossible to change.

We must break with our dualistic constructs of God and of the world – constructs that are hierarchical and tend to exclude the "other" as less valuable; for example, God is separated from the world; man from woman; heaven from Earth; good from bad. If one is good, one cannot be bad; if one is master, one cannot be a slave, and so on.

Yet, I am convinced that this way of thinking is shifting. Today we are beginning to experience who we are in a different way – more holistically. Why? Because we are beginning to suffer because our water is dirty, our rivers and oceans are dirty, because our food isn't very good anymore. We feel great pain at such destruction. We sense at a gut level that we too are "dirty," somehow "polluted" as well. Our intuition tells us what many so-called primitive peoples have always held: that we are all in all.

The scientists are also showing us how our very "power over" is tragic because it is not only causing our own destruction as human beings, but it is destroying life itself! We humans cannot live if we destroy the rest of our body.

And so we are beginning to discover our inter-connectedness. We humans are not "Lords of Creation." Instead, we are the Earth's thought, the Earth's reflection of itself; one type of consciousness present on the planet.

Therefore, when we behold the sick body of the poor, and see the injustice they suffer, we see it as our own body. There is no other. The other is myself. We are part of one immense, pulsating body that has been evolving for billions of years – and is still evolving.

But then are you saying that there is no God, no Lord of history, no Yahweh or loving father?

I am saying that our understanding of God must change. We can no longer posit a God who is Being-unto-himself, omnipotent, above all. This image of God is no longer adequate; we can no longer give obedience to someone "up there." This is the God built by patriarchy!

Instead, our intuition tells us that we dwell in Mystery larger than ourselves. We are part of this Mystery, which, like us, is evolving. This Mystery is what we call the Divine. But this Mystery is not a being, not a person. There is no God sitting on a throne who will judge us when we die. Our brothers and sisters on this Earth are our only judges!

But is there a personal God?

If God were a person, God would be an autonomous being, which is the same thing as the patriarchal concept of God who is "above" and "over" life itself. God is not a person, but we humans are persons so this is how we tend to relate to Divine Mystery. Because we are persons, we are able to initiate a dialogue, and we personalize all our relationships. Therefore, analogously, I speak to God as a person. It is as if I were talking or praying to my double. I attribute the qualities of a person to my double, but it is my "I" talking to my "I."

But what is the fear here? There is no "one God" to manipulate, as the "mono" theists have done, by making God "one," "universal," as well as "masculine." This God is an entirely political God, a God whose main job is to *dominate* and *control*.

Holistic ecofeminism holds that God is in all – and therefore all is sacred. We speak of pan-en-theism. This is much closer to what primitive peoples have believed; there are many different ways to express our experience of Divine Mystery.

Then we have no source of revelation? The Bible is not the word of God?

We must remember that sacred books like the Bible are human productions. The Bible is not "the Word of God." It is the word of humans about God. But some texts in the Old Testament and in the New Testament recount experiences so profound, so essential to us that we say "this is the word of God." For instance, those texts that speak to us of sharing, forgiving, mercy, and compassion.

The Gospel is the story of the Jesus movement, a movement of resurrection. It is a collection of stories that recount *actions of resurrection,* of giving people life in many different ways. We are told to love our neighbor as ourselves. We are invited to love ourselves, which is relatively easy; but then we are asked to step outside our individual "I" and realize that we are not separate from our neighbor, something that is harder because it doesn't come as naturally as loving ourselves does. But we do so because we are moved to compassion to do so, not because we will be rewarded in heaven.

What you are suggesting is certainly very radical, in the sense of returning to roots. But in stripping Christianity of its patriarchal structure, what is left?

What we are trying to do is to *relativize* Christianity. It is *one* experience of how human beings explain Divine Mystery. The Jesus movement offers one response to humanity's search for meaning. But the

Christian experience is only one response, not *the* response. It is just one small key. But even if we could unite all the keys, all the responses, we still wouldn't be able to fathom the Mystery in which we live.

Patriarchy is a development of human evolution – whether or not we had to develop this way is beside the point – but we did develop patriarchy and it has been the overriding way we have organized society for over 5,000 years. Christianity is marked by patriarchy; it was born and has flourished in a patriarchal society. But the other great religions are also riddled with patriarchy: Buddhism, Islam, Hinduism are all marked with patriarchy. It is not a question of throwing out these religions, but of stripping them of their patriarchal constructs.

We are speaking here of a change in paradigms. The patriarchal paradigm has lasted for more than 5,000 years. But everywhere that paradigm is falling apart. These old clothes no longer fit. We must look for new clothes, new constructs which we probably won't live to see firmly in place. But we are called to do so by the future, by our grandchildren.

18

Ecology Is a Sistah's Issue Too: The Politics of Emergent Afrocentric Ecowomanism

Shamara Shantu Riley

BLACK WOMANISTS, LIKE EVERYONE IN GENERAL, CAN NO LONGER over-look the extreme threat to life on this planet and its particular repercussions on people of African descent.[1] Because of the race for increased "development," our world continues to suffer the consequences of such environmental disasters as the Chernobyl nuclear meltdown and Brazil's dwindling forests. Twenty percent of all species are at risk of extinction by the year 2000, with the rate of plant and animal extinction likely to reach several hundred per day in the next ten to thirty years (Worldwatch 1987, 3). Manufacturing chemicals and other abuses to the environment continue to weaken the ozone layer. We must also contend with the phenomenon of climate change, with its attendant rise in sea levels and changes in food production patterns.

Along with these tragic statistics, however, are additional environmental concerns that hit far closer to home than many Black people realize. In the United States, poor people of color are disproportionately likely to be the victims of pollution, as toxic waste is being consciously directed at our communities. The nation's largest hazardous-waste dump, which has received toxic material from 45 states, is located in predominantly black Sumter County, Alabama (de la Pena and Davis 1990, 34). The mostly African-American residents in the 85-mile area between Baton Rouge and New Orleans, better known as Cancer Alley, live in a region which contains 136 chemical companies and refineries. A 1987 study conducted by the United Church of Christ's Commission for Racial Justice found that two-thirds of all Blacks and Latinos in the United States reside in areas with one or more unregulated toxic-waste sites (Riley 1991, 15). The CRJ report also cited race as the most significant variable in differentiating communities with such sites from those without them. Partly as a result of living with toxic waste in disproportionate numbers, African-Americans have higher rates of cancer, birth defects, and lead poisoning than the United States population as a whole.[2]

214

On the African continent, rampant deforestation and soil erosion continue to contribute to the hunger and poverty rates in many countries. The elephant population is rapidly being reduced as poachers kill them to satisfy industrialized nations' ivory trade demands (Joyce 1989, 22). Spreading to a dozen African nations, the Green Belt Movement is seeking to reverse the environmental damage created by the European settlers during colonialism, when the settlers brought nonindigenous trees on the continent. As with United States communities of color, many African nations experience "economic blackmail," which occurs when big business promises jobs and money to "impoverished areas in return for these areas' support of or acquiescence to environmentally undesirable industries" (Meyer 1992, 32).

The extinction of species on our ancestral continent, the "mortality of wealth," and hazardous-waste contamination in our backyards ought to be reasons enough for Black womanists to consider the environment as a central issue of our political agendas.[3] However, there are other reasons the environment should be central to our struggles for social justice. The global environmental crisis is related to the sociopolitical systems of fear and hatred of all that is natural, nonwhite, and female that has pervaded dominant Western thought for centuries.[4] I contend that the social constructions of race, gender, class and nonhuman nature in mainstream Western thought are interconnected by an ideology of domination. Specific instances of the emergent Afrocentric ecowomanist activism in Africa and the United States, as well as West African spiritual principles that propose a method of overcoming dualism, will be discussed in this paper.

The Problem of Nature for Black Womanism

Until recently, few Black womanists gave more than token attention to environmental issues. At least in the United States, the origins of such oversight stem from the traditional Black association of environmentalism as a "white" concern. The resistance by many United States Blacks to the environmental movement may partly originate from a hope of revenge. Because of our acute oppression(s), many Blacks may conclude that if the world comes to an end because of willful negligence, at least there is the satisfaction that one's oppressors will also die. In "Only Justice Can Stop a Curse," author Alice Walker discusses how her life experiences with the Eurocentric, masculinist ideology of domination have often caused her to be indifferent to environmental issues:

> I think . . . *Let the earth marinate in poisons. Let the bombs cover the ground like rain. For nothing short of total destruction will ever teach them anything.* (Walker 1983b, 341)

However, Walker later articulates that since environmental degradation doesn't make a distinction between oppressors and the oppressed, it should be very difficult for people of color to embrace the thought of extinction of all life forms simply for revenge.

In advocating a reformulation of how humans view nonhuman nature, ecofeminist theorist Ynestra King states that from the beginning, women have had to grapple with the historical projection of human concepts onto the natural, which were later used to fortify masculinist notions about females' nature (King 1989, 118). The same problem is applicable to people of color, who have also been negatively identified with the natural in white supremacist ideologies.

Black women in particular have historically been associated with animality and subsequently objectified to uphold notions of racial purity. bell hooks articulates that since the 1500s, Western societies have viewed Black women's bodies as objects to be subdued and controlled like nonhuman nature:

> From slavery to the present day, the Black female body has been seen in Western eyes as the quintessential symbol of a "natural" female presence that is organic, closer to nature, animalistic, primitive. (hooks and West 1991, 153)

Patricia Hill Collins asserts that white exploitation of Black women as breeders during the Slave Era "objectified [Black women] as less than human because only animals can be bred against their will" (Collins 1990, 167). Sarah Bartmann, an African woman also known as the Hottentot Venus, was prominently displayed at elite Parisian parties. While being reduced to her sexual parts, Bartmann's protruding buttocks were often offered as "proof" that Blacks were closer to animals than whites. After her death in 1815, Bartmann was dissected, and her genitalia and buttocks remain on display in Paris (Gilman 1985). Bartmann's situation was similar to the predicament of Black female slaves who stood on auction blocks as masters described their productive body parts as humans do cattle. The historical dissection of Black women, be it symbolic or actual, to uphold white supremacist notions is interconnected with the consistent human view of nonhuman animals as scientific material to be dissected through an ideology that asserts both groups are inferior.

Because of the historical and current treatment of Blacks in dominant Western ideology, Black womanists must confront the dilemma of whether we should strive to sever or reinforce the traditional association of Black people with nature that exists in dominant Western thought. However, what we need is not a total disassociation of people from nature, but rather a reformulation of *everyone's* relationship to nature by socially reconstructing gender, class, and ethnic roles.

Environmentalism is a women's issue because females (especially those of color) are the principal farm laborers around the world, as well as the majority of the world's major consumers of agricultural products (Bizot 1992, 36). Environmentalism is also an important issue for people of color because we disproportionately bear the brunt of environmental degradation. For most of the world's population, reclaiming the Earth is not an abstract state of affairs but rather is inextricably tied to the survival of our peoples.

Womanism and ecology have a common theoretical approach in that both see all parts of a matrix as having equal value. Ecology asserts that without each element in the ecosystem, the biosphere as a whole cannot function properly. Meanwhile, womanism asserts the equality of races, genders, and sexual preferences, among other variables. There is no use in womanists advocating liberation politics if the planet cannot support people's liberated lives, and it is equally useless to advocate saving the planet without addressing the social issues that determine the structure of human relations in the world. If the planet as a whole is to survive, we must all begin to see ourselves as interconnected with nonhuman nature and with one another.

The Politics of Nature-Culture Dualism

At the foundation of dominant Western thought exists an intense ambivalence over humankind's place in the biosphere, not only in relation to one another, but also in relation to nonhuman nature. The systematic denigration of men of color, women, and nonhuman nature is interconnected through a nature-culture dualism. This system of interconnectedness, which bell hooks labels "the politic of domination," functions along interlocking axes of race, gender, species, and class oppression. The politic of domination "refers to the ideological ground that [the axes] share, which is a belief in domination, and a belief in the notions of superior and inferior, which are components of all those systems" (hooks 1989, 175). Although groups encounter different dimensions of this matrix based on such variables as species or sexual orientation, an overarching relationship nevertheless connects all of these socially constructed variables.

In discussing the origins of Western dualism, Dona Richards articulates the influence of dominant Jewish and Christian thought on Western society's conceptions about its relationship to nonhuman nature:

Christian thought provides a view of man, nature, and the universe which supports not only the ascendancy of science, but of the technical order, individualism and relentless progress. Emphasis within this world view is placed on humanity's dominance over *all* other beings, which become "objects" in an "objectified" universe. Humanity is separated from nature. (Richards 1980, 69)

With dualistic thinking, humans, nonhuman nature, and ideas are categorized in terms of their difference from one another. However, one part is not simply deemed different from its counterpart; it is also deemed intrinsically *opposed* to its "Other" (Collins 1990, 69). For instance, speciesists constantly point to human neocortical development and the ensuing civilization that this development constructs as proof of human superiority over nonhuman animals. Women's position as other in Western patriarchies throughout the histories of both psychological theory and Christian thought has resulted in us being viewed as defective men.

Women, the nonelite, and men of color are not only socially constructed as the "Others," but the elite, white, male-controlled global political structure also has the power – through institutions such as the international media and politics – to extensively socialize us to view ourselves as others to be dominated. By doing so, the pattern of domination and subjugation is reinforced. Objectification is also central to the process of oppositional difference for all entities cast as other. Dona Richards claims that in dominant Western thought, intense objectification is a "prerequisite for the despiritualization of the universe and through it the Western cosmos was made ready for ever increasing materialization" (Richards 1980, 72). Since one component is deemed to be the other, it is simultaneously viewed as an object to be controlled and dominated, particularly through economic means.

Because nature-culture dualism conceives of nature as an other that (male) human undertakings transcend and conquer, women, nonhuman nature, and men of color become symbolically linked in Eurocentric, masculinist ideology. In this framework, the objectification of the other also serves as an escape from the anxiety of some form of mortality. For instance, white supremacists fear that it will be the death of the white race if people of color, who comprise the majority of the world's population, successfully resist the current global relations of power. Objectifying nonhuman nature by technology is predicated on an intense fear of the body, which reminds humans of death and our connection with the rest of nature. By making products that make tasks easier, one seeks to have more opportunities to live one's life, with time and nature converted into commodities.

World history can be seen as one in which human beings inextricably bind the material domination of nonhuman nature with the economic domination of other human beings. The Eurocentric, masculinist worldview that dominates Western thought tends to only value the parts of reality that can be exploited in the interest of profit, power and control. Not only is that associated with nature deemed amenable to conquest, but it is also a conquest that requires no moral self-examination on the part of the prospective conqueror. For instance, there is very little moral examination by research laboratories that test cosmetics on animals, or by men who assault women. There was also very little moral examination on the part of slave owners on the issue of slavery or by European settlers on colonialism in "Third World" nations.

By defining people of color as more natural and animalistic, a political economy of domination has been historically reinforced. An example of this phenomenon is the founding of the United States and the nation's resultant slave trade. In order for the European colonialists to exploit the American land for their economic interests, they first needed to subjugate the Native American groups who were inhabiting the land. While this was being accomplished, the colonists dominated Blacks by utilizing Africans as slave labor (and simultaneously appropriating much of Mexico) in order to cultivate the land for profit and expand the new capitalist nation's economy. Meanwhile, the buffalo almost became extinct in the process of this nation building "from sea to shining sea."

A salient example of the interconnectedness of environmental degradation and male supremacy is the way many societies attach little value to that which can be exploited without (economic) cost. Because nonhuman nature has historically been viewed by Westerners as a free asset to be possessed, little value has been accredited to it. Work traditionally associated with women via cultural socialization has similarly often been viewed as having little to no value. For instance, in calculating the Gross Domestic Product, no monetary value is attached to women's contributions to national economies through reproduction, housework, or care of children.

The Role of the Environmental-isms in Providing the Foundation for an Afrocentric Womanist Agenda

While serving as executive director of the United Church of Christ's Commission for Racial Justice in 1987, Reverend Benjamin Chavis, Jr., coined the term *environmental racism* to explain the dynamics of socioeconomic inequities in waste-management policies. Peggy Shephard, the director of West Harlem Environmental Action, defines United States environmental racism as "the policy of siting potentially hazardous facilities in low-income and minority communities" (Day and Knight 1991, 77). However, environmental racism, which is often intertwined with classism, doesn't halt at the boundaries of poor areas of color. Blacks in Africa and the United States often have to contend with predominantly white environmental groups that ignore the connection between their own values and the struggles of people of color to preserve our future, which is a crucial connection in order to build and maintain alliances to reclaim the earth. For instance, because the Environmental Protection Agency is often seen as another institution that perceives elite white communities' complaints as more deserving of attention than poor communities of color, many United States social activists are accusing the EPA of "environmental apartheid" (Riley 1991, 15).

In "Granola Boys, Eco-Dudes and Me," Elizabeth Larsen articulates how race, class, and gender politics are interconnected by describing the overwhelmingly white middle-class male leadership of mainstream United States environmental groups. In addition to being indifferent to the concerns of people of color and poor whites, the mainstream organizations often reinforce male supremacy by distributing organizational tasks along traditional gender roles (Larsen 1991, 96). The realization that only we can best represent our interests, an eco-identity politics, so to speak, lays the foundation for an Afrocentric ecowomanist agenda.[5] Even though many Black women have been active in the environmental movement in the past, there appears not to be much *published* analysis on their part about the role of patriarchy in environmental degradation. The chief reason for this sentiment may stem from perceiving race as the "primary" oppression. However, there is an emergent group of culturally identified Black women in Africa and the United States who are critically analyzing the social roles of white supremacy, patriarchy, and classism in environmental degradation.

Emergent Afrocentric Ecowomanism: On the Necessity of Survival

There are several differences between ecofeminism and Afrocentric ecowomanism. While Afrocentric ecowomanism also articulates the links between male supremacy and environmental degradation, it lays far more stress on other distinctive features, such as race and class, that leave an impression markedly different from many ecofeminists' theories.[6]

Many ecofeminists, when analyzing the links between human relations and ecological degradation, give primacy to gender and thus fail to thoroughly incorporate (as opposed to mere tokenism) the historical links between classism, white supremacy, and environmental degradation in their perspectives. For instance, they often don't address the fact that in nations where such variables as ethnicity and class are a central organizing principle of society, many women are not only viewed in opposition to men under dualism, but also to other women. A salient example of this blind spot is Mary Daly's *Gyn/Ecology,* where she implores women to identify with nature against men and live our lives separately from men. However, such an essentialist approach is very problematic for certain groups of women, such as the disabled and Jews, who must ally them-selves with men (while simultaneously challenging them on their sexism) in order to combat the *isms* in their lives. As writer Audre Lorde stated, in her critique of Daly's exclusion of how Black women use Afrocentric spiritual practices as a source of power against the *isms* while connecting with nonhuman nature:

> to imply, however, that women suffer the same oppression simply be-cause we are women, is to lose sight of the many varied tools of patri-archy. It is to ignore how these tools are used by women without awareness against each other. (Lorde 1983, 95)

Unlike most white women, Black women are not limited to issues defined by our femaleness but are rather often limited to questions raised about our very humanity.

Although they have somewhat different priorities because of their different environments, Afrocentric ecowomanists in the United States and Africa nevertheless have a common goal – to analyze the issues of social justice that underlie environmental conflict. Not only do Afrocentric ecowomanists seek to avoid detrimental environmental impacts, we also seek to overcome the socioeconomic inequalities that led to the injustices in the first place.

Emergent United States Afrocentric Ecowomanist Activism

Contrary to mainstream United States media claims, which imply that African-Americans are not concerned about ecology, there has been increased environmental activism within Black communities since the early 1980s. Referred to as the environmental equity movement by Robert Bullard, predominantly Black grass roots environmental organizations tend to view environmentalism as an extension of the 1960s civil rights movement. In *Yearning,* bell hooks links environmentalism with social justice while discussing Black radicals and revolutionary politics:

> We are concerned about the fate of the planet, and some of us believe that living simply is part of revolutionary political practice. We have a sense of the sacred. The ground we stand on is shifting, fragile, and unstable. (hooks 1990, 19)

On discussing how the links between environmental concerns and civil rights encouraged her involvement with environmentalism, arts writer and poet Esther Iverem states:

> Soon I began to link civil rights with environmental sanity. . . . Be-cause in 1970 Black folks were vocally fighting for their rightful share of the pie, the logical question for me became "What kind of shape will that pie be in?" (Iverem 1991, 38)

Iverem's question has been foremost in many African-American women's minds as we continue to be instrumental in the Black communities' struggle to ensure that the shape of the social justice pie on our planet will not be increasingly carcinogenic. When her neighborhood started to become dilapidated, Hattie Carthan founded the Magnolia Tree Earth Center of Bed-Stuy in Brooklyn in 1968, to help beautify the area. She planted more than 1,500 trees before her death in 1974. In 1986, the city council of Los Angeles decided that a 13-acre incinerator, which would have burned 2,000 tons of city waste daily, was to be built in a low-income Black and Latino neighborhood in South Central Los Angeles. Upon hearing this decision, residents, mostly women, successfully organized in opposition by forming Concerned Citizens of South Central Los Angeles. While planning direct actions to protest the incinerator, the grass roots organization didn't have a formal leadership structure for close to two years Be it a conscious or unconscious decision, Concerned Citizens accepted a relatively nonhierarchical, democratic process in their political activism by rotating the chair's position at meetings, a form of decision making characteristic of many ecofeminist groups.[7]

The Philadelphia Community Rehabilitation Corporation (PCRC), founded by Rachel E. Bagby, operates a village community to maintain a nonhierarchical relationship between human and nonhuman nature for its working-class-to-poor urban Black residents. About 5,000 reside in the community, and there is communalistic living, like that of many African villages. PCRC has a "repeopling" program that renovates and rents more than 50 previously vacant homes and also created a twelve-unit shared house. PCRC also takes vacant lots and recycles them into gardens to provide food, and oversees literacy and employment programs. Hazel and Cheryl Johnson founded People for Community Recovery (PCR), which is operated from a storefront at the Altgeld Gardens housing project, after they became aware that their community sits atop a landfill and has the greatest concentration of hazardous waste in the nation. In its fight against environmental racism, PCR has insisted that the Chicago Housing Authority remove all asbestos from the Altgeld homes and has helped lobby city government to declare a moratorium on new landfill permits. PCR also successfully prevented the establishment of another landfill in Altgeld Gardens.

One Black women's organization that addresses environmental issues is the National Black Women's Health Project. The NBWHP expresses its Afrocentric ecowomanist sentiment primarily through its SisteReach program, which seeks to connect the NBWHP with various Black women's organizations around the world. On urging African-American women to participate in the environmental movement and analyze the connections between male supremacy and environmental degradation, Dianne J. Forte, the SisteReach coordinator, makes the following statement:

At first glance and with all the major problems demanding our energy in our community we may be tempted to say, "this is not my problem." If however, we look at the ominous connection being made between environmental degradation and population growth; if we look at the same time at trends which control women's bodies and lives and control the world's resources, we realize that the same arguments are used to justify both. (Forte 1992, 5)

For instance, women are increasingly being told that we should not have control over our own bodies, while the Earth is simultaneously deemed feminine by scientists who use sexual imagery to articulate their plans to take control over the Earth. Meanwhile, dominant groups often blame environmental degradation on overpopulation (and with their privileged status, usually point at poor women of color), when industrial capitalism and patriarchal control over women's reproduction are among the most pronounced culprits.

The most salient example of practical United States Afrocentric ecowomanism combating such claims is Luisah Teish, a voodoo priestess. In connecting social justice issues with spiritual practices rooted in the West African heritage, Teish articulates the need for everyone to actively eliminate patriarchy, white supremacy, and classism, along with the domination of nonhuman nature. Members of Teish's altar circle have planned urban gardening projects both to supply herbs for their holistic healing remedies and to assist the poor in feeding themselves. They have also engaged in grass roots organizing to stop gentrification in various communities.

Emergent Afrocentric Ecowomanist Activism in Africa

On the African continent, women have been at the forefront of the movement to educate people about environmental problems and how they affect their lives. As with much of the African continent, environmental problems in Kenya particularly influence rural women's lives, since they comprise 80 percent of that nation's farmers and fuel gatherers (Maathai 1991, 74). Soil erosion directly affects the women, because they depend on subsistence agriculture for their families' survival. The lack of firewood in many rural areas of Kenya because of deforestation disproportionately alters the lives of women, who must walk long distances to fetch firewood. The lack of water also makes a negative imprint on Kenyan women's lives, because they have to walk long distances to fetch the water.

However, many Kenyan women are striving to alter these current realities. The most prominent Afrocentric ecowomanist in Africa is Wangari Maathai, a Kenyan microbiologist and one of Africa's leading activists on environmental issues. Maathai is the founder and director of the Green

Belt Movement (GBM), a fifteen-year-old tree-planting project designed to help poor Kenyan communities stop soil erosion, protect their water systems, and overcome the lack of firewood and building materials.

Launched under the auspices of the National Council of Women of Kenya, the majority of the Green Belt Movement's members are women. Since 1977, these women have grown 10 million trees, 80 percent of which have survived, to offset Kenya's widespread deforestation.[8] Although the Green Belt Movement's primary practical goal is to end desertification and deforestation, it is also committed to promoting public awareness of the relationship between environmental degradation and social problems that affect the Kenyan people – poverty, unemployment, and malnutrition. However, one of the most significant accomplishments of the GBM, Maathai asserts, is that its members are "now independent; had acquired knowledge, techniques; had become empowered" (Maathai 1991, 74).

Another Kenyan dedicated to environmental concerns is Wagaki Mwangi, the founder and coordinator of the International Youth Development and Environment Network. When she visited the University of Illinois at Urbana-Champaign, Mwangi discussed how Kenya suffers economic and environmental predicaments primarily because her homeland is trying to imitate Western cultures. "A culture has been superimposed on a culture," Mwangi said, but there are not enough resources for everyone to live up to the new standards of the neocolonial culture (Schallert 1992, 3). She asserted that in attempts to be more Western, "what [Kenyans] valued as our food has been devalued, and what we are valuing is what they value in the West" (Schallert 1992, 3). For instance, Kenyans used to survive by eating a variety of wild foods, but now many don't consider such foods as staples because of Western influences. In the process, many areas of Kenya are deemed to be suffering from food shortages as the economy has been transformed to consumer capitalism with its attendant mechanization of agriculture.

In Kourfa, Niger, women have been the primary force behind preventing the village from disappearing, a fate that many surrounding villages have suffered because of the Sahel region's desertification. Reduced rainfall and the drying up of watering places and vegetation, combined with violent sandstorms, have virtually deprived Kourfa of harvests for the past five years. As a result, the overwhelming majority of Kourfa's men have had to travel far away for long periods of time to find seasonal work.

With the assistance of the Association of Women of Niger and an agricultural advisor, the women have laid out a small marketgarden around the only well in Kourfa. Despite the few resources at their disposal, the Kourfa women have succeeded in supporting themselves, their children, and the village elders. In response to the survival of the village since these actions, the Kourf women are now calling for increased action to reverse the region's environmental degradation so "the men won't go away" from the village (Ouedraogo 1992, 38).

Afrocentric Ecomotherists: Ecowomanist Potential?

The environmental activism of some Black women brings up the question of whether community-oriented Black women who are addressing environmental issues are genuinely Afrocentric ecowomanists or possibly Afrocentric ecomotherists.[9] According to Ann Snitow, motherists are women who, for various reasons, "identify themselves not as feminists but as militant mothers, fighting together for survival" (Snitow 1989, 48). Snitow also maintains that motherism usually arises when men are absent or in times of crisis, when the private sphere role assigned to women under patriarchy makes it impossible for the collective to survive. Since they are faced with the dictates of traditional work but face a lack of resources in which to fulfill their socially prescribed role, motherists become a political force.

Since they took collective action to secure the survival of the village's children and elders only after the necessary absence of Kourfa's men, the activism of the Kourfa women may possibly be based on a motherist philosophy. One can only conjecture whether the Kourfa women criticized the social role of motherhood in Niger as they became a political force, or if womanist consciousness emerged after their political experiences. Because of their potential to transform into ecowomanists after they enter the political realm, Afrocentic ecomotherists shouldn't be discounted in an analysis of Black women's environmental activism. For instance, Charlotte Bullock contends that she "did not come to the fight against environmental problems as an intellectual but rather as a concerned mother" (Hamilton 1990, 216). However, she and other women in Concerned Citizens of South Central Los Angeles began to notice the sexual politics that attempted to discount their political activism while they were protesting. "I noticed when we first started fighting the issue how the men would laugh at the women . . . they would say, 'Don't pay no attention to them, that's only one or two women . . . they won't make a difference.' But now since we've been fighting for about a year the smiles have gone" (Hamilton 1990, 215). Robin Cannon, another member of Concerned Citizens, asserts that social relations in her home, specifically gender roles on caretaking, were transformed after she began participating in the group's actions (Hamilton 1990, 220).

Moving Beyond Dualism: An Afrocentric Approach

In utilizing spiritual concepts to move beyond dualism, precolonial African cultures, with their both/and perspectives, are useful forms of knowledge for Afrocentric ecowomanists to envision patterns toward interdependence of human and nonhuman nature. Traditional West African cultures, in particular, which also happen to be the ancestral roots of the overwhelming majority of African-Americans, share a belief in nature worship and view all things as being alive on varying levels of existence (Haskins 1978, 30). One example of such an approach in West African traditions is the *Nyam* concept. A root word in many West African languages, *Nyam* connotes an enduring power and energy possessed by all life (Collins 1990, 220). Thus, all forms of life are deemed to possess certain rights, which cannot be violated at will.

In *Jambalaya,* Luisah Teish writes of the *Da* concept, which originates from the Fon people of Western Africa. *Da is* "the energy that carries creation, the force field in which creation takes place" (Teish 1985, 61). In the Fon view, all things are composed of energy provided by *Da.* For example, "the human is receptive to the energy emanating from the rock and the rock is responsive to human influence" (Teish 1985, 62). Because West Africans have traditionally viewed nonhuman nature as sacred and worthy of praise through such cultural media as song and dance, there is also a belief in *Nommo. Nommo* is "the physical-spiritual life force which awakens all 'sleeping' forces and gives physical and spiritual life" (Jahn 1961, 105).

However, with respect for nonhuman nature comes a different understanding of *Ache,* the Yoruba term for human power. *Ache* doesn't connote "power over" or domination, as it often does in mainstream Western thought, but rather power *with* other forms of creation. With *Ache,* Teish states that there is "a regulated kinship among human, animal, mineral, and vegetable life" (Teish 1985, 63). Humans recognize their *Ache* to eat and farm, "but it is also recognized that they must give back that which is given to them" (Teish 1985, 63). In doing so, we respect the overall balance and interdependence of human and nonhuman nature.

These concepts can be useful for Afrocentric ecowomanists not only in educating our peoples about environmental issues, but also in reclaiming the cultural traditions of our ancestors. Rachel Bagby states the positivity of humans connecting with nonhuman nature, a view that is interwoven in her organization's work:

> If you can appreciate the Earth, you can appreciate the beauty of yourself. The same creator created both. And if I learned to take care of that I'll also take care of myself and help take care of others. (Bagby 1990, 242)

Illustrating an outlook of planetary relations that is parallel to the traditional West African worldview, Bagby simultaneously reveals the continuous link between much of the African-American religious tradition and African spirituality.

In light of the relations of power and privilege that exist in the world, the appropriation of indigenous cultures by some ecofeminists must be addressed. Many womanists, such as Andy Smith and Luisah Teish, have criticized cultural feminists for inventing earth-based feminist spiritualities that are based on the exploitation of our ancestral traditions, while we're struggling to reclaim and defend our cultures from white supremacy. In "For All Those Who Were Indian in Another Life," Smith asserts that this appropriation of non-Western spiritual traditions functions as a way for many white women to avoid taking responsibility for being simultaneously oppressive as well as oppressed (see her article, pp. 168-71). White ecofeminists can reclaim their own pre-Christian European cultures, such as the Wiccan tradition, for similar concepts of interconnectedness, community, and immanence found in West African traditions.[10]

Adopting these concepts would transform humans' relationship to nonhuman nature in a variety of ways. By seeing all components of the ecosystem affecting and being affected by one another, such a world perspective demonstrates a pattern of living in harmony with the rest of nature, instead of seeking to disconnect from it. By viewing ourselves as a part of nature, we would be able to move beyond the Western disdain for the body and therefore not ravage the Earth's body as a result of this disdain and fear. We would realize that the Earth is not merely the source of our survival, but also has intrinsic value and must be treated with respect, as it is our elder.

The notion of community would help us to appreciate the biological and cultural diversity that sustains life. Because every entity is viewed as embodying spirituality under immanence, culture wouldn't be viewed as separate from, and superior to, nature, as it is seen in mainstream Western religions. Communalism would also aid us in reformulating the social constructions of race, gender, species, class (among other variables), which keep groups separate from one another. And finally, the environmental movement in particular would view politics as rooted in community and communally take actions to reclaim the Earth and move toward a life of interdependence for generations to come.

Notes

I would like to acknowledge the help that Carol Adams has given me with this essay. Her reading suggested valuable changes in the structure of the paper as well as clearing up minor flaws in writing. She also suggested some references that would augment my claims.

1. Alice Walker's definition of womanist is a feminist of color who is "committed to the survival and wholeness of entire people, male *and* female" (Walker 1983a, xi-xii). University of Ibadan (Nigeria) English senior lecturer Chikwenye Okonjo Ogunyemi contends that "black womanism is a philosophy that celebrates black roots . . . It concerns itself as much with the black sexual power tussle as with the world power structure that subjugates blacks" (Ogunyemi 1985, 72). Since feminism often gives primacy to gender, and race consciousness often gives primacy to race, such limitations in terminology have caused many women of color to adopt the term *womanist,* which both Walker and Ogunyemi independently coined in the early 1980s. Although some of the women in this paper refer to themselves as feminists rather than womanists, or use both terms interchangeably, I am using the term *womanist* in an interpretative sense to signify a culturally identified woman of color who also critically analyzes the sexual politics within her respective ethnic group.

2. For a discussion of how toxic waste has affected the environmental health of United States Black communities, see Day and Knight (1991).

3. Robert Bullard (1990) contends that the mortality of wealth involves toxic waste dumping to pursue profits at the expense of others, usually low-income people of color in the United States. Because this demographic group is less likely to have economic resources and political clout, it can't fight back as easily as more affluent communities that possess white skin privileges. I think this term is also applicable to the economic nature of toxic dumping in "Third World" countries, which are basically disempowered in the global political process.

4. For an ecofeminist text that makes a similar claim, see King (1989).

5. My definition of an Afrocentric ecowomanist is a communalistic-oriented Black woman who understands and articulates the interconnectedness of the degradation of people of color, women, and the environment. In addition to articulating this interconnectedness, an Afrocentric ecowomanist also strives to eradicate this degradation. For an extensive discussion of Afrocentrism, see Myers (1988).

6. An example of this distinction can be seen in Davies (1988). In her article, Davies only discusses the interconnections between gender and nature and completely avoids analyzing how such variables as ethnicity and class influence the experience of gender in one's life.

7. For several descriptions of the political decision making within feminist peace organizations, see the essays in Harris and King (1989).

8. It is noteworthy that the seedlings come from over 1,500 tree nurseries, 99 percent of which are operated by women. In addiction, the women are given a small payment for the trees that survive.

9. In comparison to an Afrocentric ecowomanist, I define an Afrocentric ecomotherist as a communalistic-oriented Black woman who is involved in saving

the environment and challenging white supremacy, but who does not challenge the fundamental dynamics of sexual politics in women's lives.

10. For instance, Starhawk, a practitioner of the Wiccan tradition, has written about her spiritual beliefs (1990).

Part III

Postmodern Horizons

19

Ecology, Science, and Religion: Toward a Postmodern Worldview

John B. Cobb, Jr.

THE ECOLOGICAL MOVEMENT IS RELIGIOUS, AND BIBLICAL THOUGHT (LIKE most religious thought), from which Christianity arose, is ecological. But on the whole, the ecological movement is not Christian and contemporary Christianity is not ecological. The explanation lies in the participation of Christianity in the modern worldview. If, as I believe, the ecological movement is a prime bearer of an emerging postmodern worldview, this movement is important for Christians.

In this essay I: (1) discuss "worldview" in its intimate connection with both science and religion; (2) describe the roles of science and religion in the rise of the modern worldview; (3) propose that the ecological movement is supporting the emergence of a new worldview; (4) indicate two candidates for this new ecological worldview; and (5) point out implications for understanding the divine. I do this as a Christian theologian, but one who has rejected the modern as well as the premodern forms of Christian faith.

I. Science, Religion, and Worldview

Both an assumption and a conclusion of this essay is the view that compartmentalization of thought is always artificial. This view runs against the grain of twentieth-century teaching, which has gone through great pains to clarify the differences among disciplines, levels of thought, or "language games." Special emphasis has been placed on the difference between religion and science. For some, the concern has been to protect a realm of religious discourse from the criteria appropriate to science. For others, it has been to show the vacuity of religious thought.

To accomplish either of these goals, science must be defined more and more narrowly. Increasingly, "science" appears to occur only where a discipline, its conceptuality, and its methods are well established and can be applied to new data. On this view, the formation of a science, the working out of its conceptuality, and the determination of appropriate methods cannot themselves be "science." The great paradigm shifts cannot be "science." Indeed, because the majority of what is most interesting in the history of science cannot be separated from speculative philosophy and questions of worldview, it cannot be "science," according to this view. Furthermore, speculative philosophy and worldview cannot be separated from religious belief. In a recent essay on which I am here quite dependent, David Griffin has summarized the impressive evidence that, in the formation of what we know as modern science, explicit commitments to particular forms of Christian theology played a large role.[1] Denying that an antireligious conviction played a comparable role in developing positivistic views of science is difficult.

In the context of the history of global human thought, this recent Western passion for compartmentalization appears eccentric. In Greece, in China, in India, in the Middle Ages of Europe, in Muslim Spain and the Near East, no such compartmentalization was conceivable. It was certainly not envisioned or desired by such founders of modern science as Bacon, Descartes, and Newton. It arose in the nineteenth century for particular historical reasons, and its role as orthodoxy in the twentieth century is profoundly unstable.

The normal human condition is to live out of a relatively unified understanding of the nature of things, which is partly conscious while being partly and unconsciously taken for granted. The new consciousness resulting from historical study of worldviews along with the encounter of alternative living worldviews has brought more of this unconscious material into consciousness, thereby relativizing every worldview, making all problematic. Because religion traditionally has involved the celebration, articulation, and practical implications of a worldview, the relativizing of worldviews also involves the relativization of all the religious traditions of humankind. Individual freedom to transcend worldviews entails individual freedom to decide about aspects of religious belief that were once simply given.

The matter is not, however, quite so simple. Those who distance themselves from commitment to worldviews are not without a point of view. Sometimes this point of view can be readily recognized by an observer as itself a worldview of a quite conventional sort. For example, some of those who deny commitment to any worldview and its accompanying religious meaning for life are, in fact, committed to a mechanist worldview, which is as problematic as any other. Others, however, may be committed to the impossibility of any unifying vision, holding that any worldview transcends the capacity of the human mind or belies the actual nature of things. This commitment, too, leads to a total way of thinking and responding to the issues of the day, thereby resembling a worldview. But it will be better to speak of it as an antiworldview and an antireligion. Of course, it may allow room for religion in another sense, for example, an apophatic mysticism or a Christianity that has redefined itself as dissociated from any worldview.

Worldviews are always and necessarily universal generalizations made from some aspect or aspects of the world as experienced. An organic worldview generalizes from observed organisms. A mechanist worldview generalizes from observed machines. A spiritualist worldview generalizes from particular qualities of human experience. A dualistic worldview may generalize from both human self-experience as mind and human experience of the world as matter. When a worldview is articulated philosophically, the claim is made that the really real things are of the sort, or sorts, posited.

Stephen Pepper has called worldviews *world hypotheses.*[2] When we become conscious of alternative worldviews, thereby recognizing them in their relativity, we can adopt one or another in this form. But we should beware of the notion that hypotheses are held, even by the most detached scientists, in a fully open way. Most of the hypotheses, at least the important ones, elicit considerable commitment, such that they are not quickly set aside because of apparent disconfirmation. At the level of world hypotheses, these commitments are very strong indeed. Even extensive disconfirmation does not cause ready abandonment of such hypotheses, whether they are religious, antireligious, or nonreligious.

I find this true in my own case. In general, I fancy that I am quite open to evidence and prepared to make adjustments in my beliefs in its light. However, my worldview entails that the future does not actually exist and can have no causal efficacy in the present; I am also convinced that the present has some capacity to determine itself. Although many aspects of the future are now determined, I conclude that the future in its entirety and in its exact shape is not now determined and therefore cannot now be known, even by God. If I were eager to check all this out as an interesting hypothesis that I entertained in a detached way, I would no doubt study the evidence for precognition carefully. I have not done so. I am prejudiced against it. I will go to considerable lengths to explain it in terms satisfactory to my present world hypothesis. Where evidence resists such explanation, I will resist acknowledging its validity. In short, it would take overwhelming evidence to dislodge me from my "hypothesis." I think, therefore, it is better to speak of it as a conviction.[3]

I can provide some justification for my resistance to evidence in this area. My conviction seems to work very well with regard to much other evidence. It proves fruitful in new areas as I try to apply it. The world hypotheses that are supported by the idea of perfect precognition seem less fruitful or satisfactory with respect to other evidence. In addition, I have invested myself, and my personal identity, so fully in this "hypothesis" or conviction that my self-image and my pride are very much involved. My religious faith and practice are also bound up with this conviction. Nevertheless, my worldview and my religious faith both require that I not cling to them forever in the face of evidence that they are false. They would cease to be what they are if I were forced to acknowledge that they blinded me to the truth. Change is possible, but such change would be a radical conversion, and conversions do not come easily.

I have stated this quite personally so as to express my understanding of what goes on in the establishment and change of worldviews and antiworldviews. They are enormously resistant to change. A great deal is at stake. We must collectively move (and are to some extent moving) from mechanistic and dualistic worldviews and positivist and other antiworldviews to an ecological worldview Such a change entails profound alterations in both science and religion.

II. Science and Religion in the Rise of the Modern Worldview

The above-mentioned paper by David Griffin shows the unity of the scientific, religious, philosophical struggle that resulted in the victory of the Newtonian worldview. He shows that this victory, with its strong support for a Calvinistic theism, was short-lived, and that the term *Newtonian worldview* was transferred to a quite different, thoroughly mechanist worldview, against which Newton had himself fought vigorously. This section is derived from Griffin's work.

Three movements struggled for supremacy during the seventeenth century: the fading power of Aristotelian philosophy, the continuing power of the "magical" vision, and the emerging power of mechanistic thinking. The latter eventually won, and accordingly history has been written as if this were *the* scientific theory. The actual evidence, long-resisted and even concealed by the advocates of the mechanistic worldview, is that the magical movement provided the initial context for the rise of modern science.

This movement drew on the traditions of Pythagoras, Plato, Neoplatonism, Hermetic mysticism, and the Cabala. It was fascinated by number, and it turned to mathematics and science as the earlier Italian Renaissance had not. Ficino, Paracelsus, and Bruno were among its early leaders. It inspired also Copernicus, Kepler, and Francis Bacon.

Whereas the Aristotelian tradition had emphasized the teleological element in all things, the magical tradition went much further: it sought to ally itself with spiritual forces immanent in all things so as to bend them to human use and control. For it, nature was alive with spirit, and the explanations of natural events were to be found in these immanent spiritual forces. These forces could act at a distance as well as in proximity.

The primary objection to this tradition was not that it inhibited scientific investigation or blinded its adherents to empirical data. It did not. The primary objection was that it threatened belief in a God who transcended nature as its omnipotent creator. By seeing a miraculous aspect in many natural events, it undercut the arguments of the Christian church for validating supernatural miracles. It was for this reason that Fr. Marin Mersenne, the senior correspondent of Descartes, favored Artistotelianism over the magical tradition but saw even more promise in mechanism. Robert Boyle opposed the magical tradition because it united God with matter in a way theologically unacceptable to him. Accordingly, he denied to natural creatures any power to move themselves, attributing all power of motion to the external, omnipotent God. The physical world is purely objective matter, completely passive in relation to God. I stress that the "physical world" did not include the human mind or soul. The human mind or soul was regarded as a spiritual substance, wholly different from the bits of matter composing bodies.

Newton was influenced by both traditions, but for theological reasons he moved to the mechanistic camp. By denuding physical nature of all power of self-motion, he magnified the power of God. In gravity, he found apparent action at a distance that seemed to support the proponents of magic. In explaining this, he refused to allow any mechanistic account such as that of the Cartesians, but also any magical or animistic account. He ridiculed the idea that material bodies at a distance could exercise any influence on each other by any inherent power. The explanation had to be in terms of "spiritual forces," which meant, ultimately, God. Like Boyle, he magnified the power of God by denying power to the creatures.

The emergence of a mechanistic view of nature, which denied to nature any purpose, capacity for self-movement, or interiority, was not a necessity of science. At least, in part, it was designed to support theological voluntarism, the idea that the transcendent God imposes "His" will by fiat upon the world. Ironically, the mechanistic account of the way matter operated became so satisfactory to many people that they freed the mechanistic view from its original association with the imposed will of God and a dualistic view of human beings as composed of a spiritual soul in a mechanistic body. A world composed of purely material, and therefore purely passive, entities became completely self-sufficient. This materialistic, atheistic view came to be known as the Newtonian worldview!

This mechanistic-materialistic worldview was never adequate to the evidence, but its success in guiding theory-formation and experimentation in some areas was so great that it became entrenched as common sense. When Hume undercut it empirically, Kant reestablished it as grounded in the universal structure of mind. When this view could no longer be applied in subatomic physics, much of the scientific and philosophical community concluded that we are condemned to paradox and unintelligibility, because "reason" remained identified with mechanistic materialism. Surely this "hypothesis" had become a very powerful conviction! Even those who acknowledge that it may not be objectively true as a world-view still usually insist that there is no other alternative *methodologically* than to assume it. When we remember that modern science arose out of a quite different way of thinking, we cannot but be impressed by the success with which the victorious tradition suppressed even the memory of its opponent.

III. Ecology and the Rise of a Postmodern Worldview

The dominance of the materialistic-mechanistic worldview has never been complete. Most of its supporters have made some place for human beings outside the otherwise all-inclusive machine – for example, by at least tacitly presupposing the distinct existence of the human mind. This place was greatly enlarged and developed in German Idealism. The Romantic movement challenged the view of nature as machine, appealing to some of the intuitions that had been expressed in the magical tradition. Some biologists (vitalists) insisted that life could not be understood mechanically. Existentialists and counterculturalists deplored the effects of this worldview on human beings. Occultism flourished in reaction to it. More and more developments in physics pointed away from it. Positivists, while affirming its methodological implications, rejected it as worldview. Nevertheless, it is not a mistake to single out the ecological movement as of particular importance in helping to break the hold of the modern worldview on scientific thinking and common sense. Whereas the earlier reactions functioned chiefly restrictively and negatively, accepting the modern worldview for the most part, ecology has suggested essential ingredients for a postmodern worldview.

Ecologists are those biologists who study living things in relation to their natural environment. There they find an infinitely complex interconnectedness of living things with each other and with the inorganic world. They are impressed by the complex outworking of the effects of change in one part of the system and by the adaptability and resilience of the whole when it is not subjected to too great a stress by human intervention. But they have also been impressed by the increasing massiveness of human intervention and its often extreme degradation of once-flourishing ecosystems.

They see that these changes are often irreversible, because species die out, topsoil disappears, and weather is changed. They see that not only is the nonhuman world impoverished by these changes, but that an environment is being created that will not be able to support the increasing human population. They see that other species sometimes increase in population to the point that their environment cannot support them and then die out drastically. They see the danger that human beings will bring upon themselves a similar catastrophe. Toward the end of the 1960s, their cries of alarm finally caught the ear of the public. Although the initial response included faddish elements, a widespread change of consciousness has since occurred that is not likely to be reversed.

Once we are forced to attend to the destructive consequences of our exploitation of our environment, the facts are indisputable. Because the destruction has been vastly accelerated by the industrial revolution, we ask ourselves why in recent times we have been so oblivious. The answer is that we see what our worldview encourages us to see. We see especially through the eyes of our scientific disciplines, both natural and human, and these disciplines have all been established in the context of the materialistic or dualistic worldview. In the context of dualism, the human sciences along with ethics and theology take nature as the given stage for the human drama. They do not encourage attention to changes in the stage. In the context of mechanism nature appears as unhistorical. Hence, only those who actually went and looked noticed the changes; and, because they did not develop mechanistic theories of what they saw, they had the lowest status among the scientists.

Those who are committed to the rejection of all worldviews were at least equally responsible for the long obliviousness to this crucial feature of reality. For them there is no knowable reality apart from that which is treated in one department of knowledge or another. Nature does not have an independent existence which could allow it to have a history outside of human knowledge. The history of reality is accordingly identified with the history of human thought, which is fragmented among the disciplines. The modern university is a tribute to the success of this antiworldview, but is hardly a support for an appropriate response to the threat of catastrophe.

The majority of people, of course, have not been converted to an ecological worldview. Many people have incorporated *some elements* of the new awareness into the old ones. Systems theory has enabled those wedded to mechanism to envision far more complex machines replete with all manner of feedback loops. Dualists can talk about the crisis as fundamentally a human crisis to be dealt with by enhanced concern for justice among human beings. The opponents of worldviews can pay more attention to the discipline of ecology, while still berating the tendency for too great generalization from limited data. In the public realm, the issues raised by ecologists must compete for attention with those that come from other sources, especially immediate economic concerns and military policy.

Nevertheless, there are others for whom the vision of the interconnectedness of all things has become the inclusive context within which the other sciences, as well as issues raised by economic needs and military policy, are viewed. This change of vision has been for some a fundamental conversion, for others, a development of already strong intuitions. At this point, ecology becomes a worldview. The remainder of this chapter explores two forms of this worldview: the first, very briefly; the second, to which I subscribe, at greater length.

IV. Two Ecological Worldviews

The first ecological worldview is sometimes called *deep ecology.*[4] It stresses the interdependent and unified character of the ecosystem as a whole. It is in this total system rather than in individual creatures that value lies. The individuals exist as participants in this whole and have value as they contribute to the complex network of relations which is the whole. To this whole, a strong sense of sacredness attaches itself; to its violation, a strong sense of evil.

Deep ecology entails a drastically different understanding of the place of the human from that of the heretofore dominant views. Especially in the West, the emphasis has been on human separateness from nature. This separateness is especially accentuated in dualism. But evolutionary theory can also encourage a view of humanity as the supreme product of nature for whose sake the remainder exists. This view can corroborate the basic ideas of Biblical believers. In all of these views, human beings stand in some measure above nature (or, at least, above the rest of nature) and rightfully shape it to human purposes. Their basic understanding of themselves is of how they transcend nature rather than of how they belong to it.

The deep ecologists reject all of this as human pretension that is not only false but also the cause of our destructive behavior. In truth, they say, the human species is one of many, neither better nor worse than the others. It has its place in the ecosystem as a whole and can have its value as contributory to it. But humanity has no special value, and its pretense to have special value has led to its massive violations of that ecological order on which its good, and all good, depend.

Deep ecology, like most worldviews, is a profoundly religious vision. Among traditional religious doctrines it comes closest to pantheism but, if it is pantheism, it is pantheism in a new form. Its rituals and practices are only beginning to be worked out, but that it has radical implications for all of life cannot be questioned. Indeed, the implications are so shattering with respect to all that we have inherited from our civilized ancestors that one wonders how widely the worldview can be assimilated.

The second form of ecological worldview does not depart as radically from the Western tradition. It calls for a modification of science and religion but retains recognizable continuity with existing trends and in some ways returns to classical religious sources. Instead of focusing initially on the whole, it attends primarily to the individuals comprising it. I call this the *postmodern ecological worldview.*

A very simple idea impressed upon us by ecology is that things cannot be abstracted from relations to other things. They may be moved from a natural set of relations to an artificial one, such as in a laboratory, but when these relations are changed, the things themselves are changed. The effort to study things in abstraction from their relations is based on a misunderstanding. This misunderstanding is that things exist as independent entities and only incidentally are related to one another. This is the misunderstanding that lies at the base of the materialistic view of nature (which is shared by both the dualistic and the materialistic worldviews). This materialism is articulated philosophically in terms of "substance." A *substance* is that which depends on nothing else for its existence. It is a thing that remains fundamentally the same regardless of its relations. An atom was defined by the Greeks to be a unit of substance. Modern mechanism is built on this notion. Everything that is not an atom is nothing but a structure of atoms. The atoms are not affected by the structures in which they are arranged. The structures behave like machines and are not inherently affected by their relations to other things. They can be externally affected by other things by having some of their parts separated from others, but the character of the separated parts is not affected by this separation. The laboratory is the ideal place to do science, in this view, because it is designed for abstracting things from their relations, taking them apart, and putting them back together again, often in new ways.

The expectation of substantialist thinking would be that the properties of the compound structures, apart from shape, would be the sum of the properties of the substantial parts as they exist independently of the compound. It is now a commonplace idea that this is not so. Salt has properties other than shape not found in any of its components (when these are not structured as salt). This point is an embarrassment for mechanistic materialism, but it is glossed over as an instance of the "emergence" of properties, a quite nonmechanistic notion. The importance of arrangement of atoms in the determination of properties is so great that "structure" is now a fundamental category of analysis. This fact should not be so if the world were really composed of material substances.

An explanation for this fact is not difficult to find, but it requires that the notions of *material* and *substance* be rejected. According to this explanation – an ecological one – the properties of an atom are always the properties of that atom as its existence is determined by its relations to its environment. Atoms acquire different properties when they are arranged in different molecular structures because these different structures constitute different environments. Instead of viewing molecules as machines, we should view them as ecosystems. Science may continue to ask what properties a certain type of atom continues to have in great varieties of contexts, but it should add the question as to the diverse properties the atom acquires in different relationships. This ecological approach to the study of atoms can subsume the materialistic one, whereas the materialistic approach cannot subsume the ecological.

The situation does not change to the advantage of the idea of material substance when we shift to a still more primitive level. Indeed, it has long been recognized that ideas of material substance cannot be consistently applied at the subatomic level. Atoms cannot be understood as machines; they are much better envisioned as ecosystems.

That things are related is no news to mechanistic-materialists, but for them the relations of a material substance must be wholly external. That is, the substance is not different *in itself* because it is related. This doctrine makes understanding how atoms can acquire new properties when they are in new relationships impossible. If this is the case, the atoms must be affected by the relationships. That is, the relationships must be *internal* to the atoms; they must participate in the *constitution* of the atoms. The ecological worldview holds that all the units of reality are internally related to others. All units or individuals are constituted by their relations.

This notion of internal relations requires further reflection. Although much evidence is found for internal relatedness, a felt contradiction exists between what we first think of when we image a molecule and the notion of internal relations. I can explain this contradiction better at the familiar level of interpersonal relations. It is an oft-noted fact that I can think of another person in two ways. One way is as I experience him or her through my senses, especially vision. What I think of then is a body bounded by its skin. That body has spatial relations with other bodies and can be affected by the contact of other bodies. But it is hard to understand what it would mean to say that it is internally related to those other bodies. The relation *appears* to be external (although the behavior I observe testifies to something else). However, I can also think of other persons as ones who feel and think much as I do. In that case, I imagine them to experience objects in their environment through their senses. Those objects are then partly constitutive of, or internally related to, their experiences. Their experiences would be different if the objects in their field of vision were different. Thus, when I think of them not as objects of my experience but as subjects of their own, it is natural to think of them as constituted by their relations to others.

An ecological worldview of the sort I am here proposing requires that we adopt this double view of every real individual. Each such individual exists for my objectifying thought and experience. But each exists also as its own center of experience. In most cases this experience is not *conscious* experience. But it *is* an activity of taking account of its world and thereby constituting itself out of its relations.

If we ask why it goes against the grain of so many contemporary thinkers to attribute activity or agency to atoms and subatomic entities, the answer is not that this idea is inherently absurd. It was a very natural idea for some of those in the magical tradition whose work was foundational for modern science. It became strange only through the victory of those physicist-theologians who wanted to denude nature of all life and feeling for the sake of attributing all action to the will of God, and of keeping God wholly external to the world. The ecological worldview restores *inherent reality,* hence activity and experience, to nature.

A further point entailed by the above discussion needs to be drawn out. An activity is not an agent that acts. To think of an agent that acts is to move back to the idea of substance. The agent would have to exist first apart from the activity and to be essentially unaffected by the activity. There is no evidence of such agents in nature. The activity itself constitutes nature. The relatively enduring aspects of nature are the results of the repetitiveness of many activities. Also, the way in which one activity takes account of others may be highly unique. But for the ecological vision, behind the sensory display of apparently passive substances is a world of interrelated activities. What happens in the superficial world of passive substances is a function of what happens in the dynamic world of interrelated activities.

Perhaps the most radical implication for human self-understanding is that, just as there are no agents of activity separable from the activity in the rest of the world, so there is no self who is the subject of experience apart from the activity that is the experience in the human being. The ecological worldview here agrees with Hume and with the Buddhist analysis. There is a flow of experience that has just that richness and just that degree of identity through time that it factually possesses. There is nothing more (and nothing less).

The cellular activities throughout the human body and the acts of human experience which grow out of the complex patterns of structure in the brain are among these interrelated activities that constitute nature. This postmodern ecological vision agrees with deep ecology at that point. Human beings are, without remainder, part of the ecosystem. Everything is both subject and object, and human beings are no exception. Dualism is excluded.

This form of ecological vision also agrees with deep ecology in seeing value in the way each individual, each activity, contributes itself to all the others. But, unlike deep ecology, it also affirms the unique value of each activity in itself. This affirmation leads to a doubly differentiated valuation of individual things. They have diverse values for others, and they have diverse values in themselves. Some of the entities that have the least value for others have the greatest value in themselves and some that have the most value for others (at least in large numbers) have the least value in themselves. However, because of the fundamental character of internal relations, the realization of value in one entity tends to enhance the value of others.

The human species in overall perspective has very little value for other species in nature. The whole biosphere today would in fact be much healthier if evolution had not led to the appearance of human beings. If our species were to disappear under circumstances that did not poison the atmosphere or destroy numerous other species, we could expect a gradual recovery of the biosphere from our depredation.

But human experience has introduced into this planet dimensions of experience that are, as far as we know, impossible for other species. The qualities of enjoyment characteristic of human relationships and creativity have unique intrinsic worth. That we are fully part of nature does not undercut the distinctiveness of the values we have realized. Furthermore, in principle, according to this ecological vision, the realization of special value at one point does not take away from value somewhere else. On the contrary, it provides a new possibility of realizing values to those who come after because the value that can be realized in any act of experience is largely a function of the values of the activities that have come before it, and to which this new act is internally related.

This concluding emphasis is important in overcoming the substantialist idea that what is of value is in limited supply and that human beings therefore relate to one another and to other creatures in a primarily competitive way. There is truth to this doctrine with respect to many of the goods on which the economist focuses. But the greater goods of human relations and of aesthetic enjoyment are mutual rather than competitive. Furthermore, the person informed by the ecological vision can show that full employment and more efficient and democratic use of resources, far from being "tradeoffs," can be attained together. There are many instances of interspecies adjustment for mutual benefit throughout the ecosystem. Competition is not the ultimate principle.

However, neglecting the fact of competition would be sentimental. Individual plants compete for space and light; animals compete for habitat and food; animals kill plants and carnivores kill other animals. Life is robbery. Far more animals are born than can reach maturity. The ecosystem works well for the species, but the sacrifice of individuals is enormous.

Furthermore, the dominant human role continues to be that of mindless butchery and habitat destruction, often for minor short-term goals. Even if everyone shared the ecological vision, there would be no easy solution to the pressures of human population on remaining habitat for "wild" animals. A participant in the ecological worldview is in permanent mourning for the accelerating destruction which impoverishes us all. Nevertheless, the ecological vision does suggest new policies based on a *synergistic* rather than competitive model.

The modern worldview initially intended the unity of natural science. But this unity was always only a hope and, in fact, the natural sciences multiplied. In the substantialist perspective, one can isolate any set of elements from their context in the real world and study them analytically in their own terms. There is no necessary reference to other elements of the world. The social sciences, which grew up on the other side of the great divide between material and mental substances, multiplied in a similar fashion.

With time, the methods and conceptualities of each science became well entrenched within that science and quite differentiated with respect to others. Although there may be influences from one science on another, these are random. Basically each one models itself on the supposedly substantial character of the subject matter.

It is notorious that many of our most important questions cannot be dealt with within the confines of any existing science. For that reason they are likely to be ignored, or else misleadingly treated as if they did belong to some one of the disciplines. Occasionally interdisciplinary teams are organized to deal with such problems. But the results are only modestly encouraging. The questions need to be treated in their integrity, not as the sum of questions formulated according to the traditions of several discrete disciplines. For example, nothing is more important than charting the right course for development in third world countries. This task is generally treated as a problem in economics. But, in fact, cultural anthropology, political science, ecology, agriculture, and forestry are almost always centrally involved. Decisions reached by teams with representatives of many disciplines are usually better than those made by economists alone. But their multiple specialties do not add up to a unified picture. The practical results, humanly and environmentally, have been disastrous.

The ecological worldview tells us that our initial mistake was the supposition that we could isolate some elements from the whole and learn the truth about them in this abstraction. A conceptuality developed to deal with them in abstraction from their real embedment in the whole will not accurately describe them in that embedment. A sum of distortions based on the different abstractions of the several disciplines will not give us the truth about the concrete reality. Of course much can be learned, but the addition, for example, to economics of political theory and sociology still does not bring us very close to what is really going on in our society unless the economics is richly informed from the outset by political theory and sociology. Only a knowledge that is ecologically related to all knowledge is appropriate to a reality that is ecologically interconnected. The implications run markedly counter to most current trends.

V. The Postmodern Ecological Worldview and the Divine

This postmodern ecological worldview, like deep ecology, is profoundly religious while rejecting the modern, Newtonian God. It resembles more the magical vision against which the theological voluntarists reacted. But, unlike deep ecology, it cannot be pantheistic, because every individual has its own indissoluble reality, activity, and value in and for itself and not only for others. The Whole for which it is also a value must itself be an activity numerically distinct from all the others, although internally related to all.

The contrast of the thought of the divine in the substantialist and ecological worldviews deserves emphasis. Boyle and Newton thought of both God and creatures as substances. There could be no internal relations among them. Power is fundamentally power to cause locomotion. On this view, if creatures had the power to move themselves, they would compete with or displace the divine power. Hence, God is glorified by the denial of all capacity for self-motion to the creatures. They are held to be purely passive, that is, purely material. God is the one source of all motion.

For the postmodern ecological worldview the "Adventure in the Universe as One" is internally related to the world. That is, she is constituted by Her relations to the activity and value of the world. The more value is attained in the world, the richer is the divine life. Similarly, the creature is constituted in part by its internal relation to the Divine Eros. From Her, it receives the power of freedom as self-determination. Apart from Her, it would be at most the outcome of its relations to past events, determined by their relative strength. From Her, it receives the ability to transcend that determination by the past in light of relevant unrealized possibilities.

In this paragraph, I have used the language of Alfred North Whitehead in *Adventures of Ideas,*[5] except that I have employed the feminine pronoun. It would be more convenient simply to speak of *God,* as Whitehead did in *Process and Reality.* But that word is so heavily freighted with the meanings that apply to the Newtonian God that, at least provisionally, it is well to think in another language. In many respects, the ecological vision of the divine suggests feminine aspects as opposed to the stereotypically masculine ones of the Newtonian deity. Another alternative to Whitehead's language of Adventure and Eros is simply to speak of the *Goddess,* but that would falsely exaggerate discontinuity with the God of the Bible.

It would be possible to leave off these last paragraphs and present the ecological vision of the world with its obvious religious meaning without reference to divinity. There are those who share much of the ecological worldview I have outlined without feeling the need to speak of the divine. But I believe that approach to be truncated. At least two things are lost.

First, although the locus of value in this postmodern vision is dispersed throughout the myriad individual activities, there is a need to speak of better and worse states of the world as a whole. We are concerned to maintain a healthy biosphere replete with human life because such a world will be more valuable than one of molten rock. But that conviction is hardly intelligible unless we can say *from what perspective* it is more valuable. The appropriate perspective is the Whole. But if the Whole is a perspective, that perspective is divine, and all the parts must be constitutive for it. As many ethicists have also discovered, if we do not affirm the reality of an inclusive and impartial perspective, we must yet think as if there were one in order to make sense of our valuations.

Second, without the Divine Eros, the ecological vision tends to become static. The emphasis in ecology tends to be on repetitive patterns. But the real world *is* radically historical. There would be less reason to heed the ecologists' warning if there were not the likelihood of drastic destruction and the need for drastic new action historically. These things are hard to conceive if there be no real relevance of novel possibility initiating real freedom for alternative activity.

Clearly, this talk of the Divine adds additional religious dimensions to an already religious vision. For me, it adds to the continuity I feel with my Biblical and Christian heritage. To rescue that heritage from its bondage to the materialist and dualist substantialist forms of thought which have captured much of it in the modern world seems to me an important calling.

Notes

1. David Ray Griffin, "Theology and the Rise of Modern Science" unpubl. ms. Many of the relevant ideas have been incorporated into the Introduction to this volume.

2. Stephen Pepper, *World Hypotheses: A Study in Evidence* (Berkeley: University of California Press, 1942); *Concept and Quality* (La Salle, Ill.: Open Court, 1969).

3. See James W. McClendon, Jr. and James M. Smith, *Understanding Religious Convictions* (Notre Dame, Ind.: University of Notre Dame Press, 1975).

4. For a good statement, see Bill Devall and George Sessions, *Deep Ecology: Living as if Nature Mattered* (New York: Peregrine Smith, 1985).

5. Alfred North Whitehead, *Adventures of Ideas* (1933; New York: The Free Press, 1967). On the Divine Eros, see 11, 198, 277; the phrase "Adventure in the Universe as One" occurs on 295.

20

The Cosmic Creation Story

Brian Swimme

OUR PLANETARY DIFFICULTIES: OUR TECHNOLOGIES HAVE RESULTED IN 50,000 nuclear warheads; our industrial economies have given us ecocide on every continent; our social distribution of goods and services has given us a billion underdeveloped and starving humans. One thing we can conclude without argument: as a species and as a planet we are in terrible shape. So as we consider proposals for leading us out of this dying world, we need to bear in mind that only proposals promising an immense efficacy need be considered. Anything less than a fundamental transformation of our situation is hardly worth talking about.

And yet, given this demand, my own suggestion is that we tell stories – in particular, that we tell the many stories that comprise the great cosmic story. I am suggesting that this activity of cosmic storytelling is the central political and economic act of our time. My basic claim is that by telling our cosmic creation story, we inaugurate a new era of human and planetary health, for we initiate a transformation out of a world that is – to use David Griffin's thorough formulation – mechanistic, scientistic, dualistic, patriarchal, Eurocentric, anthropocentric, militaristic, and reductionistic.[1]

A *cosmic creation story* is that which satisfies the questions asked by humans fresh out of the womb. As soon as they get here and learn the language, children ask the cosmic questions. Where did everything come from? What is going on? Why are you doing such and such anyway? The young of our species desire to learn where they are and what they are about in this life. That is, they express an inherent desire to hear their cosmic story.

By *cosmic creation story* I also mean to indicate those accounts of the universe we told each other around the evening fires for most of the last 50,000 years. These cosmic stories were the way the first humans chose to initiate and install their young into the universe. The rituals, the traditions, the taboos, the ethics, the techniques, the customs, and the values all had as their core a cosmic story. The story provided the central cohesion for each society. *Story* in this sense is "world-interpretation" – a likely account of the development and nature and value of things in this world.

Why story? Why should "story" be fundamental? Because without storytelling, we lose contact with our basic realities in this world. We lose contact because *only* through story can we fully recognize our existence in time.[2]

To be human is to be in a story. To forget one's story is to go insane. All the tribal peoples show an awareness of the connection between health and storytelling. The original humans will have their cosmic stories just as surely as they will have their food and drink. Our ancestors recognized that the universe, at its most basic level, is story. Each creature is story. Humans enter this world and awaken to a simple truth: "We must find our story within this great epic of being"

What about our situation today? Do we tell stories? We most certainly do, even if we do not call them stories. In our century's textbooks – for use in grade schools and high schools – we learn that it all began with impoverished primitives, marched through the technical inventions of the scientific period, and culminated – this is usually only implied, but there is never much doubt – in the United States of America, in its political freedom and, most of all, in its superior modes of production. For proof, graphs of industrial output compare the United States with other countries. Throughout our educational experiences, we were drawn into an emotional bonding with our society, so that it was only natural we would want to support, defend, and extend our society's values and accomplishments. Of course, this was not considered story; we were learning the facts.

Obviously, Soviets reflecting on their educational process recall a different story, one that began with the same denigration of the primal peoples, continued through a critique of bourgeois societies, and culminated in the USSR. And the French or British, reflecting on *their* educations, remember learning that, in fact, *they* were the important societies, for they were extending the European cultural tradition, while avoiding both the superficiality of the Americans and the lugubriousness of the Soviets.

Although we told ourselves such human stories, none of us in the industrial countries taught our children cosmic stories. We focused entirely on the human world when telling our stories of value and meaning. The universe and Earth taken together were merely backdrop. The oceans were large, the species many, yes – but these immensities were just the stage for the humans. This mistake is the fundamental mistake of our era. In a sentence, I summarize my position this way: *all our disasters today are directly related to our having been raised in cultures that ignored the cosmos for an exclusive focus on the human.* Our uses of land, our uses of technology, our uses of each other are flawed in many ways but due fundamentally to the same folly. We fail in so grotesque a manner because we were never initiated into the realities and values of the universe. Without the benefit of a cosmic story that provided meaning to our existence as Earthlings, we were stranded in an abstract world and left to invent nuclear weapons and chemical biocides and ruinous exploitations and waste.

How could this have happened? How could modern Western culture escape a 50,000-year-old tradition of telling cosmic stories? We discovered science. So impressed were we with this blinding light, we simply threw out the cosmic stories for the knowledge that the sciences provided. Why tell the story of the Sun as a God when we knew the sun was a locus of thermonuclear reactions? We pursued "scientific law," relegating "story" and "myth" to the nurseries and tribes. Science gave us the real, and the best science was mathematical science. We traded myth for mathematics and, without realizing it, we entered upon an intellectual quest that had for its goal a complete escape from the shifting sands of the temporal world. As Ilya Prigogine summarizes: "For most of the founders of classical science – even for Einstein – science was an attempt to go beyond the world of appearances, to reach a timeless world of supreme rationality – the world of Spinoza."[3]

What a shock it has been to have *story reappear,* and this time right in the very center of the mathematical sciences! Someday someone will tell the full story of how "story" forced its way into the most antistory domain of modern science – I mean mathematical physics. Here I would like to indicate in broad strokes what has happened.

For physicists during the modern period, "reality" meant the fundamental interactions of the universe. In a sense, the world's physical essence was considered captured by the right group of mathematical equations. Gravity and the Strong Nuclear Interaction were the real actors in the universe. The actual course of events was seen as of secondary importance, as the "details" structured by the fundamental dynamics of physical reality. The Story of Time was regarded as secondary, even illusory – time was simply a parameter that appeared in the equations. That is, nothing was special about the time today, as opposed to some time one billion years from now. Each time was the same, for the mathematical equations showed no difference between any two times.

The best story I know concerning this dismissal of time concerns Albert Einstein. Out of his own amazing genius, he arrived at his famous field equations, the mathematical laws governing the universe in its physical macrodimensions. What most alarmed Einstein – and we must remember that here was a man who had the courage to stick to his mathematical insights no matter how shocking they might seem to the world – what most disturbed Einstein about his own equations was their implication that the universe was expanding. Such a notion made no sense in the Newtonian cosmology of a static universe, which held that the universe today is essentially the same as the universe at any other time. In Newton's universe motion could exist *in* the universe, but the idea that the universe as a whole was changing was hardly thinkable. For these reasons, Einstein's equations stunned him when they whispered their secret – that the universe is not static; that the universe is expanding each moment into a previously nonexistent space; that the universe is a dynamic developing reality.

To avoid these alarming implications, Einstein altered his equations to eliminate their predictions. If only the truth of the universe could be so easily contained! Soon after Einstein published his equations, the Russian mathematician Alexander Friedmann found solutions to Einstein's equations – these solutions were theoretical universes, some of which expanded, some of which contracted, and some of which oscillated in and out. Einstein's response to Friedmann's communication was a polite dismissal of what seemed to be an utterly preposterous mathematical fiction.

But when Edwin Hubble later showed the empirical evidence for an expanding universe, Einstein realized his failure of nerve. He later came to regard his doctoring of the field equations as the "biggest blunder of my life."[4] My point is the complete surprise this discovery was for the scientists involved. If Einstein had left the equations as he had come to them, he would have made the greatest prediction in the entire history of science. But such a leap out of a static universe into a cosmic story was simply beyond the pale for our century's greatest scientist.

Even so, we now realize – following the work of Einstein, Hubble, and others – that ours is a universe that had a beginning in time and has been developing from 15 to 20 billion years. And every moment of this universe is new. That is, we now realize that we live not in a static Newtonian space; we live within an ongoing cosmic story.

Story forced its way still further into physics when in recent decades scientists discovered that even the fundamental interactions of the universe *evolved* into their present forms. *The laws that govern the physical universe today and that were thought to be immutable are themselves the results of developments over time.* We had always assumed that the laws were fixed, absolute, eternal. Now we discover that even the laws tell their own story of the universe. That is, the Cosmic Story, rather than being simply governed by fixed underlying laws, draws these laws into the drama.

Story inserts itself still further into the consciousness of contemporary physicists when the very status of physical law is put into a new perspective. Where once we listed a set of laws that, we were certain, held everywhere and at all times, we now ponder the violations of each of these laws. A preeminent physicist of our time, John Archibald Wheeler, concludes that in nature "there is no law except the law that there is no law." Wheeler's inclination is to question our fixation with law; he demands that the details of nature be given the same attention we give to the unifying ideas. As Wheeler sings, "Individual events. Events beyond law. Events so numerous and so uncoordinated that, flaunting their freedom from formula, they yet fabricate firm form."[5]

What happens when physicists begin to value not just the repeatable experiment but history's unrepeatable events, no longer regarding each event as simply another datum useful for arriving at mathematical law but as a revelation all by itself? A reenchantment with the universe happens. A new love affair between humans and the universe happens.

Only when we are surprised in the presence of a person or a thing are we truly in love. And regardless how intimate we become, our surprise continues. Without question we come to know the beloved better and are able to speak central truths about her or him or it, but never do we arrive at a statement that is the final word. Further surprises always occur, for to be in love is to be in awe of the infinite depths of things.[6] What I am suggesting by remembering Einstein's astonishment at the time-developmental nature of the universe and by underlining Wheeler's fascination with the individual event is that scientists have entered a new enchantment. Having been raised and trained in the disenchanted world of classical Newtonian physics, they are suddenly astonished and fascinated in an altogether new way by the infinite elegance which gathers us into its life and existence.

A central desire of scientists in the future will be to explore and celebrate the enveloping Great Mystery – the story of the universe, the journey of the galaxies, the adventure of the planet Earth and all of its life forms. Scientific theories will no longer be seen simply as objective laws. Scientific understanding will be valued as that power capable of evoking in humans a deep intimacy with reality. That is, the value of the electromagnetic interaction as objectively true will be deepened by our awareness that study and contemplation of the electromagnetic interaction allows humans to enter a rich communion experience with the contours of reality in the stellar cores, as well as in the unfolding dynamics of our sun and forests.

I am convinced, finally, that the story of the universe that has come out of three centuries of modern scientific work will be recognized as a supreme human achievement, the scientific enterprise's central gift to humanity, a revelation having a status equal to the great religious revelations of the past.

Of course, these are my speculations. I may be wrong. Instead of scientists devoting themselves to a further exploration and celebration of the cosmic story, they may be entirely captured by the militaries of the planet. But I do not think so, and for a number of reasons. The one reason I mention here concerns the planetary implications of the cosmic creation story.

I discussed Einstein's resistance to highlight an obvious and significant fact of the cosmic creation story – *its power to draw humans into itself.* Einstein did not want to discover an expanding, time-developmental universe. Another famous physicist, Arthur Eddington, found the whole notion "abhorrent." But the story convinces regardless. Its appeal to humans is virtually irresistible. The cosmic creation story has the potency to offset and even to displace entirely every previous worldview. Often, this displacing of traditional stories has resulted in cultural tragedy, and this reality must be discussed. What I want to bring to the readers' attention here is that the human being, as constituted today, finds the cosmic story undeniably tied to the truth, and this is great news indeed.

For suddenly, the human species as a whole has a common cosmic story. Islamic people, Hopi people, Christian people, Marxist people, and Hindu people can all agree in a basic sense on the birth of the Sun, on the development of the Earth, the species of life, and human cultures. For the first time in human existence, we have a cosmic story that is not tied to one cultural tradition, or to a political ideology, but instead gathers every human group into its meanings. Certainly we must not be naive about this claim of universality. Every statement of the cosmic story will be placed in its own cultural context, and each context is, to varying degrees, expressive of political, religious, and cultural perspectives. But given that fact, we have even so broken through to a story that is panhuman; a story that is already taught and developed on every continent and within every major cultural setting.[7]

What does this mean? Every tribe knows the central value of its cosmic story in uniting its people. The same will be true for us. We are now creating the common story which will enable *Homo sapiens* to become a cohesive community. Instead of structuring American society on its own human story, or Soviet society on its own human story, and so on, we have the opportunity to tell instead the cosmic story, and the oceanic story, and the mammalian story, so that instead of building our lives and our society's meanings around the various human stories alone, we can build our lives and societies around the Earth story.

This is a good place to make my final comment on the meaning of *cosmic creation story.* Although with this phrase I refer in general to the account of our emergence out of the fireball and into galaxies and stars and Earth's life, I also think of the cosmic story as something that has not yet emerged. I think we will only have a common story for the human community when poets tell us the story. For until artists, poets, mystics, nature lovers tell the story – or until the poetic and mystical dimensions of humans are drawn forth in every person who sets out to tell us our story – we have only facts and theories.[8]

Most tribal communities understand the necessity of developing story-tellers – people who spend their lives learning the cosmic story and celebrating it in poetry, chant, dance, painting, music. The life of the tribe is woven around such celebrations. The telling of the story is understood both as that which installs the young and that which regenerates creation. The ritual of telling the story is understood as a cosmic event. Unless the story is sung and danced, the universe suffers from decay and fatigue. Everything depends on telling the story – the health of the people, the health of the soil, the health of the sun, the health of the soul, the health of the sky.

We need to keep the tribal perspective in mind when we examine our situation in the modern period. Instead of poets, we had one-eyed scientists and theologians. Neither of these high priests nor any of the rest of us was capable of celebrating the cosmic story. It is no wonder then that so many of us are sick and disabled, that the soils have gone bad, that the sky is covered with soot, and that the waters are filled with evils. Because we had no celebrations inaugurating us into the universe, the whole world has become diseased.

Bust what will happen when the storytellers emerge? What will happen when "the primal mind," to use Jamake Highwater's term,[9] sings of our common origin, our stupendous journey, our immense good fortune? We will become Earthlings. We will have evoked our of the depths of the human psyche those qualities enabling our transformation from disease to health. They will sing our epic of being, and stirring up from our roots will be a vast awe, an enduring gratitude, the astonishment of communion experiences, and the realization of cosmic adventure.

We must encourage cosmic storytellers because our dominant culture is blind to their value. It is not remarkable that we can obtain several hundred books on how to get a divorce, how to invest money, how to lose fat, and yet there is nothing available to assist those destined to sing to us the great epic of reality?

I suggest that when the artist of the cosmic story arrive, our monoindustrial assault and suicide will end and the new beginnings of the Earth will be at hand. Our situation is similar to that of the early Christians. They had nothing – nothing but a profound revelatory experience. they did nothing – nothing but wander about telling a new story. And yet the Western world entered a transformation from which it has never recovered.

So too with our moment. We have nothing compare to the massive accumulation of hate, fear, and arrogance that the intercontinental ballistic missiles, the third world debt, and the chemical toxins represents. But we are in the midst of a revelatory experience of the universe that must be compare in its magnitude with those of the great religious revelations. And we need only wander about telling this new story to ignite a transformation of humanity. For this story has the power to undo the mighty and arrogant and to ignite the creativity of the oppressed and forgotten. As the great Journey of the Universe breaks into human self-awareness, nothing can dam up our desire to shake off the suffocation of nationalism, anthropocentrism, and exploitation and to plunge instead into the adventure of the cosmos.

Let me end with an imaginary event – a moment in the future when children are taught by a cosmic storyteller. We can imagine a small group gathered around a fire in a hillside meadow. The woman in the middle is the oldest, a grandmother to some of the children present. If we can today already imagine such an event, we can be assured that tomorrow someone will begin the journey of bringing such dreams into practice.

The old woman might begin by picking up a chunk of granite. "At one time, at the beginning of the Earth, the whole planer was a boiling sea of molten rock. We revere rocks because everything has come from them – not just the continents and the mountains, but the trees, the oceans and your bodies. The rocks are your grandmother and your grandfather. When you remember all those who have helped you in this life, you begin with the rocks, for if not for them, you would not be."

She holds the rock before them in silence, showing each person in turn. "Do you hear the rock singing? In the last era, people thought there was no music in rocks. But we know that is not true. After all, some rocks became Mozart and showed their music as Mozart. Or did you think that the Earth had to go to Mars to learn how to play its music? No, Mozart is rocks, Mozart is the music of the Earth's rocks."

Now she slowly sinks her hands into the ground and holds the rich loamy soil before her. "Every rock is a symphony, but the music of soil soars beyond capture in human language. We had to go into outer space to realize how rare and unique soil is. Only the Earth created soil. There is no soil on the moon, There are minerals on the moon, but no soil. There is no soil on Mars. There is no soil on Venus, or on Sun, or on Jupiter, or anywhere else in the surrounding trillion miles. Even the Earth, the most extraordinary creative being of the solar system, required four billion years to create topsoil. We worship and nurture and protect the soils of the Earth because all music and all life and all happiness come from the soil. The soils are the matrix of human joy."

She points now to a low-hanging star in the great bowl of the night-sky. "Right now, that star is at work creating the elements that will one day live as sentient beings. All the matter of the Earth was created by the Grandmother Star that preceded our Sun. She fashioned the carbon and nitrogen and all the elements that would later become all the bodies and things of Earth. And when she was done with her immense creativity, she exploded in celebration of her achievement, sharing her riches with the universe and enabling our birth.

"Her destiny is your destiny. In the center of your being you too will create, and you too will shower the world with your creativity. Your lives will be filled with both suffering and joy; you will often be faced with death and hardship. But all of this finds its meaning in your participation in the great life of Earth. It is because of your creativity that the cosmic journey deepens."

She stares into the distance. In the long silence, she hears the thundering breakers on the ocean shore, just visible in the evening's light. They listen as the vast tonnage of saltwater is lifted up in silence, then again pounds up the sand.

"Think of how tired we were when we arrived here, and all we had to do was carry our little bodies up the hills! Now think of the work that is being done ceaselessly as all the oceans of the world curl into breakers against the shores. And think of all the work that is done ceaselessly as the Earth is pulled around the Sun. Think of all the work that is done ceaselessly as all 100 billion stars of the Milky Way are pulled around the center of the galaxy.

"And yet the stars don't think of this as work. Nor do the oceans think of their ceaseless tides as work. They are drawn irresistibly into their activities, moment after moment. The Earth finds itself drawn irresistibly to the Sun, and would find any other path in life utterly intolerable. What amazing work the stars and the planets accomplish, and never do we hear them complain!

"We humans and we animals are no different at all. For we find ourselves just as irresistibly drawn to follow certain paths in life. And if we pursue these paths, our lives – even should they become filled with suffering and hardship – are filled as well with the quality of effortlessness. Once we respond to our deepest allurements in the universe, we find ourselves on the edge of a wave passing though the cosmos that had its beginning 15 to 20 billion years ago in the fiery explosion of the beginning of time. The great joy of human being is to enter this allurement which pervades everything and to empower others – including the soil and the grasses and all the forgotten – so that they might enter their own path into their deepest allurement."

The light of dusk has gone. She sits with them in the deepening silence of the dark. The fire has died down to become a series of glowing points, mirroring the ocean of starlight all above them.

"You will be tempted at times to abandon your dreams, to settle for cynicism or greed, so great will your anxieties and fears appear to you.

"But no matter what happens, remember that our universe is a universe of surprise. We put our confidence not in our human egos but in the power that gathered the stars and knit the first living cells together. Remember that you are here through the creativity of others. You have awakened in a great epic of being, a drama that is 15 to 20 billion years in the making. The intelligence that ignited the first minds, the care that spaced the notes of the nightingale, the power that heaved all 100 billion galaxies across the sky now awakens as you, too, and permeates your life no less thoroughly.

"We do not know what mystery awaits us in the very next moment. But we can be sure we will be astonished and enchanted. This entire universe sprang into existence from a single numinous speck. Our origin is mystery; our destiny is intimate community with all that is; and our common species' aim is to celebrate the Great Joy which has drawn us into itself."

Rocks, soils, waves, stars – as they tell their story in 10,000 languages throughout the planet, they bind us to them in our emotions, our spirits, our minds, and our bodies. The Earth and the universe speak in all this. The cosmic creation story is the way in which the universe is inaugurating the next era of its ongoing journey.

Endnotes

1. This summary is found in the "Statement of Beliefs and Purposes" of the Center for a Postmodern World, which is available from the Center at 2060 Alameda Padre Serra #101, Santa Barbara, CA 93103.

2. Paul Ricoeur, "On Interpretation," Kenneth Baynes, James Bohman, and Thomas McCarthy, eds., *After Philosophy* (Cambridge, MA: MIT Press, 1987), 358.

3. Ilya Prigogine, *From Being to Becoming* (San Francisco: Freeman, 1980), 215. On this point in general, see David Ray Griffin, ed., *Physics and the Ultimate Significance of Time: Bohm, Prigogine, and Process Philosophy* (Albany: State University of New York Press, 1986).

4. Charles W. Misner, Kip S. Thorne, and John Archibald Wheeler, *Gravitation* (San Francisco: Freeman, 1970), 410-11.

5. Quoted by Freeman Dyson in Dean W. Curtin, ed., *The Aesthetic Dimension of Science* (New York: Philosophical Library, 1982), 54.

6. See, for example, Erich Jantsch, *The Self-Organizing Universe* (New York: Pergamon Press, 1980), 176.

7. The first to celebrate the emergence of a new creation story were Loren Eiseley in *The Immense Journey* (New York: Random House, 1957) and Teilhard de Chardin in *The Phenomenon of Man* (New York: Harper & Row, 1959). The person who first realized the cultural and planetary significance of a common creation story was Thomas Berry; see his *The New Story* (Chambersburg, PA: Anima Books, 1978). For a superb contemporary telling of the entire cosmic story, see Nigel Calder, *Timescale* (New York: Viking Press, 1983).

8. My version of the cosmic story is *The Universe is a Green Dragon* (Santa Fe, NM: Bear and Co., 1985).

9. Jamake Highwater, *The Primal Mind* (New York: New American Library, 1981).

21

The Ecological Self: Postmodern Ground for Right Action

Joanna Macy

IN A RECENT LECTURE ON A COLLEGE CAMPUS, I GAVE EXAMPLES OF actions being undertaken in defense of life on Earth – actions in which people risk their comfort and even their lives to protect other species. The examples included the Chipko, or "tree-hugging," movement among North Indian villagers to fight the lumbering of their remaining woodlands, and the Greenpeace organization's intervention on the open seas to protect marine mammals from slaughter. A student, Michael, wrote me afterwards:

> I think of the tree-huggers hugging my trunk, blocking the chainsaws with their bodies, I feel their fingers digging into my bark to stop the steel and let me breathe.
>
> I hear the bodhisattvas[1] in their rubber boats as they put themselves between the harpoons and me, so l can escape to the depths of the sea. . . .
>
> I give thanks for your life and mine . . . and for life itself. I give thanks for realizing that I, too, have the powers of the treehuggers and the bodhisattvas.

What strikes me in his words is the shift in identification. Michael is able to extend his sense of self to encompass the self of tree, of whale. Tree and whale are no longer removed, separate, disposable objects pertaining to a world "out there" but intrinsic parts of his own vitality. Through the power of his caring, his experience of self is expanded far beyond what Alan Watts termed the "skin-encapsulated ego."

I quote Michael's words not because they are unusual. On the contrary, they express a desire and a capacity arising in many people today as, out of deep concern over what is happening to our world, they begin to speak and act on its behalf.

Among those who are moving beyond conventional notions of self and self-interest, shedding them like an old skin or confining shell, is John Seed, director of the Rainforest Information Center in Australia. I asked him one day how he managed to overcome despair and sustain the struggle against the giant lumber interests. He said, "I try to remember that it's not me, John Seed, trying to protect the rainforest. Rather, I am

259

part of the rainforest protecting myself, I am that part of the rainforest recently emerged into human thinking."

This ecological sense of selfhood combines the mystical and the pragmatic. Transcending separateness and fragmentation, in a shift that Seed calls a "spiritual change," it generates an experience of profound interconnectedness with all life. This has in the past been largely relegated to the domain of mystics and poets. Now it is, at the same time, a motivation to action. The shift in identity serves as ground and resource for effective engagement with the forces and pathologies that imperil planetary survival.

A variety of factors converge in our time to promote such a shift in the sense of self and self-interest. Among the most significant are 1) the psychological and spiritual pressures exerted by current dangers of mass annihilation, 2) the emergence from science of the systems view of the world, and 3) a renaissance of nondualistic forms of spirituality.

This essay explores the role of these three factors – planetary peril, systems thinking, and nondualistic religion, specifically Buddhist teachings and practice – in promoting this shift. It is written from a conviction that a larger, ecological sense of self will characterize the postmodern world, and that without it there simply may *be* no postmodern world.

I. Personal Response to Planetary Crisis

The shift toward a wider, ecological sense of self is in large part a function of the dangers that threaten to overwhelm us. Given accelerating environmental destruction and massive deployment of nuclear weapons, people today are aware that they live in a world that can end. For example, public opinion polls indicate that over half the population expects nuclear weapons to be used, and two thirds believe that once they are used, the resultant nuclear war cannot be limited, won, or survived.[2] The loss of certainty that there will be a future is, I believe, the pivotal psychological reality of our time.

Over the past ten years my colleagues and I have worked with tens of thousands of people in North America, Europe, Asia, and Australia, helping them confront and explore what they know and feel about what is happening to their world. The purpose of this work, known as Despair and Empowerment Work, is to overcome the numbing and powerlessness that result from suppression of painful responses to massively painful realities.[3]

As their grief and fear for the world is allowed to be expressed without apology or argument and validated as a wholesome, life-preserving response, people break through their avoidance mechanisms, break through their sense of futility and isolation. And generally what they break through *into* is a larger sense of identity. It is as if the pressure of their acknowledged awareness of the suffering of our world stretches, or collapses, the culturally defined boundaries of the self.

It becomes clear, for example, that the grief and fear experienced for our world and our common future are categorically different from similar sentiments relating to one's personal welfare. This pain cannot be equated with dread of one's own individual demise. Its source lies less in concerns for personal survival than in apprehensions of collective suffering – of what looms for human life and other species and unborn generations to come. Its nature is akin to the original meaning of compassion – "suffering with." It is the distress we feel on behalf of the larger whole of which we are a part. And when it is so defined, it serves as trigger or gateway to a more encompassing sense of identity, inseparable from the web of life in which we are as intricately interconnected as cells in a larger body.

This shift is an appropriate, adaptive response. For the crisis that threatens our planet, be it seen in its military, ecological, or social aspects, derives from a dysfunctional and pathogenic notion of the self. It is a mistake about our place in the order of things. It is the delusion that the self is so separate and fragile that we must delineate and defend its boundaries, that it is so small and needy that we must endlessly acquire and endlessly consume, that it is so aloof that we can – as individuals, corporations, nation-states or as a species – be immune to what we do to other beings.

Such a view of the human condition is not new, nor is the felt imperative to extend self-interest to embrace the whole in any way novel to our history as a species. It has been enjoined by many a teacher and saint. What is notable in our present situation, and in the Despair and Empowerment Work we have done, is that the extension of identity can come directly, not through exhortations to nobility or altruism, but through the owning of pain. That is why the shift in the sense of self is credible to those experiencing it. As poet Theodore Roethke said, "I believe my pain."

Despair and Empowerment Work draws on both General Systems Theory and Buddhist teachings and practice. Both of these approaches inform our methods and offer explanatory principles in the move beyond ego-based identifications. Let us look at them in turn to see how they serve the shift to the ecological self.

II. Cybernetics of the Self

The findings of twentieth-century science undermine the notion of a separate self, distinct from the world it observes and acts upon. As Einstein showed, the self's perceptions are shaped by its changing position in relation to other phenomena. And these phenomena are affected not only by location but, as Heisenberg demonstrated, by the very act of observation. Now contemporary systems science and systems cybernetics go yet further in challenging old assumptions about a distinct, separate, continuous self, showing that there is no logical or scientific basis for construing one part of the experienced world as "me" and the rest as "other."

As open, self-organizing systems, our very breathing, acting, and thinking arise in interaction with our shared world through the currents of matter, energy, and information that flow through us. In the web of relationships that sustain these activities, there are no clear lines demarcating a separate, continuous self. As postmodern systems theorists aver, there is no categorical "I" set over against a categorical "you" or "it."

Systems philosopher Ervin Laszlo argues,

> We must do away with the subject-object distinction in analyzing experience. This does not mean that we reject the concepts of organism and environment, as handed down to us by natural science. It only means that we conceive of experience as linking organism and environment in a continuous chain of events, from which we cannot, without arbitrariness, abstract an entity called organism and another called environment.[4]

The abstraction of a separate "I" is what Gregory Bateson calls the "epistemological fallacy of Occidental civilization." He asserts that the larger system of which we are a part defies any definitive localization of the self. That which decides and does can no longer be neatly identified with the isolated subjectivity of the individual or located within the confines of his or her skin. "The total self-corrective unit which processes information, or, as I say, 'thinks' and 'acts' and 'decides,' is a *system* whose boundaries do not at all coincide with the boundaries either of the body or of what is popularly called the 'self' or 'consciousness'."[5]

"The self as ordinarily understood," Bateson goes on to say,

> is only a small part of a much larger trial-and-error system which does the thinking, acting and deciding. This system includes all the informational pathways which are relevant at any given moment to any given decision. The 'self' is a false reification of an improperly delimited part of this much larger field of interlocking processes.[6]

The false reification of the self is basic to the planetary ecological crisis in which we now find ourselves. We have imagined that the "unit of survival," as Bateson puts it, is the separate individual or the separate species. In reality, as throughout the history of evolution, it is the individual *plus* environment, the species *plus* environment, for they are essentially symbiotic. Bateson continues:

When you narrow down your epistemology and act on the premise "What interests me is me, or my organization, or my species," you chop off consideration of other loops of the loop structure. You decide you want to get rid of the by-products of human life and that Lake Erie will be a good place to put them. You forget that the eco-mental system called Lake Erie is a part of *your* wider eco-mental system – and that if Lake Erie is driven insane, its insanity is incorporated in the larger system of your thought and experience.[7]

Although we consist of and are sustained by the currents of information, matter, and energy that flow through us, we are accustomed to identifying ourselves with only that small arc of the flow-through that is lit, like the narrow beam of a flashlight, by our individual perceptions. But we do not *have* to so limit our self-perceptions. It is as logical, Bateson contends, to conceive of mind as the entire "pattern that connects." It is as plausible to align our identity with that larger pattern and conceive of ourselves as interexistent with all beings, as it is to break off one segment of the process and build our borders there.

Systems Theory helps us see that the larger identification of which we speak does not involve an eclipse of the distinctiveness of one's individual experience. The "pattern that connects" is not an ocean of Brahman where separate drops merge and our diversities dissolve. Natural and cognitive systems self-organize and interact to create larger wholes precisely through their heterogeneity. By the same token, through the dance of deviation-amplifying feedback loops, the respective particularities of the interactive systems can increase. Integration and differentiation go hand in hand. Uniformity, by contrast, is entropic, the kiss of death.

The systems view of the world, unfortunately, has not characterized or informed the uses our society has made of systems science. The advances permitted by its perceptions of pattern and its models of circuitry have been mainly employed to further values and goals inherited from a mechanistic, reductionistic interpretation of reality. Systems thinker Milady Cardamone hypothesizes that it is the feminine-like quality of the systems approach that has kept our society from fully grasping this wholistic style of perceiving the universe.[8]

Molecular biologist and Nobel Prize winner Barbara McClintock reveals, however, how practical and revolutionary the results can be when science is done from the perspective of the ecological self. Her discovery of the interactive nature of the cell, as opposed to the previously accepted master control theory, came out of her ability to see the cell and feel herself as part of the system. "I actually felt as if I were down there and these [internal parts of the chromosomes] were my friends."[9]

The Boundless Heart of the Bodhisattva

In the resurgence of nondualistic spiritualities in our postmodern world, Buddhism in its historic coming to the West is distinctive in the clarity and sophistication it offers in understanding the dynamics of the self. In much the same way as General Systems Theory does, its ontology and epistemology undermine any categorical distinctions definitive of a self-existent identity. And it goes further than systems cybernetics, both in revealing the pathogenic character of any reifications of the self and in offering methods for transcending them,

Dependent co-arising *(pratitya samutpada),* the core teaching of the Buddha on the nature of causality, presents a phenomenal reality so dynamic and interrelated that categorical subject-object distinctions dissolve. This is driven home in the doctrine of *anatman* or "no-self," where one's sense of identity is understood as an ephemeral product of perceptual transactions, and where the experiencer is inseparable from his or her experience. The notion of an abiding individual self – whether saintly or sinful, whether it is to be protected, promoted or punished – is seen as the foundational delusion of human life. It is the motive force behind our attachments and aversions, and these in turn exacerbate it. As portrayed symbolically in the center of the Buddhist Wheel of Life, where pig, cock, and snake pursue each other endlessly, these three – greed, hatred, and the delusion of ego – sustain and aggravate each other in a continuous vicious circle, or positive feedback loop.

We are not doomed to a perpetual rat-race; the vicious circle can be broken, its energies liberated to more satisfying uses by the threefold interplay of wisdom, meditative practice, and moral action. Wisdom *(prajna)* arises, reflected and generated by the teachings about self and reality. Practice *(dhyana)* liberates through precise attention to the elements and flow of one's existential experience – an experience which reveals no separate experience, no permanent self. And moral behavior *(sila),* according to precepts of nonviolence, truthfulness, and generosity, helps free one from the dictates of greed, aversion, and other reactions which reinforce the delusion of separate selfhood.

Far from the nihilism and escapism often attributed to Buddhism, the path it offers can bring the world into sharper focus and liberate one into lively, effective action. What emerges, when free from the prison cell of the separate, competitive ego, is a vision of radical and sustaining interdependence. In Hua Yen Buddhism it is imaged as the Jeweled Net of Indra: a cosmic canopy where each of us – each jewel at each node of the net – reflects all the others and reflects the others reflecting hack. As in the holographic view in contemporary science, each part *contains* the whole.

Each one of us who perceives that, or is capable of perceiving it, is a *bodhisattva* – an "awakening being" – the hero model of the Buddhist tradition. We are all *bodhisattvas*, able to recognize and act upon our profound interexistence with all beings. That true nature is already evident in our pain for the world, which is a function of the *mahakaruna*, great compassion. And it flowers through the *bodhisattva's* "boundless heart" in active identification with all beings.

Christina Feldman, like many other women Buddhist teachers today, points out that this bodhisattva heart is absolutely central to spiritual practice. It is more transformative of ego and more generative of connection than the desire to be perfect, pure, or aloof from suffering. It is already within us, like a larger self awaiting discovery.

> We find ourselves forsaking the pursuit of personal perfection and also the denial of imperfection. To become someone different, to pursue a model of personal perfection is no longer the goal. . . . Learning to listen inwardly, we learn to listen to our world and to each other. We hear the pain of the alienated, the sick, the lonely, the angry, and we rejoice in the happiness, the fulfillment, the peace of others. We are touched deeply by the pain of our planet, equally touched by the perfection of a bud unfolding. . . . We learn to respect the heart for its power to connect us on a fundamental level with each other, with nature and with all life.[10]

The experience of interconnection with all life can sustain our social change work far better than righteous partisanship; that is the teaching of Vietnamese Zen monk Thich Nhat Hanh. In Vietnam during the 1960s, he founded Youth for Social Service, whose members rescued and aided homeless, hungry, and wounded villagers on both sides of the war. From their ranks he created a nonmonastic Order called Tiep Hien, now gradually spreading in the West under the name Interbeing.

I take his poem "Call Me by My True Names" as an expression of the ecological self. To quote a few lines:

> Do not say that I'll depart tomorrow
> because even today I still arrive.

> Look at me: I arrive in every second
> to be a bud on a spring branch,
> to be a tiny bird. . . in my new nest,
> to be a caterpillar in the heart of a flower,
> to be a jewel hiding itself in a stone.

> The rhythm of my heart is the birth and death
> of all that are alive. . . .

> I am the frog swimming happily
> in the clear water of a pond,
> and I am also the grass snake who,
> approaching in silence, feeds itself on the frog. . . .

I am the 12-year-old girl,
refugee on a small boat,
who throws herself into the ocean
after being raped by a sea pirate,
I am also the pirate,
my heart not yet capable of seeing and loving. . . .

Please call me by my true names
so that I can hear all my cries and my laughs at once
so that I can see that my joy and my pain are one. . . .

Please call me by my true names
so that I can wake up. . . .[11]

IV. Beyond Altruism

What Bateson called "the pattern that connects" and Buddhists image as the Jeweled Net of Indra can be construed in lay, secular terms as our deep ecology. "Deep ecology" is a term coined by Norwegian philosopher Arne Naess to connote a basic shift in ways of seeing and valuing. It represents an apprehension of reality that he contrasts with "shallow environmentalism" – the band-aid approach applying technological fixes for short-term human goals.

The perspective of deep ecology helps us to recognize our embeddedness in nature, overcoming our alienation from the rest of creation and regaining an attitude of reverence for all life forms. It can change the way that the self is experienced through a spontaneous process of self-realization, where the self-to-be-realized extends further and further beyond the separate ego and includes more and more of the phenomenal world. In this process, notions like altruism and moral duty are left behind. Naess explains:

> Altruism implies that ego sacrifices its interests in favor of the other, the *alter*. . . . The motivation is primarily that of duty. . . . What humankind is capable of loving from mere duty or more generally from moral exhortation is unfortunately very limited. . . . Unhappily the extensive moralizing within the environmental movement has given the public the false impression that we primarily ask them to sacrifice, to show more responsibility, more concern, and better morals. . . . The requisite care flows naturally if the self is widened and deepened so that protection of free nature is felt and conceived of as protection of ourselves.[12]

Please note: Virtue is not required for the emergence of the ecological self! This shift in identification is essential to our survival at this point in our history precisely because it can serve in lieu of ethics and morality. Moralizing is ineffective; sermons seldom hinder us from pursuing our self-interest as we construe it. Hence the need to be more enlightened about what our real self-interest is. It would not occur to me, for example, to exhort you to refrain from sawing off your leg. That would not occur to me or to you, because your leg is part of you. Well, so are the trees in the Amazon Basin; they are our external lungs. We are just beginning to wake up to that, gradually discovering that the world *is* our body.

Economist Hazel Henderson sees our survival dependent on a shift in consciousness from "phenotype" to "genotype." The former, she says, springs from fear of the death of the ego and the consequent conflict between the perceived individual will and the requirements of society or biosphere.

> We may be emerging from the "age of phenotype," of separated ego awareness, which has now become amplified into untenable forms of dualism. . . . The emerging view is rebalancing toward concern for the genotype, protection of species and gene pools and for the mutagenic dangers of nuclear radiation, chemical wastes and the new intergenerational risks being transferred to our progeny, about which economists say little.[13]

V. Grace and Power

The ecological self, like any notion of selfhood, is a metaphoric construct, and a dynamic one. It involves choice. Choices can be made to identify at different moments with different dimensions or aspects of our systemically interconnected existence – be they hunted whales or homeless humans or the planet itself. In so doing, this extended self brings into play wider resources – resources, say, of courage, wisdom, endurance – like a nerve cell opening to the charge of fellow neurons in the neural net. For example, in his work on behalf of the rainforest, John Seed felt empowered *by* the rainforest.

There is the experience then of being acted "through" and sustained "by" something greater than oneself. It is close to the religious concept of grace, but, as distinct from the traditional Western understanding of grace, it does not require belief in God or supernatural agency. One simply finds oneself empowered to act on behalf of other beings – or on behalf of the larger whole – and the empowerment itself seems to come "through" that or those for whose sake one acts.

This phenomenon, when approached from the perspective of Systems Theory, is understandable in terms of synergy. It springs from the self-organizing nature of life. It stems from the fact that living systems evolve in complexity and intelligence through their interactions. These interactions, which can be mental or physical, and which can operate at a distance through transmission of information, require openness and sensitivity on the part of the system in order to process the flow-through of energy and information. The interactions bring into play new responses and new possibilities. This interdependent release of fresh potential is called "synergy." And it is like grace, because it brings an increase of power beyond one's own capacity as a separate entity.

As we awaken, then, to our larger, ecological self, we find new powers. We find possibilities of vast efficacy, undreamed of in our squirrel cage of separate ego. Because these potentialities are interactive in nature, they are the preserve and property of no one, and they manifest only to the extent that we recognize and act upon our interexistence, our deep ecology.

As David Griffin wrote of the emerging postmodern world in his introduction to an earlier volume, "the modern desire to master and possess is replaced in postmodern spirituality with a joy in communion."[14] That joy in communion is, I believe, a homecoming to our natural interexistence with all life forms, home to our deep ecology, home to the world as Dharmabody of the Buddha. And it brings with it the capacity to act with courage and resilience.

Endnotes

1. A term in Buddhism for a compassionate being.

2. See *Voter Options on Nuclear Arms Policy* (Public Agenda Foundation, 1984).

3. See my *Despairwork* (Philadelphia: New Society Publishers, 1982) and *Despair and Personal Power in the Nuclear Age* (Philadelphia: New Society Publishers, 1983, 1988).

4. Ervin Laszlo, *Introduction to Systems Philosophy* (New York: Harper & Row Torchbook, 1973), 21.

5. Gregory Bateson, *Steps to an Ecology of Mind* (New York: Ballantine Books, 1972), 319.

6. *Ibid.,* 331.

7. *Ibid.,* 484.

8. Milady Cardamone, "The Feminine Aspect of the Systems Approach," *Proceedings of the Annual Meeting of the Society of General Systems Research* (Louisville, Ky.: Society for General Systems Research, 1987), F-44.

9. Evelyn Fox Keller, "Women, Science and Popular Mythology," in Joan Rothschild, ed., *Machina Ex Dea* (London: Pergamon Press, 1983), 143.

10. Christina Feldman, "Nurturing Compassion," in Fred Eppsteiner, ed., *The Path of Compassion* (Berkeley, Calif.: Parallax Press, 1988), 31.

11. Fred Eppsteiner, ed., *The Path of Compassion* (Berkeley, Calif: Parallax Press, 1988), 31.

12. From an unpublished brochure by John Seed. See also Arne Naess, "Identification as a Source of Deep Ecological Attitudes," and "Self Realization: An

Ecological Approach to Being in the World," in John Seed, Joanna Macy, Arne Naess, and Pat Fleming, ed., *Thinking Like A Mountain: Toward A Council of All Beings* (Philadelphia: New Society Publishers, 1988).

13. See Hazel Henderson, "Beyond the Information Age," *Creation,* March/April 1988: 34-35.

14. "Introduction: Postmodern Spirituality and Society," David Ray Griffin, ed., *Spirituality and Society: Postmodern Visions* (Albany: State University of New York Press, 1988), 1-31, esp. 15.

22

The Sacrament of Creation Toward an Environmental Theology

Michael J. Himes & Kenneth R. Himes

SOMETHING IS IN THE AIR. OR IS IT IN THE WATER? A SENSE OF ECOLOGICAL crisis looms over our planet. Interest in the environment is spreading. In Washington, Congress has been at odds with the White House over how to make the next clean air legislation tougher. And, lo and behold, officials in Los Angeles have gotten so serious about air quality they have proposed a plan for cutting down pollution that could make car-pooling mandatory.

When the leaders of the seven industrialized nations met in Paris in the summer of 1989, their final communiqué gave evidence of just how "mainstream" environmentalism has become. That the president of the United States supports such ecological high-mindedness should come as no surprise. Recall the last presidential campaign when Messrs. Bush and Dukakis skirmished over who deserved to be called the environmental candidate.

For many, of course the environment has never not been an issue. Fetid garbage dumps, closed beaches, air you can see as well as breathe, the extinction of whole species – the causes for concern have long been with us. More recently interest has arisen in developing a religious response to the ecological crisis. Some have found the resources for such a theology and spirituality in Eastern thought and practice. Others, like Joseph Sittler and Ian Barbour, seek out elements of the Christian tradition for the development of a "creation-centered" perspective.

At the same time a number of critics (Arnold Toynbee, Lynn White) have argued that the Christian tradition is suspect on the matter of the environment. They argue that Judaism and Christianity have fed an anthropocentrism which, intentionally or not, demeans the rest of creation as it exalts those who are a "little less than the angels" (Psalm 8:5). Certainly Hebraic monotheism declared that all others but Yahweh were "no-gods." Included among those thus denied divine status were the deities of Greek and Roman mythology who protected streams, mountains, and forests. It is possible to see in this demythologizing a loss of reverence for nature. Christianity's contribution to the problem – its celebration of the

Incarnation – has promoted the centrality of humanity in the plan of creation and redemption and accorded secondary status to the rest of creation.

With a bit of poetic license and some ingenuity a few individuals (Thomas Berry, Matthew Fox) have sought to re-present the tradition and demonstrate a more sensible Christian attitude toward the created order. Some of this work has borne fruit, awakening among believers an interest in the environment and providing a degree of religious seriousness for addressing an issue that is more important and complex than the faddishness and trivialization which mass media politics inevitably encourages.

Despite these efforts, it is lamentable but true that the question still can fairly be asked, "What does Christianity have to say to the contemporary ecological movement?" That it has something to say is important to assert, but what it has to say is not primarily advice on public policy or clear moral judgments for settling disputes about economic growth versus ecological protection. In this regard, the Christian tradition is, in the words of Richard McCormick, "more a value raiser than a problem solver."

The values that Christianity points to in the cluster of issues raised by the environmental crisis is humankind's essential relatedness to nature, an understanding of the created order that is precisely what is at stake here. Too often the discussion over the ecosystem turns on arguments from self-interest, even if enlightened self-interest, a stance that we believe is fundamentally flawed.

Treating the environmental issue as primarily a calculation of long-term versus short-term interests maintains an attitude of instrumental rationality that is essentially part of the problem. The Jewish and Christian understanding of creation, at least in one of its strands, is profoundly insightful and potentially transformative of modern ways of addressing the crisis of creation.

The needed transformation lies at the level of our deep convictions, our world view. The relational dimension of the Jewish-Christian heritage must replace the atomized individualism of our current outlook. The mentality of consumerism, the myth of progress, and our technological mind-set are all problematic in regard to the environment; they are also symptomatic. Each is the distortion of a human good, a distortion rising from the nonrelational anthropology of our age. If our environmental sensitivity is to change, the transformation must take place at the root of the problem. But that transformation is more convoluted than might first appear.

The human abuse of nonhuman nature has spurred a harsh reaction by defenders of the environment, who exhibit a brand of ecological activism, and environmental romanticism, that borders on the antihuman. Nature is idealized. The achievements of human civilization are disparaged. The environmental romantic, however, mirrors the fundamental outlook of the technocrats. Both see humanity at odds with nature. In one case this leads to calls for more effective ways of manipulating, subduing, and dominating nature. In the other, there is opposition to technology, economic growth, and development efforts. In both cases humanity is set in opposition to the rest of creation. Either alternative is unacceptable from a relational world view. To separate nature from human culture is environmental romanticism. To consider human culture apart from the nonhuman is to invite the impoverishment of the first and the devastation of the second.

The Jewish and Christian traditions put before us a world view in which humanity is not against nature but a part of it. Neither element is rightly viewed in isolation. The exploration of this relational anthropology is the basic contribution theologians can make to the environmental movement. We can examine the traditions to see which developments have been distortions, which trajectories misguided, which insights forgotten. The constructive task is to illustrate how the resources of the Jewish and Christian heritage can be used in promoting ecological wisdom.

Lessons of Genesis

Like every myth of origin, the two Genesis stories of the beginning of all things (Genesis 1:1-2:4a and 2:4b-25) have been used to explain and justify the ways human beings relate to one another and to the nonhuman world, As narratives of how things came to be and depictions of how things were and presumably ought to be, these creation stories have been elaborated into cosmologies and theories of the soul and twisted into ideological support for male-dominance and industrial exploitation.

The first of the two stories has been the basis of both the overlordship and stewardship images for the role of humanity in the natural world. "Let us make the human being in our image and likeness. . . .God blessed them, saying to them, 'Be fertile and increase; fill the whole earth and subdue it; have dominion over the fish of the sea and the birds of the air and all the living things that move on the earth'" (Gen. 1:26 and 28). Part of the human being's likeness to God is the exercise of dominion over the rest of creation. The twin images of being given dominion and being commanded to subdue the earth and all the creatures which fill it are closely connected with sovereignty. God's sovereignty is asserted often in the Hebrew Scriptures. Here the image and likeness of God, the human being, is entrusted with sovereignty. From the perspective of the first creation myth in Genesis, without such dominion and power over the rest of creation, the human being would not be "like God."

But there is a contrasting theme in this story. "And so God created the human being in God's image; in the divine image did God create the human being, male and female did he create them" (Gen. 1:27). How is it that being created in the image of God results in the differentiation of male and female? Clearly the myth does not wish to attribute gender to God, much less dual bisexuality. The point is not that God is male or female or male and female, but that God is relational. The only God that the Hebrew tradition knows is the God who is about the business of creating; that is, the Hebrew Scriptures contain nothing about God *in se,* God considered apart from the creating God. Even in one of its creation myths, the Hebrew tradition envisions God as the God of the covenant, God in relationship. To be the image of this God, the human being must be relational. Humanity is sexed in order that human beings may be driven into relationship one with another.

This is a central theme of the second of Genesis's creation myths (2:4b-25). The dominion motive is depicted in the first human being naming all the animals that God has made and led before him "to see what he would call them" (Gen. 2:19). All other creatures will be what the human being says they are – certainly an extraordinary statement of the power over creation given by God to humanity. But the context of this conferral is the human hunger for companionship. In the first of the creation myths, the first divine judgment on humanity is that it is "very good" (Gen. 1:31). That judgment is made on humanity differentiated into male and female, relational being. The first judgment of God regarding human beings in the second myth makes this even more explicit. Having fashioned the human being from the clods of the earth and breathed the divine breath into him, God announces that "it is not good for the human being to be alone" (Gen. 2:18). Again there is the insistence that human beings are meant to be in relationship to one another. Thus, in this second creation story, companionship is the explicit ground given for the creation of the two sexes. But it is important to note not only human beings are intended for relationship to one another. This is also the reason for the creation of "the various wild beasts and birds of the air" (Gen. 2:19). The natural world is not merely intended for subjugation by human beings but for companionship.

Dominion over the earth and all that it contains, the command "to fill the whole earth and subdue it" – certainly this conveys power. Such a claim to power by human beings over all nonhuman creation contains the possibility, all too often realized, of domination and exploitation of the earth. Clearly the claim to power must be balanced by the call to responsibility, the traditional appeal to stewardship. The relationship between humanity and the rest of creation has often been cast in the Jewish and Christian traditions as that of a caretaker, one charged by God with the maintenance of the earth. The nonhuman world has been given to human beings for our good, to be used responsibly for our self-development, to answer to our purposes and thus to fulfill God's purpose in creating it. To be sure, this stewardship image prohibited wanton wastefulness, the mere exploitation of nature by humankind. The world is presented as a garden given into our care to be tended and nurtured. But undeniably the role of stewardship carries the implication that nonhuman creation is to be used.

The theme of companionship, the relationship which exists not only between human persons but between humans and nonhumans, has been largely submerged in the stewardship theme. We need to recover it. Companionship implies mutuality. It excludes the reduction of either side of the relationship to a tool of the other's purposes. Martin Buber, so deeply rooted in the biblical tradition, explored the meaning of companionship under the rubric "I-Thou." The contrasting possibility is "I-It." The reduction of "thou" to "it" results from making the other into an extension of oneself. The other becomes *mine* – *my* husband, my wife, *my* parent, *my* friend, *my* student, *my* boss. "It" can be manipulated in order to fulfill the task which I set, for "it" belongs to me. "It" has no intrinsic value, only the instrumental value that I assign it. The other as "thou" cannot be possessed, can never become *my* "thou." When recognized and respected as "thou," the other is seen to be of inherent value, to be an end and not a means to an end.

As a human being can be reduced to an "it," so a nonhuman being can become "thou," in Buber's terms. "It" can be a possession but not a companion. "Thou" is always a companion. But in what sense, other than the mythology of the second creation story in Genesis, can one speak of the nonhuman world as companion to human beings? At a time of global ecological crisis, we certainly do not need a revival of the nineteenth-century Romantic poets' personification of Nature. Indeed, such personification is the very reverse of what Buber meant by treating the nonhuman world as "thou," for instead of allowing the other to be what the other is, personification insists that the other must be what I am if I am to enter into any relationship with it. Such personification is another, more subtle way of reducing the nonhuman other to "it."

Augustine and Francis

The Catholic tradition offers two important symbols that deserve to be explored as ways of re-appropriating the biblical theme of companionship in creation: poverty and sacramentality.

In Book 9 of his *Confessions,* Augustine recounts an incident that took place shortly before the death of his mother, Monica, as they stayed at Ostia on their way home to North Africa after his baptism in Milan. Seated at a window overlooking the garden of their rented house, they speculated on the life of the saints in glory. As Augustine describes their experience, they entered into a rapturous ecstasy in which they had a foretaste of that life. Passing through all the spheres of the sun, moon, planets, and stars of their Ptolemaic universe, they came to the outermost limit of their own minds and transcended even that. All the heavenly spheres ceased their music, Augustine writes. Everything that exists by passing away, that is, all creatures, since the mark of creatureliness is temporality, fell silent after singing the song which they constantly sing: "We did not make ourselves, but were made by God who is forever" (Bk. 9:10, 25).

Eight centuries later, Francis of Assisi grasped the two central elements of this Augustinian song of all creation. As with so many charismatic men and women, the historic Francis has been lost in popular mythology. But two themes of the Franciscan legend seem rooted in Francis himself: poverty and the unity of all creatures. The singer of the Canticle of the Sun, who recognized the sun and moon, earth and air, fire and water, his own body, all animals and plants, and death itself as brothers and sisters, also entered into a mystical marriage with Lady Poverty. This Franciscan emphasis, which finds its legendary expression in Francis's preaching to the birds and the wolf of Gubbio, is grounded in one insight: all creatures are united in the depths of their being by the fact of being creatures.

The discovery of one's finiteness is the recognition of one's poverty. When one grasps the "iffiness" of one's existence, the shocking fact that the source and foundation of one's being is not in oneself, then one knows oneself as truly poor. To be poor in this fundamental sense is a definition, not a description. True poverty, the poverty of the spirit, is the realization that there is no intrinsic reason for one's being at all. In this fundamental poverty of creatureliness, there is quality. The human person has no more claim to intrinsic being than a plant or animal, a star or a stone. This is not in any way to deny the unique role which the human person plays in the divine economy. Indeed, in light of the Christian doctrine of the Incarnation, that role is one of extraordinary dignity. But the role given to humanity is as sovereignly the gift of God as is the role of every other creature. The human person is the point in creation to which the fullness of the self-gift of God can be given. But the human person has been *created* as such.

The doctrine of *creatio ex nihilo* is not a claim about *how* the universe came into being, but *why*. It is the Christian response to the question that Martin Heidegger held was the beginning of all metaphysics: why is there being rather than nothing? If the question seeks a reason within being itself, it is doomed to remain unanswered. The doctrine of *creatio ex nihilo* insists on the fundamental poverty of the universe: the universe has no intrinsic ground for existence. When all else has been said, when the heavenly spheres fall silent, Augustine knew, the great truth that must be proclaimed is that we – all of us individually and together – did not make ourselves. And so Francis saw that it was neither an act of human self-denigration nor an effusion of poetic personification to address the sun and the moon, the fire and the earth, and all animate and inanimate creatures as his brothers and sisters; it was the simple truth.

The only reason for anything to exist is the free *agape* of God. The universe exists because God loves it and wills to give God's self to it. Utterly dependent, creation is divinely gifted. Thus, to see creation as a whole or any creature in particular as what it is, namely, totally dependent on the gracious will of God, is to see revealed the grace which is its foundation in being. Since everything that is exists because of the free act of God – the overflowing *agape* that is the source of all being – then everything is a sacrament of the goodness and creative power of God.

The themes of creation and poverty intersect in the Catholic vision of sacramentality. A sacrament is not a stand-in for something else, a visible sign for some other invisible reality. The essence of a sacrament is the capacity to reveal grace, the agapic self-gift of God, by being what it is. By being thoroughly itself, a sacrament bodies forth the absolute self-donative love of God that undergirds both it and the entirety of creation. The Catholic community has recognized seven particular events as being revelatory of grace. But every creature, human and nonhuman, animate and inanimate, can be a sacrament. The more richly developed our sacramental vision, the more sacraments crowd in upon us. Francis of Assisi's interweaving of poverty with the brotherhood and sisterhood of all creatures is profoundly Catholic because it is profoundly sacramental.

This sacramental vision is by no means limited to the Roman Catholic church. When Jonathan Edwards described the marks of true conversion in his great *Treatise on Religious Affections,* he gave as the first mark of such affections that they "do arise from those influences and operations on the heart which are *spiritual, supernatural,* and *divine.*" In explanation of this first mark of the converted, Edwards wrote that "in those gracious affections and exercises which are wrought in the minds of the saints, through the saving influences of the Spirit of God, there is a new inward perception or sensation of their minds, entirely different in its nature and kind, from anything that ever their minds were the subjects of before they were sanctified." The saints, to use Edwards's term, see reality differently from the unconverted. They do not see things that others do not see; rather, they see what everyone else sees but in a different way. They see everything in its relation to God: they see it as creature. Edwards's "new inward perception or sensation" is the ability to hear the song of all creation that Augustine and Monica heard, to see the community of all creatures as creatures that Francis saw. At the risk of "catholicizing" the great eighteenth-century Calvinist, one way of describing this "new inward perception" of the Edwardsean saint is the capacity for sacramental vision.

The cultivation of sacramental vision is the richest way of recovering the companionship motif of the Genesis stories that the Christian tradition has to offer in the current global ecological crisis. The discovery that every creature, including oneself, is a sacrament of the love of God that causes all things to be provides the deepest foundation for reverencing creation. The recognition of the other as a creature and, therefore, that which exists because it is loved by God cannot occur where the other is regarded as "it." By its nature a sacrament requires that it be appreciated for what it is and not as a tool to an end; in Buber's terms, a sacrament is always "thou." Since every creature can and should be a sacrament, so every creature can and should be "thou," a companion. But this sacramental vision demands unflinching recognition of the poverty of one's own being – for many too terrible to be true – and joyful acceptance of the absolute *agape* that supports one's own being – for many too good to be true. This requires the expansion of the imagination.

Paul Ricoeur has written that "we too often and too quickly think of a will that submits and not enough of an imagination that opens itself." Seeing the world sacramentally cannot simply be commanded. However necessary it may be for the survival of the planet in our time, sacramental vision cannot be made a moral imperative. It might better be understood as a Christian aesthetic that needs cultivation. The whole of Catholic praxis is training in sacramental vision. Liturgy and social action, marriage and parenthood, prayer and politics, music and dance and the visual arts, all educate us to appreciate the other as sacramental, worthy companions of our poverty and our engracedness. They teach us to see things as they are. In Gerard Manley Hopkins's words, "These things, these things were here, and but the beholder/Wanting." At present, "beholders" are desperately wanted.

Elements of a New Ethic

If the ecological crisis is to be addressed effectively, the ethic of individualism must be replaced with an ethic of companionship. Both creation myths in Genesis agree in their depiction of the human capacity for relationship as that which makes humanity "like God." The exaltation of the individual at the expense of the community, which in its crudest form becomes the "trickle-down" theory of social responsibility, stands in contradiction to this foundational insight of the Jewish and Christian traditions. Not surprisingly, this individualist ethic has debased the image of stewardship from participation in the creative activity of God into cost-benefit analysis. While it is important to attempt to reassert the stewardship motif in its pristine form, it is also necessary to strike at the heart of the problem, to confront impoverished and impoverishing individualism with the relational anthropology of the Jewish and Christian traditions. The crisis of the environment is directly linked to the problem of humanization. For unless nonhuman beings are treated as "thou," human beings will be treated as "it." This is why the appeal to self-interest cannot yield sufficient support in responding to the global environmental crisis. Such an appeal merely reinforces the basic problem. Far more adequate and far more faithful to the Christian tradition is the reappropriation of the companionship motif of the biblical creation stories.

The religious discussion of human responsibility toward creation must move beyond stewardship for the sake of both theology and the environment. Theologically, stewardship has been open to a deist interpretation whereby God is seen as having begun creation and then handed over care of it to humanity. When the image of stewardship dominates our imagination, God can be removed from the scene as human beings are given oversight of the earth and move to center stage in the drama of creation. Too easily the duty of caring for God's world becomes the task of shaping our world. Just as stewards are not anxious for the master's presence lurking over their shoulder, so humanity is content to keep God in a distant heaven.

Companionship evokes a different attitude toward creation. This difference in attitude will be reflected in an environmental ethic grounded on a relational anthropology. Such an ethic does not spring full-blown from the companionship theme. The movement from an over-arching frame of mind to an ethical method is more complex. What the companionship motif provides is an orientation that should guide us in devising an environmental ethic.

The first point of orientation that the companionship motif provides is the desirability of a transformed context within which to develop an environmental ethic. Governed by images of stewardship and ruled by precepts based on self-interest, our moral imaginations are unable to envision an environmental ethic that is adequate to the Jewish and Christian heritage. In contrast, images of companionship encourage the moral imagination to consider that more than the good of the individual self is at stake. Once the intrinsic good of creation is seen, then approaches to the environmental crisis that treat creation only as an instrumental good for humanity become inadequate.

Basic to any ethic is a determination of the moral standing of the "other" one encounters. The reduction of creation to "it" has promoted a loss of respect for nature and an attitude of instrumental rationality. Doing justice to the environment becomes difficult when the context of decision making is so one-sided. Rediscovering the "thou" dimension of all creation provides a corrective to the tendency to relate to nature only as "it" by moving beyond the technological vision of instrumental rationality to a reawakened sacramental vision of companionship. So fundamental a reorientation alters the context for assessing our responsibility toward the environment.

The context of mutuality created by an awareness of both the poverty and the sacramentality of all the created order should yield an ethic less prone to denigrate the intrinsic worth of nonhuman creation. The poverty of the entire created order forces us to acknowledge our ties with the rest of creation in its dependence upon the creator. At the same time the sacramentality of all creation prevents any debasement of our common creaturely state. Our poverty as creatures and our dignity as sacramental mediations of divine grace must be held in tension as twin aspects of our organic connection with all creation.

The second point of orientation for an environmental ethic is an expanded notion of the common good that includes nonhuman creation. The common good, in John XXIII's classic phrase in *Mater et magistra,* embraces "the sum total of those conditions of social living whereby people are enabled to achieve their own integral perfection more fully and easily." As a way of elaborating what those "conditions of social living" entail, John went on to list an extensive roster of human rights. Both Paul VI and John Paul II have continued to use the language of human rights when discussing the common good. Theologian David Hollenbach suggests that the use of human rights in recent Catholic social teaching is a way of specifying the essential *needs, basic freedoms,* and *relationships* with others that comprise the common good and serve human dignity. In this essay we have suggested a perspective that sees the created order as an "other" with whom we have a relationship and that this relationship is part of the common good. Protecting that relationship with *nonhuman creation* is properly one of the aims of *human* rights.

Various addresses of Pius XII are also important resources for social ethics. So, for example, while not denying the right to private property, Pius made it clear that property rights are not primary but secondary. Private property is always subordinate to the more fundamental right of all people to the goods of the earth. This reiteration of the priority to be given to the universal destiny of goods contains the germ of an important insight. Pius saw the relationship of humanity to the earth and the rest of its inhabitants as basic to the common good. There is no need to protect the environment by ascribing rights to nature or individual animal species. It is humanity's fundamental human right to share in the goods of the earth that is at stake in the ecological issue. Setting this human right in the context of companionship is necessary, however, to prevent the human right to the universal destiny of the goods of creation from being interpreted according to a narrow mind-set of instrumental rationality.

The third point of orientation for an environmental ethic concerns the means whereby an expanded notion of the common good can be safeguarded and promoted. Here too the tradition of Catholic social thought has something to offer. In *Pacem in terris* John XXIII drew attention to the existence of the "universal common good." The unity of the human family was the basis for John's espousal of a common good that transcended national boundaries. In the same encyclical John noted that the "whole reason for the existence of civil authorities is the realization of the common good." The difficulty was that existing political institutions "no longer correspond to the objective requirements of the universal common good." Subsequent popes have continued John's move from a national to an international to a transnational plane when analyzing social questions.

Issues that touch upon the universal common good – and the environment is one of these – go beyond the competence of individual nation-states. It is necessary to develop vehicles that protect the well-being of the global environment. An international agreement like the Law of the Sea Treaty serves as an illustration of the kind of structure that the papacy advocates for the sake of the universal common good. In contrast, the tendency to define narrowly the self-interest of a nation – as the Reagan administration did in opposing the Law of the Sea Treaty or as Japan has done in resisting fishing and whaling treaties – remains a major obstacle to building effective vehicles for the universal common good.

The language of the common good challenges political arrangements not only at the level of transnational issues. Ours is a nation that has prized individual liberty and has a strong attraction to free market economics. But we cannot avoid asking what social mechanisms on a national level must be devised so that the varied activities of citizens are directed to the common good, understood as including the good of creation. Romantic calls for simpler lifestyles or ideological reliance on purely voluntary measures are simply insufficient. Debate on the specific nature of these necessary mechanisms requires political leadership notably lacking at all levels of government.

No proposed environmental ethic can avoid confronting the pressing question of the relationship between ecology and ecoomic development. Are ecological concerns to be traded off for the creation of jobs in poor areas? Or vice-versa? Is industrialization to be discouraged in nations with undeveloped economies for the sake of preserving certain animal and plant species? The common good cannot be a mere abstraction which prescinds from specific social and historical conditions. Building a shared understanding on the matter of the common good and the place accorded to the environment among other goods is a crucial enterprise for true development.

In *Redemptor hominis* John Paul II opposes a false development that is "dilapidating at an accelerated pace material and energy resources, and compromising the geophysical environment. . . ." This critique of forms of development that ignore the earth's ecosystem echoes an earlier position articulated by many third-world hierarchies. At the 1971 Synod the bishops stated that "such is the demand for resources and energy by the richer nations, whether capitalist or socialist, and such are the effects of dumping by them in the atmosphere and the sea that irreparable damage would be done to the essential elements of life on earth, such as air and water, if their high rates of consumption and pollution, which are constantly on the increase, were extended to the whole of mankind."

Donal Dorr has suggested that the episcopal view helps explain the use of the strong language about exploitation that is found in many third-world pronouncements about the international economic system. For too long the presumption was that the task was to "raise" poorer nations to the level of production and consumption found in richer countries. The 1971 Synod pointed out, however, that such a view, whatever other failings it has, ignores the abuse of the environment that has accompanied development based on the first-world model. This development has come at the price of exploitation, directly the exploitation of the earth.

An indirect form of exploitation is the overuse of the universal goods of the earth for the benefit of a few, penalizing people in nations where economic development was slow in occurring. The earth cannot sustain everyone at the level of consumption found in the first-world. The first nations to undergo modern industrialization have used more than their fair share of the earth's resources. Nations seeking economic development now must compensate for the abuses of those who benefited from earlier exploitation of the earth. According to third-world leaders, the limits now proposed on development constitute an exploitation of poor nations. No consensus yet exists on how to reconcile ecological concerns and developmental needs, but some headway in resolving them is a *sine qua non* if the environmental movement is to make progress.

Getting It Right

An attitudinal shift is foundational for dealing with the environmental crisis, and theology has a leading role to play in this endeavor. The main contribution of the church in the ecological crisis should be to foster a correct attitude toward all of God's creation. The motif of companionship is an important initial stage for establishing the imperative of a new way of relating to the created order. Without that starting point, the problems of developing a politics and economics cognizant of the ecological common good will be multiplied.

There is the danger that the language of companionship could be understood as simply fostering romantic forms of opposition to technology. But a simplistic "back to nature" movement fomenting broad opposition to technology is a distortion of a proper theology of creation. Technology is an outgrowth of our own human nature as creative beings. Unless we do violence to ourselves, technology will continue. What is needed is the wisdom to direct the process of technological change, not to stop it. The primacy of ethics and politics over technology must be asserted. First, we must assess the human goods that technology must serve. Second, the political process is the arena in which many of the moral choices will be worked through and implemented. Effective political action must follow careful ethical reflection. To fail in either of these realms is to permit technology to slip beyond human direction. In order to guide change there must be a sense of the goods that are to be sought and an appreciation of the ranking of goods that may conflict. Only then can we know what goods technology must serve, what policy choices are to be made, at what price, and what institutional arrangements are required for implementation. From the outset, however, the scale of goods will be skewed unless humanity's relations with nature include an awareness of the "thou-ness" of creation.

Although, we believe, the retrieval of the companionship theme and a deepened commitment to the common good tradition are required criteria for the development of an environmental ethic, other criteria are also essential. The Jewish and Christian understanding of creation should not be wedded to any economic ideology. Neither capitalism nor socialism in their historical realizations differ in the way they view creation and humanity's relation to it. Both Adam Smith and Karl Marx had a strong bias toward instrumental rationality. At the same time, neither system should be dismissed as inevitably inhospitable to environmental concerns. Whether or not a sacramental vision of creation can take root in either approach remains to be seen. In both systems what must be addressed is the proper balance between the environment and economic development. Here the magisterium's theme of true development is a reminder that economic growth must be based on a model that is ecologically sustainable. In this regard the World Council of Churches' call for a criterion of sustainable efficiency strikes an important note for future decision making.

In addition, the criterion of social justice cannot be lost in the struggle for ecological responsibility. A simple disavowal of economic growth may perpetuate injustice to humans in the name of nonhumans. Ecology has to do with the relationship of organisms to the total environment, including other organisms of the same or different species. Ecological balance has unquestionably been lost in the way that human beings have treated nonhuman nature. Righting the imbalance, however, cannot entail injustice to fellow human beings for the sake of other species. Poorer nations will not be willing to forego economic development at the behest of wealthier nations, who have belatedly seen the results of their own assaults on nature in the quest for more and more expansion. To avoid a new imbalance, an environmental ethic must be informed by a careful analysis of the demands of economic justice.

Justice in economic development, economic growth premised on sustainable efficiency, and a heightened role for the environment in our understanding of the common good are three vital elements in any environmental ethic. But seeing the world rightly precedes our ability to act wisely and justly. The first task before us, that which theology can assist, is to revision all beings as united in their createdness, given to one another as companions, sacraments of "the love that moves the sun and other stars."

23

Healing Our Brokenness: The Spirit and Creation

Grace M. Jantzen

CHRISTIAN THEOLOGY HAS FOR CENTURIES BEEN IN A GRIP OF A SERIES OF interlocking and destructive dualisms. Because Christianity has strongly affected the shape of Western culture, these dualisms are pervasive in the thought structures throughout the parts of the world historically dominated by that culture, even when those thought structures are not seen as specifically religious. In this article I wish to show, first, the set of interconnected dualisms and something of the intellectual roots of these destructive fragmentations. I then wish to argue that these are not a series of innocent intellectual mistakes, but are founded in vested interests of power and control, rationalized and legitimized by misguided theology, and ultimately rooted in fear. Finally, I shall make some suggestions towards the healing of these divisions, based on a solidarity with the Spirit of God in her work of the renewal of all creation.

I. Fragmentation

The basic theological dualism is the split between God and the material universe. The doctrine of creation *ex nihilo* is usually centered on an understanding of God as pure spirit, utterly other than the material universe which is created by divine *fiat*. This world, thus created and set apart from God, is essentially matter (minds are introduced by a separate act of divine creation, as we will shortly consider), and the attributes of matter are the polar oppositions of the attributes of God. God is the omnipotent living one; matter is lifeless and powerless, utterly passive to the forces exerted upon it. God is all-knowing; matter is mindless, irrational. God is goodness itself, matter in itself is without value, mere stuff. Given these polarities, it is no wonder that one of the ways God has been named in Western theology is as the Wholly Other, the one who is in every respect different from material creation and shares nothing in common with it.[1]

The cosmic dualism that places God and the world at opposite ontological poles is often taken for granted as essential to the Christian doctrine of creation rooted in scripture. Actually, however, the situation is much more complex. The doctrine of creation *ex nihilo* is nowhere found in the Bible, and indeed is at odds with those Bible stories of creation which portray God's creation not as making the world out of nothing but rather we forming cosmos out of chaos by the presence of the divine Spirit. It was in the early Christian era that the doctrine of creation, much influenced by a rather hastily baptized Platonism, began to take for granted a cleavage between spirit and matter that was both an ontological distinction and a distinction in value as well. God as Spirit is good; matter, seen as the opposite of spirit. is not good.

The dualism between God and the world reflects and is reflected by a dualism of mind and body in the human person. Again, this mind-body division has deep roots in Platonic thought (though much of its modern foliage is due to the influence of Descartes) and was taken up into Christian theology by early thinkers as diverse as Origen and Augustine. Mind (or soul) is seen to be the real person; the body is its prison house from which it can hope to be released only by death to enjoy an incorporeal immortality no longer shackled by the demands and clamours of physicality. The real self (soul or mind) is akin to God, specially created by God and breathed into the material body; the body is a part of the physical universe, dust from dust, to which it will return. Thus for instance Augustine said:

> Not in the body but in the mind was man made in the image of God. In
> his own similitude let us seek God: in his own image recognize the
> Creator.[2]

Accordingly, the mind, made in the image of God, reflects the attributes of God. As God is life, so the mind is the life or animating force of the person; a human body without a mind ("where the soul has departed") is a corpse. As God is omniscient, so the mind is the organ of knowledge and wisdom, reflecting on finite scale the infinite wisdom of God. The body, by contrast, shares in the irrationality of the material world. As God is omnipotent, so, on finite scale, the mind is powerful, exerting its strength through the force of will on the body which, left to itself, shares the inertia of matter. The mind, being the real self made in the image of God, is of infinite and eternal value; the eventual crumbling of the body to dust is no loss.[3]

Yet that is not quite the whole story, even on a strongly dualist analysis. The body, irrational and powerless as it seems, nevertheless exerts a pull of its own, a resistant weight to the things of the spirit. Through bodily desires for food, drink, sleep and comfort, distractions and demands are placed on the soul. This is especially the case with the

sexual desires of the body, where physical desires are capable of completely dislodging the mind from its pursuit of wisdom. Thus the body,
and with it the whole material order, reveals itself not simply as an inert
innocent lump, but as having a kind of negative power of its own, especially strong and sinister in the case of sexuality. It is the life-long task
of every person to free ourselves – that is, our minds – from these clamours and pulls of our bodies, using, if necessary, sharp discipline and as-
cetical techniques.

Again, I would not wish to give the impression that this portrayal is
the only possible Christian understanding of personhood or indeed of
sexuality; far from it. I have argued elsewhere that central Christian doctrines of creation, incarnation and salvation require a very different conceptualizing of personhood and sexuality.[4] Nor do I think that the asceti-
cal practices of Christian monasticism, in particular in its emphasis on
chastity, were uniformly negative about sexuality: in at least some cases,
for example, the possibility of living together in celibate communities
was a radical counter-cultural alternative for women whose society perceived them largely as bearers of children.[5] The qualifications notwithstanding, however, a negative Christian theology of the physical, and its
outworking in body-despising attitudes and practices cannot be denied,
and are anchored in a mind-body dualism that parallels the cosmic dualism between God and the world.[6]

Now, the psychological dualism of mind and body was further projected as a dualism between male and female, giving a rationalization and
theological justification for the misogynism pervading Western culture.[7]
According to Augustine, only men (and then only their minds) were made
in the image of God; women were made in the image of man, from man's
rib, and to serve his needs.[8] The male is identified with the mind and
with God; the female with the body and the material universe. Just as the
mind is the rational and the body the irrational, so it is between the man
and the woman: male rationality is set over against female ignorance, an
ignorance exacerbated by the typically female characteristic of feeling.
Thus men are wise; women are prey to fluctuating emotions. These emotions are seen to be rooted in the woman's body, particularly in her menstrual cycle, and therefore in her sexuality. Though the woman is perceived as weak and vulnerable, and the man as strong and dominant, it is
nevertheless also the case that female sexuality is sinister and invidious,
always lurking to prey upon the unwary man, undermine his rationality
and unseat his control. Therefore the man must dominate the woman, who
must be subordinate to him and serve him as the body and sexuality must
be subdued in the service of the mind. The same principle of danger that
lurks in physicality generally is embodied in the sexual temptation that
women represent to men made in the image of an asexual (but yet normatively male) God.

It is easy to see that this male-female dualism identifies women strongly with the material, the earth. The male principle of rationality and mastery, by contrast, is identified with the technological dominance of nature. Just as men by their rationality master their bodies, feelings, and women, so technology is the rational mastery of nature by males.[9] The biblical writings offer a vocabulary of *subduing* the earth and *subordinating* women: the extent to which mastery of the earth is identified with violent sexual conquest of women is evident in the much-used modern phrase "the rape of nature." While those who use this phrase are pointing to the inappropriateness of such violence, it still indicates that the earth and the female are identified with each other, and presumably that males stand in a dominant relation to both, even if that dominance should be less overtly violating. The irony is staggering: all human beings are born of women, and all derive ultimately from "Mother Earth"; yet men have sought to reverse this dependency and bring women and the earth into subjection to themselves. Hence the mind-body dualism and the male-female dualism generate an ecological crisis of technological proportion as the technological dominance of nature proceeds; and in the background is the theological rationalization of a cosmic dualism between a God of ultimate value and a material universe of no intrinsic worth.

Male dominance, however, is not restricted to nature; and the same dualistic pattern that results in an alienating split can be seen in other situations of mastery. Just as there is a fracturing of technology and nature, so also there is an assumption of "godlike" power, rationality and right by Western males over people of other races who are (or can be rendered) powerless. Imperialism in every form, whether military, intellectual, or economic, finds a ready justification in a dualistic ideology which sees power vested in the rational, male-dominated society. This is also the dualist basis of racism, which splits white people from people of colour, and indeed of slavery and oppression of every form, which splits master from servant and rich from poor. In each case the assumed superiority of the former is used to despise and exploit the resultant weakness of the latter. It is no coincidence that it is Western society with a Christian theological heritage that has been much to the fore in aggressive and oppressive imperialism, regularly offering theological justification for its exploitation of non-white races and non-Christian cultures.

That is not to say that all oppressions rooted in dualisms are the same. It has been rightly remarked, for instance, that the universal oppression of women by men is in important respects different from the oppression of black people by white people, not least in the fact that white women are no less racist than white men and historically have enthusiastically participated in injustice towards black women and men.[10] The oppression of a white woman in a top administrative position in a London office, dressed in shoes and clothes which restrict freedom of movement, and expected to wear perfume, make-up and jewelry to be sexually attractive to her male colleagues (and yet at fault as a seductress if the attraction develops into an affair) is utterly different from the oppression of the Asian women working in sweatshops a few streets away.

Significant as these differences are, however, I suggest that the fundamental basis of both is a dualism which vests dominance and rationality ultimately in white Western men (whose ideology has been internalized by, *inter alia,* many white Western women) to dispose of as kindly or as harshly and in whatever forms they see fit. To the extent that this is true, it goes back to the identification of the male with the mental and with God, and therefore with rationality, value and power, as over against the "other," whether in terms of sex, race, class, or culture, who is (or can be made) weak, and is thus "given" to men for conquest and exploitation in whatever civilized or uncivilized form they choose.

Christianity has colluded with this oppressive structuring not only by providing its ideological underpinnings but also in some structural dualisms of its own. Branches of the church differ, but in many of them there is still a very strong dualism between clerical and lay people, with the former regarded as having the authority and the truth on their side, and the latter as being the weak and ignorant flock who must be told what to think and what to do. Significantly, the branches of the church with the most strongly institutionalized hierarchy are also the branches that find it hardest to allow women to be ministers, in many cases still refusing their ordination. Once we have noticed the way in which the fundamental dualisms on which Western culture rests perpetuate themselves in increasingly alienating structures, this stance by the male-dominated ecclesiastical hierarchies is unsurprising; and it becomes clear that what is needed is not simply such changes as would permit women to be ordained into the existing structures, but a fundamental change in the structures themselves and a whole revisioning of the church and all humankind along holistic rather than dualistic lines.[11] I will return to this in the third section.

II. Innocent oppression?

From the way in which I have thus far presented the series of interconnected dualisms one might suppose that they were rooted in simple intellectual mistakes, with unfortunate effects but without evil intent. On this view, it was in part because of the early church's preoccupation with Greek thought – a preoccupation wholly understandable and even laudable in the cultural context of the early Christian centuries – that theologians like Origen, Augustine and Jerome defined the doctrine of creation in overly Platonic categories, and developed their anthropological understanding along lines which drew too strong a contrast between the material and the spiritual. The other dualisms in the series, male/female, technology/nature, mastery/slavery, clerical/lay follow from these initial mistakes in a logical or at least understandable sequence. Hence any oppression which has resulted from these mistakes (and on this view the oppression is usually perceived as balanced by very considerable benefits which have accrued to women, non-whites, lay people, etc.) is unfortunate but should not be judged too harshly.

In my view, however, the situation is quite different. I do not at all deny that there is a certain deductive sequence in the parallel dualisms which I have outlined; indeed the logical parallels have been part of my point. Nor do I wish to underestimate the extent to which the mind-body dualism and its cosmic counterpart are rooted in Greek metaphysical categories. But I suggest that whereas the God-world split is logically prior to the other dualisms and provides the basis for their theological rationalization, it is naive to suppose that this doctrine of ontological dualisms is itself a result of neutral, objective scholarship detached from all vested interests and pursuing theological truth for its own sake. There has been plenty of recent work developing and using a "hermeneutic of suspicion": I suggest that it can be applied fruitfully to the Christian doctrine of creation *ex nihilo* and the sequence of parallel dualisms which anchor themselves in it. One need only ask who perpetrates this sort of thinking, and from what position, and what they would stand to lose by reconsidering it, to make us highly dubious of the claim that the dualisms are a result of neutral, objective thought incorporating some unfortunate but innocent intellectual errors.

This suspicion is strengthened by the fact that there is nothing at all new in my presentation of the dualisms: it has all been said before. Theologians of the stature of Paul Tillich and Karl Rahner have been pointing out the deficiencies in an anthropology based on Platonic-Cartesian dualism and showing that Christian theological categories rooted in a doctrine of incarnation require a more holistic approach.[12] Along with this has been a theological reconsideration of the relationship of God to the material universe, rejecting the idea of a God wholly removed from the physical world in favour of a view which gives more prominence to divine immanence.[13] Theologians have had available the work of secular thinkers like Lévi Strauss, who have shown the parallels between (male) Western society's view of nature and its understanding of women, other races, and the colonialized.[14] The two have been brought together powerfully in feminist analyses, notably those of Rosemary Radford Ruether.[15]

For more than a decade the analysis of parallel dualisms and their theological and human inadequacies have been widely available; yet in important respects they have made very little impact. Large branches of the church still refuse to ordain women, and even in those who do, the ordination is usually in terms of existing structures of power and control of the clergy over against the laity. Theologians and the ecclesiastical hierarchies have hardly been to the fore in championing the dismantling of the technology/nature dualism, often being at best a reluctant late-comer in addressing urgent ecological issues. Even worse is the Western church's recent record on calling into question the economic, military and cultural imperialism of the North Atlantic over exploited peoples. Christianity has been more likely to emphasize "enterprise" and "success" than to challenge militarism and consumerism, more willing to offer theological justifications of nuclear weapons than to support the women of Greenham Common or even to take them seriously. The moral preoccupations of the churches have been far more with keeping control of people's sexual practices (witness the endless and often repressive debates and policies about contraception, abortion, homosexuality and divorce) than in dismantling the dualisms that perpetuate racism, sexism and poverty. One of the most striking characteristics of Christianity of the North Atlantic in the recent past has been its increasing tendency to privatization and thereby its alignment with and perpetuation of the status quo.[16]

Why should this be so? How is it that well-intentioned and well-informed Christians, many of them in positions of intellectual or administrative power in the churches, have done so little and appeared so reluctant even to acknowledge let alone deconstruct the structures of fragmentation? It is not, as I said, out of ignorance: the analysis has long been available. Neither is it that the laity form a lump of inert resistance: many have joined, for instance, in campaigns for nuclear disarmament, the ordination of women, and environmental concerns. Yet all too often they are then regarded with suspicion and even hostility by the established churches and theological institutions, at best tolerated as fringe or marginal activities for Christians to engage in and at worst seen as having nothing to do with the real work of the church (whatever that is: saving souls, perhaps, and preserving the nuclear family). There are, thankfully, exceptions; but their presence only heightens the question of why it is that the churches are not at the forefront of an intellectual and practical campaign to dismantle unjust structures perpetrated by dualisms that have long been recognized to be theologically untenable.

It appears obvious that the dualisms which perpetuate the privatization of religion and the vested interests of the powerful do not derive merely from a series of intellectual errors which have not yet been rectified by properly qualified academics. Indeed, the extent to which the dualisms reflect and carry forward these vested interests should make us skeptical not only about them but about the very idea of neutral, objective intellectual endeavor patiently seeking truth without personal preference or passion. It is a truism too frequently ignored that all thinking is done by thinkers; and in the world as we know it thinkers are not disembodied, timeless, isolated minds, but embodied people with a history and a culture, who therefore can think only from the particularity of their own perspectives with all their in-built biases.

This is not to say that thought cannot be correct: from the fact that thinking is inevitably *affected* by the perspective of the thinker it by no means follows that it is wholly *determined* by that perspective and is therefore without validity. The phenomenon of vision provides a parallel: we see from where we are, and can do no other. From the fact that our vision is limited and affected by our perspective it does not follow that what we are seeing is not really there or even that it is utterly different from how we see it. But when we suppose that our vision is *not* particular, when we neglect the stance that generates our perspective and suppose that what we see is the whole, universal reality without need of appraisal that takes the character of our own stance into critical account, then we are liable to serious error.

Now, this is as true for theological thinking as for anything else: theologians think from particular personal and cultural perspectives, and our thought is inevitably affected by them. But Western Christian theologians have been singularly reluctant to recognize the particularity and partiality of our thinking, treating the products of our reflection as though they came from a stance of neutrality and universality, even though the idea of a "universal stance" is literally a contradiction in terms. We have been slow to accept the implications of the message of liberation theologians that "academic theology has tended to emerge from the dominant groups of society and be entrenched on the side of the status quo in various situations throughout the world."[17] Instead, the theologies of liberation which regard this as a fundamental premise of theological analysis – feminist, black, Latin American, etc. – are themselves regularly treated as fringe or marginal by the theological and ecclesiastical establishments of Western Christendom, with the presumption that those establishments are the normative "centre" in reference to which the "margins" can be defined.

When we take this seriously with reference to the series of dualisms outlined above, it becomes obvious to what extent theologians, emerging, as Boesak says, "from the dominant groups of society," have a vested interest in providing a theological rationalization for the dualisms rather than getting on with the real work of dismantling them and constructing in their place a theology of integration and justice. In fact, although the sequence of justification of the dualisms proceeds from the split between God and the world, the sequence of their construction is, I suspect, different.

As I have said, the doctrine of creation ex *nihilo,* usually seen as primary datum for a theological doctrine of God wholly other than the world, is not in the Bible, and was a theological construct using Greek philosophical ideas. It is at least arguable that, far from being a doctrinal given to which all else must conform and from which the sequence of dualisms followed, it was itself constructed as a theological justification for patriarchy. The dominant group of ruling class males constructed a world-view which set them apart as normative humanity, over against the "other" – women, other races, the poor, the earth – and then fashioned in their own image a God of ultimate value, power and rationality over against the disvalue, passivity and irrationality of the opposite side of the duality.

Of course I do not mean that this was done deliberately in the sense that theologians set about with conscious intent to construct a theological rationalization for patriarchy. But what I do mean is that as ruling-class males increasingly identified themselves over against the "other" over whom they took power, so the "other" of the various dualisms began to be a series of look-alikes because of the perspective from which they were defined. As Ruether puts it:

> A repressive view of the alien female was also the model for the inte-
> riorization of other subjugated groups, lower classes, and conquered
> races. Subjugated groups are perceived through similar strategies, not
> because they are alike, but because the same dominant group (ruling-
> class males) are doing the perceiving. All oppressed peoples tend then
> to be seen as lacking in rationality, volition, and capacity for autonomy.
> The characteristics of repressed bodiliness are attributed to them: pas-
> sivity, sensuality, irrationality and dependency.[18]

And in the same categories as the subjugated groups came, as we have seen, the body, feeling, and even the earth itself. When men of that perspective construct a theology using Greek conceptual structures, and perpetuate it through the patriarchal centuries of Western Christendom, it is hardly surprising that God will turn out to be the omnipotent, omniscient male of ultimate value, wholly other than the material universe of "his" fiat which is given to "man" to subdue. It is the classic instantiation of Boesak's comments on the provenance of academic theology and its entrenchment on the side of the status quo.

This in itself however does not make it false, even if it raises our suspicions. As I have said, the mere fact that our perspectives are particular does not mean that it is impossible for them to be correct. But as already pointed out, there has been for some time solid theological argument showing their inadequacies and suggesting alternatives, and yet these have been largely ignored as serious theological positions, let alone as part of popular Christian education.

This makes it necessary to look more closely at the vested interests of power and control which the sequence of dualisms serves to illustrate and legitimate. It is a striking fact that the recognition of a desire to control – even the recognition that that desire is inappropriate – does not of itself diminish the desire. For example, it is well known in Western Europe that our prosperity is built on the oppression of poorer countries, and that that is unjust; and yet the structures of that oppression are if anything stronger than they were a decade ago. Similarly, while many men recognize the injustice of patriarchy and might even be sympathetic to feminism, little is actually being done to change the male domination of society in which most scientific, technological, business and political decisions are made by men, usually set free to do so by a whole pyramid of supporting women, from a wife who looks after home and children, irons shirts and prepares meals, to the secretary, administrative assistant, telephonist, and cleaning lady in the office.

Why is this the case? Why is there such reluctance to get serious about structures that are recognized to be corrupt, and to dismantle them together with the faulty thinking that props them up? How is it that vested interests have such a binding power over people and societies? Is it sheer wickedness? There *is* wickedness in the structures, to be sure, but how does it get its purchase? At a conscious level, most people want to be fair and decent; yet the corruption persists, along with a great reluctance to take it seriously enough to do anything about it.

It is this great reluctance, I suggest, which gives us a clue to a deeper analysis. Whenever there is such great resistance to knowing something that in itself is obvious, or facing the practical implications of something that on one level cannot be denied, it is very likely that at least one ingredient of that resistance is fear. We refuse to know because we are afraid to know. At some deep level we feel fundamentally threatened. This need not be the only ingredient, of course; it can coexist with the sheer inconvenience that would accrue from renouncing the structures of injustice, and a whole ideology which supports them. Yet I suggest that fear is fundamental to the resistance, and indeed to the ideology itself.

This becomes clearer when we look at several of the dualisms in turn. Why should it be deemed essential that the body, especially sexuality, should be rigidly controlled? Surely it is because of fear of sexuality *out* of control. Why should white people – say, in South Africa – cling to a system of apartheid? Surely it is because of fear of what would happen if the black population were no longer in their control. Why is it necessary for dominant white males to keep a very tight rein on their feelings? Surely it is because the strength of those feelings is terrifying. And there is no shortage of misogynist literature showing that women are dominated because they are seen to present a threat to men; or that technology is pursued with such ferocity in order to bind the earth.

Now, if the need to control is rooted in fear and insecurity regarding the element to be controlled (sexuality, feelings, women, other races, the earth), this fear will not be eliminated by the simple recognition that the control is unjust. Indeed, the recognition of the injustice of patriarchy, or of minority oppression, is far more likely to produce guilt than to produce change, as long as the fear on which the injustice is based is not dealt with. Indeed, this guilt is all too likely to find relief in reinforcing the intellectual rationalizations and legitimations of the very dualisms on which the injustice is built. I suggest that the paralysis in theology, the churches, and Western society generally is in large part due to fear. Until this fear is healed, no amount of castigation is likely to have the least good effect.

But what is this fear about? Are feelings, sexuality, women, other races, the earth really threatening? Will they really do harm? The previous quotation from Ruether can be helpfully adapted here: all these subjugated groups are perceived as threatening, not because they are all alike, let alone because they are inherently sinister, but because they are being defined by the same group: dominant males. Characteristics of fearsomeness are attributed to them, not because they are fearsome, but because those who are defining them are afraid, and are projecting their own fear on to them.

But if the things themselves are not inherently fearsome, where does the fear originate? I have already used the term "projection": I suggest that the source of much of the fear, and hence of the whole sequence of dualisms, originates with an alienation of the bodily dimension of male selfhood that has not been welcomed. The self must then be defined as other than this split-off dimension; and this definition sets up a series of "others" whose definition as other and fearsome is a projection of the split-off aspect of the definer. Ultimately the sequence of dualisms together with their theological ratification are a result of this fear, self-alienation and projection. Until this is dealt with, no amount of intellectual theology, however brilliant, and no amount of prophetic denunciation, however merited, will begin to shift the structures of oppression. They cannot, because the oppressors are themselves oppressed, rigid with fear, paralyzed. And often too frightened even to recognize it.

III. "God has not given us a spirit of fear"

What can be done about it? Perhaps the least helpful thing to say to someone in the grip of fear – especially if that fear is at an intellectual level recognized to be irrational – is that they ought not to be afraid. The fear is real enough, and unwelcome, and cannot be banished by moralizing. And yet it is also the case that these fears are not a product of the Spirit of God. Indeed the Holy Spirit, as portrayed in scripture, is the spirit of encouragement and boldness and creative integration, not a spirit of alienation or repression. Perhaps the greatest need of the Christian

churches of the West is a new encounter with the Spirit of God, both intellectually and practically, not simply at a privatized personal level but
at a structural level, to deconstruct the edifices of oppression and their
theological props by dissolving the fear and threat upon which they are
based. Since our need to control is rooted in our fear and insecurity, it is
the healing love of the spirit of God to which we need to be exposed.

But this will not come about by magic, or by wishing it were the
case, or by privatized charismatic experience divorced from political
analysis and action. My immediate impulse as an academic theologian
who has pursued the argument this far is to urge the development of a
new theology of the Spirit, searching the scriptures and the tradition with
a special eye for the way in which the Spirit liberates from fear and
brings about integration and healing, not simply at a private "mental
health" level but in terms of all the alienating dualistic structures which
we have been considering. The understanding of the Spirit of God immanent in the created world dismantles the cosmic dualism that sets God
apart from the universe. The Spirit of God in the incarnation liberates us
from fear of the body and sexuality. The Spirit poured out upon all flesh,
women and men, slaves and free, deconstructs myths of superiority and
fearsomeness, and enables mutuality and inclusiveness.

All this is true; and I would in no way belittle the importance of an
intellectual engagement with the theology of the Spirit. Yet I doubt
whether this is the place to start. I have argued at length that the structures of oppression and the sequence of alienating dualisms on which
they rest are not a result of innocent intellectual mistakes but rather arise
out of vested interests of power and control, ultimately based on fear. But
if it is the case that our wrong thinking is a product of this fear and its
projections, then it is highly unlikely that we will get our thinking right
unless we begin from a *practical* confrontation with the fears, by way of
a radical renunciation of the control mechanisms it spawns, not as an intellectual exercise merely, no matter how worthy or theologically correct,
but in concrete commitment to the poor and weak and despised. When we
begin to give priority of attention and to hold ourselves accountable not
to the powerful but to the powerless, and when we begin deliberately to
make changes in our life-styles and ecclesiastical structures reflecting this
solidarity, the effect on our thinking and theologizing will inevitably be
more profound than any amount of insulated intellectual activity could
bring about.

If this is correct, then what we need much more than a new theology of the Spirit is a new practical commitment within the tradition of
Christian spirituality, learning how to proceed from the women and men
of the Christian tradition who show in their lives the challenging and integrating fruits of the Spirit, and who offer models of living by the Spirit
of liberating love in a diversity of concrete situations. As we take seri-

ously the need to reverse the patterns of alienation by practical solidarity with the split-off other, the way in which the giants of Christian spirituality model this praxis takes on an absorbing interest far removed from saccharine hagiography.

One example must suffice to clarify my meaning. The story is well known of Francis of Assisi ministering to the leper who then turns out to be Christ: it is often told as an illustration of Francis's holy generosity and its reward. But the real point of the story is very different. As told by Bonaventure following Francis's biographer Thomas of Celano, Francis was for a long time utterly revolted by lepers with a revulsion born of fear and fastidiousness. Whenever he encountered a leper he would hold his nose, send his servant to give alms, and ride away as rapidly as possible. This fear and revulsion was still very much a part of him when he felt himself constrained by the Spirit of God not simply to send token alms from a distance, but to get off his horse and kiss the leper, offering the solidarity of an embrace.

With that embrace Francis was given to himself. He acknowledged and received to himself the fear and revulsion he had projected on to the leper, and found that the leper, the alien other, was Christ to him, giving back to him the dimensions of himself from which he had alienated. Francis of Assisi did not first love the lepers and then begin to care for them; he began, in spite of his revulsion, to care for them, and thus was healed by their love. The story is at least as much about Francis's healing and reintegration as it is about any good done to the leper; the leper becomes a Christ figure because through him Francis is made whole in a way which is fundamental for his whole subsequent pattern of thought and life.[19]

Like Francis, much of our need to dominate is built on revulsion born of fear. Since this is at the root of our need to control, our greatest lack is not in the first instance intellectual. What we need is to expose ourselves to the healing love of the Spirit of God, which will be ministered to us, not abstractly, but precisely through those whom we have feared, and have rejected because of that fear. Far from this being a matter of detached "doing good" to them, the whole-making of all of us and the survival of the earth is at stake.

The sequence of dualisms shows the sequence of splits in consciousness particularly as defined by dominant males and largely internalized in Western Christian mentality, both male and female. As such it is also the sequence of fear. This fear can be relieved, and the fragmentation healed, not so much by word or theory but by embrace, deliberate practical solidarity with the "other" side. In our thinking and in our policies, individually and corporately, we need a real commitment in each case to the "underside" of the dualism, to begin the process of reintegration by what may seem at first like overcompensation, giving priority of attention and accountability to our bodiliness and sexuality, to our feelings, to the people of colour, women, the laity, other cultures and faiths, the earth itself. We need to learn together to get in touch with the vulnerable dimensions of ourselves that we have split off, not to eliminate them or control them, but to integrate them and allow them to be the basis for the sensitivity of the Spirit of God to each other and to our vulnerable world.

Endnotes

1. Cf. my *God's World, God's Body,* ch. 3, London, Darton, Longman & Todd, and Philadelphia, Westminster, 1984.

2. Augustine, *Commentary on the Gospel of John,* XXIII. 10.

3. Cf. Origen, *On First Principles,* 3.6.6.; *Against Celsus,* 3.41f.; 4.56f.; Thomas Aquinas, *Summa Theologiae,* Ia. 93.3.

4. In *God's World, God's Body, op. cit.,* ch. 1.

5. Cf. Peter Brown, "The Notion of Virginity in the Early Church," in Bernard McGinn & John Meyendorff eds., *Christian Spirituality 1: Origins to the Twelfth Century,* New York, Crossroad, 1987, pp. 427-443.

6. Cf. Rosemary Radford Ruether, *Sexism and Godtalk: Towards a Feminist Theology,* chs 3 and 6, London, SCM, 1983.

7. This is not to minimize the misogyny of other cultures, which have different rationalizations. Cf. Mary Daly, *Gyn/Ecology: the Metaethics of Radical Feminism,* chs 3-5, London, Women's Press, 1979.

8. Rosemary Radford Ruether, *New Woman/New Earth: Sexist Ideologies and Human Liberation,* New York, Seabury Press, 1975, p. 72: Eleanor Commo McLaughlin, "Equality of Souls, Inequality of Sexes: Women in Medieval Theology," in Rosemary Radford Ruether ed., *Religion and Sexism: Images of Women in the Jewish and Christian Traditions,* New York, Simon & Schuster, 1974.

9. Cf. Carol MacCormack, *Nature, Culture and Gender,* Cambridge University Press, 1980, p. 6: also her "The Experience of Wholeness: the Limits of Dualism," Essex Hall Lecture, 1988, London, Unitarian Publications, 1988.

10. Cf. Angela Davis, *Women, Race and Class,* London, Women's Press, 1982.

11. *New Woman/New Earth, op. cit.,* pp. 75-6.

12. Paul Tillich, *Systematic Theology,* Vol. I, University of Chicago Press, 1951, part II; Karl Rahner, *Foundations of Christian Faith,* London, Darton, Longman & Todd, 1978, part I.

13. John Macquarrie, *Principles of Christian Theology,* London, SCM Press, rev. ed. 1977, chs 5, 9 and 10; cf. my *God's World, God's Body.*

14. Claude Lévi-Strauss *Structural Anthropology,* Vol. 1, New York, Basic Books, 1963; Vol. II, London, Allen Lane, 1977.

15. E.g. in *New Woman/New Earth.*

16. Cf. Rosemary Radford Ruether, "Religion and Society: Sacred Canopy vs. Prophetic Critique," in Ellis and Maduro eds., *The Future of Liberation Theology: Essays in Honour of Gustavo Gutierrez,* Maryknoll, Orbis, 1989. Her analysis also applies to Thatcherite Britain and other right-wing European countries.

17. Allan Boesak, preface, in Charles Villa-Vicencio ed., *On Reading Karl Barth in South Africa,* Grand Rapids, Eerdmans, 1988, p. vii.

18. *New Woman/New Earth, op. cit.,* p. 4.

19. Bonaventure, *The Life of St. Francis,* I.5.6, in *Bonaventure,* Classics of Western Spirituality, New York, Paulist Press, and London, SPCK, 1978, pp. 188-190.

24

Six Characteristics of a Postpatriarchal Christianity

Jay McDaniel

Abstract. Christianity is best understood not as a set of timeless doctrines, but as a historical movement capable of change and growth. In this respect, Christianity is like a science. Heretofore, most instances of Christianity have exhibited certain ways of thinking that, taken as a whole, have led to the subordination of women (and the Earth and animals as well) to men in power. This article describes these ways of thinking, then contrasts six ways of thinking and acting that can inform post-patriarchal Christianity and science.

Keywords: value-hierarchical thinking; value-pluralistic thinking; unilateral power; relational power; dualistic thinking; nondualistic thinking; feminist theology; post-patriarchal theory; God.

FOR AT LEAST FOUR THOUSAND YEARS THE CREEDS, CODES, AND CULTS OF the world's major religions have been controlled by men. Men, not women, have been the primary social and imaginative engineers of Judaism, Christianity, Islam, Hinduism, Buddhism, Taoism, Confucianism, and Shintoism. Consider, for example, a list of prime movers upon whom introductions to the world religious so often focus: Abraham, Moses, Jesus, and Muhammad in the West; Gautama, Mahavira, Sankara, and Ramanuja in India; Confucius, Mencius, Lao-tzu, and Chuang-tzu in China; and Shinran, Honen, Dogen, and Nichiren in Japan. Of course, women have contributed to the development of the world religions, but they have not been equal partners. More often than not they have been helpmates, working in homes and behind the scenes to help men in positions of leadership, and all too often – as the histories of European witch burning, Indian widow burning, and Chinese foot binding attest – they have been, victims. Mary Daly does not exaggerate in saying that for at least four thousand years patriarchy has been, and still is, "the prevailing religion of the entire planet." As she puts it, "all of the so-called religions legitimating patriarchy are mere sects subsumed under its vast umbrella/canopy" (1978, 39).

For most feminist philosophers and theologians the word *patriarchy* has two meanings. It refers to a social system in which men rule women economically, politically, and culturally; and it also refers to a way of thinking and feeling, guided by a conceptual framework, that supports and legitimates this social system. This way of thinking and feeling can be internalized by women as well as by men, and it may or may not be a subject of conscious reflection. As philosopher Karen Warren explains, "whether we know it or not, each of us operates out of a socially constructed mind set or conceptual framework, i.e., a set of beliefs, values, attitudes, and assumptions which shape, reflect, and explain our view of ourselves and our world" (1987, 6). When I use the word *patriarchy* in this essay, I mean it primarily in the second sense.

The ideas and images within a patriarchal conceptual framework need not be about women in order to affect women. Instead, they may deal with the nature of the human self, or the good life, or the world as a whole, or God. When in the West, for example, Christians have imaged God as male, that very imagery, though apparently referring to the divine rather than the human, has nevertheless suggested to many men, and to women as well, that women are less godlike than men and, hence, that women are rightly subjugated to men. And when the good life has been imaged as one that is in complete control of nonhuman nature, that very image, though apparently referring only to nature, has led to the view that women, too, are to be controlled or tamed, because they have been symbolically identified with nature.

Furthermore, as writers such as Rosemary Ruether have shown, it is not exclusively women who have been detrimentally affected by patriarchy. At least in the West, images that have supported male rule over women have also supported the rule of rich over poor, race over race, culture over culture, and humanity over nature. The attitudes that have enabled sexism to persist also enable classism, racism, cultural chauvinism, and anthropocentrism to persist.

As the work of Warren suggests, this is because Western patriarchal thinking has been characterized by three features: value-hierarchical thinking, a logic of domination, and certain conceptual dualisms.

Value-hierarchical thinking consciously or subconsciously tends to categorize differences – for example, between men and women, or rich and poor, or light skin and dark skin, or humanity and nature – in terms of the spatial metaphor "up" versus "down," evaluating one group as *higher* than, and thus *superior to,* the other. Warren does not argue that evaluations of superior and inferior are inevitably illegitimate; indeed, she deems a nonsexist society superior to a sexist one. Rather, she proposes that Western patriarchal thinking has been prone to draw hierarchical distinctions *at the expense* of recognizing and appreciating valuable forms of diversity. Western patriarchal thinking has been prone to rank differences at the expense of appreciating them. Amid this tendency, women and others have been seen and treated as inferior. They have been viewed not simply as different from the men in power, but as inferior to them.

A logic of domination issues from value-hierarchical thinking, and that "explains, justifies, and maintains the subordination of an 'inferior' group by a 'superior' group on the grounds of the alleged inferiority or superiority of the respective group" (1987, 6). In the process, it justifies the right of one group to exercise unilateral power over the other. From the perspective of the one exercising unilateral power, the power may be for good or ill; but in either case it is power *over* rather than power *with*. In the West this is the power that God has been said to have in relation to the world: the power to influence without being influenced, to shape without being shaped. It is also the power, Warren claims, that many men in the West have thought they ought to exercise over women and nature, people of color, and the poor.

Conceptual dualisms are dichotomized items of reflection (human and nonhuman, mind and body, self and other, history and nature, reason and emotion) in which the items are conceived as essentially independent and mutually exclusive. To think in terms of dualisms is to think in terms of mutually external substances, or self-enclosed atoms, and of either/or rather than both/and. It is to believe, for example, that reason and feeling are essentially independent from one another and that one must be either rational or emotional, not both; or that the self and the world are mutually external and that one must love either the self or the world, not both. Often, Warren suggests, hierarchical thinking has been applied to conceptual dualisms, so that one side of the dualism is valued "up" and the other "down." Warren avers that women and others have often been associated with items on the "down" side – with feeling rather than reason, with body rather than mind, with nature rather than history. In the process they have been subjugated to the "higher" powers: to men, who have been associated with mind, reason, and history.

To criticize patriarchy is not to suggest that patriarchal social systems have been bereft of created goods. In the West alone, witness the music of Bach, Mozart, and Beethoven; the literature of Chaucer, Dante, and Shakespeare; the painting of Michelangelo, Rembrandt, and Picasso; the philosophy of Plato, Aristotle, and Marx; and the science of Newton, Darwin, and Einstein. These goods emerged out of, and with the support of, patriarchal social arrangements. Consider also the countless lives of unnamed men and women, from all walks of life, who have lived and died amid patriarchal social arrangements with satisfaction and who have found meaning in patriarchy. It would be simpleminded – and patriarchal – to draw a sharp line between patriarchy and post-patriarchy, and then to treat one as unambiguously good compared to the other, which is unambiguously evil. Patriarchy is not the root of all evil, and all evil will not be eliminated in an elimination of patriarchy. Every social system and way of thinking has involved, and will involve, both good and evil.

To criticize patriarchy, however, is to recognize that opportunities for cultural achievement in patriarchal social systems have not been equally shared and that social benefits have been won at great cost, in lives and well-being, to *many* women, to *many* poor, to *many* people of color, to *many* animals, and to *much* land. For the victims of patriarchal social arrangements, the benefits and achievements have not outweighed the costs. Feminists rightly hope for something better in the future. They call for the envisionment of alternative, post-patriarchal perspectives that can help guide us, women and men alike, beyond an age of male rule and its attendant oppressions toward an age of greater peace, justice, and ecological sustainability.

It is with the envisionment of such alternative perspectives, aligned with hope for alternative futures, that theology is most pertinent. For the task of theology – at least of Christian theology, influenced by prophetic biblical traditions – is not simply to interpret inherited symbols of thought; its task is to imagine new and hopeful ways of thinking and feeling in light of existing needs in the present. It is to exercise what biblical scholar Walter Brueggeman calls "the prophetic imagination," whose task is "to nurture, nourish, and evoke a consciousness and perception alternative to the consciousness and perception of the dominant culture around us" (1978, 13). Of course, in the latter decades of the twentieth century Christian theology has very little influence in secular colleges and universities around the world. When theologians speak, few academicians listen. But some forms of Christian theology have considerable influence outside secular colleges and universities. They influence faculties in seminaries, who in turn influence church leaders, who in turn influence religious communities. Religious communities are formidable influences in the world today, and Christians alone number almost a quarter of the world's population. Thus one of the least prestigious intellectual endeavors in the academy is one of the most influential in the world. For this reason, it is important that theology seek to become post-patriarchal. In Christianity, the possibility of a full-fledged post-patriarchal theology will for long remain an ideal rather than a reality, but it is an ideal worth striving toward, and it *is* being striven toward. Even today, some theological perspectives come closer than others to approximating it.

What ideas might constitute contemporary approximations of post-patriarchal vision? And what role do women have, on the one hand, and men, on the other, in shaping these ideas? The purpose of this essay is to answer these questions. In the first of its three sections I introduce Christian feminist theology for the general reader and discuss the roles of women and men in the development of post-patriarchal perspectives. Section I is written for those in the natural and social sciences, and the humanities as well, who are interested in gender bias in society but unaware of attempts to overcome it in religious thought. Sections II and III, for both specialist and nonspecialist, show how "process theology" creates post-patriarchal religious perspectives and, finally, the six characteristics of a post-patriarchal orientation.

I. The Roles of Women and Men
in Creating Post-Patriarchal Theologies

As suggested above, patriarchal thinking in the West has involved value-hierarchical thinking, a logic of dominance, and conceptual dualisms. Although these traits are not necessarily characteristic of patriarchal thinking throughout the world – a Buddhist culture, for example, might evince patriarchal thinking that emphasizes interconnectedness and relationality rather than atomized dualisms – patriarchal thinking, whatever its content, functions to legitimate and support male rule.

Androcentrism as a Universal Characteristic of Patriarchy

Despite the possibility of variation in patriarchal thinking, one aspect of it seems universal: its conceptual frameworks are almost always male centered, or androcentric, in two related ways. First, they repress and devalue women and women's experience as source of insight and vision for both women and men. Second, they absolutize male experience as representative of human experience in general. These two aspects of androcentrism constitute the gender bias that has often been characteristic of the world's major religions.

The devaluation of women and women's experience in Western religious thought has been well documented, from Paul's injunction that married women should remain silent in church, because they can get their spiritual food from their husbands (1 Cor 14:33-36), through Aquinas's view (following Aristotle) that women are misbegotten males, to Ignatius of Loyola's view that Satan conducts himself "like a woman," in that he is weak before a show of strength but a tyrant if he has his will. Moreover, such devaluation is also characteristic of Eastern religions and ethics: in Confucianism, for example, a woman's role is to serve her parents, husband, and husband's parents, along the way producing sons for her husband. And the Buddha had to be persuaded, against his inclinations, to allow creation of an order of nuns, on which he laid special regulations and subordinated to monks. For Gautama and Confucius as for Paul and Loyola, the experiences of women did not rank equally with those of men.

The second characteristic of androcentric thinking – the absolutization of male experience – has been part of the very method of much global theology and philosophy. In his description of his method of philosophizing, Thomas Hobbes, the Western philosopher, captures the nature of the androcentric method. He writes that "from the similitude of the thoughts and passions of one man to the thoughts and passions of another, whosoever looketh into himself, and considereth what he doth when he does think, opine, reason, hope, fear, etc. . . . he shall thereby read and know what are the thoughts and passions of all other men upon like occasions" (quoted in Zimmerman 1987, 21). It does not seem to have occurred to Hobbes that his experiences may have been shaped by his gender and may not represent those of women. The result of such one-sided universalization is that norms are established that, though imposed on and internalized by women, are not necessarily relevant to them – or even to other men.

In Western theology, which until recent times has been almost completely created by men, sin has often been identified with pride, and virtue with self-sacrificial love. The men who proclaimed this – Reinhold Niebuhr and Paul Tillich, to give two examples from the twentieth century – have usually believed that their claims are relevant to all humans under any circumstances. However, drawing from studies of women's experience, theologians such as Valerie Saiving, Sue Dunfee, and Judith Plaskow, have pointed out the limitations of such thinking. They show that self-sacrificial love may be relevant to men who have a positive self-regard and a strong ego, but it is much less relevant (and sometimes destructive) to women and powerless men who suffer from negative self-regard and need, if not an ego to be sacrificed, a self to be possessed. For them, one-sided emphasis on the virtues of self-sacrificial love leads to an underdevelopment or negation of self. In the Christian tradition, had women been cocreators of theology, such androcentric one-sidedness might have been avoided.

Feminist Theologies and Post-patriarchal Theologies

Why has androcentrism prevailed in so many of the world religions? The reasons are complex. From different ends of the political spectrum come such explanations as cultural conditioning, male conspiracy, female complicity, biological determination, or various combinations thereof. *Whatever* the reason, one thing is clear: slowly but surely, among creative minorities in the religious world, things are changing.

Feminist theologies often are *critical,* which means they attempt to unmask the gender biases of classical theologies. They are also *constructive,* which means they attempt new understandings of self, world, and the divine. These new understandings speak to the experiences of women in ways that patriarchal religious opinions have not. To speak *to* the experience of women is to illuminate where women have been under patriarchy and to show where they can be after patriarchy. In terms of world religions, such "speaking" is unique. Most male-designed theologies have spoken about and for women, but they have not.spoken *to* women in terms women have defined.

In many instances, to speak *to* the experience of women is really to speak *about* the experience of men. Many feminist theologies do this by attempting to understand how and why men have been responsible for, and influenced by, patriarchy. They describe male behavior, and in so doing they often imagine the intentions, attitudes, and dispositions of men. Although an understanding of male intentions is not the primary aim of feminist theology, it is important. If male rule is to be overcome, it must be understood, and if it is to be understood, men must be understood. To understand men is not simply to know how they behave; it is to know how they think and feel. Of course, generalizations are dangerous, because men (like women) are different within societies, and from one society to another, and from one individual to another. It is important to point out, however, that feminist theology is for the most part a white woman's movement and thus subject to racial limitations. But generalizations are inevitable and important; without them, there is no insight.

Sometimes, as in Ruether's thought, feminist theologies attempt to speak to the experience of men. Explicitly or implicitly, they indicate post-patriarchal ways of thinking, feeling, and acting by which men's lives might be informed. This, too, is an act of imagination, and a hopeful act, because men have also been victimized by patriarchal machismo. By conforming to patriarchal images of "masculinity," men have denied themselves a realization of their full humanity. They have been strong at the expense of being vulnerable, rational at the expense of being emotional, assertive at the expense of being receptive. This is not to say that women are by nature vulnerable, emotional, and receptive; rather, it is to say that whatever women are by nature (which is best left for women to decide), men also need such qualities.

Given the originality and promise of feminist theologies for men as well as women, it is understandable that men might want to join women in creating feminist theologies. Unfortunately, they – we – cannot. Despite the terminology, feminist theology does not mean only theology that speaks to women, and perhaps to men; it also means it speaks from the experience of women as women. Feminist theologies are created by women from women's experience as partially shaped by, and partially transcendent of, patriarchy. These theologies may speak truths that are relevant to men, but they speak these truths as they emerge from woman's experience. It would be as difficult, arrogant, and self-deceptive for a man to do feminist theology as for a North American to do Latin American liberation theology or for a white to do black theology.

What, then, can men do? It is important that they do something, for (barring an unforeseen shift in power relations throughout the world) it is doubtful that patriarchy can be transcended without male cooperation. In religion, men can (first and most important) internalize the insights of feminist theologies and attempt to rid their vision and practices of gender bias. This takes time, patience, study, openness to change, receptivity to criticism, and willingness to relinquish power. Second, men can attempt to construct perspectives that see beyond patriarchy. Although men cannot construct feminist theologies, they can attempt to construct post-patriarchal theologies.

A post-patriarchal theology is critical of gender bias and its ways of thinking, and attempts to construct ideas and images that point to ways of living – for women, men, and both – that supersede patriarchy. Post-patriarchal feminist theologies are created by women out of women's experience; some are intended to be relevant to women alone, others are intended to be relevant to men and women, and both types are indispensable for men who wish to construct post-patriarchal religious perspectives.

As yet, there is no name for the theology created by men in response to, and in solidarity with, feminist theologies. Nor is there an accepted name for male-envisioned post-patriarchal theology. There is, however, a resource for such theology, and it is called process theology.

II. Process Theology as Postpatriarchal Theology

Process theology itself has been in process. Most of its advocates have been men, but it is increasingly used by women for developing feminist theologies.

What do feminists find helpful about process theology? In general, as Penelope Washbourn explains, both process and feminist thought attempt "to revise the fundamental categories of the Western tradition" in similar directions (Washbourn 1981, 85). Both criticize a static, hierarchical social order and advocate an alternative "participatory" social order; both deplore the absolute power of God and propose alternative ways of envisioning the Divine; both criticize atomistic understandings of the self and propose, instead, that the human self is both relational and self-creative; both criticize dualisms between humanity and nature and insist, instead, that humanity is part of nature; both criticize anthropocentric ethics and emphasize, instead, the intrinsic value of all living beings, human and nonhuman.

This process theology is in a unique situation. It offers a conceptual bridge on which women and men can travel separately – and, if they wish, together, in conversation with one another – to attempt to move from patriarchy to post-patriarchy. Of course, the bridge is built as it is traversed. Planks already laid by men may have to be replaced and many (if not most) of the planks that have not yet been laid will be laid by women. Moreover, there is no guarantee that, even at a conceptual level, the other shore will be reached or that, if reached, it will make a difference. Whether process perspectives take hold in seminaries and religious communities remains to be seen. But the attempt is worth considering, because it shows what a post-patriarchal Christianity, guided by a post-patriarchal theology, might look like.

Christianity as a Changing Tradition

Women and men who are developing process post-patriarchal orientations acknowledge that a post-patriarchal Christianity, envisioned by process theologians or other feminist thinkers, is a *new* Christianity. Although it may be influenced by what Rosemary Ruether calls "usable traditions," both biblical and postbiblical, orthodox and unorthodox, and Christian and non-Christian, it synthesizes aspects of these traditions in unprecedented ways. It involves ways of thinking, feeling, speaking, and acting that cannot be traced to, and in some respects diverge from, the dominant traditions of the Christian pasts.

Thus the question arises: Is a new Christianity still Christianity? Process theologians believe it is. They argue that Christianity always has been, and ought to be, an ongoing process, capable of growth and development, rather than a settled and fixed fact that repeats its past. It is a historical movement, pluralistic and developmental from its beginnings, rather than a set of timeless abstractions. To participate in this contemporary movement is not necessarily to repeat the past; it may be to help inaugurate a new future.

This is not to suggest that Christians should forget the past. On the contrary, they should remember it, if only not to repeat it. Nor is it to suggest the past is never worthy of repetition; indeed, it can sometimes serve as a resource for, and judge of, the present. For example, whole generations of Christians in capitalist societies have fallen from (rather than advanced beyond) the socialism of early Christian communities. And in many ways patriarchal Christians have fallen from (rather than advanced beyond) the egalitarian Christianity of the original Jesus movement (Fiorenza 1983). To say that Christianity is capable of growth is not to say that it has always grown in a positive direction. Sometimes it has regressed, and subsequent generations sometimes have much to learn from prior generations.

To say that Christianity is capable of growth, however, is to say that, in the last analysis, Christians must evaluate themselves and determine what is and is not to be called Christian on the basis of future hopes rather than past achievements. Even when the past is appreciated as a resource, it must be appreciated because it is resourceful for the future, not because it is an unquestionable authority in its own right. To treat it as an unquestionable authority is to fall into an idolatry of tradition, thereby obstructing the possibility of new life.

Process thinkers contend that authentic Christian life is formed by an anticipated future rather than a settled past, a future that is partially realizable in the present and toward which humans are beckoned by God. This is a future for which Jesus seems to have yearned as he healed the sick and announced "good news" to the poor. It is a future of *shalom* – of love and justice among people, of harmony with nature and communion with God. This means that, in the interests of *shalom* for women as well as men and in faithfulness to a God who perpetually beckons toward *shalom*, Christians can repent (or turn around) from ways of thinking, feeling, and acting that their predecessors often embodied. They can repent from patriarchy, and thereby effect a transformation of the tradition in which they participate, enabling it to move beyond what it has been toward what it can be.

A post-patriarchal theology is not the only way, however, in which this transformation occurs. In addition to new ways of thinking, new forms of worship are required, as are new ways of speaking and new modes of social interaction. Religion, Christianity included, is much more than theology. Nevertheless, theology is important because it helps guide people toward new ways of thinking, feeling, and acting.

III. Six Characteristics of a Postpatriarchal Christianity

To understand post-patriarchal modes of thinking, feeling, and acting, we should consider six aspects of a post-patriarchal Christianity as seen in a process theology: (1) value-pluralistic thinking and care, (2) a logic of relational power, (3) a nondualistic approach to reason and feeling, (4) the self as creative, relational, and dynamic, (5) nature as evolutionary and ecological but not mechanistic, and (6) God as Heart.

The first three aspects pertain not so much to notions of the self, world, or God but to dispositions – that is, to the styles of thinking and modes of feeling that are encouraged in process post-patriarchal theologies. To understand these dispositions, recall Karen Warren's argument that, in the West, the patriarchal mind-set has been disposed toward value-hierarchical thinking, a logic of domination or unilateral power, and certain forms of conceptual dualism. She also believes that these habits of mind have led to an oppression of women and of powerless men, people of other races and religion, fellow animals, and the earth. Process theologians agree, and they point out that classical Christian ways of thinking, including some biblical ways of thinking, have been similarly disposed. They propose for our internalization three alternative dispositions, as follows.

Value-Pluralistic Thinking and the Importance of Care. The first of these three dispositions is value-pluralistic thinking, which can be best understood by comparing it to a traditional form of hierarchical thinking in Christianity, or the thinking that has given rise to Christian exclusivism. Until recently, Catholics have claimed that outside the Church there is no salvation, and Protestants have claimed that outside Christianity there is no salvation. To be a Christian has been to hold to a set of principles and practices labeled Christian at the expense of appreciating, and being transformed by, other peoples and other insights. Christianity has been valued "up" at the expense of "other Ways," which have been valued "down."

Process theologians propose, instead, that a post-patriarchal Christianity is a "Way that excludes no ways." It is disposed to recognize and appreciate a plurality of life-paths, life-styles, and life-orientations, which is to say that it is inclined toward value-pluralistic rather than value-hierarchical thinking. The phrase "Way that excludes no ways" is borrowed from John Cobb, who proposes that the Way of Christianity can (and ought) to be one in which different forms of value – discovered among non-Christian religions, in women, and in nonhuman forms of life – are appreciated and in which Christians are "creatively transformed" as they recognize and affirm these different values (Cobb 1975, 22). Indeed, Cobb identifies the living Christ with the transformation that emerges from an embrace of pluralism.

Of course, there are limits for Cobb as there are for all process theologians. Tolerance must be a principled tolerance; at some point, hierarchical thinking is necessary. Life-orientations that promote the well-being of women as well as men, for example, are higher and worthier of affirmation than those that promote men at the expense of women. But there can be *many* life-enhancing life-orientations – African as well as Asian, Latin American as well as North American, Oceanic as well as European, rural as well as urban, homosexual as well as heterosexual, female as well as male. None of these Ways need be absolutized; all have capacities for evil as well as good. Yet each can have beauty and integrity in its own right, and each can add to our lives and to the divine Life. A post-patriarchal Christianity is a Way that hierarchizes as a last, not a first, resort.

Out of this desire not to exclude others a deep concern for justice emerges. To be "open" to other people is not simply to acknowledge their right to exist, it is to be influenced by them. It is to listen to others, to hear them on their own terms, to feel their feelings, to share their destinies, and to revision one's perspective with theirs in mind. A post-patriarchal Christianity is particularly open to those who are excluded by the societies in which they live: the victims, the outcasts, the forgotten, the unwanted, the marginalized, the despised, the poor. The consequence of such openness is a hunger for justice. This hunger does not issue from abstract principles, understood to derive from an inscrutable God or a transcendent rationality, but from connectedness with those who suffer. It issues from care.[2]

Care of this sort has often been identified in the West with "the feminine." Feminists, of course, object to this stereotype because they recognize that it has given a one-sided and distorted notion of women's capacities and because it was created by men. In fact, "the feminine" in the West – like "the feminine" in many other cultures – has been male-defined; it has been the "patriarchal feminine." Post-patriarchal Christians need not dwell on whether care is feminine or masculine. Instead, they propose that it is (or can be) human: responsiveness to others that can be embodied by women and men.

Relational Power. A life of care is by no means powerless, given the notion of power that post-patriarchal Christians find most meaningful. According to Karen Warren, the power emphasized in Western patriarchy is unilateral power: the power of complete control over another. Feminists such as Audre Lord and Susan Griffin insist that this is the power men desire to exercise over women and nature. These women propose, as do process theologians, that another kind of power is more desirable and more in touch with reality.

In process theology this alternative form is called relational power – or, as Rita Nakashima Brock speaks of it, "erotic power" (1988, 25). Such power lies within the depths of our relations to ourselves, to our bodies, to others, and to the world. It is erotic because it is imbued with Eros, a yearning to be as richly related to others as possible and therein discover the fullness of life. A post-patriarchal Christianity will emphasize that women and men can find fulfillment in and through relational rather than unilateral power. Relational power has two inseparable aspects. First, it is a power to receive influences from the past, from other people, and from the surrounding world. Webster's dictionary gives a definition of power as "the capacity for being acted upon or undergoing an effect"; however, this understanding – power to receive influences – is neglected in English parlance because, for us, *power* ordinarily connotes control over others. Despite the distortion of the word by the image of control, we recognize a kind of strength in people whose minds are so open that they can receive and then integrate many intellectual influences, or whose hearts are so open that they can hear and understand different kinds of people without being narrow and intolerant. We recognize strength in those who can feel deeply, who can share in the sufferings and joys of others, who can affirm the uniqueness of each individual as an added dimension of richness in their own lives. This strength is the receptive side of relational power. It is the power to be open-minded and openhearted, and to be changed in the process. The antithesis of defensiveness, it is the strength to be creatively vulnerable.

In its second aspect, relational power is the power to determine one's destiny, to express oneself creatively, and thereby to influence others. Thus relational power bears a resemblance to unilateral power because it affects the world, yet it differs in a very important way. Unilateral power aims to control others in a way that subverts their creativity and thereby minimizes opportunities for reciprocal influence. By contrast, relational power aims to influence others in a way that appreciates and inspires their creativity and invites their influence.

In Alice Walker's novel *The Color Purple* (1984), Celie's dominating and abusive husband had unilateral power over her; relational power is the power that Shug, Celie's newfound lover, had with her. Those who have read the novel will recognize that Shug was by no means weak and nonassertive. She had a powerful effect on Celie, yet her power in relation to Celie neither sought nor obtained full control. Rather, it influenced Celie in a way that inspired Celie's creative response. It empowered Celie, and was empowered in turn by the unpredictability of Celie's response.

The role of surprise, of unpredictability, in relational power is important. Whereas in unilateral power the good to be achieved in control is predicted by the one seeking control, thus limiting outcomes, in relational power the good emerges from the relationship itself. For this reason a central feature of relational power in human interactions is risk: the risk that if one is not in complete control of the other, richer experiences can emerge for oneself and the other (paradoxically) than if one is in full control. Fear is the primary obstacle to such risk.

Post-patriarchal Christians need not hope for a world in which unilateral control is eliminated; some unilateral power is inevitable in human relations and in relations between humanity and the rest of nature. Rather, they can hope for a world in which relational power is maximized and unilateral power minimized. They can hope for a world in which "true power" – that is, the most desirable form of power – includes vulnerability as well as creativity, dependence as well as self-expression, and being affected as well as affecting. Such power (as will be suggested) is concordant with divine power.

Nondualistic Thinking and the Importance of Feeling. In addition to value-pluralistic thinking and relational power, post-patriarchal Christians will emphasize nondualistic thinking. This does not mean, however, that they will oppose all distinctions; one can think nondualistically and yet make important distinctions between things – say between the psyche and the body, or between humanity and nature, or between God and the world. To emphasize nondualistic thinking is to oppose the assumption that the "things" to be distinguished are atomistic and, hence, exist in independence from one another, or that one of them exists in absolute independence from the other. Dualistic thinking is atomistic thinking.

The alternative is nondualistic, or relational, thinking. To think in this way is to recognize that, logically and indeed ontologically, every actuality – whether material or psychological, secular or sacred, human or nonhuman, terrestrial or celestial – exists in relation to, and hence in partial dependence on, countless other actualities. This recognition is profoundly Buddhist; it is also, from the vantage point of some scientists, profoundly scientific. It is no accident that in developing their theological orientations process theologians have been shaped by, and indebted to, insights from Asia, from modern biology, and from modern physics. As do most Buddhists and many scientists, process thinkers submit that there are no independent substances, no self-enclosed atoms, no isolated "things." Although human beings and other animals are partially self-determining, their self-determination lies not in transcending influences but in integrating influences. Even freedom is freedom-in-relation. To think nondualistically is to recognize the radically relational character of all existents and thus to move beyond the many dualisms that characterize so much of patriarchal Christianity.

The emphasis of process theology on nondualistic thinking has implications even for the way in which thinking is conceived, if by *thinking* we mean reason and if by *reason* we mean discursive reason. Among the many dualisms that process theologians propose to overcome in a post-patriarchal Christianity is that between reason and feeling. In the West, reason has often been conceived as a solely cognitive activity, independent of, rather than dependent upon, feeling. It has been presumed that (a) rational thought is a nonaffective activity, devoid of passion, intuition, or emotion, and (b) feeling and emotion have no cognitive content. These presuppositions have affected the ways in which men and women are approached, because masculinity has often been identified with autonomous, rational thought and femininity with nonautonomous, vulnerable feeling.

Process theologians propose alternatives to all of these assumptions. They suggest that reason is infused with forms of feeling: whenever one reasons, one *feels* the presence of ideas and *enjoys* their clarity, or is *perplexed* by their ambiguity, or *appreciates* their aesthetic richness, or *judges* them to be false, or *intuits* their truth value. Enjoyment, perplexity, appreciation, judgment, and intuition are forms of feeling that are responsive to images and ideas. In their way, they are no less affective than feelings that are responsive to sense perception. Rational affections differ from other forms in that the data to which they are responsive are internal rather than external, mental rather than physical.

Furthermore, process theologians suggest that nondiscursive feelings – that is, feelings that are not emotional responses to abstract ideas – can have cognitive value in their own right. Consider, for example, the many feelings that accompany our perceptions of the natural world: feelings of beauty and wonder, mystery and awe, fear and delight. In an intuitive way, we learn something about nature through such feelings, even though they are not immediately responsive to intellectualized abstractions or controlled by rational processes. Consider also the feelings that absorb us in dreams, when we are open to preconscious and prereflective dimensions of experience. Here, too, we learn something about nature: the nature of our subconscious minds. A process epistemology includes more than reason among its avenues for knowing. As David Griffin explains, "human experience is not limited to sensory and conscious experience, and human knowing includes not only intellectual operations but also affective, aesthetic, symbolic, imaginal, and bodily operations, which are equally important" (Griffin 1987a, 123 – 36).

Griffin's description of human cognition is meant to be free from gender bias. As with all process thinkers, he believes that, for men and for women, knowing is – or can be – affective, aesthetic, symbolic, imaginal, and bodily as well as rational. A post-patriarchal Christianity emphasizes the cultivation of each and all of these forms of knowledge.

The Self as Creative, Relational, and Dynamic. Of course, human beings are more than knowers, they are *experiencers* – and there is more to being an experiencer than knowing. There is doing, willing, hoping, trusting, fearing, dreaming, yearning, breathing, loving, remembering, forgetting, laughing, crying, and dying. Whether or not these experiences have cognitive value, they are the very content of a life as lived from the inside. They have aesthetic value (when enjoyed) even if they lack cognitive value. The question arises: What is it – or better, who is it – that suffers or enjoys these experiences? What or who is the human self? A post-patriarchal Christianity must arrive at some way of viewing the human self that is relevant to the experiences and possibilities of women and men, and here the work of one process thinker, Catherine Keller, is particularly helpful. In *From a Broken Web: Separation, Sexism, and Self* (1986) Keller points out that in patriarchal Christianity, as in much of the West, the self has often been construed in nonrelational, atomistic terms – as a soul cut off from the world by the boundaries of the skin or, in post-Christian settings, as a "mind" that resides in the body, separated from an "objective" world. This way of conceiving the self – as an atomized, autonomous, disembodied, unrelational substance of one sort or another – has had destructive consequences for both women and men.

For men, it has been destructive in that it has supported the ideal of complete autonomy, which has inhibited the realization of intimacy and equality. An atomistic understanding of selfhood has undergirded the idea than a man achieves authentic identity only if he is clearly distinguishable from others and from the surrounding world. The concept of the isolated ego has "codified the notion that only separation – under the banner of 'independence' and 'autonomy' – prepares the way" for authentic existence (Keller 1986, dustjacket). Drawing from the work of Nancy Chodorow, Keller speculates that in Western societies the male's impulse for separation may stem from an early age, when boys have had to separate themselves from their mothers (Chodorow 1978). The conception of self as isolated ego may itself be a projection of the male experience of the separated self, and this can change only after the social structures have changed.

For women, the conception of self as isolated ego has also had destructive consequences, in two ways. First, as embodied by men, it has led to the view of women as "other." Of course there are important senses in which women *are* "other" in relation to men. Men must learn that each woman – and perhaps women in general – has unique values *as* a woman, values "other" than those readily realized (or realizable) by men. But the "otherness" of such values is not the otherness of an object upon whom unilateral power is exercised, the otherness of an object to be controlled. When men have been influenced by the ideal of the autonomous self, they have approached women as objects to be controlled by that self.

The second way in which the conception of self as isolated ego has had destructive consequences for women pertains not so much to adoption of this conceptuality by men but to its adoption (or counteradoption) by women. If the only option for conceiving of self is the isolated ego, a woman is in a double bind. On the one hand, she can be a patriarchal self, in which case she, like men, seeks to become separate from the world: an autonomous ego cut off from the world by the boundaries of her skin. On the other hand, she can think of herself in opposite and complementary terms: as an utterly relational self whose sole value lies in being of service to, and dependent on, others and whose primary ideal is self-sacrifice or selflessness. In the latter instance, which is common under patriarchal circumstances, she becomes the counterpart to the male ego: the one possessed by the possessor. Keller speaks of this counterpart as the "soluble" self, that is, the self that has been dissolved into relational bondage.

Keller recognizes that in response to the dilemmas of a soluble self, women often seem to opt for an autonomous ego. "Often we hear women say that first, or finally, they must get separate individuality and develop their own autonomy: an especially pressing motive among women coming up to breathe after long immersion in marriages, families, and disappointing love affairs" (Keller 1986, 3). From the point of view of an observer, and perhaps from the point of view of a woman, "separate individuality" can be a traditionally masculine ego pattern. But Keller does not believe that this is the aim of most women who seek autonomy. She does not believe that most women, in seeking "an empowering center in themselves and often furious at the sums of selfhood drained away in futile asymmetries, are actually repudiating connectedness." Rather, they "desire worlds – places of inner and outer freedom in which new forms of connection can take place. "Their hope is that in these worlds they can "range through an unlimited array of relations – not just to other persons, but to ideas and feeling, to the earth, the body, and the untold contents of the pressing moment." In other words, "women struggling against the constraints of conventionally feminine modes of relation desire not less but more (and different) relation: not disconnection, but connection that counts" (Keller, 1986, 3).

The image of self as autonomous ego does not allow for this "connection that counts." Given the inadequacy of the image for women and for men, Keller says that "something new is needed" (Keller 1986, 4). Using process categories of thought, she offers an alternative way of conceiving the self that eliminates the double bind for women and provides a more hopeful option for men. It is to think of the self as an ongoing, multifaceted, and ever-changing process of experiencing, each moment of which is a creative synthesis of many worlds. To understand this, let us examine figures 1 and 2.

Figure 1 illustrates the "autonomous ego" view of the self, represented by a box that has an identity (internal space) apart from its relations to its body and the environment. Those who think this way recognize that the self is conditioned by the body, by the extrabodily environment (including other people, artifacts, plants and animals, land, and the atmosphere), and by experiences. The solid lines from "environmental influences," "bodily influences," and "past experiences" represent these influences. However, at least with respect to extrabodily environment and also, perhaps, the body, advocates of the autonomous ego understand this conditioning on the analogy of two self-enclosed billiard balls colliding with a third called the self. The self they envision is not internally related to environment or the body, so that its connections with the body and environment are essential to its identity; rather, it is externally related to the body and environment, which is to say that it could "be what it is" even if those relations were different. The fact that "influence lines" from society and body are broken rather than solid indicates that these relations are external to the identity of the self rather than internal. In principle, the self and all its experiences could be transplanted into a new body and environment, and be the same self.

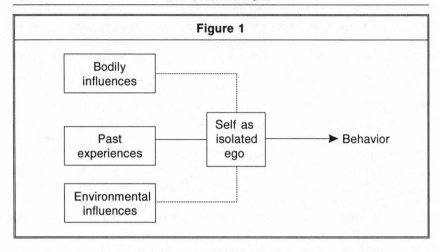

Figure 1

Bodily influences

Past experiences

Environmental influences

Self as isolated ego

→ Behavior

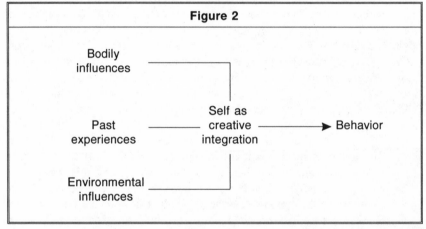

Figure 2

Bodily influences

Past experiences

Environmental influences

Self as creative integration

→ Behavior

Figure 2 illustrates Keller's alternative to this way of thinking, so that the self is not self-enclosed. The lines from the body, the environment, and experiences are solid, representing the fact that the self's relations to these realities are internal to its own identity and existence. Moreover, these relations are not simply causal connections discerned by an objective observer from a third-person perspective; they are feelings enjoyed or suffered from a first-person perspective. From Keller's point of view, the self "feels" or "takes into account" body environment, and experiences both consciously and subconsciously, and thereby is "connected" with them. Not just the feelings, but the items felt, enter the self's constitution, becoming part of its identity. The environment and the body are just as much part of the self as the self's own experiences. From this perspective it would make no sense to speak of the self as transplanted into a new body and remaining unchanged in the process. In either a new body or a new world, the self is a new and different self.

To emphasize the relationality of Keller's perspective, however, is only half the story. For her as for all process thinkers, the self is not simply a synthesis of connections to body, environment, and experiences; it is a *creative* synthesis of these relations. If an omniscient observer knew all factors from the body, environment, and past that influence the self, that observer could not predict with certainty how the synthesis would occur or what the behavioral outcome would be. In the depths of the self is an act of decision, of cutting off certain possibilities for integrating "the many into one" and thereby actualizing other possibilities. This decision, too, is part of the self. The self's creativity lies not in being independent of connections with others but in creatively determining the quality and style of that dependence. Freedom is how many influences become one self, and to be free is to be creatively dependent.

Both because the self is free yet profoundly dependent on changing circumstances, the self is fluid and dynamic. It is not a settled and static thing or entity that owns or possesses feelings and decisions; rather, it is an ongoing process of feeling and deciding from one second to the next, one minute to the next, one hour to the next, one day to the next. As soon as a moment of creative synthesis occurs, it becomes a past experience, to be integrated by successive instances of creative synthesis. Thus a person's sense of continuity is largely a function of memory. In fact, the self can be thought of as a verb rather than a noun – a pilgrimage rather than a destination, a journey rather than a stopping place. From this perspective, one can never step into the same river twice, not because the river changes but because the self changes.

The fact that the self changes – that its very existence and identity can be different from one moment to the next – means that people can grow beyond their pasts, can become new persons. This is quite important for women and men who seek existences and identities different from those into which they have been conditioned by patriarchy. Such women and men can never be fully or absolutely disconnected from their pasts, but they can creatively integrate past influences in ways that transcend their destructive power.

Keller believes that the process model of the self is true to the nature of human existence, including women's experience. She agrees with Sheila Davaney, who writes that "the process perspective reflects and affirms the feminist understanding of women as subjects" (Davaney 1980, 4). Both agree that human subjects are creative and relational, and that the image of the self as an isolated ego is ontologically misguided.

Yet from Keller's perspective, as from that of Davaney, ontology is by no means the most important issue. A creative-relational view of the self commends itself, not simply because it approximates truth of the way things are but because it offers a promising ideal of the way things can be. The ideal is to live a life consistent with the very nature of the self: to be, and allow others to be, creatively relational. Of course, not any relations will do; they must be "connections that count" (Keller 1986, 3). Such connections involve relational rather than unilateral power, and they involve mutual care. Keller's hope – and that of a post-patriarchal Christianity – is that women and men alike can enjoy "connections that count" without discrimination on the basis of gender.

More than that, the hope is that women and men can enjoy such connections in and through healthy affirmations of their gender. Part of what must be integrated into the life of a creative and relational self is gender itself. For most of us, gender identity is partly the result of body chemistry, partly the result of social conditioning, and partly the result of decisions we have made in the past and are making in the present. How much our gender is the result of body chemistry and social conditioning is a matter of serious and important debate. However, regardless of the outcome of this debate, freedom plays a role. At least in part, we choose what it means "to be a man" or "to be a woman." As Mary Daly's appropriation of words like *hag* and *bitch* attests, inherited meanings of *woman* can be changed by women themselves, in which case the meaning of "being a woman" changes. In the lives of an individual and a society, gender identities can evolve. Keller and other process theologians propose "new ways of being male [and] new ways of being female" that, in the immediacy of the present, we can begin to create.

Nature as Evolutionary and Ecological, but Not Mechanistic. The human self as described in the previous section is inseparable from nature. To say that it is partly free is not to suggest that the self is supernatural; it is a nonmechanistic way of conceiving nature: it sees human freedom as a sophisticated evolutionary expression of (rather than a sophistical exception to) what is happening in other animals, in living cells, and in submicroscopic matter. In a process post-patriarchal theology, as in most forms of feminist theology, other biological organisms also are creative, relational, and dynamic. The natural world is evolutionary and ecological but not mechanistic.

The affirmation that nature is not mechanistic has important implications for a post-patriarchal religious orientation. The metaphor of the mechanistic worldview is that nature is *like a machine,* that it is like a vast assemblage of lifeless, atomized particles in motion that can and should be used exclusively for human beings. In *The Death Of Nature: Women, Ecology and the Scientific Revolution,* a historian of science, Carolyn Merchant, explains how this metaphor functioned in the scientific revolutions of the sixteenth and seventeenth centuries to sanction an exploitation of nature, unfettered commercial expansion, and a new socioeconomic order that subordinated women. Merchant reminds us that under the dominance of this metaphor nature was approached (in the words of Francis Bacon) as something to be "bound into service" and made a "slave." She also reminds us that much of the imagery Bacon used in stating the objectives and methods of the new science derived from witch trials of his day. Under the scrutiny of science, Bacon implied, Mother Nature is to be hounded much as witches are hounded. Both are to be subdued, interrogated, and conquered (Merchant 1985,169).

Despite revolutions in science, the metaphor of nature as machine prevails in much science today. As Merchant puts it, "The mechanistic approach to nature is as fundamental to the twentieth-century revolution in physics as it was to classical Newtonian science" (Merchant 1985, 291). This means that contemporary science, despite its many accomplishments, often advances a way of thinking that has a destructive effect on human and nonhuman life. Illustrative of this destruction is the fact that 100 to 200 million animals die each year in laboratories around the world, often under conditions of severe stress and pain, with little protest from the global scientific community (Ryder 1985, 79). The animals are dispatched, in part, because they are viewed as machines that can be "bound into service" for human ends. Thus science plays no small role in encouraging a mechanistic understanding of life.

Like every process theologian, Merchant believes there is a viable and socially necessary alternative to the machine metaphor, that the human future – and that of the earth and all its creatures – may depend on our learning to see and think of nature as a *living organism* rather than a *machine* (Merchant 1985, 289). She points to the philosophy of Whitehead as an important example of what it might mean in a contemporary context to understand nature organically rather than mechanistically, and it is by this Whiteheadian alternative that process post-patriarchal theologies are shaped.

Although advocating an organic rather than a mechanistic understanding of nature, process theologies are by no means antiscientific. Indeed, they are deeply influenced by (among other things) evolutionary thinking. From astrophysicists and cosmologists, process theologians have learned to affirm, and to integrate into a religious orientation, the idea that the universe is the result of a 10 to 15 billion-year process of cosmic evolution that continues, and from evolutionary biologists they have learned to affirm, and again integrate into their religious orientation, the idea that life is also the result of an evolutionary process that continues into the present. Moreover they recognize, with several speculative physicists, that there may well be other forms of life on other planets surrounding other stars, and they insist, as do most biologists, that even in terms of life on earth there is no reason to assume that human life is the exclusive aim or goal of the biological process. A process post-patriarchal

Christianity recognizes that humans are by no means the sole locus of value, or the sole end, of cosmic and terrestrial evolutionary developments. All living beings, not just human beings, have intrinsic value.

In addition to evolutionary theories, process theology is influenced by quantum mechanics and relativity theories in physics, by ecology and cognitive ethology in biology, and by thermodynamics in physical chemistry. Indeed, most process theologians submit that a dialogue between religion and science, in which religious perspectives are partially shaped by insights from science, is essential to the future of religion. Post-patriarchal Christianity must be scientifically informed.

Yet the dialogue with science is, and must be, both ways. Even as post-patriarchal Christians learn from science, they must be critical of the mechanistic worldview by which much science is motivated. The argument of process thinkers such as John Cobb and the biologist Charles Birch is that science can proceed in terms of, and indeed be advanced by, an alternative "organic" worldview such as that proposed by Whitehead. Science would thereby contribute more richly to the liberation of life that is sorely needed in our time.

For life to be liberated, process theologians believe, the very concept of life must be liberated from the mechanistic interpretation (Birch and Cobb 1981; Griffin 1987a). In a process context, *mechanistic* refers to one or a combination of five perspectives: (1) deterministic, in which happenings are understood to be caused by powers from the past; (2) utilitarian, in which value is understood to be instrumental rather than intrinsic; (3) devitalized, in which the depths of physical matter are understood to be lifeless and inert rather than lifelike and creative; (4) reductionistic, in which living wholes are understood to be reducible to nonliving parts; and (5) dualistic, in which a sharp line is drawn between spirit and matter, supernatural and natural, mind and body, thought and feeling, and self and world. To say that nature is like a machine is to think in terms of one or several of these points of view.

The organic worldview advocated by process thinkers stresses alternative ideas, some of which include insights from mechanisms that run counter to mechanistic perspectives. Process thinkers emphasize (1) that present happenings are the result not only of causative powers from the past but come about from creative impulses in the present that are guided by final causes from the future. This means that nonhuman organisms, such as human beings, are partially creative and, hence, partially unpredictable in the ways they respond to and integrate environmental and bodily influences. In addition, process thinkers propose (2) that nonhuman organisms (from living cells to porpoises) are of intrinsic value in and for themselves, even as they are of instrumental importance to others, (3) that physical matter is more alive than dead in its ultimate depths, (4) that living wholes, such as the human self or an animal psyche, are very much influenced by (and yet more than) the parts of which they are composed, and (5) that reality, although in many respects pluralistic and manifold in its domains and dimensions, is better characterized as interdependent and interfusing than as dualistic and dichotomized. In the latter respect, a process understanding of nature is very similar to a Buddhist orientation. For process thinkers as for Buddhists, nature is a seamless web of interdependent realities which includes ourselves.

It is important to note that some scientists – David Bohm in physics, for example, Ilya Prigogine in physical chemistry, and Donald Griffin in biology – have adopted aspects of an organic orientation. This suggests that the concept of nature in science may be changing in ways intimated by process thinkers. It is precisely this kind of creative transformation in science that should parallel creative transformation in religion. A post-patriarchal Christianity can best be complemented by a post-patriarchal – that is, a post mechanistic – science.

God as Heart. Women and men seeking liberation from male rule are no less part of living nature and evolution than other living beings, whether human or nonhuman. They, like other creatures, are drawn by goals or purposes for living with some satisfaction relative to the situation at hand; in post-patriarchal Christians, the situation at hand is of course patriarchy. The goal is to live with greater satisfaction than has been available under patriarchy. Christians and others rightly name this satisfaction *shalom* – that dynamic and relational peace that is the fullness of life in relation to other people, nonhuman nature, and the divine spirit.

The five characteristics of post-patriarchal Christianity (mentioned above) are strategies for achieving an approximation of *shalom*. They are also the characteristics that might sustain *shalom* once it is approximated. Our assumption is that *shalom* can be approached and sustained if Christians and others (1) begin to embody value-pluralistic thinking and its care; (2) begin to cherish and embody relational more than unilateral power; (3) cultivate nondualistic thinking and realize its inseparability from feeling; (4) see the self as creative and relational rather than as isolated ego; and (5) appreciate, with the help of a postmechanistic science, the natural world as organic and evolutionary.

The hope for *shalom is* not a hope for eternal life. Indeed, a characteristic of most feminist theologies is that they advocate acceptance of finitude, and perhaps this is as it should be, for even if *shalom is* approximate, human lives in particular and human life in general will not extend into the indefinite future. In all likelihood the human species, like all species, will eventually become extinct, either before or when the energy of the sun is exhausted. The quest for post-patriarchal existence is not for existence beyond finitude, but for quality of existence amid finitude.

What motivates this quest? Many, of course, are motivated by the necessity of finding an alternative to situations under patriarchy to escape suffering. But process theologians suggest something else: people are also motivated by the possibility of *shalom* within their subjective experience. It is as if within all people is a beckoning light, a small voice that calls them beyond the person they have been (and perhaps beyond the person society tells them they ought to be) toward the person they can be if they are true to themselves. The metaphorical *light* and *voice* refer to an attractant within each person, lure toward self-actualization (including gender affirmation) in community with other people, with nonhuman nature, and with the divine spirit. This lure is also present in nonhuman life; it is that power by which nonhuman organisms live from moment to moment with some satisfaction relative to *their* situations. From a process perspective, this lure is God, or at least one aspect of God.

Feminists who are influenced by process theology disagree on whether the word God can be used in a post-patriarchal Christian setting. For some – Rita Nakashima Brock and Catherine Keller, for example – the word is too tainted with images of an exclusively masculine deity, or a cosmic moralist, or an all-powerful autocrat to be useful. For others – Marjorie Suchocki and Nancy Howell, for example – the word is still helpful and at present, indispensable for naming the sacred reality (Suchocki 1982; Howell 1988). But all agree that the sacred reality is not exclusively male, nor is it a cosmic moralist or an all-powerful autocrat. They also agree that whether or not the word God is used, new and different words are needed to name the sacred reality, words such as lover and friend, light and life, mother and daughter, water and fire, earth and eros. Christians and others are at a stage in which experimentation in naming and describing God is required and in which, for some, the word God must be abandoned.

Amid this experimentation, a word that may be helpful (and upon which we shall focus) is Heart. In a post-patriarchal context, the divine mystery can be named, and felt, as Heart. In post-patriarchal process theologies, the word Heart has been used most systematically and creatively by Rita Nakashima Brock (1988), who uses it to refer not to the Divine but to relational power as enjoyed and exercised by humans. She speaks of patriarchy as being brokenhearted and of post-patriarchy as a yearning for and internalization of relational power, or heart. Because in process theology the divine mystery is the most inclusive example of relation power, Heart – with an uppercase *H* – can name this mystery.

The word Heart is meant to complement and enrich other words traditionally used in process theology to name the divine mystery, words such as mind, consciousness, subject, and self. In process theology, God is described as a cosmic, omnipresent Subject who feels and responds to worldly events as they occur and whose subjectivity is an ever-changing yet ever-constant creative integration of worldly events. In this sense, God is a Self who includes and is affected by all selves. Just as a human self creatively integrates bodily influences so that what happens in the body happens in the self, the divine Self creatively integrates everything that happens in the universe so that what happens in the universe happens in the divine Self. God is the mind of the universe, it has been said, and the universe is the body of God.

The mind-body analogy has distinct advantages over patriarchal ways of thinking about God. The latter have often focused on metaphors such as parent-child (particularly father-child) or artisan-artifact (creator-created) that stress a mutual externality between God and the world. In *Models of God: Theology for an Ecological, Nuclear Age* (1987), Sallie McFague shows how destructive these metaphors can be, because they can wrongly suggest that all power lies with a creator God and that what happens in the world need not affect this God unless "he" chooses to be affected. As McFague makes clear, for a post-patriarchal and postmechanistic religious orientation the mind-body analogy can rightly suggest that God and the world are related through mutual dependence and creativity.

Still, as Brock points out, the mind-body analogy may have disadvantages if "mind" suggests reason divorced from feeling or thought divorced from care. In this case the word mind is too cold, too masculine, too oriented toward Logos at the expense of Eros, too patriarchal. Naming God *Heart* can complement, if not replace, the language of God as mind. According to the Oxford English Dictionary, *heart* "means mind in the widest sense, including the functions of feeling and volition as well as intellect" (1970, 159). The intentions of process thought can be better realized if we speak of God as the Heart of the universe, and universe as the body of this Heart.

The word *heart* has additional meanings and associations that tell us something about the Divine as understood in a process context. One meaning is "center of vital functions" or "seat of life" or "life itself." For example, when we say that "our hearts were gladdened" by good news or "our heart was in our hands," we mean our innermost being by "heart," the center of our lives, our life itself. In a process context, the divine lure is the seat of life, in the sense of being that within each human (and non-human) by which the will to live with satisfaction and wholeness is elicited. It is no accident that at the interface of theology and biology John Cobb and Charles Birch speak of the divine mystery as the Life (with an uppercase *L*) by which all other lives (with a lowercase *l*) are enlivened (1981, 183-202). To speak of the divine mystery as Heart is to highlight its connection with life.

A second meaning of heart is "center" or "core" or "middle." We speak of "getting to the heart of the matter," and by this we mean getting to the center of an issue, the middle of it. As a metaphor for God, Heart in this sense suggests that the divine mystery is at the core or center of the universe, and of life itself, rather than above or outside. This need not imply that the divine mystery is not in some ways transcendent. Indeed, from a process perspective the mystery *is* transcendent. It is a relational Self – with consciousness, purposes, creativity, and care – that includes all selves. Yet this Self is within us, in the center of our lives, rather than outside or external to us. We experience divine transcendence not so much as external authority over us but as an inexhaustible font of possibilities within us: a wellspring of potentialities by which, if we are creatively responsive, our lives (and those of others) are fulfilled. Sin misses the mark of responding to these possibilities, missing the mark of responding to God within us. God within us is the Heart of our hearts.

A third way the word heart is used is to refer to feelings of sympathy, understanding, compassion, and care. We speak of caring people as "full of heart," and by this we mean that they have deep love and affection for others. For process thinkers the divine mystery is heartfelt in this sense, and in two ways. The cosmic Heart is active in the world as a lure, which is one way its love is expressed; it is also receptive of the world as an all-empathetic consciousness, which is the other way its love is realized. It is bipolar, both yin and yang. In its bipolarity, Heart is the ultimate expression of relational power. It is potentially the most influential power in the universe, although its influence depends on worldly response; and it is the most vulnerable power in the universe. In the latter respect, Heart feels the feelings of living beings, suffering their sufferings, enjoying their joys, sharing in their destinies in ways much deeper than we can imagine. Moreover, it does all this in a pluralistic way. Its empathy is responsive to each life on the latter's terms: to the amoeba on its terms, to the herring gull on its terms, and to a human on her or his terms. The divine mystery is "all heart," not only because it is imbued with empathy but because it is also receptive of diversity. It is the Heart that includes all hearts.

Inasmuch as it is responsive to living beings on their own terms and humans are among the beings to which it is responsive, the divine Heart is personal as well as transpersonal. It can be referred to as He or She, as well as It. (I have used *it* to avoid gender bias, but the language of He or She can be used as well.) In different contexts and for different people, either or both words may be meaningful. For some, the image of a tender, caring father – the *Abba* addressed by Jesus – can be helpful (fathers, too, can have hearts.) For many post-patriarchal Christians, however, She may be more appropriate than He, given the history of patriarchal God-language in the West. In fact, the divine Heart bears much greater resemblance to the creative and relational self envisioned by feminists such as Catherine Keller than to the autonomous ego exemplified in most characters portrayed by Sylvester Stallone. God is much more like Shug Avery in *The Color Purple* than She is like Rambo. She is strong, but her strength is tender and it lies in being creatively relational rather than absolutely independent. For those who have been oppressed by patriarchal imagery or who have used such imagery to oppress others, the divine spirit is best conceived not as a father "who art in heaven" but, as Sallie McFague suggests, as a mother, lover, or friend.

For process thinkers, the life well lived is open to the divine Heart. Openness of this sort is faith, and an art rather than a science. It involves trust in a Presence who cannot be manipulated or exhausted by conceptual formulas or religious doctrines. The fruits of openness include value-pluralistic thinking, care for others, hunger for justice, relational power, a union of thought and feeling, discovery of one's self as creatively integrative, appreciation of nature as organic and evolutionary, and reverence for life. It is the hope of process theologians that the religions of the world, Christianity included, can evolve into traditions that nourish and encourage these fruits. Of course they also hope that all religions, each in its own way, can become post-patriarchal. Post-patriarchal theologies within Christianity are a sign that such a transformation can occur.

In this paper I have explained the nature and function of post-patriarchal theology and I have illustrated one version of it: a process post-patriarchal perspective. In fact, in Christianity and elsewhere many versions of post-patriarchal theologies are needed – some created by women, some by men, and some created jointly. If such changes in religious self-understanding are to influence society, they must be complemented and enriched by new ways of thinking in other sectors of society, including scientific communities. In our time the lure of the divine Heart is toward new, imaginative visions that elicit compassion as well as understanding. "Where there is no vision," the Bible tells us, "the people perish." The question of our age is whether such vision will emerge in time to stem the tides of ecological destruction, social injustice, and war. It is good for us, and for God, that the future is open to new vision.

Notes

1. For an example of a philosophical ethic centered in care, see Nel Noddings *Caring: A Feminine Approach to Ethics and Moral Education* (Berkeley: Univ. of California Press, 1984).

References

Birch, Charles, and John B. Cobb, Jr. 1981. *The Liberation of Life. From Cell to Community.* Cambridge: Cambridge Univ. Press.

Brock, Rita Nakashima. 1988. *Journeys by Heart: A Christology of Erotic Power.* New York: Crossroad.

Brueggeman, Walter. 1978. *The Prophetic Imagination.* Philadelphia: Fortress Press.

Chodorow, Nancy. 1978. *The Reproduction of Mothering: Psychological Theory and Women's Development.* Berkeley: Univ. of California Press.

Cobb, John B., Jr. 1975. *Christ in a Pluralistic Age.* Philadelphia: Westminster Press.

Daly, Mary. 1975. *The Church and the Second Sex. (With a New Feminist Postchristian Introduction by the Author.)* San Francisco: Harper and Row.

_____. 1978. *Gyn/Ecology: The Metaethics of Radical Feminism.* Boston: Beacon Press.

Davaney, Sheila Greeve, ed. 1980. "Introduction." *In Feminism and Process Thought: The Harvard Divinity School/Claremont Center for Process Studies Symposium Papers.* Lewiston, NY: Edwin Mellen Press.

Dunfee, Sue. 1982. "The Sin of Hiding: A Feminist Critique of Reinhold Niebuhr's Account of the Sin of Pride." *Soundings* (Fall), 316-27.

Fiorenza, Elisabeth Schüssler. 1983. *In Memory of Her: A Feminist Reconstruction of Christian Origins.* New York: Crossroad.

Griffin, David R., ed. 1987a. *Physics and the Ultimate Significance of Time: Bohm, Prigogine, and Process Philosophy.* New York: State Univ. of New York Press.

_____. 1987b. "Report on the Conference "Toward a Post-Modern World." *Center for Process Studies Newsletter* 11(1): 5-12.

Howell, Nancy. 1988. "The Promise of a Process Feminist Theory of Relations." *Process Studies* 17(2): 78-87.

Keller, Catherine. 1986. *From a Broken Web: Separation, Sexism and Self.* Boston: Beacon Press.

McFague, Sallie. 1987. *Models of God: Theology for an Ecological Nuclear Age.* Philadephia: Fortress Press.

Merchant, Carolyn. 1985. *The Death of Nature: Women, Ecology and the Scientific Revolution.* San Francisco: Harper and Row.

The Oxford English Dictionary. 1970. Vol. 5. Oxford: Clarendon Press.

Plaskow, Judith. 1980. *Sex, Sin and Grace: Women's Experience and the Theologies of Reinhold Niebuhr and Paul Tillich.* Washington, D.C.: University Press of America .

Ryder, Richard D. 1985. "Speciesism in the Laboratory." *In Defense of Animals,* ed. Peter Singer. San Francisco: Harper and Row. cf. R.D. Ryder 1975, *Victims of Science.* London: Davis Poynter.

Saiving, Valerie. 1979. "The Human Situation: A Feminine View." In *Womanspirit Rising: A Feminist Reader in Religion,* ed. Carol Christ and Judith Plaskow. San Francisco: Harper and Row.

Suchocki, Marjorie Hewitt. 1982. *God Christ-Church: A Practical Guide to Process Theology.* New York: Crossroad.

Walker, Alice. 1982. *The Color Purple.* New York: Washington Square Press.

Warren, Karen. 1987. "Feminism and Ecology: Making Connections." *Environmental Ethics* 9:3-20.

Washbourn, Penelope. 1981. "The Dynamics of Female Experience: Process Models and Human Values." In *Feminism and Process Thought: The Harvard Divinity School/Claremont Center for Process Studies Symposium Papers,* ed. Sheila Greeve Davaney. Lewiston, NY: Edwin Mellen Press.

Zimmerman, Michael E. 1987. "Feminism, Deep Ecology, and Environmental Ethics," *Environmental Ethics* 9:21-24.

25

An Earthly Theological Agenda

Sallie McFague

I TEACH A SURVEY COURSE IN CONTEMPORARY THEOLOGY THAT COVERS THE 20th century. When I took a similar course as a divinity student at Yale in the late '50s, it had considerable unity. We studied the great German theologians whose names began with "B" (seemingly a prerequisite for theological luminosity) – Barth, Bultmann, Brunner, Bonhoeffer – and, of course, Tillich. They were all concerned with the same issues, notably reason and revelation, faith and history, issues of methodology and, especially, epistemology: how can we *know* God?

More recent theology has no such unity. The first major shift came in the late '60s, with the arrival of the various liberation theologies, which are still growing and changing as more and different voices from the underside of history insist on being heard. While what separates these various theologies is great (much greater than what separated German theology and its American counterparts), one issue, at least, unites them: they ask not how we can know God but how we can change the world. We are now at the threshold of a second major shift in theological reflection during this century, a shift in which the main issue will be not only how we can change the world but how we can save it from deterioration and its species from extinction.

The extraordinary events of the past year or so, with the simultaneous lessening of cold-war tensions and worldwide awakening to the consequences of human destruction of the flora and fauna and the ecosystem that supports them, signal a major change in focus. Perhaps it is more accurate to say that the focus of the liberation theologies widened to include, in addition to all oppressed human beings, all oppressed creatures as well as planet earth.

Liberation theologies insist rightly that all theologies are written from particular contexts. The one context which has been neglected and is now emerging is the broadest as well as the most basic: the context of the planet, a context which we all share and without which we cannot survive. It seems to me that this latest shift in 20th-century theology is not to a different issue from that of liberation theologies, but to a deepening of it, a recognition that the fate of the oppressed and the fate of the earth are inextricably interrelated, for we all live on one planet – a planet vulnerable to our destructive behavior.

The link between justice and ecological issues becomes especially evident in light of the dualistic, hierarchical mode of Western thought in which a superior and an inferior are correlated: male-female, white people-people of color, heterosexual-homosexual, able-bodied-physically challenged, culture-nature, mind-body, human-nonhuman. These correlated terms – most often normatively ranked – reveal clearly that domination and destruction of the natural world is inexorably linked with the domination and oppression of the poor, people of color, and all others that fall on the "inferior" side of the correlation. Nowhere is this more apparent than in the ancient and deep identification of women with nature, an identification so profound that it touches the very marrow of our being: our birth from the bodies of our mothers and our nourishment from the body of the earth. The power of nature – and of women – to give and withhold life epitomizes the inescapable connection between the two and thus the necessary relationship of justice and ecological issues. As many have noted, the status of women and of nature have been historically commensurate: as goes one, so goes the other.

A similar correlation can be seen between other forms of human oppression and a disregard for the natural world. Unless ecological health is maintained, for instance, the poor and others with limited access to scarce goods (due to race, class, gender or physical capability) cannot be fed. Grain must be grown for all to have bread. The characteristic Western mind-set has accorded intrinsic value, and hence duties of justice, principally to the upper half of the dualism and has considered it appropriate for those on the lower half to be used for the benefit of those on the upper. Western multinational corporations, for example, regard it as "reasonable" and "normal" to use Third World people and natural resources for their own financial benefit, at whatever cost to the indigenous peoples and the health of their lands.

The connections among the various forms of oppression are increasingly becoming clear to many, as evidenced by the World Council of Churches' inclusion of "the integrity of creation" in its rallying cry of "peace and justice." In the closing years of the 20th century we are being called to do something unprecedented: to think holistically, to think about "everything that is," because everything on this planet is interrelated and interdependent and hence the fate of each is tied to the fate of the whole.

This state of affairs brought about a major "conversion" in my own theological journey. I began as a Barthian in the '50s, finding Barth's heady divine transcendence and "otherness" – to be as invigorating as cold mountain air to my conventional religious upbringing. Like many of my generation, I found in Barth what appeared to be a refreshing and needed alternative to liberalism. But after years of work on the poetic, metaphorical nature of religious language (and hence its relative, constructive and necessarily changing character), and in view of feminism's critique of the hierarchical, dualistic nature of the language of the Jewish and Christian traditions, my bonds to biblicism and the Barthian God loosened. Those years were the "deconstructive" phase of my development as a theologian.

My constructive phase began upon reading Gordon Kaufman's 1983 Presidential Address to the American Academy of Religion. Kaufman called for a paradigm shift, given the exigencies of our time – the possibility of nuclear war. He called theologians to deconstruct and reconstruct the basic symbols of the Jewish and Christian traditions – God, Christ and Torah – so as to be on the side of life rather than against it, as was the central symbol of God with its traditional patriarchal, hierarchical, militaristic imagery. I answered this call, and my subsequent work has been concerned with contributing to that task.

While the nuclear threat has lessened somewhat, the threat of ecological deterioration has increased: they are related as "quick kill" to "slow death." In other words, we have been given some time. We need to use it well, for we may not have much of it. The agenda this shift sets for theologians is multifaceted, given the many different tasks that need to be done. This paradigm shift, if accepted, suggests a new mode of theological production, one characterized by advocacy, collegiality and the appreciation of differences.

Until the rise of liberation theologies, theology was more concerned with having intellectual respectability in the academy than with forging an alliance with the oppressed or particular political or social attitudes and practices. There was a convenient division between theology (concerned with the knowledge of God) and ethics (a lesser enterprise for action-oriented types). Theologians were also usually "solo" players, each concerned to write his (the "hers" were in short supply) magnum opus, a complete systematic theology. As the deconstructionists have underscored, these theologians also strove to assert, against different voices, the *one* voice (their own – or at least the voice of their own kind) as the truth, the "universal" truth.

Our situation calls for a different way of conducting ourselves as theologians. Like all people we need, in both our personal and professional lives, to work for the well-being of our planet and all its creatures. We need to work in a collegial fashion, realizing that we contribute only a tiny fragment. Feminists have often suggested a "quilt" metaphor as an appropriate methodology: each of us can contribute only a small "square" to the whole. Such a view of scholarship may appear alien to an academy that rewards works "totalizing" others in the field and insisting on one view.

The times are too perilous and it is too late in the day for such games. We need to work together, each in his or her own small way, to create a planetary situation that is more viable and less vulnerable. A collegial theology explicitly supports difference. One of the principal insights of both feminism and postmodern science is that while everything is interrelated and interdependent, everything (maple leaves, stars, deer, dirt – and not just human beings) is different from everything else. Individuality and interrelatedness are features of the universe; hence, no one voice or single species is the only one that counts.

While I realize that the focus for this series is on how one's mind has changed, the way mine has changed demands that I focus not on mapping my individual journey but on specifying how our minds ought to change, both now and in the future. If advocacy, collegiality and difference characterized theological reflection and if the agenda of theology widened to include the context of our planet, some significant changes would occur. I will suggest three.

First, it would mean a more or less common agenda for theological reflection, though one with an almost infinite number of different tasks. The encompassing agenda would be to deconstruct and reconstruct the central symbols of the Jewish and Christian traditions in favor of life and its fulfillment, keeping the liberation of the oppressed, including the earth and all its creatures, in central focus. That is so broad, so inclusive an agenda that it allows for myriad ways to construe it and carry it out. It does, however, turn the eyes of theologians away from heaven and toward the earth; or, more accurately, it causes us to connect the starry heavens with the earth, as the "common" creation story claims, telling us that everything in the universe, including stars, dirt, robins, black holes, sunsets, plants and human beings, is the product of an enormous explosion billions of years ago. In whatever ways we might reconstruct the symbols of God, human being and earth, this can no longer be done in a dualistic fashion, for the heavens and the earth are *one* phenomenon, albeit an incredibly ancient, rich and varied one.

If theology is going to reflect holistically, that is, in terms of the picture of current reality, then it must do so in ways consonant with the new story of creation. One clear directive that this story gives theology is to understand human beings as earthlings (not aliens or tourists on the planet) and God as immanently present in the processes of the universe, including those of our planet. Such a focus has important implications for the contribution of theologians to "saving the planet," for theologies emerging from a coming together of God and humans *in and on the earth* implies a cosmocentric rather than anthropocentric focus. This does not, by the way, mean that theology should reject theocentrism; rather, it means that the divine concern includes *all* of creation. Nor does it imply the substitution of a creation focus for the tradition's concern with redemption; rather, it insists that redemption should include all dimensions of creation, not just human beings.

A second implication of accepting this paradigm shift is a focus on praxis. As Juan Segundo has said, theology is not one of the "liberal arts," for it contains an element of the prophetic, making it at the very least an unpopular enterprise and at times a dangerous one. The academy has been suspicious of it with good reason, willing to accept religious studies but aware that theology contains an element of commitment foreign to the canons of scholarly objectivity. (Marxist or Freudian commitments, curiously, have been acceptable in the academy, but not theological ones.) Increasingly, however, the hermeneutics of suspicion and deconstruction are helping to unmask simplistic, absolutist notions of objectivity, revealing a variety of perspectives, interpretations, commitments and contexts. Moreover, this variety is being viewed as not only enriching but necessary. Hence the emphasis on praxis and commitment, on a concerned theology, need in no way imply a lack of scholarly rigor or a retreat to fideism. Rather, it insists that one of the criteria of constructive theological reflection – thinking about our place in the earth and the earth's relation to its source – is a concern with the *consequences* of proposed constructions for those who live within them.

Theological constructs are no more benign than scientific ones. With the marriage of science and technology beginning in the 17th century, the commitments and concerns of the scientific community have increasingly been determined by the military-industrial-government complex that funds basic research. The ethical consequences of scientific research – which projects get funded and the consequences of the funded projects – are or ought to be *scientific* issues and not issues merely for the victims of the fall-out of these projects. Likewise, theological reflection is a *concerned* affair, concerned that this constructive thinking be on the side of the well-being of the planet and all its creatures. For centuries people have lived within the constructs of Christian reflection and interpretation, unknowingly as well as knowingly. Some of these constructs have been liberating, but many others have been oppressive, patriarchal and provincial. Indeed, theology is not a "liberal art," but a prophetic activity, announcing and interpreting the salvific love of God to *all* of creation.

A third implication of this paradigm shift is that the theological task is not only diverse in itself (there are many theologies), but also contributes to the planetary agenda of the 21st century, an agenda that beckons and challenges us to move beyond nationalism, militarism, limitless economic growth, consumerism, uncontrollable population growth and ecological deterioration. In ways that have never before been so clear and stark, we have met the enemy and know it is ourselves. While the holistic,

planetary perspective leads some to insist that all will be well if a "creation spirituality" were to replace the traditional "redemption spirituality"
of the Christian tradition, the issue is not that simple. It is surely the case
that the overemphasis on redemption to the neglect of creation needs to be
redressed; moreover, there is much in the common creation story that calls
us to a profound appreciation of the wonders of our being and the being
of all other creatures. Nonetheless, it is doubtful that such knowledge and
appreciation will be sufficient to deal with the exigencies of our situation.

The enemy – indifferent, selfish, shortsighted, xenophobic, anthropocentric, greedy human beings – calls, at the very least, for a renewed
emphasis on sin as the cause of much of the planet's woes and an emphasis on a broad and profound repentance. Theology, along with other institutions, fields of study and expertise, can deepen our sense of complicity
in the earth's decay. In addition to turning our eyes and hearts to an appreciation of the beauty, richness and singularity of our planet through a
renewed theology of creation and nature, theology ought also to underscore and elaborate on the myriad ways that we personally and corporately have ruined and continue to ruin God's splendid creation – acts
which we and no other creature can knowingly commit. The present dire
situation calls for radicalizing the Christian understanding of sin and evil.
Human responsibility for the fate of the earth is a recent and terrible
knowledge; our loss of innocence is total, for we know what we have
done. If theologians were to accept this context and agenda of their work,
they would see themselves in dialogue with all those in other areas and
fields similarly engaged: those who feed the homeless and fight for animal rights; the cosmologists who tell us of the common origins (and
hence interrelatedness) of all forms of matter and life; economists who
examine how we must change if the earth is to support its population; the
legislators and judges who work to advance civil rights for those dis-
criminated against in our society; the Greenham women who picket nuclear plants, and the women of northern India who literally "hug" trees to
protect them from destruction, and so on and on.

Theology is an "earthly" affair in the best sense of that word: it
helps people to live rightly, appropriately, on the earth, in our home. It is,
as the Jewish and Christian traditions have always insisted, concerned
with "right relations," relations with God, neighbor and self, but now the
context has broadened to include what has dropped out of the picture in
the past few hundred years – the oppressed neighbors, the other creatures
and the earth that supports us all. This shift could be seen as a return to
the roots of a tradition that has insisted on the creator, redeemer God as
the source and salvation of all that is. We now know that "all that is" is
vaster, more complex, more awesome, more interdependent, than any
other people has ever known. The new theologies that emerge from such
a context have the opportunity to view divine transcendence in deeper,

more awesome and more intimate ways than ever before. They also have the obligation to understand human beings and all other forms of life as radically interrelated and interdependent as well as to understand our special responsibility for the planet's well-being.

My own work takes place within this context and attempts to add a small square to the growing planetary quilt.

26

Feminist Perspectives on Science: Implications for an Ecological Theology of Creation

Anne M. Clifford

> As man proceeds toward his announced goal of the conquest of nature,
> he has written a depressing record of destruction, directed not only
> against the earth he inhabits but against the life he shares with it.
> Rachel Carson, *Silent Spring*, p. 85

Ecology was once discussed by only a handful of scientists, but that began to change when Rachel Carson wrote *Silent Spring* over thirty years ago. Her book grew out of her desire to communicate to the public the destructive ecological effects of indiscriminate use of pesticides. *Silent Spring* poignantly brought concern for ecology into the homes of millions in the United States, and to distant parts of the world as well.[1] Since Carson first sounded the warning of the irreversible consequences of environmental exploitation, ecology has become a broadly shared concern. This was apparent in 1990 when the twentieth anniversary of Earth Day was celebrated as a media event to usher in "the decade of the environment."

In spite of the efforts of numerous concerned persons around the world, humans continue to inflict our planet with pollution, deforestation, ozone destruction, endangerment of plant and animal species, and resource depletion. To remedy these many modern ills, a full-scale collaborative effort is needed. Recognition of this is growing, as the United Nations Conference on Environment and Development (popularly known as the "Earth Summit") held at Rio De Janeiro in June 1992 made evident.

In the midst of rising concern for the environment, ecofeminism has drawn attention to the interconnectedness of the domination of women and of nonhuman nature which has resulted in the ecological crisis.[2] Most ecofeminists would be in agreement with Rosemary Radford Ruether's articulation of this connection:

> Women must see that there can be no liberation for them and no solution to the ecological crisis within a society whose fundamental model of relationships continues to be one of domination. They must unite the demand of the women's movement with those of the ecological move-

ment to envision a radical reshaping of the basic socio-economic relations and the underlying values of . . . society. The concept of domination of nature has been based from the first on social domination . . .
starting with the basic relation between men and women.[3]

In the nearly two decades since Ruether's words appeared in print,
feminist scientists and philosophers have done a considerable amount of
critical research into the foundations of modern science. My purpose in
this essay is to explore possible intersections between feminist perspectives on science and ecological theology of creation. My guiding
questions for this exploration are: 1) How has science, especially traditional – male – epistemologies of science, contributed to the ecological
crisis? 2) What can feminist perspectives on science offer as a viable alternative? 3) What are the implications of these findings for an ecological theology of creation?

Theologians and scientists, male and female, need to become companions in responding to the ecological crisis, if nature, human and nonhuman, is to survive on this planet. Since both the drive for scientific
progress through domination over nature, and the theological retreat from
nonhuman nature into a personal faith in salvation have contributed to the
crisis, alternatives to these stances must be explored and appropriate
transformations of discourse and practice must be implemented.

Faith in a Creator God is deeply connected to ecology, but this connection, like the one cited by Ruether, has not been as obvious in the past
as it is today. The manner in which the Genesis creation stories have
been abused as proof texts for the domination of nature (Gen 1) and of
women (Gen 2-3) makes the task all the more difficult. Biblically rooted
beliefs about creation have had a profound impact on the thinking and
practice of Western society. But Western thinking and practice have also
impacted the interpretation of biblical texts. At this point of global crisis
the meaning of biblical creation must be explored in tandem with ecology, a branch of science that is often highly critical of the thinking and
practices of much of Western science and technology.

The term "ecology" has been in existence for well over a century;
historians of science trace it to German biologist Ernst Haeckel's *The
Natural History of Creation* (1868). Haeckel proposed the term "ecology" for a sub-discipline of zoology which would investigate the totality
of relationships between an animal species and its inorganic and organic
environment.[4] The meaning invested in "ecology" by Haeckel is flawed
by today's standards because he gave preference to animal species over
plants and macro-organisms over micro-organisms. Today, ecology studies the interrelationships among all forms of life. Its goal is the understanding of the mutual interdependence of species and the promotion of a

balance between all the inhabitants of the complex eco-system called earth.

Although Haeckel is credited with coining the term "ecology," in the nineteenth century important groundbreaking work in this field was done by a woman at MIT. Ellen Swallow did an extensive study of water, air and food purity, sanitation and industrial waste disposal. This was an important ecological study for the time, because it dealt with these areas, not as discrete questions, but rather as a mosaic of inter-twined problems that adversely affect human beings. At the time Swallow's work was classified as "home economics" rather than as science, probably because it was done by a woman.[5] The classification of her work in a field regarded as proper to women served to trivialize her research. It illustrates gender bias and the social domination of men in the scientific community and in the society at large. In the late nineteenth century the "cult of domesticity" held considerable influence on all aspects of North American culture; science was no exception.

In the 1960s Rachel Carson's work in ecology was similarly subject to gender bias and attempts to trivialize her contribution. Initially, Carson had major difficulties finding publishers for her works. After the publication of *Silent Spring*, spokespersons for the pesticide industry claimed that Carson's study should be disregarded because she lacked a doctorate and was not affiliated with a major research institution.[6] While it is true that Carson did not have a doctorate, she did, however, have an undergraduate degree in biology from Chatham College and a master's degree in zoology from John Hopkins University, where she also taught. It was not in the artificial environment of the university laboratory, but rather in the natural habitats of plants and animals as an employee of the Fish and Wildlife Service that Carson formulated her scientific questions and pursued her ecological research.

Aside from Rachel Carson, there are few women of note in the field of ecology and in the natural sciences. Since so few women have been full players in scientific fields, women have been unable to develop alternatives to the paradigms of the male-dominated scientific community. "Normal Science," to borrow a term coined by Thomas S. Kuhn, is the practice of science that is accepted by a particular scientific community.[7] Kuhn points out that to be a participant in the scientific community and gain the status as "scientist," the student "joins men who learned the bases of their field from the same concrete models."[8] The use of "men" here is more than a generic term for persons accepted into the scientific community. Traditionally, membership in the scientific community involved mentoring of men by men. As a result, women could not set the boundaries of what counts as scientific knowledge or decide how that knowledge would be articulated, nor could they contribute significantly to the decisions about what questions were to be researched.[9]

I draw attention to this fact because it is germane to the critical appraisal of traditional epistemologies of science by women scientists and philosophers of science today. These women speak from an awareness that few women have ever been in a position to influence science in theory or in practice. Many women in the sciences are asking: Is women scientists' approach science different from that of men? Some have responded to this question with a resounding yes; others with more qualified positive responses. Still others have said no. It is not possible to survey these differences here; however, I will note the significance of the locus of this question. It is being asked by women from within a traditionally androcentric community of discourse that has placed the scientific and the feminine in opposition.[10] Further, the ambiguity and complexity of the question emerges when one considers that in the past women scientists often disavowed their gender as a variable in their scientific performance in the hope of gaining equity with men. In the patriarchal political climate of the scientific community, difference could easily translate into inequality and therefore, exclusion from the community of scientists.[11]

Epistemologies of Science: A Feminist Appraisal

Epistemology is concerned with the ways of knowing and explaining phenomena, rather than with particular research questions. In the scientific fields, epistemology is attentive to how scientists go about theorizing. The obvious role of an epistemology is explanatory, but it also serves to justify theories and the metaphors chosen to articulate them. In traditional epistemologies of science, rigid boundaries are placed around science, in a way that sets it apart from other disciplines and from the broader culture and its values. These boundaries are based on the conception of science as an objective knowledge about nature. This empiricist conception still manages to persist, even in an era in which quantum physics and the principle of indeterminacy have thrown into question a mechanistic or positivistic world view. In the objectivist conception the scientist as agent entirely disappears. The result is that scientific language endows science with an aura of depersonalized authority. Furthermore, the way language often is used in scientific writing denies the relevance of time, place, social context, authorship and personal responsibility.[12]

Feminist philosophers of science have taken issue with this approach to science. They argue that an epistemology will be incomplete and seriously flawed, unless it gives attention to the presuppositions and biases that are at work in what counts as "normal science." One result of the claim of science to objectivity is that it renders gender difference invisible. Philosopher of science Sandra Harding critically appraises the pseudo-gender-neutrality in science by drawing attention to some major questions. For example, if scientific methodology is intent on eliminating gender bias from the results of its research, why has it left undetected so much sexist and androcentric bias?[13] Evelyn Fox Keller provides a response: the exclusion of the feminine from science has been historically constitutive of the standard definition of science as objective, universal, impersonal and masculine.[14] This definition allows science to maintain its epistemic authority and to insure its power in the broader society.

Harding also raises a question about the very idea of woman as scientist, as knower.[15] Feminist epistemology asks: in a male-dominated field is this not a contradiction in terms? If knowledge is supposed to be based on experience, and male dominance of science has insured that women's experience is viewed as different from men's and not a subject of consideration, then women's experience does not count as fruitful grounds from which to generate scientific problems or test scientific evidence. As long as scientific epistemology does not attend to gender as a social construction with major consequences for what counts as scientific knowledge and in what questions are addressed, it will continue a false universalizing of male experience.

Until recently, gender questions have been absent from discussions about what counts as scientific knowledge and about how scientific paradigms operate in practice. Attention to gender difference indicates that the boundaries used to set science apart from the other realms of our societal and cultural life are artificial and misleading. Science is a socially constructed human activity that is not only decided through interaction among the community of scientists, but is also formed by interaction with the broader social order, a social order which determines the authority given to knowledge and to the meaning and significance of gender, race, and class.

Feminist Appraisal of the Root Metaphors of Science

A critical appraisal of the root metaphors that are standard in "normal science" requires an examination of both the origins of what counts as scientific knowledge and the attitudes of scientists toward nonhuman nature. This examination will take the form of an exercise in deconstruction that scrutinizes the beginnings of modern science, in order to identify the gender biases on what would be included and excluded from scientific knowledge, and on how that knowledge would be expressed in scientific discourse. This exercise will illustrate the historical interconnectedness of the social construction of gender and of science.

Of particular interest for the topic of ecology are Francis Bacon, often characterized as the "father of modern science," and Charles Darwin, the "father of evolutionary biology." The purpose of examining the science of Bacon and Darwin is to show how the scientific theories and epistemologies of these significant figures were influenced by the attitudes of the societies in which they participated. These societies not only shaped how Bacon and Darwin engaged in scientific inquiry, they affected how they articulated their findings.

Francis Bacon (1561-1626), a scientist and philosopher of science, has received the title "father of modern science" for his role in the development of scientific methodology. Bacon, perhaps more than any other scholar of his era, helped to set the scientific revolution in motion. Rejecting the authority of traditional philosophy, Bacon wanted to replace speculative metaphysical thought about the nature of reality with a mode of inquiry that would allow people to verify the truths of science by reading nature's books. Bacon likened his method of scientific research to a kind of mechanical engine of discovery, fueled by experiment and observation.[16]

The goal of Bacon's new experimental science was the competence to dominate and control nature. Why does domination and control become the goal of Bacon's science? Carolyn Merchant, in *The Death of Nature*, provides a response by examining the linguistic metaphors of Bacon's scientific treatises in the context of his social and political world.[17] A metaphor is a figure of speech that conjoins the semantic fields of unrelated words in such a way as to create new meaning. According to Merchant, Bacon extensively used gender metaphors in a patriarchal manner and conjoined them to natural science. Bacon gave a new twist to patriarchal thought patterns that can be traced to the ancient Greeks: woman represented the body, the natural, the disordered, the emotional, the irrational; man represented the soul, epitomizing objectivity, rationality, culture and control. Bacon pushed these gender stereotypes still further. He viewed nature not only as a female, but as a wild and uncontrollable female to be subdued and controlled. This attitude of dominance contrasted with the gender stereotyping of a different form found in the literature of the Renaissance which viewed nature as an organism to be revered. The organic metaphor for nature as nurturing mother, common in sixteenth-century England, found itself in competition in the seventeenth century with the metaphor of a wayward woman who needed to be subdued. Although the image of nurturing earth did not vanish, it was superseded by new imagery which emphasized domination. The witch, symbol of the violence of nature, raised storms, caused illness, destroyed crops, obstructed generation, and killed infants. Disorderly woman, like chaotic nature, needed to be controlled.[18] The male biases prevalent in seventeenth century England affected the assumptions, methods and interpretations of Bacon's science. During Bacon's time religiously motivated witch trials were commonplace. Suspected witches were tried for copulating with the devil. Determining whether or not a woman was guilty of this crime required a

thorough physical examination. In England several hundred women were
identified as witches and were put to death in 1644-45. Merchant argues
that one plausible reason for witch trials was the maintenance of control
of women by men in power in the society.[19]

There is ample evidence for arguing that the metaphors for nature in
Bacon's epistemology originated, at least in part, in the witchcraft trials
of his day. Bacon's mentor was King James I, a strong supporter of anti-
witchcraft legislation in both England and Scotland. Influenced by the
witch trials ordered by James I, Francis Bacon transformed tendencies already in existence in his own society into a total program advocating the
control of nature for the benefit of "man." Bacon formulated a new ethic
sanctioning the exploitation of nature. Through the methods of scientific
inquiry Bacon envisioned that disorderly, active nature would be forced to
submit to the questions and experimental techniques of his new science,
just as the suspected witches had been forced to submit to the probing of
their accusers.[20] The practices associated with the inquisition of witches
permeated his descriptions of nature and his metaphorical style, and were
instrumental in his transformation of the earth, as nurturing mother and
womb of life, into a source of secrets to be extracted for economic advantage.

Bacon supported his emphasis on the control of nature through his
interpretation of chapter two of Genesis, the second story of creation.
Merchant draws from several of Bacon's works for his theological interpretation of the role of science.[21] She points out that Bacon interpreted
the fall from the garden of Eden (caused by the temptation of a woman),
as the human race's loss of dominion over creation. Before the fall, there
was no need for power or dominion, because Adam and Eve had been
made sovereign over all other creatures. In the state of dominion man
was like unto God. Only by digging further into the mine of natural
knowledge could mankind recover that lost dominion. Although woman's
inquisitiveness may have caused man's fall from his God-given dominion,
man's relentless interrogation of another female, nature, could be used to
regain it. Bacon wrote: "I am come in very truth leading to you nature
with all her children to bind you to her service and make her your
slave."[22] We have no right to expect nature to come to us. Instead she
must be taken and subdued by force.

Bacon's choice of sexist metaphors served to establish male authority as integral to the practice and the epistemology of science. The gender
terms chosen by Bacon resulted in science assuming the role of a dominating patriarchal male and nature a subordinate female. These ideas
were not generated in a cultural vacuum and have had a far-reaching impact. Bacon's bold sexual imagery is a key feature of the modern experimental method – the constraint of nature in the laboratory, dissection by
hand and mind, and the penetration of nature's hidden secrets. Merchant

illustrates how scientists still use gender imagery today in such phrases as "the hard facts," "the penetrating mind," and "the thrust of the argument" of scientists.[23] Merchant concludes that Bacon's image of nature as female to be controlled and penetrated has served to legitimate the exploitation and the rape of the earth's natural resources by science and technology.

> Nature, as active teacher and parent has become a mindless, submissive body. Not only did this new image function as a sanction, but the new conceptional framework of the Scientific Revolution – mechanism – carried with it norms quite different from the norms of organicism. The new mechanical order and its associated values of power and control would mandate the death of nature.[24]

Sandra Harding, in her comments on Merchant's analysis of the paradigmatic metaphors of Baconian science, contends that there is reason for considerable concern about the intellectual and moral structures of modern science when we think about how misogynous it is in its inception. Both nature and scientific inquiry have been conceptualized in ways modeled after rape and torture – on men's most violent and misogynous relationships to women – and this modeling has been advanced as a reason to value science.[25] The result of such conceptualizations is the ecological crisis.

Evelyn Fox Keller finds Bacon's sexual metaphors more subtle than do Merchant and Harding. Keller argues that for Bacon the aim of science is not to violate, but rather to master nature by following its dictates. Keller states, however, that "these dictates include the requirement, even demand, for domination" of nonhuman nature by scientists.[26]

The obvious conclusion from the analysis of Merchant and the reflections of Harding and Keller is that modern science, which traces its origins to Bacon, was influenced by the patriarchal biases prevalent in the broader society. The result has been the promotion of the domination of nature both in the metaphors of scientific theory and in the candidates for scientific research, with devastating results for nature. This antagonistic relationship is evident in science as a whole and particularly in biology. Since ecology is directly related to the biological sciences and the question of the survival of plant and animal species, an examination of the linguistic constructs that Charles Darwin used to explain his findings is crucial.

Charles Darwin (1809-82) developed the almost universally accepted theory of the evolution of species. Darwin is often portrayed as an innovative thinker who swam against the social stream. His theory of evolution ran counter to the determinism of the science of his day, because it included chance and change. It also conflicted with the interpretation of origins in the first chapters of Genesis, widely accepted by nineteenth-century British Christians. Although revolutionary from some perspectives, his theory of the process of evolution through the "natural selection" of characteristics that contribute to the survival of the fittest, exhibits substantial congruence with the social, economic and political ideology of his time.[27]

Darwin's evolutionary theory, presented in *The Origins of Species* (1859), highlights two themes: scarcity and competition. He borrowed these themes from Thomas Malthus' *An Essay on the Principle of Population* (1789), which he read in 1838.[28] From Malthus, Darwin accepted an analysis of the effects of scarcity of resources on British society. Malthus reasoned that scarcity of food would result in competition among people which would affect the composition of successive generations. In this idea, Darwin found a basis for his evolutionary theory. He expanded Malthus' human populations theory and reconceptualized it as a principle about the rest of the natural world. Following Malthus' logic, Darwin reasoned that in the course of competition among individuals, those best suited to an environment would be able to produce healthy offspring. Through inheritance their characteristics would predominate in the next generation.[29] Darwin's theory of "natural selection" is a transformation of Malthus' socio-economic theory.

Michael Gross and Mary Beth Averill draw attention to the specific classist purposes of Malthus' work. Malthus opposed the movement to better the economic lot of the poor by means of proposed "poor laws." He argued that such generosity allowed the unfit (the poor) to reproduce, indeed to reproduce faster than the upper class which showed more moral restraint. He predicted that as a consequence humanity would deteriorate.[30]

In their commentary on Darwin's appropriation of Malthus' positions, Gross and Averill note that Malthus' beliefs were sustained by what they believe to be a typical attribute of patriarchal thought: objectification of, rather than identification with, the "other," in this instance the members of the poorer classes. While the exigencies of survival were a source of dismay for Malthus, who saw in scarcity and competition the decline of English aristocracy under the provisions of the "poor laws," for Darwin they were positive in their consequences for the evolution of plant and animal populations. Darwin saw struggle and competition as essential facts of nature. Gross and Averill observe:

> Darwin thus employed struggle rhetorically "for convenience sake," casting every significant interaction in nature in the language of competition within and among the species, and the struggle between organism and its environment.[31]

The theory of evolution based on struggle and competition among species is widely accepted today. The interpretation of nature as battleground, and life as essentially a competitive struggle with limited places at the top, results in a hierarchically ordered world. Evolutionary theory not only changed the course of biology, but also shaped notions of how science progresses. Its influence on fields ranging from sociology, political science, and anthropology to philosophy and Protestant liberal theology is beyond dispute. Given its wide acceptance, does Darwinian evolution adequately account for the data in nature? Or is it an attempt to impose a particular notion of economic and political order on nature in keeping with the perspectives of nineteenth-century Victorian society?

Gross and Averill argue that evolutionary theory centered on struggle for the survival of the fittest does not adequately represent the complex interrelationships among all forms of life. Darwin's evolutionary theory is a cultural product of the nineteenth-century British society's patriarchal concern with the problem of disorder in the reproductive process of the poor and the desire to control it.[32]

In analyzing the linguistic metaphors chosen by Bacon and Darwin, I do not mean to imply that science since their groundbreaking work has completely accepted these metaphors. There are dissenting voices among scientists. But these metaphors have often been used without question, and, as a result, have been given a certain elevated status of empirical objectivity, where none is warranted.

Feminist Epistemology for Reconstructing Science

Through critical analyses of the linguistic patterns of Baconian and Darwinian science, feminist thinkers have brought to light the patriarchal and androcentric biases in their assumptions, methods and interpretations. These exercises in deconstruction make it clear that science is a socially produced body of knowledge and a cultural institution. An important question remains: How can we make science a holistically human, rather than an androcentric project? The response to this question requires a reconstruction that attempts to incorporate aspects of women's experience. Obviously, what is involved in this process is not only a challenge to "normal science" in the Kuhnian sense, but also an argument for revolutionary reformulation of what constitutes science. Clearly, an exhaustive reformulation is beyond the scope of this paper, or the expertise of this writer. Nevertheless, I would like to suggest that the question that needs to be addressed in carrying out this task is: What is required in scientific inquiry to incorporate women's experience into a more adequate and more holistic human epistemology?

This question is not an easy one to answer. One problem of course is that there is no clear consensus among feminist thinkers in science and the academic disciplines as a whole, on what constitutes "women's experience." Debates center on what is particular to biological sex, and what is due to gender as it has been constructed by society. What does seem to be widely accepted by feminist scientists and philosophers of science is the need to reconceptualize science, its methods, theories and goals in a way that places the scientist on the same plane as the questions being researched.

Feminist philosophers of science who subscribe to this stance argue that scientific research designed and practiced by women (and by feminist men) would be different from science which is done in the Baconian and Darwinian paradigms. Obviously, a scientist or philosopher of science who identifies herself (himself) as a feminist is explicitly taking a critical stance vis-á-vis androcentic bias in science. Evelyn Fox Keller and Ruth Bleier critique Baconian scientific methodology and metaphors by attacking any science which assumes a dualistic, detached attitude about the object of study. Rather than avoid subjectivity, scientists who incorporate a feminist approach are explicit about their personal assumptions, methods and values.[33] In a reconstructed feminist epistemology of science, the scientist is not seen as an impersonal authority standing outside and above nature and human concerns, but a person whose thoughts and feelings, logical capacities and intuitions are all relevant and involved in the process of discovery.

In company with Keller and Bleier, Elizabeth Fee proposes that the incorporation of a feminist epistemology in science would result in the removal of the rigid boundaries that separate the subject of knowledge (the knower) and the object of that knowledge. The elimination of the subject/object dualism, used to legitimate the domination of nature would result in a change in the goals of science.[34] Rather than seeking to dominate and control nature, goals which have resulted in ecological disaster, science would concern itself with listening to nature, guided by questions about how human society can restore harmony with its natural environment.

It follows that in a feminist epistemology, nature is conceptualized as active rather than passive, a dynamic and highly complex totality requiring human cooperation and understanding. The recognition of the complexity of nature is a good starting point for a reconstruction of evolutionary theory to counter Darwin's emphasis on scarcity and competition. Unfortunately, the limitations of the underlying principles of Darwin's thought have seldom been criticized by scientists. Gross and Averill's survey of literature in the field of ecology indicates that current research projects rarely challenge the fundamental principles of scarcity and competition.[35] This selective bracketing out of other factors is a consequence of the androcentricism of the biological sciences.

A major manifestation of androcentric bias is the emphasis on the role of dominant males in biologically determining the survival of mammals. While it is true that in many species of mammals mating is determined by fierce struggle among males, it is not true for all species, especially for primates. Female researchers are gathering new data guided by questions that were previously not raised. For example, Elizabeth Fisher's observations have led her to challenge conceptions of population regulation among higher primates which assume competition among dominant males. Fisher notes that in animals where reproduction involves complex social interactions, females play a role equal to or greater than that of males in determining the genetic constitution of the next generation. Generally, the females determine which males they will accept as mates.[36]

Data on primates, such as that gathered by Fisher, challenge the assumption that the survival of all mammal species demands competition among males for dominance. The universalizing of the pattern of male dominance and female subordination is an example of the androcentricism of evolutionary theory. Harding points out that it is men who have been preoccupied with finding the continuities between men and males in other species, and between women and females in other species. This has provided men with a basis for linking evolutionary hypotheses with biological determinist claims about the roles appropriate for each gender in society.[37]

Furthermore, competition cannot account for variations in specific characteristics in species that arise continually both through the recombination of genetic characteristics during sexual reproduction and by the introduction of altogether new variations by mutation. Darwinian evolution is one-dimensional and linear. It imposes a static explanation of winners and losers on fundamentally dynamic and complex processes. What evolutionary theory based on competition ignores is a number of other processes: nurturance, tolerance, and collectivism. Environments are constantly undergoing change, and both species' characteristics and population distribution respond and lead to further change. What is needed is the creation of better models for evolutionary change which will be more responsive to the data and which will better facilitate new ways of addressing ecological problems.[38]

One such model is that of Barbara McClintock, a biologist who was awarded a Nobel Prize in medicine and physiology in 1983. McClintock's major contribution was her theory of transposition, which she developed from her research into the cytogenetics of corn plants. Evelyn Fox Keller captures McClintock's model for doing science in the phrase: "a feeling for the organism."[39] McClintock describes her work as an attempt to listen to what an organism has to say. McClintock cautions scientists to resist the temptation to impose an answer on their research. The scientist must listen by identification with the organism. To do this the scientist needs to develop a capacity for an empathetic union with that which is to be known.[40]

Integral to McClintock's unique approach to scientific research is her conception of nature. She does not view nature as a passive, mechanical object ruled by externally imposed law, but as alive, growing, internally ordered and resourceful. In a sense McClintock's understanding of nature presupposes an organic model with multiple patterns of interrelationships. McClintock's attitude towards nature sharply contrasts with the rigid dualism of subject and object.

Keller believes that had it not been for her scientific accomplishment, McClintock may have been dismissed as a romantic. Instead she discovered a different approach to genetics, one that recognizes the complexity of interacting systems, including the interrelationships of observer to observed, cell to organism, and organism to environment. Her theory of transposition brought the problem of genetic inheritance into dialogue with the problem of the development of organisms in response to their environments.[41] To understand the life of an organism one must understand not only its genetic blueprint (DNA) but also the relationship of the organism's genes to the environment. Every organism is a complex interdependent relationship – an interaction of individual cell and organism and of the organism and its environment. There is nothing static and linear about the development of organisms – the environment affects them and they in turn their environment.

Keller points out that McClintock never identified herself as a feminist. Born in 1902, McClintock did much of her groundbreaking research in the 1930s and 40s. Typical of women scientists of her era, she viewed science as a gender-free undertaking. But in doing scientific research she relied on intuition, feeling, and a sense of connectedness and relatedness, attitudes that are repudiated by stereotypic (male) science.[42]

In particular, McClintock's perspective has important implications for science in an era of heightened awareness of our ecological crisis. "Feeling for the organism" rules out an objectivist conception of science and exhorts the scientist to adopt a more holistic approach to scientific research. Her reconstructed understanding of the scientist's relationship to nature is founded on respect for difference among individual subjects. It offers clues into how to promote the survival of species through active empathy, rather than contribute to their demise through control and domination.

"Feeling for the organism" rejects domination as the role of science. It lends itself to ecology because it focuses on forms of interrelatedness, emphasizing harmony, and complexity. It attempts not only to transcend the dualism of subject/object, but also insists on the need to unite the two. In addition, I believe that research guided by feeling for the organism avoids the Kantian dichotimization of reason/emotion. While it argues for the recognition of the scientific validity of the subjective, it also unites the cognitive and affective domains in scientific inquiry.

Implications For an Ecological Theology of Creation

What are the implications of feminist critical appraisals of traditional – male – science and the manner in which women, such as Barbara McClintock, engage in scientific research, for ecological theology of creation? One obvious implication is the removal of the rigid boundaries that separate the scientific community from the other communities that make up society, including theologians. One possible outcome of the removal of these boundaries could be fruitful and transforming dialogue among scientists, philosophers of science, and theologians. Such a dialogue would be historically significant, when one reflects on the fact that Darwin's theory of evolution led many scientists and theologians to treat each other as adversaries. This adversarial relationship contributed to the separation of science and theology in the twentieth century. Theologians relinquished nonhuman nature to scientists, who in turn viewed theology as having no relevance for the study of nature. As a result, the majority of theologians focused their attention on theological anthropology or theology of history and neglected creation.[43]

The separation of science and theology into distinct epistemic communities took place after Bacon had interpreted the Genesis creation texts in a manner that gave a "religious legitimation" to science's domination of nature, the unruly female. The use of Genesis creation texts to rationalize the domination of nature has been criticized by historian Lynn White in an essay that is widely regarded as a classic in ecological literature.[44] According to White's analysis, the Christian doctrine of creation is at the root of the ecological crisis caused by Western science and technology. The Genesis creation texts authenticate humanity's dominance over nature as part of God's plan. As a result, Christianity not only established a dualism of humanity and nature, but it also fostered science and technology as the instruments for the exploitation of nature.

White's position has some obvious resonance with the feminist critique of Bacon's use of patriarchal metaphors. Both critique the relationship of domination and its legitimation on either religious or gender-related grounds.

The text that has been most often cited as a charter or proof text for human domination of nature is Genesis 1:26-30. Why has this been the case? According to Dorothee Soelle, this is due to the tendency of Christianity to interpret this text as symbolizing God's complete separateness from the world (nature) and, as a result, has elevated God's transcendence to an extreme. God's immanence in the world has been downplayed in order to eliminate any form of pantheism. In Soelle's judgment, the distant transcendent God is a projection of a patriarchal world view and its ideal of an independent and self-sufficient king. In the modern period, emphasis on divine transcendence has contributed to human domination of nature by science and technology. The human, as made in the image of a transcendent God, is depicted as radically different from nature. This distinction has contributed to humanity's loss of awareness of and reverence for what humans share with earth's other life forms.[45]

A close examination of Genesis 1:1-2:4a is called for to see if the text itself necessarily sanctions the domination of nature by humans – scientists. At the outset it is important to note that there is no Hebrew word for "nature" in the Tanakh. The idea of nature as a unity first appeared in classical Greek thought. In its modern usage, "nature" refers to the natural order outside of humanity. This understanding of nature would have been completely foreign to the authors of Genesis 1.

Biblical scholars widely share a consensus that the first chapter of Genesis comes from the Priestly tradition of the Babylonian Exile Period (ca 550 BCE). The text emphasizes God creating the world by bringing order out of chaos.[46] Its six-day structure was adapted from the Babylonian myth *Enuma elish*, but given a unique accent by the Jews, expressed in the words: "And God saw that this was good." Nahum M. Sarna argues that what is significant about this text is that the world is declared to be a "very good world." This "very good world" is ordered by God in such a way that the interrelationship of organisms with their environment and with each other is harmonious and mutually beneficial.[47] In his judgment, the original condition of the earth has a great deal to do with humanity's special charge to fill the earth and master it (v. 28).

In Genesis 1:26-27, on the sixth day of creation the human (*ádam*) is created, following the animals. Sarna interprets the significance of humans' sharing the sixth day of creation with animal life as underscoring the earthiness of humans and their solidarity with other forms of animal life.[48] This earthy kinship is also symbolized in the second Genesis story of creation by the formation of humans and other animals from the same element, the earth (2:7, 19).

In Genesis 1 humans are not only created in solidarity with animal life, they are also created in the image and likeness of God. Sarna argues that there is a connection between resemblance to God, as God's image, and the gift of human dominion of the earth's resources. The terminology "in our image, after our likeness" used to describe humanity is derived from Middle Eastern regal vocabulary. Humans image God by carrying out the function of God's representative. The charge to rule the earth and its life forms is in keeping with humans as "the image of God." What does it mean for humans to rule as God's representative? Sarna provides a response to this question which challenges human domination:

This power, however, cannot include the license to exploit nature bane-
fully, for the following reasons: the human race is not inherently sovereign, but enjoys its dominion solely by the grace of God. Furthermore,
this model of kinship here presupposed is Israelite, according to which
the monarch does not possess unrestrained power and authority; the
limits of his rule are carefully defined and circumscribed by divine law,
so that kingship is to be exercised with responsibility and is subject to
accountability.[49]

In Sarna's commentary on Genesis 1, concern for the environment is
very much in evidence. This concern has also prompted some Christian
theologians to counter the domination interpretation of dominion by proposing dominion as "stewardship" of creation. At the core of this interpretation is the idea that to be God's representative is to act as the Divine
King's steward, like a trustee of property.

A chief proponent of dominion as stewardship is Douglas John Hall.
He interprets the Genesis 1 *imago Dei* symbol in the categories of identification and differentiation.[50] He explains identification as the solidarity
of humans with all earth's creatures. His approach is similar to Sarna's
interpretation of the significance of animals and humans being created on
the sixth day. Differentiation is the category Hall uses to highlight *imago
Dei*, as indicating human transcendence over nonhuman creation. He develops the latter by proposing that inherent to the human being as *imago
Dei* is not the sanction to dominate nature, but rather the God-given vocation of stewardship of the environment.

Hall proposes a radically Christocentric interpretation of *imago Dei*
and stewardship by focusing on the Lordship of Christ as the exemplar
for human beings' relation to the world.[51] He stresses that Christ's Lordship is expressed, not as mastery over creation, but as the service of sacrificial love. Christ, in his exercise of dominion, is what the human, as
created in the image of God, is called to enact.

This interpretation of dominion as stewardship focused on Christ is
thought-provoking and worthy of consideration. It offers a corrective to
conceptions of God as sovereign King and dominating Other associated
with Genesis 1. I do not believe, however, that it sufficiently reconceives
humanity's relationship with nonhuman nature. I find Hall's proposal to
be problematic on several fronts: (1) The Lordship of Christ has a history
of imperial interpretation that has often muted its association with Jesus'
sacrificial love. To his credit, Hall recognizes this difficulty and gives it
attention, but I don't believe that he sufficiently resolves it. Since human
imperialism vis-á-vis nature has resulted in the ecological crisis we are
now facing, the imperialism associated with the symbol of Christ's Lordship deserves more serious consideration than Hall gives it. (2) In Hall's
interpretation, humanity is placed in a type of redeemer role where nonhuman nature is concerned. Although Hall does argue for humanity's

identification (solidarity) with the rest of creation, identification with Christ, the Lord and Savior of the world, lends itself to a triumphalistic otherness. If the human vocation is conformity to Christ's saving Lordship, are humans still really in solidarity with nonhuman nature? It seems to me that nonhuman nature remains unavoidably subordinate and "other" in its relationship to its human saviors. (3) In my reading of Hall's argument for dominion as stewardship, I do not find that it sufficiently attends to the fact that we humans *are* the ecological crisis; it is we who are the major cause for the imbalances in the ecosphere. This is the legacy of the paradigm of control of nature through science and technology. By what right do we envision ourselves as the stewards of creation, when nonhuman nature could take care of itself without us? In addition, emphasis on human stewardship of creation can too easily imply instrumental management of nonhuman nature, as if it was property primarily for human use and benefit.

As a first step in the search for an ecological theology of creation responsive to feminist perspectives on science, I propose that Genesis 1:1-2:4a be examined as a part of the eleven-chapter introductory unit of the Torah. Perhaps more light can be shed on the biblical understanding of "dominion" in this context. In the account of Noah and the flood (Gen 6:9-9:29),[52] we find another type of creation story. In this story human wickedness creates an ecological disaster of worldwide proportions. The just man Noah, along with his wife and family, are chosen to act as God's representatives in a special exercise of dominion. In this context, dominion means attending to the survival of the animals who are also beloved creatures of God. After the flood, God indicates that a reckoning will be required from humans and the same will also be required from every beast (9:1-4). God establishes a covenant with Noah's family and their descendants and also with every living creature that is with them – birds, cattle and every wild beast (9:9-11).[53] There is an inherent relational interdependence in this covenant. The Noachic covenant is a symbol of the unbreakable bonds among all creatures and their Creator. The perpetual sign of the covenant is God's "bow in the clouds" (9:13). Consequently, humans and animals are covenant partners with God and are ever-reminded of this with the appearance of a rainbow.

Is there anything that can be drawn from this that responds to White's critique? First of all, the exploitation of nonhuman nature and the resulting destruction of the balance of nature at human hands are not the result of the gift of dominion, but of humanity's disregard for the order of the universe which has its source in God. Secondly, the central affirmation that the Creator is the God of the covenant contains an inherent critique of God as a dominating transcendent Other, and places God's dominion in the context of a mutual relationship. The language of covenant is in tension with the language of domination. In a covenant relationship God is not a dominating ruler outside the world; rather God is intimately connected to the world and to its inhabitants.

Practically speaking, what does being a covenant partner with other life forms mean for us today? To truly be a covenant partner with non-human nature rules out a stance of domination. In an age of ecological crisis, I believe that creation theology can be transformed by bringing mutual covenant partnership into dialogue with the understanding of nature operative in some scientific work. I have already noted that Barbara McClintock's research tenet "feeling with the organism," reflects an understanding of nature which presupposes an organic model with multiple patterns of interrelationships that include the scientific researcher. The organic model of science offers a corrective to human imperialism over nonhuman nature and provides rich prospects for theological understanding of the human as a covenant partner with the rest of creation.

Sally McFague, a feminist theologian who has made ecology her focal concern, describes an organic ecological model as "one that unites entities by symbiotic, mutual interdependencies, creating a pattern of internal relations."[54] McFague's model stands in contrast to objectivist models which separate entities dualistically and hierarchically. Her organic model is predicated on a mutuality that recognizes all entities as having intrinsic worth and not only instrumental value for humans.

McFague theologizes about this organic model in the evocative metaphor, "the world as God's body."[55] In the light of the dominant image of God as sovereign over creation, this is a radical metaphor for re-envisioning the relationship between God and the world. In this metaphor the entire universe is envisioned as expressive of God's very being: "*the* 'incarnation'."[56] It is this metaphor that she believes best expresses the God-world relationship for our time.

McFague's proposal is a critique of the monarchical understanding of the God-world relationship which puts distance between God and the world. The embodiment of God as the world overcomes that distance, and the emphasis on control and the God-world dualism that accompanied it. McFague is cautious not to give a pantheistic understanding to this metaphor. God cannot be reduced to the world, any more than we humans can be reduced to our bodies.

To ground the metaphor of the "world as God's body" biblically, McFague proposes a remythologizing of the suffering love of the cross of Jesus[57] and the risen Jesus as "a permanent presence in our present."[58] She argues that these are signs of the abiding and caring presence of God in the world.

This does not mean, however, that McFague neglects the biblical doctrine of creation. In the context of her reflections on God as mother she gives some attention to creation and to some of the problems with its modern biblical interpretation. The Enlightenment era interpretation of the

Genesis creation texts is defective because it supports dualism and hierarchy. God is distinct from the world and spirit superior to matter. She
finds the image of God as fashioning the world, either intellectually by
word or aesthetically by craft, to be inadequate for it depicts God as totally different and totally distant from creation. As an alternative model
she images creation as a physical event in which the universe is "bodied
forth" from the womb of God.[59] If we were to follow the logic of this
image, however, it seems that the world is God's child and not actually
God's body.[60] So has McFague really overcome the distance between God
and the world that she believes is so important in an ecological age?

In the context of her treatment of God as Mother-Creator McFague
briefly notes that the biblical Wisdom literature depicts Wisdom as a female figure involved in creation.[61] She indicates that in Sophia she does
not see the dualism that later became dominant in the tradition. However, she does not develop the God-Sophia-Creation theme.

As a basis for an ecological theology of creation, I propose to explore what the biblical Wisdom literature might have to offer. I see this
as an important supplement to the creation-covenant theme of Genesis 9
that I have already treated. In Wisdom literature there are several passages that describe wisdom as intimately connected with creation. For
example Proverbs declares that by wisdom God founded the earth (3:19).
Although the female character of wisdom is not evident in this text, in
many of the Wisdom literature's creation texts wisdom is presented as a
female with strong intimations of divinity. For this reason, I will render
wisdom as Sophia, the Greek term that makes the female character explicit.[62]

The association of Sophia and creation is developed in detail in
Proverbs 8:22-31. In this text creation is the arena where God's presence
is revealed. Here Sophia replaces the royal representative imagery of
Genesis 1.[63] It is Sophia who is the source for the order and meaning of
the world. In this poem, Sophia speaks in the first person and describes
herself as the very first of God's works, brought forth before the creation
of any reality (vs. 22-26). Further, when God performed the work of the
world's creation, Sophia was present. Sophia in this passage is presented
in a way that is unique in Wisdom literature. Preexistent Sophia is not of
the ordinary created order. Paradoxically, she is both outside creation and
also within it, as the instrument of the production of creation.[64] She participates in the activity of creation: "When he marked out the foundations
of the earth, then I was beside him . . . " (vs. 29-30).[65] In further probing
Sophia's role in creation, we find that she is the model or exemplar of
Yahweh's works. This is what it means for Sophia to be the "master
worker" (v. 30).[66]

The poem concludes with Sophia rejoicing in God, the world and
the human race. This makes Sophia the center of a threefold relationship.

In a sense, it is she who is the bow in the sky, for she spans the distance between God, the world and human beings. Claudia Camp points out that any hint of dichotomizing between God and nature, and sacred and profane are overcome in the female imagery for wisdom.[67] Sophia goes on to give a clear directive: "Hear instruction and be wise, and do not neglect it" (v. 33). Listening to her instructions is the key to finding wisdom.

The preexistence of Sophia and her participation in the creation of the world are themes also found in Job 28 and Sirach 24. Job 28 raises the question: " . . . where shall wisdom be found?" (v. 12). The theme of personified Wisdom is participation in the work of creation is hinted at. The hiddenness of Sophia within creation is stressed (vs. 20-22). It is God who has placed her within creation (vs. 23-27). Sophia cannot be gotten for gold or silver (v. 15). To find her it is necessary that one depart from evil (v. 28). In Sirach 24 the origins of Sophia are described in a manner similar to that of Proverbs 8:22-31. "I came forth from the mouth of the Most High" (Sir. 24:3). She describes herself as very ethereal: "mistlike" she covers the earth (24:3), much as the spirit of God came over the waters of chaos (cf. Gen 1:2). However, what is unique about Sophia in Sirach is her identification with the Torah (24:23). Ben Sira links creation with the Law and therefore with the covenant relationship.

In the Wisdom of Solomon, the Sage begins by saying explicitly that wisdom inheres in creation (1:7). In a later lengthy passage Sophia is presented as a divine character with a cosmic function (6:12-11:1). She is not just the Creator at the beginning. She is part of the ongoing creative process. In Wisdom 7:22-8:1, it is Sophia, who acts as the artisan who fashions all things (cf. Prov. 8:30), and teaches humanity about the structure of the world, the nature of animals and the varieties of plants (7:17-22). Her teachings, therefore, are broader than the Law (cf. Sir. 24:23); they take on encyclopedic proportions. Further, Sophia penetrates all spirits (v. 23) and indeed all things because of her purity (v. 24). In reflecting on this passage, Roland Murphy points out that in this text her "cosmological ubiquity comes into play."[68] Sophia is the way in which God is present to the world and to humans.

The close relationship of Sophia to creation is further spelled out in Wisdom 8:1: " . . . She orders all things well." She is immanent in creation. In the opening verses of the chapter that follows, we find a prayer directed to God with this address:

O God of my ancestors and Lord of mercy,
who have made all things by your word,
and by your wisdom have formed humankind
to have dominion over the creatures you have made . . . (9:1-2).

As the prayer unfolds the reader is reminded of Sophia's immanence in creation. It is Sophia who knows God's works and was present when God made the world. Therefore, she understands what is pleasing in God's sight and what is right according to God's design. It is to her that we are to look for the meaning of "dominion." It is by her that people will be saved (v. 18). Perhaps there is some justification for asserting that it is also by her that creation, as a whole, will be restored to ecological harmony.

Conclusions

I realize that what I have presented does not adequately address the immensity of the ecological crisis that we face. What has been accomplished in this essay is far more modest. Hopefully, I have succeeded in initiating a process of further dialogue and collaboration that will contribute to the more radical transformation that is needed.

No solution to our ecological crisis will be forthcoming until sexism is rooted out of our patterns of thinking and acting. The critical feminist appraisal of the metaphors and concepts of traditional Baconian science and Darwinian evolution theory has brought to light how pervasive the androcentric bias of traditional science is. In Bacon's conceptualization of science, the domination of nonhuman nature and of women are arbitrarily linked. In Darwin's theory of "natural selection" both sexist and classist biases are in evidence.

As an alternative to these androcentric perspectives is Barbara McClintock's approach to biological research – as "a feeling for the organism." While McClintock does not provide us with a complete epistemology of science, she does provide a viable method of research that makes empathetic listening to nonhuman nature central. Learning to listen from within nature is basic to true ecological consciousness.

In exploring the possible connections between the feminist perspectives on science and creation theology, I began with Genesis 1:1-2:4a, the creation text that is most often cited as a proof text for human domination (exploitation) of nonhuman nature. As a corrective to approaches that lend themselves to human mastery of nonhuman nature in the name of God or of Christ, I have proposed the covenant partnership of humans with nonhuman nature in the story of the Noachic covenant (Gen 9:8-17), because it emphasizes the solidarity of human and nonhuman nature in relationship to God. For a further basis for an ecological theology of creation I have looked to Sophia creation texts. The Divine Sophia is often at the heart of creative activity in biblical Wisdom literature. The Sophia creation texts provide a corrective to the dualistic/dominating conceptions of the relationship between the divine and creation, and human and nonhuman nature commonly associated with Genesis 1. In making this proposal, I do so with the recognition that Sophia is a complex and somewhat ambiguous figure. In some texts she is present at the beginning of creation, but she is neither clearly distinct from the Creator nor from creation. In other texts, Sophia inheres in Creation; it is she who makes all things new, and orders existence.

In closing, it seems fitting to note that in the biblical Wisdom literature Sophia is found primarily through effort and discipline (Sir. 4:17; 6:18-36; Prov. 4:10-27; 6:6; Wis. 1:5; 7:14). This effort and discipline requires that we conceive of reality in new ways and make choices in life that will embody those new conceptions. In our present era, if we are to find Sophia in our world, new root metaphors must be sought for making the divine order intelligible. I believe that the admonition to listen to Sophia and to study her ways is very much akin to McClintock's empathetic "feeling for the organism." With willingness to be challenged beyond both traditional science and its epistemology and traditional interpretations of biblical texts, we must listen to nonhuman nature speak its wisdom of ecological harmony. It will take real discipline to listen to Sophia speak by allowing ourselves to "feel" with creation in a stance of prayerful openness to the discovery of divine order.

Listening to Sophia obviously requires of us an active commitment to restore the sacred covenant partnership with nature's life forms that we humans have broken. It requires of us the abandonment of the dualistic and hierarchical understandings of reality that put us, as humans, in transcendent domination over (and against) nonhuman nature, as if we were its royal rulers. Nature is neither an unruly female to be tamed by science and technology for human benefit, nor an evolving saga of competition at the expense of others. Rather it is a complex web of life in which we humans are a vital thread. To really listen to Sophia immanent within nature as God's creation means we must attempt to be attuned to the inner dynamism of our complex global ecosystem and discover ourselves as humans in continuity with it.

Endnotes

1. Rachel Carson, *Silent Spring* (Boston: Houghton Mifflin Co., 1962). This work has also been published in Great Britain, France, Spain, Norway, Sweden, Holland, Japan, Israel and Yugoslavia.

2. Françoise d'Eaubonne introduced the term *ecofeminisme* in *Le feminisme oú la mort* (Paris: Pierre Horay, 1974). Since the term was first coined it has been used in a variety of ways. It is beyond the scope of this paper to address these differences.

3. Rosemary Radford Ruether, *New Women/New Earth: Sexist Ideologies and Human Liberation* (New York: Seabury Press, 1975), 204.

4. Hans Magnus Enzensberger, "A Critique of Political Ecology," in *Ideology of/in the Natural Sciences,* ed. Hilary Rose and Steven Rose, (Cambridge, Mass.: Schenkman Publishing Co., 1980), 136.

5. Sue V. Rosser, "Feminist Scholarship in the Sciences: Where Are We Now and When Can We Expect a Theoretical Breakthrough?" in *Feminism and Science,* ed. Nancy Tuana, (Bloomington: Indiana University Press, 1989), 4.

6. Hilary Rose argues that the initial dismissal of Rachel Carson and the ecology movement shows the reluctance of masculine science to give over its domination. See "Beyond Masculinist Realities: A Feminist Epistemology for the Sciences," in *Feminist Approaches to Science,* ed. Ruth Bleier, (New York: Pergamon Press, 1986), 59.

7. Thomas S. Kuhn, *The Structure of Scientific Revolutions,* vol. 2, *The International Encyclopedia of Unified Science,* 2nd ed. (Chicago: University of Chicago Press, 1970), 10.

8. *Ibid.,* 11.

9. The National Science Foundation provides statistical reasons for why women scientists have not played a role in establishing the reigning paradigms in the scientific communities. According to a 1980 NSF report, of the people who received their doctorates in the natural sciences in the 1960s 62.8% of the men were full professors, while only 36.5% of the women were. While the ladder for men is graduate student, post-doctoral fellow, research associate, assistant professor, associate professor and full professor, most of the women, who had not abandoned their fields, were hired as research associates and remained at that level. This NSF study is cited by Vivian Gornick in *Women in Science, Portraits from a World in Transition* (New York: A Touchstone Book, 1983), 73-75. A 1986 NSF report, *Women and Minorities in Science and Engineering,* indicates that women's participation in the sciences have increased somewhat, but women still face lower salaries, and lower rates of promotion and tenure than men, 86-300.

10. Evelyn Fox Keller, "The Gender/Science System: or, Is Sex to Gender as Nature Is to Science?" in *Feminism and Science,* 37.

11. *Ibid.,* 35.

12. For insightful treatments see Ruth Hubbard, "Introductory Essay: The Many Faces of Ideology," in *Ideology of/in the Natural Sciences,* xiv-xv; Kathryn Pyne Addleson, "The Man of Professional Wisdom," in *Discovering Reality, Feminist Perspectives on Epistemology, Metaphysics, Methodology, and Philosophy of Science,* ed. Sandra Harding and Merrill B. Hintikka, (Boston: D. Reidel Publishing Co., 1983), 165-186 and Lynn Hankinson Nelson, *Who Knows: From Quine to a Feminist Empiricism* (Philadelphia: Temple University Press, 1990).

13. Sandra Harding, "Is There a Feminist Method?" in *Feminism and Science,* 23.

14. Evelyn Fox Keller, "The Gender/Science System," 42.

15. Harding, "Is There a Feminist Method?" 23-24.

16. Peter Urbach, *Francis Bacon's Philosophy of Science: An Account and a Reappraisal* (La Salle, Ill.: Open Court, 1987), 1-20.

17. Carolyn Merchant, *The Death of Nature: Women and the Scientific Revolution* (New York: Harper and Row, 1980), 164-190 and passim.

18. *Ibid.,* 127.

19. *Ibid.,* 138-140.

20. *Ibid.,* 164.

21. *Ibid.,* 170. Merchant cites "Novum Organum," part 2 in Francis Bacon, *Works,* 4: 247 and "Valerius Terminus," *Works,* 3: 217, 219, ed. James Spedding, Robert Leslie Ellis and Douglas Heath (London: Longmanns Green, 1870), and "The Masculine Birth of Time," in *The Philosophy of Francis Bacon,* ed. Benjamin Farrington, (Liverpool, England: Liverpool University Press, 1964), 62; 170, 317 n.13.

22. *Ibid.,* 170. This quote is from Bacon, "The Masculine Birth of Time," 62.

23. *Ibid.,* 171.

24. *Ibid.,* 190.

25. Sandra Harding, *The Science Question in Feminism* (Ithaca, N.Y.: Cornell University Press, 1986), 116.

26. Evelyn Fox Keller, *Reflections on Gender and Science* (New Haven: Yale University Press, 1985), 37.

27. Ruth Hubbard, "Have Only Men Evolved?" in *Discovering Reality,* 45.

28. *Ibid.,* 51. Hubbard indicates that she found this information in Darwin's autobiography.

29. Michael Gross and Mary Beth Averill, "Evolution and Patriarchal Myths of Scarcity and Competition," in *Discovering Reality,* 75.

30. *Ibid.,* 74.

31. *Ibid.,* 75.

32. *Ibid.,* 81.

33. Evelyn Fox Keller, *Reflections on Gender and Science,* 7-12; and Ruth Bleier, "Introduction" in *Feminist Approaches to Science,* ed. by Ruth Bleier, (New York: Pergamon Press, 1986), 1-17, passim.

34. Elizabeth Fee, "Critiques of Modern Science: The Relationship of Feminism to Other Radical Epistemologies," in *Feminist Approaches to Science,* 47.

35. Gross and Averill draw attention to several ecological research projects carried out in the late 1970s, "Evolution and Patriarchal Myths of Scarcity and Competition," 76-80.

36. *Ibid.,* 84. Gross and Averill cite the research of Elizabeth Fisher, author of *Women's Creation* (Garden City, N.J.: Anchor/Doubleday, 1979).

37. Harding, *The Science Question in Feminism,* 100.

38. Gross and Averill suggest that a more reliable understanding of nature would be gained by thinking in terms of concepts central to feminist thought which would accurately reflect the natural order. They suggest plentitude and cooperation, "Evolution and Patriarchal Myths," 81-86. I have not included a treatment of their suggestion in this paper, because I believe that what they propose may be a too facilely constructed female myth to replace the male myth which they have demythologized.

39. Evelyn Fox Keller indicates that Barbara McClintock often used this phrase in describing her conception of scientific research. *A Feeling for the Organism* (San Francisco: W.H. Freeman and Co., 1983), 198. McClintock died on September 2, 1992; she was ninety years old.

40. *Ibid.,* 198-204.

41. Keller. *Reflections on Gender and Science,* 167-172.

42. Keller notes that whether or not McClintock identified herself as a feminist, she does display attitudes which many feminists associate with the female gender, attitudes which Keller argues she likely internalized along with her core gender identity. "The Gender/Science System: or, Is Sex to Gender as Nature Is to Science?" 37-38.

43. Within the limits of this essay it is not possible to delve into the relationship between science and theology. It is important, however, to note that the adversarial relationship about which I speak was concentrated on Darwin's evolutionary theory, because it was perceived to be in conflict with the first chapters of Genesis. For more, see my "Creation" in *Systematic Theology, Roman Catholic Perspectives,* vol. 1, ed. Francis Schüssler Fiorenza and John P. Galvin, (Minneapolis: Fortress Press, 1991), 219-246.

44. Lynn White, Jr. "The Historical Roots of Our Ecological Crisis," in *Ecology and Religion in History,* ed. David Spring and Eileen Spring (New York: Harper and Row, 1974), 24-28. This essay was first published in *Science* 155 (1967), 1203-07. It has been republished many times in environmental and ecological literature.

45. Dorothee Soelle with Shirley A. Cloyes, *To Work and to Love, A Theology of Creation* (Philadelphia: Fortress Press, 1984), 14-19. This insight has been highlighted by many feminist theologians, including Rosemary Radford Ruether who draws attention to the transcendence and separateness of God from creation in *Sexism and God-Talk, Toward a Feminist Theology* (Boston: Beacon Press, 1983), 76-79.

46. John L. McKenzie, "Aspects of Old Testament Thought," in *The New Jerome Biblical Commentary,* ed. Raymond E. Brown, Joseph A. Fitzmyer and Roland E. Murphy (Englewood Cliffs, N.J.: Prentice Hall, 1990), 1292-1293.

47. Nahum M. Sarna, *The JPS Torah Commentary of Genesis: The Traditional Hebrew Text and the New JPS Translation* (Philadelphia: The Jewish Publication Society, 5749/1989), 13.

48. *Ibid.*

49. *Ibid.,* 12-13.

50. Douglas John Hall, *Imaging God: Dominion as Stewardship* (Grand Rapids: Wm. B. Eerdmans Publishing Co. and New York: Friendship Press, 1986), 178-183. (Readers will, no doubt, recognize the Hegelian roots of his categories.)

51. *Ibid.,* 183-187.

52. This story is a combination of the Yahwist and Priestly traditions redacted into a coherent unity; chapter 9:1-17 is believed to have Priestly origins. See Richard J. Clifford, S.J. "Genesis," in *The New Jerome Biblical Commentary,* 15.

53. Richard J. Clifford has drawn attention to the extension of the covenant to animal life in Genesis 9 in providing a negative response to the question raised in the title of a recent article: "Genesis 1-3: Permission to Exploit Nature?" *Bible Today* 26 (1988), 135.

54. Sally McFague, *Models of God: Theology for an Ecological, Nuclear Age* (Philadelphia: Fortress Press, 1987), 11. McFague mentions White's critique in n. 10 on page 68, but she does not address it in depth.

55. *Ibid.,* 61.

56. *Ibid.,* 62.

57. *Ibid.,* 72.

58. *Ibid.,* 59.

59. *Ibid.,* 110.

60. McFague, herself, notes this problem with her interpretation of creation as being bodied forth from God; see 110-11.

61. *Ibid.,* 115.

62. The word for wisdom in Hebrew is *hokmah;* it is *sophia* in Greek. Both are feminine gender. In focusing on the divine Sophia, I find myself at odds with Rosemary Radford Ruether's rejection of Sophia. Ruether believes that the Hebrew tradition has limited Sophia to the status of an attribute of the male God. (*Sexism and God-Talk.* Boston: Beacon Press, 1983), 57. My position is more in keeping with that of Elisabeth Schüssler Fiorenza whose research has led her to conclude that Sophia is the God of Israel expressed in the imagery of a goddess. See *In Memory of Her* (New York: Crossroad, 1983), 133-135.

63. For a thorough survey of the question of female personification of Wisdom in the book of Proverbs see Claudia V. Camp, *Wisdom and the Feminine in the Book of Proverbs* (Decatur, Ga.: Almond Press, 1985). Camp's research notes that the feminine Wisdom figure in Proverbs 8:22-31 may be patterned after the Egyptian goddess Maat. This goddess is the favorite child of the god Re; she came down to earth at the beginning of time as the embodiment of cosmic order and the preserver of the law. During the Hellenistic period, Maat became identified with the Egyptian goddess Isis, 29-41.

64. Bruce Vawter, "Proverbs 8:22, Wisdom and Creation," *Journal of Biblical Literature* 99 (1980), 214-15.

65. This text and subsequent biblical passages cited are taken from the *New Revised Standard Version: The New Oxford Annotated Bible,* ed. Bruce M. Metzger and Roland Murphy, (New York: Oxford University Press, 1991).

66. The Hebrew term is *'mwn.* Its meaning has been a subject of debate. It has sometimes been rendered as crafts[wo]man, as darling, or even as nursling. See Roland E. Murphy, *The Tree of Life: An Exploration of Biblical Wisdom Literature* (New York: Doubleday, The Anchor Bible Reference Library, 1990), 136. Murphy indicates that, in his opinion, the author of the Wisdom of Solomon understands *'mwn* of Proverbs 8:30 as "artisan or crafts[wo]man, or maker of all." Thus she is identified with God, 143.

67. Camp, 289.

68. Murphy, 143.

27

Experience and God

Mary Heather MacKinnon

HUMAN EXPERIENCE AND KNOWLEDGE OF GOD ARE KEY CONCERNS OF contemporary Christian theology.[1] With the rise of historical conscious-ness, believers and non-believers alike seek to know more about how God reveals God's self to and through human experience, what constitutes an experience of God, what is the locus of one's experience of God, how ex-perience of God informs one's faith and one's way of being in the world, and how contemporary experience of God relates to traditional Christian understandings of God. This essay examines how various contemporary theologians attempt to answer these questions.

In his book, *Experiencing God All Ways and Every Day*, J. Norman King begins his discussion with these questions: "Is there anything we touch upon in our deepest experience to which the word 'God' might cor-respond? What are the most suitable ideas and words to express and in-terpret this experience?"[2] King declares that God is the Presence we touch upon in our deepest human experience, and he begins with the sup-position that God is experience of transcendent reality, ineffable mystery, something more and beyond the human, rather than the experience of a mere void in life.[3]

Basing his thought on an interpretation of the work of Karl Rahner, King suggests that "the question of God is *the* human question" and that experience of God is common to all persons, but that there is no univer-sal naming of this experience.[4] The primary moments of experience of God for King occur in such dimensions of life as "silence in solitude, re-sponsible freedom, generous love, death and enduring meaning, social involvement, guilt and forgiveness."[5] The dynamic within these experiences appears to be the involvement of one's whole being in the discovery of that ultimate mystery toward which human life universally longs and is directed.[6]

For King, lived experience of God is experience of the presence of God as totally Other. God can neither be reduced to nor be separated from human experience.[7] In the Christian tradition, King claims:

> God is what we touch upon in our deepest human experience. We touch here not on an empty abyss but a self-bestowing source of the

fullness of life even out of death. God is the presence within at the core of our being which is totally other and embodied in the man Jesus. God as immanent is Spirit; God as transcendent is Father; God as incarnate is Son.[8]

King's approach is deductive if the task, as he describes it, is to explore human experience to find what in one's experience "corresponds" to already established theological notions of God. For a Christian, the naming of one's experience of God appears to mean that one interprets the data of human experience in such ways as to verify the reality of God as described by traditional Christian beliefs and doctrines. Does a deductive approach, however, speak sufficiently to contemporary Christians who raise questions concerning the function of traditional Christian images and doctrinal statements about God? What happens in the experience of revelation to the raw data of human experience of God? How can this data be named and interpreted inductively?

Denis Edwards approaches his study, *Human Experience of God*, from much the same perspective as J. Norman King.[9] In addition to the thought of Karl Rahner, Edwards draws upon the work of John of the Cross. Edwards begins with a concern that the Roman Catholic tradition restore its attention to the role of experience in faith instead of continuing its sixteenth-century Tridentine preoccupation with dogmatic theology. Like King, Edwards starts from the premise that "God is not an object in the world but a reality transcending all actual and possible objects."[10]

Preservation of the notion of God's transcendence is central to Edward's understanding of human experience of God. He writes:

> There is a tradition in theology which is hesitant to speak of the human experience of God. There are important reasons for this. One of them is the need to preserve God's transcendence, and any theological language that fails to safeguard this transcendence is automatically and rightly suspect. Where experience is taken to mean the same thing as knowledge or comprehension, then the phrase "experience of God" is rightly called into question. I hope to make clear that experience and conceptual knowledge are not the same thing. It is possible to show that while we do not have access to God's inner being, and while God always transcends our intellectual comprehension, yet we can and do experience the presence and activity of this Holy One in a pre-conceptual way.[12]

For his understanding of "experience," Edwards draws upon the work of John E. Smith who claims that experience is always double dimensional. It "involves both encounter and the interpretation of the encounter. There is always the reflective conceptual awareness of what we experience, but this points back to the original experiential encounter."[13] All human experience is mediated, interpreted, and subjective. Experience of God is always mediated because it occurs in and through everyday experience.[14] One's experience of God comes through events which in turn are mediated through one's own consciousness in such a way that any immediate sense of God is never entirely unmediated.

Edwards proposes three ways in which the human experiences reality: sense, intellect, and preconceptual experiences.[15] God transcends sense and intellect. Experience of God, therefore, is always preconceptual experience, because any human conceptualizations about God are necessarily inadequate images of incomprehensible and ultimate mystery. Like King, Edwards claims that there is a universal dynamism within the human that moves the human toward an infinity that remains mysterious.

The moments of the experience of mystery are much the same as those distinguished by King. Edwards describes moments of "grace" which in turn are understood as "the experience of something which transcends us, which breaks in upon our day to day existence in a mysterious way, and which we experience as a gift given to us."[16] These moments of grace occur either in positive experiences of a fullness and richness which the human cannot attribute to oneself (interpersonal love, childbirth, creativity, forgiveness, beauty of nature), or in negative experiences of human limitation and finitude (vulnerability, death, failure, loneliness, alienation).[17]

Edwards echoes Rahner's understanding of the mysticism of everyday life, but the influence of John of the Cross is also evident in the following distinctions:

> "Mystical experience," of course, is experience of God. But mystical experience is usually, and properly, equated with contemplative moments in prayer. Experience of God as I want to speak of it is wider than this, including both contemplative prayer and pre-conceptual experiences of God that occur because grace is poured out in our everyday lives and in our hearts. Some theologians have extended the word "mysticism" to cover our daily experience of God's grace and they speak of the "mysticism of everyday life." It seems preferable, however, to speak of experience of God as a broad term with mystical experience keeping its traditional meaning as one kind of experience of God, that which occurs in contemplative prayer.[18]

In much the same way as King, Edwards argues that Christian experience of God is dependent upon and in some way derived from Jesus' own encounter with his Father. In addition, Edwards identifies many principles of authentic experience of God among which he includes the characteristics trinitarian, ecclesial, mystical, social, and personal.[19] Edwards writes:

> The best procedure is not to describe God and then ask where we experience such a God. Rather, we must first ask where it is in human life that a person experiences moments of mystery and transcendence, and then we can draw upon the traditional, powerful word "God" and use

> this to speak of the one toward whom such experiences point. Then we
> can look to the Gospel of Jesus to illuminate our understanding of
> God. . . . In the first place it can be said that any genuine experience of
> God will resonate with what we learn from the Gospels. For a Chris-
> tian all experience of God depends upon and is in some way derivative
> from Jesus' own experience of his Father as Abba.[20]

What then is the relationship of this traditional, powerful word "God" to
present human experience of God? How does the traditional Christian
symbol of God resonate with what one learns today from the Gospels? In
what way is Jesus' *Abba* experience universally normative of Christian religious experience?[21]

John F. Haught commences his exploration into the common ground
of human discourse about God with the question: *"What* is God?"[22] He
asks whether there is anything identifiable and universal to human experience "to which the name `God' might possibly refer."[23] In this way,
Haught appears to approach his study about human experience of God in
the same deductive manner and with the same presuppositions as King
and Edwards. Haught focuses his discussion of human experience of
God, however, on the description of God "the divine." Haught claims
that speaking of God in gender-neutral rather than gender-specific images
allows one to explore ultimacy from theist and/or non-theist perspectives.
In this way, Haught proposes to locate transcendence in the ordinary life
experiences of "depth, future, freedom, beauty, and truth."[24] Haught's
sources include theologians and philosophers such as Paul Tillich, Alfred
North Whitehead, Paul Ricoeur, Bernard Lonergan, and Karl Rahner.[25]

Haught concludes that any metaphor for God must come back to the
word "mystery" as the final and only satisfactory way to name one's human experience of "the `whatness' of God."[26] All other metaphors are in-
adequate. If God is experienced primarily as ultimate mystery, human
experience of God is experience of "the inexhaustible depths of reality."[27]
To speak of God as mystery, however, is not to speak of God as that
which is as yet humanly unsolved or unknowable. For Haught, much like
King and Edwards, to speak of God as mystery is to name the locus of
God as resting in the positive and/or negative experiences of life which
evoke a sense of human limitation and contingency. Furthermore, our relationship to mystery is what defines and determines what it means to be
truly human:

> It is our fundamental openness to mystery that sets us apart from the
> animal and grounds the self-transcendent nature of our lives. It is our
> openness to mystery that constitutes the foundation of our freedom and
> liberates us from the slavery of mere normality. It is because of our
> capacity for mystery that we experience the uneasiness and anxiety that
> provoke us to move beyond the status quo and to seek more intense

beauty and more depth of truth. In short, mystery is what makes a truly human life possible in the first place.[28]

It follows that the role of religion is to encourage human openness to the reality of mystery which our social and cultural patterns have repressed or distorted.

Haught does not examine the role of Christian tradition and human experience of God or that of any other religious tradition. He does stress that the word "God" is essential to theistic religion, and "it cannot be dropped completely from our Western vocabulary for naming the mysterious dimension of our existence."[29] Where Haught intersects with traditional Christian naming of the experience of God is in his emphasis that mystery has a personal, gracious, and self-giving nature.[30] Similarly, the traditional descriptions of the transcendent and immanent dimensions of Jesus' Abba experience appear reflective of Haught's notion of the nearness and remoteness of God:

> In fact there is no contradiction between the absence and the nearness of God, and God's absence may even be understood as essential for the sake of the nearness. The unavailability of the divine is a necessary condition for the intimacy of God with the world and human persons. By not intruding into or forcing itself upon the world and personal subjects the divine mystery can be understood as caringly involved with the world. Concerned that the world not lose its integrity by being absorbed into the divine or diluted into an overbearing divine "presence," God "withdraws" from the world and persons in order to let them be. This withdrawal is not, however, an abdication but rather a selfless and humble self-distancing undertaken in order to be more involved in the world and with persons than any specific localized or objective presence would permit. The divine must withhold presence precisely in order to bestow intimacy. The self-absenting of God is essential in order to give the world its autonomy and human subjects their freedom. In this sense the absence and inobviousness of mystery may be understood as the other side of its intimacy with us.[31]

For Haught, all experience of God is in essence an experience of mystery. To name God and one's experience in this way is to avoid narrow, anthropomorphic ideas of ultimacy and to understand the reality of God as beyond human definition and control.[32] But how does one describe one's experience of God if God is experienced as ultimate mystery that chooses to be intimately involved in the world by being freely absent? If God withholds presence in the world, how is the activity of God evident and operative in the world? What determines for the human that God is gracious and personal? If God is essential mystery, then how does one relate to God? What happens to Christian anthropomorphic God-language in Haught's gender-neutral notion of the "divine"?

Written prior to Haught's text, James J. Bacik's *Apologetics and the Eclipse of Mystery* reads as an interesting sequel to Haught.[33] Bacik proposes that all human consciousness necessarily experiences self-awareness in relation "to an encompassing mystery which is both the source and goal of human activity."[34] Throughout his book, Bacik develops a theoretical framework and various models for a contemporary mystagogy by examining several aspects of the work of Karl Rahner. His concern is with what he describes as the eclipse of mystery and with the vindication and/or recognition of the presence of mystery as universal to human experience.

Bacik offers a critical analysis of many of the suppositions about mystery upon which Haught appears to base his study of human experience of God. Similarly, Bacik develops key theories about human questioning and freedom that relate to the works of King, Edwards, and Haught: (1) there is a mysterious depth to human experience; (2) this mystery draws the human to it and is experienced as gratuitous and gracious; (3) this mystery can be related to and named by the Judeo-Christian understanding of God revealed in Jesus Christ. If what Bacik suggests is true, why in our times is there such a tremendous "eclipse of mystery"? If experience of ultimate mystery is primary to human experience, why is there a pressing need to awaken the human to this experience? Is human experience of mystery really "eclipsed," or do traditional doctrines and religious language about God merely fail to name contemporary human experience of the reality of God?

In *The Experience of God: An Invitation to Do Theology*, Dermot A. Lane examines the role of experience in theology from a perspective similar to the preceding writers.[35] Rahner's transcendental anthropology permeates Lane's emphasis that God is present in our deepest experiences of "aloneness, freedom and responsibility, love and encounter, death and hope."[36] Lane's thesis is that "God comes to us *in* experience. We receive God in experience. We do not project, create, or posit God in experience. Rather we find God, already there ahead of us, in human experience."[37] Religious experience is conscious discovery of "that which was already there in our experience but which we failed to acknowledge explicitly in the first instance."[38]

Because he understands human experience of God to be bound intimately to the process of conscious human knowing, Lane emphasizes that all religious experience is historically conditioned and biased. Because human knowing does not take place in a vacuum, doctrines and beliefs dialectically shape and determine religious experience. Lane's concern is that theology "maintain a critical correspondence between doctrine and experience" and that a "fundamental unity, therefore, should obtain in all instances between experience and doctrine. In this way, the credibility of doctrine is advanced by human experience and experience becomes the source of new religious knowledge."[39]

What Lane highlights resonates with the views of many liberationist theologians on the role of experience in faith. Lane writes: "Most of all, the theology of faith will have to reflect more critically on its indissoluble relation with God's gracious revelation, past and present, which addresses us *in* human experience and *in* the interpretations of that experience . . . ."[40] The nature and interpretation of experience are pivotal concerns of liberationist theologians, especially feminist theologians who seek "to identify how exclusively masculine perspectives on masculine experience have shaped systematic thought in theology and to identify aspects of women's experience which provide resources for a fuller understanding of human experience."[41] Consequently, many theologians are calling into question traditional patriarchal and universal notions of experience of God by demanding that the world heed the experience of those oppressed by classicism, sexism, racism, militarism, poverty, colonialism, and clericalism.

Jon Sobrino represents the voice of the marginalized and the oppressed who attempt to name and to interpret their experience of God from what Sobrino identifies as the self-manifestation of God in real history.[42] Honesty with and fidelity toward the real constitute for Sobrino the prerequisites for human experience of God and the activity of faith.[43] What Sobrino and liberation theologians most challenge are white, Western, middle-class, North American assumptions concerning the nature and function of universal human experience of God. This influence is identified well by David Tracy who states:

> . . . the voices of the others multiply – all those considered "non-persons" by the powerful but declared by the great prophets to be God's own privileged ones. All the victims of our discourses and our history have begun to discover their own discourses in ways that our discourse finds difficult to hear, much less listen to. Their voices can seem strident and uncivil – in a word, other. And they are. We have all just begun to sense the terror of that otherness. But only by beginning to listen to those other voices may we also begin to hear the otherness within our own discourse and within ourselves. What we then might begin to hear, above our chatter, are possibilities we have never dared to dream.[44]

When Christian theologians, as Tracy suggests, move to the margins to listen for contemporary experience of God, they encounter not only new voices from within the Christian tradition but other than Christian voices as well. This presents a myriad of challenges for Christian theologians to articulate their christocentric and biblical understandings of experience of God amid growing theological questions concerning the uniqueness of the entire Judeo-Christian tradition and God's revelation in

Jesus Christ. On what basis can Jesus Christ be deemed the primary source of experience of God through whom all revelation takes place and is complete? How does contemporary human experience of God dialogue with other monotheistic and/or polytheistic namings of God? In any religious tradition what constitutes an authentic experience of God, and who decides what is authentic?[45]

In *Women at the Well: Feminist Perspectives on Spiritual Direction*, Kathleen Fischer examines faith and experience from the conviction that Christianity's exclusive use of male God-language has restricted the God experience of all persons.[47] She writes as a Christian feminist theologian who believes that reconstruction of the Christian tradition is not only possible but necessary. Since language expresses and interprets experience through symbols, then all male symbols for naming one's experience of God condition one to understand God as male. Language describes one's experience, but one's experience is similarly shaped and conditioned by language.

Because male experience has been the dominant lens by which the Christian tradition has named all human experience of God, Fischer advises that it is imperative for women to name their experience of God out of their own experience so that inadequate metaphors be challenged and revisioned. Fischer also cautions that no image "functions in exactly the same way for every individual."[48] Women and men must let go of predominantly male language and give voice to their own experience of God and discover its power and importance in shaping their experience of God, self, and the interrelatedness of all of life.[49]

Although not a theological work, *Women's Ways of Knowing*[50] offers several epistemological insights which relate to the present discussion of human experience of God. In *Women's Ways of Knowing*, the authors study the effects of patriarchal bias and social conditioning on women's cognitional and personal development. Although their work is gender-specific, there is a growing conviction that their critique applies both to women's and men's experience in various ways.

Women's Ways of Knowing provides an interesting psycho-social study of women's patterns of learning. The authors identify five main categories in women's development:

> Silence, a position in which women experience themselves as mindless and voiceless and subject to the whims of external authority; received knowledge, a perspective from which women conceive themselves as capable of receiving, even reproducing, knowledge from the all-knowing external authorities but not capable of creating knowledge on their own; subjective knowledge, a perspective from which truth and knowledge are conceived of as personal, private, and subjectively known or intuited; procedural knowledge, a position in which women are invested in learning and applying objective procedures for obtaining and

communicating knowledge; and constructed knowledge, a position in which women view all knowledge as contextual, experience themselves as creators of knowledge, and value both subjective and objective strategies for knowing.[51]

What do these insights suggest about human knowledge and experience of God? In traditionally all-white, Western, male-dominated Christian churches, how does one learn about God and give voice to that experience? How have patriarchal, androcentric values suffused or silenced human experience? What more do we need to know about learning in order to learn about God in our lives?[52]

Another theologian who calls for the transformation of patriarchical metaphors which limit and distort contemporary experience of God is Sallie McFague. In her book, *Models of God: Theology for an Ecological, Nuclear Age,* McFague declares that: "I have come to see patriarchal as well as imperialistic, triumphalist metaphors for God in an increasingly grim light: this language is not only idolatrous and irrelevant – besides being oppressive to many who do not identify with it – but it may also work against the continuation of life on our planet."[53] McFague explores experience of God in terms of human relating and suggests that our way of naming this experience be open to new metaphors for God such as "mother," "lover," and "friend." Her work presupposes the Christian tradition and seeks to revision traditional trinitarian notions of God beyond "father," "son," and "spirit."

McFague's work also highlights the growing critique of dualistic, anthropocentric, hierarchical, and androcentric images for God. In human experience, is God experienced primarily as person? How does one speak of a personal God in terms of human experience, if to be human is to be female or male? How is role definition, e.g., parent, friend, descriptive of human experience of God? How thoroughly does anthropocentrism condition or distort human experience of God?

These and ensuing questions are guiding the search of many theologians to identify the ingredients of an ecological theology that will help Christians to name experience of God in light of the discoveries of contemporary science and today's ecological crisis. Often influenced by the work of geologian Thomas Berry, numerous theologians are concerned that the human join its voice with all the other living voices of the universe, such that human experience never be viewed as anthropomorphically separate or distinct from its cosmic integrity with all life forms. If the human community has come, therefore, to a new cosmic consciousness of what it means to be human, how then does this awareness relate to human experience and consciousness of God?

Berry offers a new vision of God's revelation that acknowledges a psychic-numinous dimension in all of reality such that the earth itself is

the primary mode and locus of divine presence.[54] Berry calls for openness to more than the anthropocentric experiences of ultimate mystery
found in human ecstasy and/or pain. For Berry, experience of the divine
encompasses "the world of life, of spontaneity, the world of dawn and
sunset and starlight, the world of soil and sunshine, of meadow and
woodland, of hickory and oak and maple and hemlock and pineland forests, of wildlife dwelling around us, of the river and its well-being." In
the story and reality of the universe, Berry claims, the human experiences
"the reality and values that evoke in us our deepest moments of reflection, our revelatory experience of the ultimate mystery of things."[55]

What Berry proposes, however, is not a mere romantic appreciation
of all creation. Rather, he calls for a cosmic consciousness and vision of
the interconnectedness and interrelatedness of all of life. Here especially,
Berry's cosmology calls into question patriarchical and hierarchical-dual-
istic notions of the locus, nature, and experience of God. How does the
traditional Christian symbol of God function if the earth constitutes one's
primary experience or revelation of God? Does the universe constitute
God (pantheism) or is the universe permeated with the presence of God
(panentheism)? What happens to classical metaphysical notions of God
as "eternal, immutable, impassable being" in light of the time-developmental processes of the universe, or the differentiation, subjectivity, and
communion which Berry sees as constitutive of the entire universe?[56] As
the human awakens to a deeper ecological self-consciousness, can traditional theological understandings of divine transcendence and immanence
function holistically? What are the theological implications of Berry's
thought if no one reality, though distinct, is ever unrelated to or separate
from the whole of reality, and all of reality is always in existence?

Jay B. McDaniel is one theologian who attempts to speak of experience of God in ways which recognize an ecological understanding of the
interdependence and interconnectedness of all things. McDaniel draws
upon the work of Berry and on a holistic interpretation of reality to express his understanding of "the face and voice of the Divine" in his two
major works, *Of God and Pelicans* and *Earth, Sky, Gods and Mortals.*[57]

Using the resources of process theology, McDaniel moves from
classical redemption/salvation emphases to dynamic creation/relation assumptions about God. He stresses that process theology offers styles of
thinking and modes of feeling which challenge out-moded, uniform,
mechanistic, hierarchical, and dualistic understandings of the self, world,
and God.[58] He contends that "Christians and others are at a stage in
which experimentation in naming and describing God is required and in
which, for some, the word God must be abandoned."[59]

McDaniel's understanding of divine mystery is grounded in what he
describes as "relational panentheism" and he suggests that one way to image God is by the use of the word "heart."[60] God is the heart of the uni-

verse and all other creatures are the body of this heart.[61] In McDaniel's body/heart analogy, God is a living ecological Whole in whom the long-ings of all of creation are fulfilled.[62] For McDaniel, the word *heart* speaks of relational power, vitality, centricity, affectivity, lure, and receptive diver-sity.[63] What happens, however, to traditional Christian doctrines about a per-sonal God when language such as "heart" describes experience of God? If God is experienced as "relational power, vitality, and centricity," can experi-ence of dynamic relationship be differentiated from experience of cosmic functionality and dynamic organicism? Does activity constitute being?

Although unanswered questions abound, this brief theological litera-ture review suggests several conclusions about human experience and knowledge of God. First, contemporary experience of God is conditioned significantly by a fundamental shift in human perception of reality and that language plays a critical role in this shift in consciousness. Second, theological language functions critically as both expression and interpreta-tion of human experience. While theological language names religious experience, religious experience generates theological language. Third, a critical task of current theological inquiry is to uncover what form of lan-guage best speaks to and is expressive of contemporary human experience of God. Fourth, current theological inquiry must determine the relation-ship of that language to traditional Christian doctrines about God in light of the grave dissonance recognized between traditional theology and con-temporary lived experience of faith.

In sum, Christian theology faces critical questions about the nature, function, and role of human experience in relation to traditional christo-centric and biblical understandings about human experience and the word "God." Of considerable uncertainty is how classical trinitarian and chris-tological doctrines remain functional and descriptive of contemporary hu-man experience of the nature, locus and activity of God. Furthermore, there is pressing concern as to whether the traditional Judeo-Christian symbol of God can be sufficiently reenvisioned in order for it to function within contemporary "understandings of the development of the cosmos, the evolution of life, and the movements of human history."[64]

In conclusion, perhaps there is an eternal wisdom for contemporary theologians in the caution, "Be still and know that I am God (Psalm 46:10)," and a direction for theological investigation in the advice of Karl Rahner:

> If we are to speak of the experience of God today we must, in the very nature of the theme we have set ourselves to explore, presuppose two points:
>
> 1. That there is such a thing as an experience of God, and
> 2. That it has a special and peculiar quality of its own, which it derives from our contemporary situation.[65]

Endnotes

1. See Donald L. Gelpi, *The Turn to Experience in Contemporary Theology* (New York: Paulist Press, 1994); Anthony F. Krisak, "Theological Reflection: Unfolding the Mystery," in *Handbook of Spirituality for Ministers,* ed. Robert J. Wicks (New York: Paulist Press, 1995): 308-329; and George P. Schner, "The Appeal to Experience," *Theological Studies* 50 (March 1992): 40-59. The centrality of experience to Christian theology is highlighted well by Edward Schillebeeckx who is quoted by Timothy G. McCarthy, *The Catholic Tradition: Before and After Vatican II 1978-1993* (Chicago: Loyola University Press, 1994): 127: "Christianity is not a message which has to be believed, but an experience of faith which becomes a message, and, as an explicit message, seeks to offer a new possibility of life experience to others who hear it from their own experience of life."

2. J. Norman King, *Experiencing God All Ways and Every Day* (Minneapolis: Winston Press, 1982): 5.

3. *Ibid.,* i, 7-8.

4. *Ibid.,* 5-6.

5. *Ibid.,* 7-8.

6. *Ibid.*

7. *Ibid.,* 144

8. *Ibid.,* 15

9. Denis Edwards, *Human Experience of God* (New York: Paulist Press, 1983).

10. *Ibid.,* ix.

11. *Ibid.,* 5.

12. *Ibid.,* 7.

13. *Ibid.,* 65.

14. *Ibid.,* 9-13.

15. *Ibid.,* 28.

16. *Ibid.,* 29-38

17. *Ibid.,* 14. For Rahner's "mysticism of everyday life," see Karl Rahner, "Reflections on the Experience of Grace," *Theological Investigations 3: The Theology of the Spiritual Life* (New York: Seabury Press, 1967): 86-90.

18. See Edwards, 132-35, for his eighteen characteristics of true experience of God.

19. *Ibid.,* 15, 63.

20. For further study, see Dermot Lane, *Christ at the Centre: Selected Issues in Christology* (New York: Paulist Press, 1991), and Maryanne Stevens, ed. *Reconstructing the Christ Symbol: Essays in Feminist Theology* (New York: Paulist Press, 1993).

21. John F. Haught, *What Is God? How to Think about the Divine* (New York: Paulist Press, 1986): 1.

22. *Ibid.*, 3.

23. *Ibid.*, 5.

24. *Ibid.*, 10.

25. *Ibid.*, 115.

26. *Ibid.*, 117.

27. *Ibid.*, 124.

28. *Ibid.*, 126.

29. *Ibid.*, 6, 126.

30. *Ibid.*, 130-31.

31. *Ibid.*, 8-9.

32. James J. Bacik, *Apologetics and the Eclipse of Mystery: Mystagogy According to Karl Rahner* (Notre Dame: University of Notre Dame Press, 1980).

33. *Ibid.*, xiii.

34. Dermot A. Lane, *The Experience of God: An Invitation to do Theology* (New York: Paulist Press, 1981).

35. *Ibid.*, 23.

36. *Ibid.*, viii.

37. *Ibid.*, 15.

38. *Ibid.*, 22-23.

39. *Ibid.*, 89.

40. Ellen Leonard, "Experience As a Source for Theology," *CTSA Proceedings* 43 (1988): 48.

41. Jon Sobrino, *Spirituality of Liberation: Toward Political Holiness* (Maryknoll, New York: Orbis Books, 1988): 21.

42. *Ibid.*

43. Quoted by Leonard, 60.

44. See Sandra M. Schneiders, "The Bible and Feminism," and Mary Catherine Hilkert, "Experience and Tradition – Can the Center Hold?" in Catherine Mowry LaCugna, ed. *Freeing Theology: The Essentials of Theology in Feminist Perspective* (New York: HarperSanFrancisco, 1993): 3-57, 59-82.

45. Kathleen Fischer, *Women At the Well: Feminist Perspectives on Spiritual Direction* (New York: Paulist Press, 1988): 53.

46. *Ibid.*, 58.

47. *Ibid.*, 61. For a detailed study of the use of women's experience and female imagery as a resource for describing the Christian experience of God, see Elizabeth A. Johnson, *She Who Is: The Mystery of God in Feminist Theological Discourse* (New York: Crossroad, 1992).

48. Mary Field Belenky, et. al., *Women's Ways of Knowing: The Development of Self, Voice and Mind* (New York: Basic Books, Inc., 1986).

49. *Ibid.,* 15.

50. Significant to this inquiry but beyond presentation within the scope of this essay is the work of Bernard J. F. Lonergan on the relationship to theology of patterns of conscious human knowing. See especially *Method in Theology* (New York: The Seabury Press, 1972), and *Insight: A Study of Human Understanding* (San Francisco: Harper & Row Publishers, 1958[1957]).

51. Sally McFague, *Models of God: Theology for an Ecological, Nuclear Age* (Philadelphia: Fortress Press, 1987): ix. See also McFague, *The Body of God: An Ecological Theology* (Minneapolis, Fortress Press, 1993).

52. For development of this understanding see Thomas Berry, "The Divine and Our Present Revelatory Moment," in *Befriending the Earth: A Theology of Reconciliation Between Humans and the Earth,* eds. Stephen Dunn and Anne Lonergan (Mystic, Connecticut: Twenty-Third Publications, 1991): 3-28, and Berry, "The Gaia Theory: Its Religious Implications," in *ARC* 22 (1994): 7-19.

53. Thomas Berry, *The Dream of the Earth* (San Francisco: Sierra Club Books, 1988): 176.

54. *Ibid.* Avery Dulles offers an extensive analysis of the existence and nature of revelation in his book, *Models of Revelation* (New York: Image Books, 1983). Study of Dulles' third model, Revelation as Inner Experience, shows that the Rahnerian authors considered in this paper appear to focus on revelation as the self-manifestation of God in the depths of the human spirit. Berry and other liberationist writers seem to operate more from Dulles' fifth model, Revelation as New Awareness, which sees revelation as a breakthrough to a higher level of consciousness as humankind is drawn to a fuller participation in divine creativity. Dulles' presentation on symbolic mediation (131-154) offers an interesting hypothesis in light of feminist claims that we need to re-envision our traditional religious symbols and images for God.

55. Berry, *Dream of the Earth:* 134-135, and *Befriending the Earth:* 15-16. For further discussion of the relationship of contemporary experience to classical theism and trinitarian theology which goes beyond the limits of this essay, see the following creative works: Catherine Mowry LaCugna, *God For Us: The Trinity & Christian Life,* (New York: HarperSanFrancisco, 1991); Elizabeth A. Johnson, *She Who Is,* and "The Search for the Living God." John M. Kelly Lecture. Toronto: The University of St. Michael's College, 8 March 1994.

56. Jay B. McDaniel, *Of God and Pelicans: A Theology of the Reverence for Life* (Louisville, Kentucky: Westminster/John Knox Press, 1989) and *Earth, Sky, Gods and Mortals: Developing an Ecological Spirituality* (Mystic, CT: Twenty-Third Publications, 1990).

57. McDaniel, "Six Characteristics of a Postpatriarchal Christianity," *Zygon* 25 (June 1990): 197.

58. *Ibid.,* 212.

59. McDaniel, *Pelicans:* 27.

60. *Ibid.,* 48-49

61. *Ibid.,* 48.

62. *Ibid.,* 212-216.

63. Gordon D. Kaufman, "Nature, History and God: Toward an Integrated Conceptualization," *Zygon* 27 (December 1992): 379.

64. Karl Rahner, "The Experience of God Today," in *Theological Investigations* XI, trans. David Bourke (New York: Seabury, 1975): 149.

28

Toward a Theological Perspective on the Implicate Order of David Bohm

Moni McIntyre

IN PONDERING THE WORK OF DAVID BOHM, RENEE WEBER DESCRIBED A curious paradox of our times: "the more nearly physics approaches the twenty-first century, the closer it seems to get to the cosmology of the remote past. Thus, the scientific discoveries of our own time are moving us toward ideas in many ways indistinguishable from those held by the sages and seers of India and Greece."[1] For example, one can see two very different developments in human thought since the time of Heraclitus of Ephesus and Parmenides of Elea, ancient Greek thinkers who predate Plato and Aristotle. The followers of Heraclitus include such diverse groups and individuals as native peoples of North America and mystics,[2] Taoists,[3] Albert Einstein, and David Bohm. These persons see the world as a dynamic, interrelated, nonhierarchical whole. They believe change is the fundamental principle of the universe.

The earlier followers of Parmenides, however, including those in the tradition of Plato and Aristotle as well as those who write and believe in the teachings of the traditional Christian churches, perceived the world as hierarchical and perfectly ordered with human beings occupying the dominant role after God and angels. They related most easily to a transcendent and unchanging God who keeps all things in their proper order. God, people, and the world are related in an organic whole. Aristotle and Aquinas are among the chief spokespersons for this world view.

The idea of the atom grew out of attempts to compromise the views of Heraclitus and Parmenides. The unchanging Being, the Greek atomists believed, was manifest in the basic building blocks which were the smallest indivisible units of matter. These atoms were passive and believed to be dead particles that moved around presumably by spiritual but external forces. Capra notes that "in subsequent centuries, this image became an essential element of Western thought, of the dualism between mind and matter, between body and soul."[4]

In contrast to the organic view of Aristotle and Aquinas, a picture of the world as static and mechanistic emerged. With the help of observation as well as reason, scientists concluded that human beings are related to the rest of nature and not separate beings created by God. In this picture human beings were seen to be as grains of dust in a huge universe of material bodies (galaxies, stars, etc.), each of which is ultimately composed of atoms and molecules that can be compared to parts of a giant machine. As far as anyone has been able to determine, this machine does not constitute a whole with meaning. Each part exists independently and interacts blindly through the forces it exerts on the other parts. Human beings are insignificant; meaning amounts to the significance each person can give to what he or she does since the universe is indifferent to human affairs. The notion of God is used to fill gaps in scientific accounts. This line of thought reached its zenith in physics in the nineteenth century and has come to permeate most of modern science and technology. In the late twentieth century, this God-of-the-gaps is often used, among other things, to justify particular right-wing ideologies.

David Bohm was one physicist who rejected the limitations that a mechanistic world view imposes. Part I of this chapter is a consideration of the place of mechanism in history as sandwiched between the older organic world view and the newer quantum theory. Part II identifies Bohm as a contemporary scientist who has played a major role in the development of the "new physics." Part III offers some challenges of Bohm's thought to contemporary religious thinkers.

Part I: The Decline of Mechanism

David Bohm described the main feature of the mechanistic order in this way:

> the world is regarded as constituted of entities which are *outside each other*, in the sense that they exist independently in different regions of space (and time) and interact through forces that do not bring about any changes in their essential natures. The machine gives a typical illustration of such a system of order.[5]

He contrasts the mechanistic model to the organicist model:

> ... in a living organism, for example, each part grows in the context of the whole, so that it does not exist independently, nor can it be said that it merely "interacts" with the others, without itself being essentially affected in this relationship.[6]

The influences of mechanism can be felt all over the globe. This particular approach to the world became especially prominent during the last century when it seemed to dominate the earth, although it can be traced back to the seventeenth-century observations and conclusions of Sir Isaac Newton (1642-1727) and his contemporaries.[7] Because it was in physics that mechanism became most prominent, it is worthwhile to examine the shape it took there in order to understand the beginnings of this pervasive world view. In so doing we can recognize the inherent limitations of mechanism that have led to alternative world views.

In the first place, mechanism reduces the world to a set of basic elements, e.g., atoms, electrons, protons, quarks, which are seen to operate in various fields, e.g., electromagnetic and gravitational. These particles have an *external* relationship to one another since the fundamental nature of each one is to be independent of the other. Elements, therefore, are related but not interrelated, i.e., they are like parts of a machine which interact mechanically. The fundamental nature of one entity does not fundamentally alter the fundamental nature of any other entity.

The mechanistic world view may be contrasted with the organic world view of Aristotle and Aquinas which sees the parts of the world related *internally*. The fundamental nature of each part of the organism is such that it may be fundamentally altered when another part is disturbed. (One need only consider the Pauline image of the body of Christ for an example of how the writers of the Christian scriptures made use of the organic model.) Whereas the mechanistic world view recognizes the existence of organisms, they are understood to be at base *externally* related parts operating in a mechanistic manner.

This mechanistic view of the world is not something that can be proven. On the contrary, persons must accept this radical reductionism as an article of faith. Until this century there seemed to be little reason to doubt the truth of mechanism's claims. Bohm noted that "the Newtonian form of insight worked very well for several centuries but ultimately (like the ancient Greek insights that came before) it led to unclear results when extended into new domains."[8] In fact, Ian Barbour states that in the last century theoretical physicist "Lord Kelvin asserted that a person does not really understand something until he has a mechanical model of it."[9] With the advent of the relativity and quantum theories, Lord Kelvin's assertion, which worked for his time, has been found to be of little use to high energy physicists in our time.

The theory of relativity was revolutionary because it destroyed the mechanistic synthesis that Newtonian physicists had come to regard as true. Whereas traditional physics divided the world into matter and energy while giving priority to matter, Einstein claimed that these were different forms of one reality. In particular, Einstein's ideas altered our conception of particles in a drastic way. No longer do we regard particles as solid bits of matter which form the basic building blocks of the rest of matter. Instead, we now speak of fields that spread continuously through space. Bohm concluded that

> the idea of a separately and independently existent particle is seen to be, at best, an abstraction furnishing a valid approximation only in a certain limited domain. Ultimately, the entire universe (with all its

"particles," including those constituting human beings, their laboratories, observing instruments, etc.) has to be understood as a single undivided whole, in which analysis into separately and independently existent parts has no fundamental status.[10]

Like Heraclitus, then, the universe of Einstein as understood by Einstein and his followers is one unbroken whole in flowing movement. The claims of the mechanistic world view that small bodies move in empty space can no longer be substantiated in the face of the relativity theory.

Einstein retained some of the elements of mechanism in his relativity theory, however. For example, he maintained that fields interact only *locally* with one another, i.e., one field could only be affected by another field which was connected to it or separated by an extremely short distance. Still, this field theory was a significant step beyond the conventional mechanistic world view.

Quantum theory is another major contribution of Einstein to modern physics which, along with relativity theory, forced scientists to adopt a much more subtle and holistic model of the universe.[11] The demise of mechanism's reign became certain with this new development. Quantum theory differs from the relativity theory in that "all action, all motion, is in discrete indivisible units, called *quanta*. (Hence the name, quantum theory)."[12]

Capra explains how the action of quanta contradicts the classical notion of movement in physics:

> The subatomic units of matter are very abstract entities which have a dual aspect. Depending on how we look at them, they appear sometimes as particles, sometimes as waves; and this dual nature is also exhibited by light which can take the form of electromagnetic waves or particles.[13]

The "dual aspect" to which Capra refers is an important feature in breaking the hold of mechanism upon the thought of physicists. Because any system can demonstrate wave-like or particle-like features depending upon its environment, mechanism's theory of solid particles clearly cannot stand. This tendency of an element to vary according to conditions is much more akin to what one would expect of a living and even conscious being than a machine.

Unlike the relativity theory, the quantum theory provides for *non-local* connection.[14] In other words, whereas both in classical physics and in the relativity theory strong connections can only occur either when two surfaces or basic elements contact one another or are extremely close together, quantum theory holds that basic elements or fields may be disturbed by other basic elements or fields even when they are not in close proximity. This has enormous ramifications: (a) if it is true that all elements of the universe are somehow indivisibly connected, then the world cannot be divided into independently externally related parts; (b) the fundamental nature of each part depends upon its environment; and (c) the nature of any part may depend to a large extent upon what is happening in distant regions of space.[15]

Such observations and speculations which are commonplace among nuclear physicists do not touch the lives of those who have no need to operate at such a high level of refinement. For most persons, including the scientists who predate the quantum theory, the level of refinement achieved by classical physics is sufficient. It is only since the advent of sophisticated equipment and very complicated theories that we have come to realize the limitations of a perception of the world which accounts for only *external* relationships between and among entities.

Another feature of subatomic existence that physicists have discovered is that one cannot apply classical laws to the behavior of particles since they merely exhibit tendencies to exist. Gone is the complete determinism of Newtonian physics. No one can predict with certainty where a subatomic particle will be at a certain time, or how an atomic process will occur. Scientists can only predict the odds. They must reckon with wavelike patterns of probabilities which ultimately represent probabilities of interconnections rather than probabilities of things.

In sum, the adherents of mechanism maintain that entities are solid and affect each other only *externally* and *locally*. Those who hold the quantum theory, on the other hand, believe that the fundamental nature of entities shifts with the environment and that relationships between and among entities are *internal* and *nonlocal*.

In the next section I will consider David Bohm's theory of the implicate order which he saw as a corrective to the randomness of the quantum theory. First, however, I will give a brief biographical sketch of David Bohm and describe his early approach to science and philosophy.

Part II: David Bohm and the Implicate Order

The son of a furniture dealer, David Bohm was born in Wilkes-Barre, Pennsylvania in 1917. He studied physics at the University of California with J. Robert Oppenheimer. He retired from Birkbeck College at the University of London, England where he was a professor of physics. He died suddenly in 1992.

Even as a young man, Bohm was reluctant to separate the fields of science and philosophy:

> I learned . . . that many of my fundamental interests were what other people called philosophical and that scientists tended to look down on philosophy as not being very serious. This created a problem for me, as I was never able to see any inherent separation between science and philosophy.

Indeed in earlier times, science was called *natural philosophy* and this corresponded perfectly with the way I saw the whole field. . . . Although I was quite capable of mastering these mathematical techniques [in graduate school] I did not feel it was worth going on with, not without a deeper philosophical ground and the spirit of common inquiry.[16]

Bohm became acquainted with the work of Niels Bohr through Oppenheimer. Bohr's concept of the oneness of the universe made a big impression on Bohm and was an overriding concern of Bohm's until his death.

Perhaps best known for his early work on the interactions of electrons in metals, Bohm "showed that their individual, haphazard movement concealed a highly organized and cooperative behavior called plasma oscillation. This intimation of an order underlying apparent chaos was pivotal in Bohm's development."[17] It is this pursuit of order in the universe that took him beyond the randomness of quantum mechanics which gives only the probability of an experimental result.[18]

The notion of order is common both to the ancient Greeks and classical physics. For example, the order of the Greeks consisted of increasing perfection from earth to the heavens. Each part along the way strives to reach its proper place and to fulfill its appropriate function in the whole. This kind of order, however, is completely irrelevant to Newtonian physicists. The notion of order that matters for them is the mechanical order which Descartes introduced that can be worked and expressed mathematically in terms of coordinates.[19]

When Bohm began to consider what relativity and quantum theory had in common, he realized that they both maintain an unbroken wholeness of the universe. Although each theory does it in a radically different way, the common element between them is the notion of unbroken wholeness. Bohm wondered if it would be possible to develop a new order that would be suitable for thinking about the basic nature of the universe as unbroken wholeness. Clearly such an order would be different from that of the ancient Greeks and the Newtonian physicists.[20]

Bohm wrote a great deal on the notion of order.[21] He concluded that a general and explicit definition of order is not actually possible: "You cannot define order (I will take this for granted): order exists; order is perceived. But we can develop certain notions of order."[22] We rely mainly on our perceptual experience for this tacit sense of order.

The lens serves as a common analogy for the mechanistic order. For example, "in normal photography a lens is used to focus light from an object, so that each small section of the object is reproduced in a small section of the photographic plate."[23] This point-to-point correspondence emphasizes the notion of point as fundamental in the sense of order and supports the idea that the world is in fact constituted of several parts or points which interact externally and locally. Telescopes, micro-

scopes, and very sophisticated cameras have thus reinforced the mechanistic way of thinking.

Bohm suggested that the hologram is a good analogy for the new
order which he proposed. The hologram (from the Greek words meaning
"whole" and "to write") "makes a photographic record of the interference
pattern of the light waves that have come off an object."[24] Bohm explained that

> the key new feature of this record is that each part contains information
> about the *whole object* (so that there is no point-to-point correspon-
> dence of object and recorded image). That is to say, the form and
> structure of the entire object may be said to be *enfolded* within each
> region of the photographic record. When one shines light on any re-
> gion, this form and structure are then *unfolded*, to give a recognizable
> image of the whole object once again.[25]

The hologram, then, illustrates the kind of order Bohm calls implicate,
which affirms the internality of the whole to each "part" of the universe,
such that "one may say that everything is enfolded into everything."[26]
This contrasts with the unfolded or explicate order illustrated by the lens,
which is the order given mathematical expression in the Cartesian coordinates and which remains dominant in current physics.

The notion of the enfolded or implicate order is central to Bohm's
science and philosophy. He saw the hologram as a good analogy of his
idea because it parallels how the implicate order is relevant to the quantum behavior of matter. But it is only a static record. In fact, there is a
constant dynamic pattern of waves coming off an object and interfering
with the original wave. Within that interference pattern of movement,
many objects are enfolded in each region of space and time. Whereas
classical physics claims that reality is actually little particles that separate
the world into independent elements, Bohm proposed the reverse: the
fundamental reality is the enfoldment and unfoldment, and these particles
are abstractions from that.

Bohm developed other examples to demonstrate the properties of his
new theory of the implicate order. One popular example Bohm used is
that of a drop of insoluble ink placed in viscous fluid, such as glycerine
or treacle, between two concentric glass cylinders. If the outer cylinder
is turned very slowly, the ink will get spread out in a band and finally
become invisible. If the cylinder is backward, the glycerine will draw
back into its original form and the ink drop will be visible again.

Bohm believed that the movement of all matter can be discussed in
terms of this folding and unfolding. He called this "*the holomovement*,
which is an unbroken and undivided totality."[27] Everything emerges by
unfoldment from the holomovement, then enfolds back into the implicate
order. Bohm called the enfolding process "implicating" and the unfolding
"explicating." For Bohm, "the implicate and explicate together are a

flowing, undivided wholeness. Every part of the universe is related to every other part but in different degrees."[28] The holomovement is Bohm's metaphor for the essence of new order which abolishes dualism and replaces it with a pervasive monism and holism. In this way Bohm pushed "forward" toward the ancient claims of both the Eastern and Western wisdom traditions which held that the nature of reality is flux.

Bohm's holomovement presses for a unified field theory in which even the knower is integrated within the process, enacting, recording, and observing it. John B. Cobb, Jr. explains why both the quantum particle theory and the quantum field theory are inadequate for Bohm's thinking: "Bohm's deepest dissatisfaction with the dominant form of quantum theory is that it remains at the phenomenal level. He wants to know not only how to predict what the appearances will be under certain circumstances but also what is going on whether observed or not."[29] Bohm believed that quantum phenomena can be interpreted realistically. As Robert John Russell indicates, Bohm "sees the idea of a second quantum potential and a super-implicate order as legitimate alternatives to the field theory approach which will eventually lead to testable predictions and carry the additional philosophical advantage of allowing a realistic interpretation of nature."[30] The implicate order can thus be seen as a corrective to the quantum theory in that it is a realistic and not just a phenomenalistic approach to reality.

Bohm described the movement within the implicate order in this way: ". . . all matter, animate and inanimate, unfolds from a greater whole and folds back again into it, in an endless process of replication of forms that are similar but different."[31] There are impressive conclusions that follow from this line of thought. For example,

> there is no absolutely sharp "cut" or break between consciousness, life, and matter, whether animate or inanimate [although] each of these can be analyzed in thought as categories with a degree of relative independence upon each other. This makes it possible for each to be studied, up to a point, in its own right.[32]

I will discuss consciousness and matter in greater detail in Part III.

Bohm wished his readers to be cognizant of the difference between "parts" and "fragments." The former are intrinsically related to the whole whereas the latter have been broken up or smashed as a watch that has been smashed by a hammer. Parts are relatively stable, independent, and autonomous sub-wholes.

Bohm pointed out that fragmentation "arises when an attempt is made to impose divisions in an arbitrary fashion, without any regard for a wider context, even to the point of ignoring essential connections to the rest of the world."[33] While there can be useful instances of fragmentation, e.g., at a quarry where a geologist smashes rocks in order to discover certain properties, Bohm was concerned about the destructive aspect of frag-mentation which "disposes the mind to regard divisions between things as absolute and final, rather than as ways of thinking that have useful-ness."[34]

N. Max Wildiers expresses a similar concern about the damaging ef-fects of fragmentary thought as they have manifested themselves in mechanism. He identifies the modern age's problem as that of an out-moded theology which continually withdrew from the world. Wildiers explains:

> It is precisely in the concept of hierarchical order that this fossilization process can be clearly seen. What was once an imaginative concept that stimulated man's intellectual, moral, and political activity, was on account of the new view of the cosmos gradually deprived of its intrin-sic value, and it finally became a meaningless notion incapable of evoking a response in modern man.[35]

The problem with the hierarchical order is that it split what should not have been split. It divided the world into fragments and set up arbitrary divisions between matter and spirit, man and woman, and opened the door to sexism, classism, and racism. This is what Bohm pointed to – but did not explore – in his treatises on wholeness and fragmentation. Clearly, there are religious implications in his thinking on these matters. I will consider these in the next section.

By way of summary, we can see that David Bohm was no ordinary physicist who looked only for measurable results of his work. From his youth he could not separate the issues of science and philosophy, and we see that in his later years he still sought their relationship. His early fas-cination with order persisted even to the development of his own "impli-cate order," the end of which is, after all, eternity.[36] The implicate order, according to Bohm, is an improvement over the quantum theory because it is applicable to the level of realism as well as the phenomenal level.

In Part III I will examine some of the theological implications of Bohm's thought and look at some critiques of his work offered by phi-losophers and theologians.

Part III: The Theological Implications of Bohm's Thought

Ian Barbour believes that David Bohm's work is "ripe for theologi-cal interpretation, since concepts such as cosmos, wholeness, fragmenta-tion, and implicate order are extended as integrating metaphors to all of experience."[37] Indeed, Barbour believes that through the work of Bohm "can come new language for God and human nature, for estrangement and community, for religious experience in contemporary culture."[38]

In this section I will consider the impact that Bohm's thought has had on theological studies, although, as Robert John Russell points out, the theological implications of Bohm's work have scarcely been tapped: "Clearly, though the theological dimensions to Bohm's work are relatively unexplored, as Bohm's scientific ideas continue to develop and change, their religious implications will require careful tracking."[39] The following survey is intended to acquaint the reader with the potential that waits to be developed as we look at the beginnings of the implications of Bohm's ideas on God, the human person, and the world.

A. God

Bohm understood himself to be a physicist and was therefore quite cautious about making theological statements. He was aware, however, that others had extracted elements of his writings and examined them for their religious implications. For example, while some writers wished to equate the holomovement with God, Bohm wrote: "I myself would prefer to regard this as no more than an analogy or a metaphor, that may be useful for giving insight, but that should not be taken too literally."[40]

Ted Peters discusses the question of the divinity of the holomovement and notes that it "performs the job done by God in the Descartes' system."[41] It is commonly agreed that Bohm was pursuing religious questions, although he was not providing theological answers. Peters observes that "whether or not Bohm himself engages in theological inquiry, we must recognize that talk about the whole suggests talk about God. To raise the question of the whole of reality is to ask about the divine."[42]

To be sure, Bohm did have unmistakably theological notions about the personal nature of the ultimate ground:

> . . . I feel that all emerges from some ultimate ground. When I see the immense order of the universe (and especially the brain of man), I cannot escape feeling that this ground enfolds a supreme intelligence. Although it is not quite so evident, I would say also that this intelligence is permeated with compassion and love.[43]

John B. Cobb, Jr. notes that in the Indian traditions there is a tendency to separate the "unutterable ultimate" and the personal God. Cobb concludes that "in a general way what [Bohm] calls the ultimate ground corresponds with the impersonal absolute, whereas what he calls the whole resembles the personal God."[44] He reasons further: "If this is so, then perhaps intelligence and compassion should be relocated in the whole, with the ground understood to be beyond all distinctions except as it expresses itself in and is qualified by the whole of which it is the ground."[45] Cobb believes that by separating these two notions of the divine and thus making the impersonal absolute distinct from the personal deity, intelligence and compassion can be relocated in the whole and consequently preserve both of the elements in Bohm's thinking, i.e., the whole and the ultimate ground can be preserved. Furthermore, in making this distinction, Cobb is "persuaded that a convincing vision can be formed, and that within the vision the Christian testimony can be heard anew and with greater power."[46] Cobb does not develop the details of this vision in this article.

Robert John Russell sees Bohm as a panentheist. Russell believes that Bohm's ideas "point to transcendent, even self-transcending, features of nature which could correspond to divine presence. Hence on balance Bohm is probably closest to a panentheistic and impersonal conception of God."[47] Russell does not believe that Bohm's view of nature leads one to conclude that God is personal, although his notion of nature as a gift of a loving and redeeming God does not rule out this idea.

David Ray Griffin criticizes Bohm for wavering among three visions of God, namely, the Vedantist-Neoplatonic way, the Thomistic way, and the Whiteheadian way.[48] In so doing, Griffin maintains, Bohm "[contradicted] our deepest intuitions about time, freedom, and causation."[49] Griffin suggests that Bohm should reformulate his notion of wholeness by strengthening his idea of the holomovement. Bohm could do this without equating God with the dynamic activity of enfolding and unfolding. Instead, God would become the all-inclusive, intelligent, compassionate embodiment of the holomovement. Bohm did not take up Griffin's suggestion. Instead, in words which breathe a kind of mysticism, Bohm described the experience of meaning for beings within the explicate order:

> . . . the explicit order, which dominates ordinary "common sense" experience as well as classical physics, appears to stand by itself. But actually this is only an approximation and it cannot be understood properly apart from its ground in the primary reality of the implicate order, i.e., the holomovement. All things found in the explicate order emerge from the holomovement and ultimately fall back into it. They endure only for some time, and while they last, their existence is sustained in a constant process of unfoldment and re-enfoldment, which gives rise to their relatively stable and independent forms in the explicate order.[50]

The freedom of God is an especially difficult issue in this discussion. Mechanistic determinism had no room for divine initiative and freedom. God could either be immanent within the system but bound by it (as in the thought of Spinoza), or outside of it and irrelevant to it (as in Deism). God could not be both immanent and free. Bohm, however, did not ask the question of the freedom of God in the familiar way of the thinkers of these other ages. His stress was on inter-relatedness and inter-connections. What is fundamental is the infinite complexity of nature and not determinacy or indeterminacy. We cannot satisfactorily reduce nature to familiar categories. To speak of the freedom of God, therefore, is outside of Bohm's realm.

To summarize the foregoing, it is quite clear that Bohm did not care to settle the theological questions that arose from his thoughts on the holomovement. Correspondingly, many writers believe that there are important questions that arise out of Bohm's thought that need to be addressed. There seems to be a consensus among these writers that one must take Bohm on his own terms and not attempt to twist his ideas around previously articulate dogmas that have been worked out by scholars operating within a different world order. For to do that would likely do violence to the possibilities that lie in wait for future scholars who would be willing to grapple with the raw data of a new age and face another situation not unlike that of Galileo in which a person's thoughts are condemned before they are even understood.

B. The Human Person

Three aspects of the human emerge as primary in Bohm's thought: consciousness, morality, and language.

1) *Consciousness.* Bohm may be presenting a new model for consciousness as well as a new model for cosmology. He regards consciousness as an essential feature of the holomovement, and he claims that much of our experience suggests that the implicate order is natural for understanding consciousness since consciousness is enfolded in each individual. For example, the movement of the implicate order is apparent in consciousness when it is shared between persons as they look at an object and verify that it is the same object. Any high level of consciousness is a social process and evokes the implicate order. Language, which is social, i.e., outside of an individual, evokes meaning which is inside of a person.

Meaning, according to Bohm, is the bridge between consciousness and matter: "meaning enfolds the whole world into me, and vice versa – that enfolded meaning is unfolded as action, through my body and then through the world."[51] Bohm believes that an understanding of how neurotransmitters carry meaning and affect the immune system could be the beginning of a different attitude to mind and life itself. He maintains that "meaning *is* being! So any transformation of society must result in a profound change of meaning. Any change of meaning for the individual would change the whole because all individuals are so similar that it can be communicated."[52]

Renee Weber describes Bohm's concept of consciousness in terms of "psychological atom-smashing" in which the thinker is the atom. Just as enormous quantities of energy are released in physical atom-smashing, so too in this analogy there is a tremendous amount of multi-dimensional energy released when the conscious mind is smashed or freed: "Such a process provides consciousness with direct access to that energy, leading it to experiential certitude, based on inner empiricism, that the ultimate nature of the universe is an energy of love."[53] We are seeing a convergence of thought among mystics of the East and West as well as contemporary physics. As Weber points out, "the challenge for the individual locus of consciousness is to provide the condition that allows the universal force to flow through it without hindrance."[54] For this to happen one must realize that one will never reach final truth. The acceptance of this fact will open the way to insight.[55] The result of this kind of insight can be the transformation of the earth.

Furthermore, Bohm extended his thought to include the connection between consciousness, self-awareness, and human freedom:

> I propose that self-awareness requires that consciousness sink into its implicate (and now mainly unconscious) order. It may then be possible to be directly aware, in the present, of the actual activity of past knowledge, and especially of that knowledge which is not only false but which also reacts in such a way as to resist exposure of its falsity. Then the mind may be free of its bondage to the active confusion that is enfolded in its past. Without freedom of this kind, there is little meaning even in raising the question as to whether human beings are free, in the deeper sense of being capable of a creative act that is not determined mechanically by unknown conditions in the untraceably complex interconnections and unplumbable depths of the overall reality in which we are embedded.[56]

I will take up the question of human freedom in the next section on morality.

2) *Morality*. The greatest evil in Bohm's mind is fragmentation because it destroys the attitude of wholeness that is so necessary not only to perceive reality correctly but to upgrade the care that we give to our world. Bohm identified some of the evils that have come about because of our fragmentary thought patterns and way of life: "Thus, as is now well known, this way of life has brought about pollution, destruction of the balance of nature, over-population, world-wide economic and political disorder, and the creation of an overall environment that is neither physically nor mentally healthy for most of the people who have to live in it . . . ."[57]

David Ray Griffin explains that "David Bohm's passion is to overcome fragmentation."[58] Griffin speaks of the "modern vision" which

> has reinforced the egotistical and tribal tendencies of us humans to think that the welfare of the individual person or at least group (social, cultural, religious, and/or economic) can be promoted by ignoring (or even defeating) the welfare of all the others.[59]

These evils have been identified with patriarchy by several authors who root the problem in the basic dualism of Aristotelian philosophy. One such writer is theologian Rosemary Radford Ruether whose understanding of fragmentation and wholeness is similar to that of Bohm: "We must postulate that every religious idea begins in the revelatory experience. By *revelatory* we mean breakthrough experiences beyond ordinary fragmented consciousness that provide interpretive symbols illuminating the means of the *whole* of life."[60] Ruether and several others identify explicit links between the exploitation of women and the devastation of the earth. They cite fragmentation as a primary cause of such separation and destruction[61] and point out the inevitable consequences of patriarchy, i.e., racism, sexism, and classism. Although Bohm never drew such explicit connections between his implicate order and ecofeminism, there is ample evidence that the views of Bohm and Ruether would have been compatible.

Like Ruether and some of the other ecofeminists, Fritjof Capra examines the tradition of the goddess which predates patriarchy. It has wholeness for its base unlike the dualistic origins of patriarchy. Capra believes that the feminist movement, with its emphasis on wholism and the ability to trace humanity to a time before the advent of patriarchy, is bringing about the "slow and reluctant but inevitable decline of patriarchy" which has been around for "at least three thousand years."[62] The breakdown of patriarchy coincides with a growing awareness of the need for a holistic approach to several disciplines including moral theology.

Renee Weber describes the radical implications of Bohm's vision of the implicate order for ethics:

> The *roots* of disturbances in the culture will be considered to lie within the implicate order – though not in the deep-structure where only order is possible – somewhere within the collective consciousness of [humankind] . . . . The paradox, of which Bohm is aware, seems to be that, although the "sorrow of mankind" may be a universal field, its purification is an individual task, requiring self-transformation.[63]

Weber notes that "this model of cosmos and consciousness, although revolutionary, is not new. It forms the content of the wisdom traditions of India and Greece."[64]

While Bohm posited a radically new understanding of morality, I believe that he still left room for individual and collective human responsibility. In speaking of the implicate order, he stated that

> For the human being, all of this implies a thoroughgoing wholeness, in which mental and physical sides participate very closely in each other . . . . Extending this view, we see that each human being similarly participates in an inseparable way in society and in the planet as a whole.[65]

Although human beings are intimately bound to the rest of the planet, they do not lose their individual identity and freedom to explore new approaches to mind and matter. Without doubt there is more to explore, and, presumably, there is a sensible wholeness beyond human comprehension. It seems plausible that Bohm would not have relinquished the notion of human freedom even as he argued for an implicate order which is his theory of the whole. A constant in his thinking is the "irreducible contingency"[66] of his whole approach, one that certainly leaves room for human culpability.

3) *Language*. Bohm examined the role language has played in bringing about the debilitating sort of fragmentation in thought and action described above. He identified the typical subject-verb-object pattern as participating in our stagnation since the emphasis in such a pattern is on the nouns and not on the verbs. Bohm experimented with what he called the "rheo-mode" and attempted to rework the English language in order to place the emphasis on the verb and thus help to eliminate the fragmentation with which we have become accustomed. Bohm was fully aware that such a major reorganization in the language would create a major upheaval if it were ever imposed.[67]

Bohm's cautions are worth noting, however. How we speak is how we think. Paul Knitter explains that "the very structure of our language prevents us from grasping that we *are* our relationships."[68] Knitter makes the same connection as does Bohm regarding our use of nouns and verbs. Knitter states that "we begin our thinking and speaking with nouns that are then followed by verbs; the subject generally must precede the predicate . . . . We are not first of all individuals who later relate; rather it is our relating – how we do it and with whom or what-that makes us (or gives us the semblance of being) individuals."[69] Knitter cites Bohm's implicate order as a way of describing our interrelatedness.[70]

Other scholars have been very vocal in pointing out the problems associated with the use of imprecise and androcentric language. For example, Sandra Schneiders has taken up this subject as it pertains to biblical scholarship.[71] Theologians would do well to consider not only grammar and syntax but also their selection of words to make sure that fragmentation does not inadvertently occur. The use of inclusive language is obviously a first step in this very complex process.

C. The World

Bohm's understanding of the world has major implications for theology. At bottom is the assertion that all matter and energy are interrelated. All is one and in flux. There are, of course, subwholes which may be studied in their own right, but the primary reality is the whole. I will consider the implications of this on the notion of eternity since it occupies a major position in the physics and philosophy of David Bohm.

Eternity for Bohm is not "a whole (or totality) of time, but rather . . . the *quality* of the wholeness of time."[72] Eternity is "a standpoint outside of time rather than something that contains a fore-knowledge or predetermination of the whole of time. That is to say, eternity contains time, and yet, it does not *determine* the future completely in terms of the past, nor in terms of something given statically that rules over all time."[73] For Bohm, eternity is "the most immediate ground of the being of everything."[74] Bohm is talking about a creative process that cannot be completely described and one that is fraught with paradox.

The notion of eternity is tied up with the fate of human beings in traditional theology. Time is linear, and life follows death. For Bohm, however, humans are always alive in some form. We are part of the farthest stars and the smallest atoms. Bohm's theory of nonlocal correlation transcends linear time and renders unreal the distinction between past, present, and future. Once nonlocality is extended from space to time, Bohm realizes that "the concept of nonlocal action over time introduces new difficulties for understanding causality in its usual sense."[75] All of this has direct bearing on traditional theological understandings of creation, salvation, redemption, resurrection, grace, and justification, none of which Bohm chooses to explore.

To think in Bohm's terms is to pose new questions and allow the old ones to dissolve. Whereas traditional Christian religions believe that eternity is a mode of existence not subject to time, Bohm believes that *"eternity* means the depths of the implicate order, not the whole of the successive moments of time."[76] Bodily death does not bring on a cessation of consciousness nor does consciousness leave time at the moment of death and become somehow absorbed into eternity. Bohm gladly admits that there are many unanswered questions in his treatment of eternity.

Conclusion

This brief introduction to the thought and theological implications of the work of David Bohm supports several conclusions reached by contemporary thinkers in ecology and theology. Among the most prominent are the following: (a) The world is charged with meaning; (b) ". . . that they all may be one" (John 17:22) is as contemporary an idea now as it ever was; and (c) change is a fundamental reality.

a. In contrast to the mechanistic world of the previous centuries, many of today's ecologists and theologians argue in favor of a world imbued with meaning. They find unacceptable the claim that reality is either illusory or random. The physics of David Bohm, with its corrective to the randomness of quantum physics, offers the possibility – indeed the promise – that science will endorse the impulse toward ultimate meaning, i.e., that at the heart of reality is a compassionate strength capable of enfolding all that is.

b. The great prayer for unity recorded in the gospel of John gains new meaning for those who subscribe to the thinking of David Bohm. The unity imagined by Bohm is of a magnitude most likely not fathomed even by Jesus himself. The potential of this longing is captured by Passionist priest and geologian Thomas Berry in his reflection upon the Gaia hypothesis, a theory which posits that the earth is a living organism:

> In our discussion of the Gaia Theory there is need, it seems, for a cosmology of Gaia as well as a biology of Gaia for, ultimately, everything in the universe finds its context of interpretation within the universe. Within the phenomenal world, only the universe itself is a self-referent, a text without context. This cosmology of Gaia is especially necessary as a context for any religious interpretation of our subject. Religious experience itself seems to emerge out of the wonder that strikes the human mind as it experiences the inexplicable grandeur of the natural world about us.[77]

As Berry implies, physics is only one area in which scientific study has touched philosophical inquiry. Chemistry and biology are also being probed for their revelatory possibilities of the whole. Significant investigation into the role of religion and emergent scientific perspectives has occurred during this century. Both Bohm and Berry offer creative – if controversial – visions of the reaches of human thought and the created order. Neither writer claims to have fully comprehended the dimensions and mysteries of the universe, but the unity of the universe is undeniable, they believe.

c. The ancient insight of Heraclitus, i.e., that the world is in constant flux, is clearly reestablished in the findings and conjectures of Bohm's post-Newtonian physics. Process theologians have attempted to apply this concept to the deity, and they have met with mixed success among traditional theologians who continue to hold out for an immutable God. Bohm's work invites reflection on the notion of a God who unfailingly changes. The holomovement, insofar as one may accurately draw conclusions from it about God, is *movement*. This challenges the traditional notion of an impassible and immutable Being who is outside the created order. One cannot easily reconcile a stable God outside as well as within a dynamic universe.

David Bohm's implicate order is one of the most creative and visionary torches we have which can guide us into the future. Bohm believed that we cannot reach the final truth. His thought has the potential to keep us humble and searching with care and dignity.

Endnotes

1. Renee Weber, "Reflections on David Bohm's Holomovement: A Physicist's Model of Cosmos and Consciousness," *The Metaphors of Consciousness,* ed.

by Ronald S. Valle and Rolf von Eckartsberg (New York: Plenum Press, 1981), pp. 122-23.

2. Mystics face the same dilemma as contemporary physicists, i.e., they want to communicate their knowledge but are constrained by traditional language. Werner Heisenberg describes the situation for quantum physicists: The most difficult problem . . . concerning the use of the language arises in quantum theory. Here we have at first no simple guide for correlating the mathematical symbols with concepts of ordinary language; and the only thing we know from the start is the fact that our common concepts cannot be applied to the structure of the atoms." Quoted by Fritjof Capra in *The Tao of Physics: An Exploration of the Parallels between Modern Physics and Eastern Mysticism* (Toronto: Bantam Books, 1975), pp. 32-33.

3. Capra notes that "Heraclitus is often mentioned in connection with modern physics, but hardly ever in connection with Taoism. And yet it is this connection which shows best that his world view was that of a mystic and thus, in my opinion, puts the parallels between his ideas and those of modern physics in the right perspective." (Tao of Physics, p. 104).

4. Capra, *The Tao of Physics,* p. 6. Capra also describes the members of the ancient Milesian school who believed that matter was alive. They did not distinguish between animate and inanimate, matter and spirit.

5. David Bohm, *Wholeness and the Implicate Order* (London: Routledge and Kegan Paul, Ltd., 1980), p. 173.

6. *Ibid.*

7. Ian Barbour states that "the concepts of Newtonian physics, which had been so superbly successful in astronomy and mechanics, were increasingly adopted as an all-encompassing metaphysical scheme." *Issues in Science and Religion* (New York: Harper & Row, 1966), p. 36.

8. Bohm, *Wholeness and the Implicate Order,* p. 4.

9. Barbour, *Issues in Science and Religion,* p. 159.

10. Bohm, *Wholeness and the Implicate Order,* p. 174.

11. Although Einstein constructed most of the relativity theory himself, it took more than twenty years for scientists to fine tune the quantum theory.

12. David Bohm, "The Implicate Order: A New Approach to the Nature of Reality," *Beyond Mechanism: The Universe in Recent Physics and Catholic Thought,* ed. by David L. Schindler (Lanham, MD: University Press of America, 1986), p. 18.

13. Capra, p. 55.

14. For a recent discussion of Bohm's notion of nonlocality, see Chapter 7 "Nonlocality" in *The Undivided Universe: An Ontological Interpretation of Quantum Theory* by David Bohm and B. J. Hiley (London: Routledge, 1993), pp. 134-159.

15. For a comprehensive view of the quantum theory and the way it relates to classical physics, see David Bohm's "Classical and Non-Classical Concepts in the Quantum Theory," in *Physical Reality: Philosophical Essays on Twentieth-*

Century Physics, ed. by Stephen Toulmin (New York: Harper & Row, 1970), pp. 197-216.

16. David Bohm and F. David Peat, *Science, Order, and Creativity: A Dramatic Look at the Creative Roots of Science and Life* (Toronto: Bantam Books, 1987), pp. 3-4.

17. John Briggs and F. David Peat, "Interview: David Bohm," *Omni* 9 (January 1987): 70. Bohm gives an account of the development of his thought in "Hidden Variables and the Implicate Order," *Zygon* 20 (June 1985): 111-121.

18. Michael Audi has studied the "hidden variable theory" of Bohm and concluded that "examination of Bohm's theory will reveal that the motivation behind hidden variable theories is the restoration of determinism and that such a restoration is misguided, i.e., unjustified on present evidence," in *The Interpretation of Quantum Mechanics* (Chicago: University of Chicago Press, 1973), p. 72. Audi's comments reveal the lack of understanding and agreement among scientists concerning theories by Bohm and others who push conclusions they cannot observe. As we have seen, however, Bohm regards the conclusions of classical physics as an "article of faith" as well.

19. For a summary of the contributions of René Descartes, see Fritjof Capra, *The Turning Point: Science, Society, and the Rising Culture* (Toronto: Bantam Books, 1982), pp. 56-63.

20. Audi emphasizes that what Bohm proposes in contrast to what has gone before is a difference of substance: ". . . [the] alternative proposed by Bohm to the standard quantum theory is nothing like a mild, minor modification. It is a drastic, radical reinterpretation, postulating a new, hitherto undetected field which the standard theory presumes does not exist. Bohm's theory is a quasi-classical, deterministic theory in which the individual paths of individual particles are in principle calculable, whereas the standard theory is inherently deterministic. Bohm's theory must be regarded as a distinct new theory" (Audi, *The Interpretation of Quantum Mechanics,* p. 75).

21. See, for example, *Wholeness and the Implicate Order,* pp. 115-118, and *Science, Order, and Creativity,* pp. 104-150.

22. David Bohm, "The Implicate Order: A New Order for Physics," *Process Studies* 8 (Summer 1978), p. 73. In another place Bohm notes that "the notion of order is so vast and immense in its implications, however, that it cannot be defined in words. Indeed, the best we can do with order is to try to `point to it' tacitly and by implication, in as wide as possible a range of contexts in which this notion is relevant," *Wholeness and the Implicate Order,* p. 115.

23. Bohm and Peat, p. 175.

24. Bohm, *Wholeness and the Implicate Order,* p. 177.

25. *Ibid.*

26. *Ibid.*

27. *Wholeness and the Implicate Order,* p. 151.

28. Briggs and Peat, *Omni,* p. 72.

29. John B. Cobb, Jr., *Beyond Mechanism,* p. 39.

30. Robert John Russell, "The Physics of David Bohm and Its Relevance to Philosophy and Theology," *Zygon* 20 (June 1985), p. 145. For Bohm's explanation of the super-quantum potential, see "Hidden Variables and the Implicate Order," *Zygon* 20 (June 1985), pp. 119-121.

31. Bohm, "The Implicate Order," p. 28.

32. Bohm and Peat, *Science, Order and Creativity,* p. 211.

33. *Ibid.,* pp. 15-16.

34. Bohm, "The Implicate Order," p. 36.

35. N. Max Wildiers, *The Theologian and His Universe: Theology and Cosmology from the Middle Ages to the Present* (New York: Seabury Press, 1982), p. 160.

36. David Bohm, "Time, the Implicate Order and Pre-Space," p. 199.

37. Ian Barbour, "Editorial," *Zygon* 20 (June 1985): 107. Not all writers agree on the import of Bohm's writings for theological discussion, however. For example, Robert John Russell criticizes Anglican theologian and physicist John Polkinghorne's interpretation of Bohm's work both for its scientific and philosophical content. Russell accuses Polkinghorne of misunderstanding Bohm's writings. See Robert John Russell, William R. Stoeger, and George V. Coyne, eds. *Physics, Philosophy and Theology: A Common Quest for Understanding* (Vatican Observatory: Vatican City State, 1988), p. 371n.

38. *Ibid.* B. D. Josephson, "Science and Religion: How to Make the Synthesis?" *Perkins Journal* 36 (Summer 1983): 33-39, has made a similar point: "If what Bohm is doing with unmanifest order can be combined with the mathematics of intelligence, we'll be well on the way to integrating God and his domain into the framework of science," p. 38.

39. Robert John Russell, "A Response to David Bohm's 'Time, the Implicate Order and Pre-Space,'" *Physics and the Ultimate Significance of Time,* ed. by David Ray Griffin (Albany: State University of New York Press, 1986), p. 215.

40. Bohm, "Hidden Variables and the Implicate Order," p. 123.

41. Ted Peters, "David Bohm, Postmodernism, and the Divine," *Zygon* 20 (June 1985): 206.

42. *Ibid.,* p. 210.

43. Bohm, "Hidden Variables and the Implicate Order," p. 124.

44. John B. Cobb, Jr., "Bohm's Contribution to Faith in Our Time," *Beyond Mechanism,* p. 50.

45. *Ibid.*

46. *Ibid.*

47. Russell, "The Physics of David Bohm and Its Relevance to Philosophy and Theology," p. 153.

48. David Ray Griffin, "Bohm and Whitehead on Wholeness, Freedom, Causality, and Time," *Zygon* 20 (June 1985), pp. 174-178.

49. *Ibid.,* p. 190.

50. Bohm and Hiley, *The Undivided Universe*, p. 382.

51. Briggs and Peat, "Interview," *Omni*, p. 74.

52. *Ibid.*

53. Weber, p. 128.

54. *Ibid.*, p. 131. In this article Weber explains how Bohm has worked with Krishnamurti to expand the implications of his thought to extend to consciousness and the idea of the holy. For a discussion of how the East and West have responded to the conditioning of consciousness, see Bohm and Peat, *Science, Order and Creativity,* pp. 255-260 in which the authors discuss further implications of Krishnamurti's impact on Bohm's thought.

55. For a discussion of Bohm's notion of insight, see David Bohm, "On Insight and Its Significance for Science, Education, and Values," *Education and Values,* ed. by Douglas Sloane (Columbia, New York: Teachers College Press, 1980), pp. 7-22.

56. David Bohm, "Time, the Implicate Order and Pre-Space" in *Physics and the Ultimate Significance of Time,* p. 205. In an appendix to this essay, Bohm attaches a beautiful and cogent reflection on freedom (see pp. 201-208).

57. Bohm, *Wholeness and the Implicate Order,* p. 2.

58. Griffin, "Bohm and Whitehead on Wholeness, Freedom, Causality, and Time," p. 165.

59. *Ibid.*

60. Rosemary Radford Ruether, *Sexism and God Talk: Toward a Feminist Theology* (Boston: Beacon Press, 1983), p. 13. See also her recent work, *Gaia and God: An Eco-Feminist Theology of Earth Healing* (San Francisco: HarperSanFrancisco, Francisco, 1992).

61. As noted elsewhere in this volume, ecofeminism is an area of study that considers the unfortunately similar treatment sustained by both women and nature. For other examples of available literature in this field, see additional readings in this area: Carol Adams, ed., *Ecofeminism and the Sacred* (New York: Continuum, 1993) and Irene Diamond and Gloria Feman Orenstein, *Reweaving the World: The Emergence of Ecofeminism* (San Francisco: Sierra Club Books, 1990).

62. Capra, *The Turning Point,* p. 29.

63. Weber, "Reflections on David Bohm's Holomovement," p. 135.

64. *Ibid.*

65. Bohm and Hiley, *The Undivided Universe*, p. 386.

66. *Ibid.*

67. Bohm, *Wholeness and the Implicate Order,* p. 47.

68. Paul Knitter, *No Other Name?: A Critical Survey of Christian Attitudes Toward the World Religions* (Maryknoll, New York: Orbis Books, 1985), p. 8.

69. *Ibid.*

70. *Ibid.*

71. See Sandra M. Schneiders, "The Bible and Feminism" in *Freeing Theology: The Essentials of Theology in Feminist Perspective,* ed. by Catherine Mowry LaCugna (San Francisco: HarperSanFrancisco, 1993), pp. 31-57; see also Schneiders' most recent book, *The Revelatory Text: Interpreting the New Testament As Sacred Scripture* (San Francisco: HarperSanFrancisco, 1991). In the latter volume, Schneiders, relying on the work of Gadamer and Ricoeur, has done an extensive study of the notion of language and the transformative power of the words we regard as sacred text.

72. David Bohm, "Comments on the Papers," *Beyond Mechanism,* p. 129.

73. *Ibid.,* p. 134.

74. *Ibid.,* p. 142.

75. Bohm, *The Undivided Universe,* p. 238.

76. Bohm, "Reply to Comments of John Cobb and David Griffin," *Physics and the Ultimate Significance of Time,* p. 199.

77. Thomas Berry, "The Gaia Theory: Its Religious Implications," *ARC: The Journal of The Faculty of Religious Studies* McGill: 22 (1994): 7.